John H. B. Nowland

Early Reminiscences of Indianapolis

John H. B. Nowland

Early Reminiscences of Indianapolis

ISBN/EAN: 9783337289973

Printed in Europe, USA, Canada, Australia, Japan

Cover: Foto ©Suzi / pixelio.de

More available books at **www.hansebooks.com**

EARLY REMINISCENCES

OF

INDIANAPOLIS,

WITH

SHORT BIOGRAPHICAL SKETCHES

OF ITS EARLY CITIZENS,

AND OF A FEW OF THE PROMINENT BUSINESS MEN OF THE PRESENT DAY.

BY JOHN H. B. NOWLAND.

"I have a work to do,
 A work I must not shun;
One path I will pursue,
 Until my aim be won;
What others do I need not ask,
Enough for me I know my task."

INDIANAPOLIS:
SENTINEL BOOK AND JOB PRINTING HOUSE.
1870.

Entered according to Act of Congress, in the year 1870,

BY JOHN H. B. NOWLAND,

In the Clerk's Office of the District Court of the United States for the District of Indiana.

DEDICATION.

THE dedication of a book is generally considered as a compliment and mark of respect from the author to a personal friend, and significant of pure and disinterested friendship.

Although the writer of this has many old friends worthy of such consideration, yet he can not in one work bestow it upon all. He has, however, selected from among the number one who is well worthy this slight testimonial of regard; and would that the work was more worthy to be dedicated to one who was his early friend; rejoiced in his prosperity, and ever cheered him in adversity; the companion of his youth, and for years the inmate of the same house, and who in a treacherous world has never deserted him.

I therefore respectfully inscribe "Early Reminiscences of Indianapolis, with Short Biographical Sketches of its Early Citizens, and a few of the Prominent Business Men of the present day," to EDWIN J. PECK, the steadfast friend, the honest man, and the devoted Christian.

THE AUTHOR.

INDIANAPOLIS, March 1, 1870.

PREFATORY REMARKS.

WHEN a writer assumes to give reminiscences or sketches from personal knowledge or observation, he will have to use the personal pronoun I oftener than might seem to be in good taste. In this I hope the reader will pardon me, as I have to depend almost entirely upon my personal knowledge and observation for the facts of this history for the first five years after the settlement of Indianapolis.

There are few, very few, persons now living who were here previous to the year 1825; of that class of old citizens several have died within a few years, therefore I have to depend upon my own impressions for reminiscences prior to the year named. Those impressions, however, were formed at a very early period of my life (six years of age), and at a time when once stamped upon the young mind, are indelible and can never be erased. They are, indeed, more fresh in my memory to-day than others that occurred but a few years since; for their correctness I would appeal to any person living here at that time.

Therefore, I shall write what I know, and what I have seen of Indianapolis, from 1820 to 1870; and try to convey to the reader an idea of what Indianapolis was in its incipient state.

The sudden rise, the energy of its population, the excellence of its institutions, its railroad facilities, the whole character of its people and prosperity, render Indianapolis prominent among the cities that have recently sprung into existence throughout a land notable for individual enterprise; and being most happily endowed with the natural advantages of climate and soil, makes it one of the most desirable cities of the great West. It is, therefore, meet that its present population and the country should know something of its beginning, and of those to whom they are indebted for converting it from a howling wilderness to its present state of prosperity and social happiness, before the last of those old pioneers shall have passed away.

The origin and condition of a city which has so recently become prominent among the chief cities of the Union, is a subject calculated to awaken attention among minds inquiring the effects of government, and other causes, on the destinies of the human race.

As I remarked before of the pioneers of the wilderness, there are but few spared to enjoy the prosperity they contributed so much to produce. They can not look with apathy upon such exertions as will tend to perpetuate the history of the past; while the rising generation among us will naturally entertain a curiosity to know something of the men that founded and established the city of their birth and residence.

Indianapolis, situated as it is in the midst of one of the finest agricultural and grain growing countries of the great West, it is not astonishing or surprising it has made the rapid stride to prosperity and wealth it has within a few years. It has only been about fifteen years since there was adequate facilities for the transportation of the great surplus of the country to market. Since that time its march has been onward.

It is not my purpose, in this work, to attempt to show, from the central location of Indianapolis, its great advantages over other cities of the West. I leave that task for more able and wiser heads than mine. My object is merely to give reminiscences and sketches of its first settlers, and snatch from oblivion its past history, and sketches of those who have contributed so much to develop the resources of the country, and the great drawbacks against their energy, enterprise and industry they had to contend with. 'Tis with the past I expect mostly to deal, in a plain, unvarnished way; if it answers no other purpose, it may serve as a landmark for some future historian.

In giving a correct history of the times, I will have to refer to some characters and circumstances the fastidious reader may think unworthy of notice. But I assure them I do not have to draw upon my imagination to find them; the characters were a part and parcel of the population, the circumstances a portion of the history; "truth is stranger than fiction," and these reminiscences would be incomplete without them.

Could the first settlers of Indianapolis, who for forty years "have slept the sleep that knows no waking," upon the banks of White River, awake to consciousness, how they would wonder and stare to see the village of log cabins they left, transformed into a city of sixty thousand inhabitants; its twelve railroads centering into one common depot; its thirty or forty magnificent temples dedicated to the worship of the only true and living God; its gorgeously decorated saloons of pleasure and fashion, almost unequaled in tales of fairy land; its hundreds of wooden steeds that canter or gallop at the will of the riders;—would they not, like Rip Van Winkle, when he inquired for Jacob Stein, ask for something they had left behind?

Since I commenced writing these short sketches, I have recurred so often to names once familiar, and to scenes of my early youth and school-boy days, when there was not a cloud to obscure my sun, nor a ripple upon my sea of life, when every brook and tree were as old acquaintances, I have been ready to exclaim with the poet,

"O! would I were a boy again,
When life seemed formed for sunny years."

The reader will pardon me, I hope, if I use some of the cant phrases and other expressions of the "early settlers." I would here remark, "I have no friends to reward nor enemies punish." What I know, and what I have seen of Indianapolis, I shall write as General Jackson construed the Constitution, "as I understand it." Therefore, if there are any who think I have not given their name the prominence they would wish, it will be the fault of their history, and not of my pen.

In this work I will attempt to show the great variety of characters found in the early settlers of this city, and what I know personally of its history for fifty years.

EARLY REMINISCENCES.

SELECTION OF THE CAPITAL.

THE act of Congress of April, 1816, granting Indiana admittance into the Union, also donated four sections of unsold public lands as a permanent seat of government, or capital of the new State.

In consequence of the central portion of the State yet belonging to the Indians, the selection of the land was postponed and not made until the summer of 1820. The Legislature that assembled in the winter of 1819-20, appointed ten commissioners, viz., Stephen Ludlow, John Conner, John Gilliland, George Hunt, Frederick Rapp, John Tipton, Joseph Bartholomew, Jesse B. Durham, William Prince, and Thomas Emerson, to make the selection.

Frederick Rapp and other members of the commission from the Southern part of the State, met at Vincennes about the middle of May, 1820, preparatory to joining the others, at the house of Wm. Conner, on White River, and near where the location would most likely be made.

Matthias R. Nowland (the father of the writer), and his brother-in-law, Andrew Byrne, had been visiting some friends and relatives in Lawrence County, Illinois. On their return home, they happened at Vincennes at the time that portion of the commission were about to start to the upper White River, or the newly acquired territory, to carry out the objects for which they were appointed.

My father and uncle were persuaded and induced to join and accompany the party. The first settlement they found, after entering the new purchase, was at the Bluffs of White River, where there were about a half dozen families settled, including that of Jacob Whetzel, near whose cabin they encamped one day to rest themselves and jaded horses. At this point the commission was not yet full; those that were there were very much pleased with the country, and afterwards proposed revisiting that place and giving it a more thorough examination.

The next stopping place or camping ground was on the east side of Fall Creek, at its junction with White River. Here they also remained one day, and most of them were favorably impressed. My father told them if the location was made here he would not only move out to it in the fall, but would try and induce other Kentuckians to join him. At that time there were about four or five families here, viz., Hardings, Wilson, Pogue, and McCormicks, all of whom had come that spring.

My father and uncle remained at the camp at Fall Creek, while the others went to join their associates at the house of Wm. Conner, near where Noblesville now stands.

The whole commission now for the first time being together, they proceeded to examine Mr. Conner's favorite locality, which was near the present site of Noblesville. Very few favored that place, and the whole party returned to their old camp at the mouth of Fall Creek.

After a few days' further examination, this site was almost unanimously chosen on the 7th of June, 1820, and the whole delegation were greeted by the few families here with demonstrations of joy, and their scant stores of provisions freely divided with the commissioners.

I shall never forget the tears shed in my father's family when he returned home and announced his intention of removing to the new purchase in Indiana. This news was not long in finding its way to the ears of his numerous friends, who did all in their power to dissuade him from carrying out his intentions. They told him that he would never be permitted by the Indians to reach White River, if he started; that he was endangering the lives of his whole family; in short, every argument was used to deter him from attempting so hazardous an undertaking; but all arguments were of no avail; his mind was made up the moment the selection of the site was made by the commissioners.

PREPARATIONS FOR AND REMOVAL TO THE NEW PURCHASE.

My father immediately set about making preparations for removing. He had no difficulty in selling his suburban residence of ten or twelve acres, and realized quite a handsome amount to begin with in a new country. He disposed of every article of wood or iron furniture that was not indispensable, or that could possibly be done without. He then loaded a large six-horse wagon with heavy necessary furniture and provisions sufficient for the winter use.

The beds and bedding, and most of the clothing, were so arranged and packed as to be carried on the backs of horses. Feather beds were rolled up and tied together in such a way that one would rest on each side of the horse, forming a platform on the back of the animal, where one or two children could ride. My mother and grandmother were provided with single horses and side saddles, and when the whole caravan was in motion, would remind a person of a cavalcade of Bedouins, or Arabs. In this way, about the middle of October, 1820, we left our home in Frankfort, Kentucky, to seek our fortune among strangers, in a wilderness whose population was almost entirely savage.

As a start in a journey is the main point, and when started

half accomplished, my father only intended to go seven miles the first day and stop at the house of an old friend, at the Sulphur Springs, to which point we were accompanied by several of his friends, who held high carnival during the evening. In parting with friends, all of whom were there to see us start, there was none more deeply affected or showed more heartfelt sorrow than the old negro woman who had nursed all my father's children. When parting with my mother, she fell on her knees, and prayed that God would watch over and protect her old mistress, and her children, from the tomahawk of the wild "Ingins," which brought tears to the eyes of all present. This good old woman would have come with us, but was deterred only by the fear of the Indians. My sister, now Mrs. S. H. Patterson, of Jeffersonville, and myself, were placed on the platform made by feather beds, on the back of one of the horses. In descending a steep hill the first day we started, the horse stumbled, landing her and myself on the rocky road, with beds on top of us.

In about four days we reached the Ohio, at the mouth of the Kentucky River. Here we encountered the first difficulty of any moment. The ferry-boat had left the spring before for parts unknown. Fortunately the river was quite low, and the only possible way of getting over was to unload the wagon and take it to pieces, and ferry over in a skiff a portion at a time. The running gear was taken over in this way and put together; then the large body or bed was floated over; then the furniture was taken over and reloaded, and the horses swam over; and last the family were ferried over the evening of the second day, and camped for the first time in Indiana, on the north bank of the Ohio River.

The ferryman at that time was George Ash, well known in frontier history, having, when a child, been taken prisoner and raised entirely by the Indians. He lived on the Indiana side, could scarcely speak a word of English, wore rings in his ears and nose, and dressed in Indian style. Although he had a very good house, he had not a chair or bedstead in it, and lived in every way like a savage.

From Ash's Ferry, as it was then called, we went by way of Versailles to Napoleon, in Ripley County; this occupied two days. Although we had an open road, it was quite hilly and rough. At Napoleon we camped near the house of William Wilson, son of Isaac Wilson, living at that time in this place, of whom I will speak in another sketch. Here we bought corn, and had it ground into meal on a small hand-mill belonging to Mr. W. This occupied one day. Here ended the road, and commenced Berry's Trace, which had to be cut out before the large wagon could get along.

The first house from Napoleon was that of Montgomery, on "Flat Rock," about nine miles above where Columbus now stands. Here we were detained one day in consequence of the wagoner having foundered one of his horses. While here we were overtaken by Henry Bradley, his brother William, and Bob Sacre, who had agreed to meet us at the mouth of the Kentucky River. This acquisition in numbers and strength, with three additional trusty rifles, was truly encouraging, and gave confidence to the whole party, especially two young men, James Graves and Nathaniel Jones, who had begun to show signs of fear soon after we crossed the Ohio River, so much so my father was afraid they would take the back track.

From Montgomery's the next house was that of Captain John Berry, father of Colonel Nineveh Berry, now of Madison County. Mr. Berry lived at the mouth of Sugar Creek, on Blue River, about three miles from where Edinburg now is There also we stopped one day and replenished our stock of fresh meat by the purchase of a hog, and one of the party, I think Mr. Henry Bradley, killing a fine buck. My father had stopped at Mr. Berry's in the summer, and formed quite an attachment for him.

About the time we were there, a circumstance happened that gave name to a creek in that vicinity, which it now bears, and will, I suppose, as long as water runs in its bed. Nineveh Berry, then quite young, had killed a deer; with the deer on his shoulder and gun in his hand, he attempted to cross the creek on a log; the bark of the log slipped, throwing Mr. B., deer and gun into the water. When he went home, he told his father the circumstance, who immediately named the creek Nineveh.

The next day we reached the house of Loper, which was where Berry's Trace crossed that of Whetzell's, about three miles southwest of Greenwood. This place is now owned by William Law. It may be proper here to say there are two places in Johnson County, known as where Loper's cabin stood. This point is where his first house was. He afterwards sold this place, and built another cabin about five miles east of it, on a creek now known as Hurricane. We stayed at Loper's on the night of the third of November. The next morning set in a violent snow storm. Mr. Bradley proposed to my father to take the family on horseback, and go on and have them a warm dinner by the time they would arrive with the wagon. This he did, and we arrived about twelve o'clock, the fourth day of November, at the house of that good old Samaritan, Isaac Wilson, which was on the northwest corner of the State House Square. About four o'clock Mr. B. and friends came in with the wagon.

It was on this evening, my little eyes (as old Johnny Ewing would say) first opened upon a live "Ingin," of which I had heard so much. I had gone to the river with the teamster to help him water his horses. At the river one of the Hardings detained me to ask questions about the "new comers," what their names were, and where from. By the time I had answered the various questions, the teamster had reached the wagon; the horse I was riding was very restive, and finally threw me. I jumped up, and followed along the path; when about where Miekel's brewery stands, I met a "big Injun." I don't know which was the worst scared, he or I; but I suppose I was. I did not stop to ask him any foolish questions, or compliment him upon his warrior-like appearance; but I think I made about as good time between that and the wagon as there is on record. One yelp and a few jumps took me to the wagon. What became of him I did not look back to see. And here commences what I know and have seen of Indianapolis.

FIRST WINTER IN INDIANAPOLIS.

We found Mr. Wilson with quite a large family of his own, although he told my father he would be welcome to the use of one of his two cabins until such time as he would be able to build one for himself; but that a Quaker from Wayne County, named Billy Townsend, had been out and raised a cabin and covered it, but had neither cut out a door, window, or place for a chimney. It was situated in the middle of Kentucky avenue, about midway between Illinois and Tennessee streets.

My father did not take the liberty of cutting out the doors and chimney, lest he would not get them in the place the owner wished; so he pried up two corners of the house and took out the third log from the bottom, which would, by climbing, be sufficient for ingress and egress. A few boards were removed from the middle of the roof for the escape of smoke, the fire being built in the middle of the room on the ground, there being no floor. This house had neither "chinking or daubing." My mother lined the inside walls by hanging up rag carpeting, which rendered it quite comfortable for the short time we occupied it. The whole entire male population were prompt to tender their services to assist in building a cabin of our own; this, with seven men already at my father's command, enabled him in a few days to have a comfortable cabin, which he built on the west bank of the ravine (where the canal now runs), about midway between Washington and Maryland streets.

At this cabin of Townsend's, the men enjoyed very much the going in and out of my grandmother. She was quite a large but short woman, pretty near as thick as she was long, and none enjoyed the fun more than the old lady herself.

Our new cabin was eighteen by twenty feet square; the chimney, which was in the east end, would take in a "back log" eight feet in length, and a "fore stick" ten feet. There were two doors, one on the north, and the other on the south side, opposite. These doors were made in this way to facilitate the making of fires. The back sticks were about eighteen inches in diameter; one end was placed on a sled called a "lizard," to which the horse was hitched, and driven through the house until the log was opposite the fire-place, and then rolled to its place in the fire; and so with the fore stick; and the smaller fuel carried in and placed on top; the two large sticks would last about twenty-four hours.

Although this was one of the coldest winters ever experienced in this country, the ground covered with snow from the time we arrived here (4th November) until the first of March, we lived as comfortable and contented as "Friday and Robinson Crusoe;" there were "none to hinder or make us afraid," with the exception of our dusky neighbors—they were pretty quiet during the winter.

The day before Christmas of that year, one of our household killed a turkey in front of our door, and where Washington street crosses the canal, that weighed twenty-three pounds before it was dressed. It was so fat that the fall from the top of the tree burst it open.

About four o'clock, Christmas morning, we were awakened by a salute from eight or ten rifles, and the cry of "Get up,

Kaintuck; we want some of that old peach brandy and honey;" which my father understood very well to be some excellent peach brandy he brought from Kentucky, of which they had drank freely while building our cabin. When he opened the door, the entire male portion of the Harding and McCormick population stepped into the cabin, and gave three cheers for "Old Kaintuck, the new comer."

After paying the brandy the highest compliment in their power by drinking freely of it, they went to and saluted the inmates of the different cabins in a similar way. There was no petty jealousy in the people at that day; all seemed on an equality; indeed, they seemed to think their only safety from their dusky neighbors was in unity and harmony—all seemed as members of one common family.

There were several accessions of families during that winter. A large portion of them were from Kentucky, among which were Robert Wilmot, George Buckner, Maxwells, Cowans, Daniel Shaffer (the first merchant), and many others. It was a noticeable fact that when one of the settlers should visit his old home, it would be followed by an increase of the population from that locality.

The two Messrs. Bradley stayed pretty much all winter, and assisted in clearing land preparatory for raising a "crap" the ensuing summer.

AN INDIAN ATTEMPTS TO CUT A DOOR DOWN.

One bright, sunny Sunday morning, about the middle of March, 1821, my father and myself took a walk to the river. When within about fifty yards of the house of John McCormick (which stood where the toll-house now stands, at the east end of White River bridge), we heard cries of "Help! Murder!" etc., coming from the house. We ran, and by the time we got there several men had arrived.

It appears a well known and desperate Delaware, known as Big Bottle (from the fact that he generally carried hung to his belt a very large bottle), had come to the opposite bank of the river, and demanded to be brought over. Mr. McCormick not being at home, his wife refused to take the canoe over for him, knowing that he wanted whisky, and when drinking was a very dangerous Indian.

He set his gun down against a tree, and plunged into the river and swam over, and when we reached the house was ascending the bank, tomahawk in hand, preparatory to cutting his way through the door, which Mrs. McCormick had barricaded, At the sight of the several men he desisted from his intention, and said he only wished to "scare white squaw." He was taken back to his own side of the river in the canoe, and admonished that if he attempted to scare the white squaw again her husband would kill him. This rather irritated him, and he flourished his scalping-knife toward her, and intimated by signs from her head toward his belt, that he would take her scalp; but he never did, as I saw it on her head a few weeks since. She now lives in Johnson County, two miles north of Waverley. The husband of this woman, John McCormick, built this house, the first in this place, February 26th, 1820, when commenced the first settlement of Indianapolis; although it has been asserted by some that George Pogue was here and settled in 1819, which I am prepared to show, by the most indubitable evidence, is not the case, and that John McCormick was the first, and that it was the latter part of February, 1820, and then followed, that spring, the Harding families, Wilsons, Pogues, which were about the only families here when we came on the fourth of November of that year.

Robert Wilmot, the second merchant, had a small stock of goods and Indian trinkets, and for a short time carried on a trade with the Indians; but a little circumstance occurred

Indian Attempts to Cut a Door Down. 19

that frightened him, and he soon returned to Georgetown, Kentucky, his former residence.

A Delaware Indian, named Jim Lewis, had pledged some silver hat-bands to Wilmot for goods, and was to return in two moons and redeem them. His word he kept, but when he came back Wilmot had sold them to another Indian, which exasperated Lewis so he threatened W. that if he ever found him going to his corn-field alone he would take his scalp. This frightened him so much that he never would go alone, but often requested and was accompanied by the late Doctor Livingston Dunlap. So fearful was he that Lewis would execute his threat, he sold out, and, as before stated, returned to Kentucky, as it was pretty generally known that Lewis was the murderer of the white man found near the Bluffs on an island of White River. This threat against Wilmot had a tendency to alarm and put on their guard other settlers.

That spring my father made sugar at an old Indian sugar camp (many of the trees are yet standing), at the south-east end of Virginia avenue. He was alone at night boiling the sap. He discovered coming direct to him, and only about thirty steps distant, a man he at once took to be Jim Lewis. He raised his rifle, pointed it at the man, and directed him to stop. The person threw up his hands, and cried out, "Don't shoot, Nowland, it is Harris." It turned out to be an old friend from Kentucky, named Price Harris, who had just arrived that evening, and wished to go out to the camp that night. He wore a white hat, which my father took for the silver bands Lewis wore on his hat. After this threat, for some time the settlers did not feel secure, and every little incident created alarm.

The supposed murder of George Pogue by the Indians, about this time, increased the alarm, and put the settlers more on their guard than they had ever been. A full account of the disappearance of Mr. Pogue, or all that was ever known of it, I will give in the next sketch. One writer says he was killed about daylight on a certain morning. How he found that out I am at a loss to understand, as those who lived here at the time never knew he was killed at all, although the circumstances are pretty strong that he came to his death by the hands of the Indians. After reading the next sketch the reader will be enabled to judge for himself.

GEORGE POGUE

Was a large, stout man, very dark complexion, black hair, very broad shoulders, and was, at the time he disappeared, about fifty years of age. His dress was something like that of a "Pennsylvania Dutchman," broad brim, black wool hat, and a drab overcoat, with several capes. To look at the man, you would think he defied all the "Injuns" in the "New Purchase." His cabin was built on the south-east bank of the creek that took its name from him, at the east end of the Donation, and near where Governor Noble's residence afterwards stood. He was a blacksmith by trade, and the first of that trade to enter the "New Purchase." He, like most all that were here in his day, was directly from "in yonder on White Water."

About the first of April, 1821, a straggling Wyandotte Indian, known to the settlers, as well as Indians, as "Wyandotte John," stopped at the house of Mr. Pogue about twilight one evening, and requested to stay all night. Mr. Pogue did not like to keep him, but thought it best not to refuse him, as he was known to be a very bad and desperate man, having left his own tribe in Ohio for some offense, and was now living among the different Indiana tribes. His principal lodging-place the previous winter was a hollow sycamore log, that lay under the bluff, and just above the east end of White River bridge. On the upper side of this log he had hooks (made by cutting the forks or limbs of the trees), on which he hung his gun; at the end of the log that lay next to the water he built his fire, which rendered this log about as comfortable as most of the cabins. I well remember it as I have described it. After John had something to eat, Mr. Pogue, knowing him to be traveling from one Indian camp to another, inquired of John if he had seen any white man's horses at any of the camps. He said he had left a camp of Delawares that morning (describing their place to be on Buck Creek, about twelve miles east, and near where the Rushville State Road now crosses said creek), and that he had seen horses there with iron hoofs (meaning that were shod), and described the horses so as to lead Mr. Pogue to believe they were his. Although he had described the horses very accurately, Mr. Pogue was afraid that it was a deception to lure him into the woods, and mentioned his suspicions to his family.

When the Indian left his house next morning, he took a direction toward the river, where nearly all the settlement was. Mr. Pogue followed after him some distance, to see whether he would turn his course or not toward the Indian camps, and found that John kept a direct course toward the settlement.

Mr. Pogue returned to his house, took his gun, and with his dog set out for the Delaware camp, and was never seen or heard of after. It is not true that he was seen near the Indian camp, or that gunshots were heard in that direction, or that his horses and clothing were seen in the possession of the Indians; although there can be but little doubt that the Wyandotte told him true, and that he found his horses in the hands of the Delawares, and in trying to get possession of them got into a difficulty with the Indians, and was killed— at least such was the prevailing opinion here at the time, but any certainty as to his fate was never known, and of course at this late day never will be. The settlers made a thorough search through all the Indian camps within thirty or forty miles, but never saw or heard anything of him.

In the summer of 1840, the writer employed John Pogue, son of George, to build a log cabin for the use of the Tippecanoe Club. While there at work I asked John what his opinion was as to the fate of his father. He said, "he was killed beyond a doubt at the Delaware camp on Buck Creek. The summer after my father left home, I was hunting south of our residence. I heard the report of a rifle, which was but a few steps from me. Knowing it to be from the gun of an Indian, I directed my steps immediately to it, before he would have time to reload his gun, as I had sworn to kill every Indian I met alone in the woods. A few steps from where I first heard the crack of the rifle, I saw a large, tall Indian reloading his rifle. I took a sure aim, and down came Mr. 'Injun.' I was surprised, when I went up to him, to find he had my father's hat on."

In answer to my question why he never let it be known at the time, he said he was afraid he would be prosecuted for the murder. He said he and his brother Tom went out at night, and brought the Indian to their corn-field and buried him. This story could not have been true, as the Indian would have been missed by his friends, and a disturbance made about it. John Pogue had got to be quite dissipated, and sometimes hardly knew what he said himself.

I do not think there are any of the children of George Pogue now living, at least not in this country. The last of the family, Bennett, removed to some of the Western States, and I understand died soon after.

I have endeavored to give a true account of the mysterious and first incident of note connected with the settlement of this city.

JOHN McCORMICK

Was the first white man that settled in this city. He arrived here on the twenty-sixth day of February, 1820, and built his cabin on the bank of White River, about ten steps below the east end of the National Road bridge. His two brothers, Samuel and James, helped him to move out and build his cabin. James' family arrived here on the seventh of March; Samuel did not bring his family until the next fall.

Mr. McCormick kept the first tavern in the place, and entertained the commissioners a part of the time when they were here for the purpose of selecting a site for the seat of government. He was very expert with a gig, and could fill a canoe with the most choice fish in a few hours. He frequently gigged the inferior kinds to feed to his hogs.

Mr. McCormick was the first man to leave the fort at Connersville, and build a house for a residence, about the year 1813, and there remained until his removal to this place. He died at his residence on the bank of the river in the year 1825. His widow married a man named King, and moved within one mile of the bluffs of White River, where she yet lives, a widow the second time.

Samuel and James McCormick lived in this county many years—Samuel on the farm now owned by Charles Garner, on the west bank of the river, at the crossing of the Crawfordsville State road. From there he moved to Hendricks County, near Cartersburgh, and there died in June, 1867.

James McCormick died in this county many years since, and left a large family of children, most of whom live in Hendricks County, where their mother also resides.

John McCormick, eldest son of Samuel, yet lives one mile west of the city, on the National Road, and is in the nursery and gardening business.

The three elder McCormicks were considered honest and industrious men, and respected in their neighborhood. There has been considerable said and written as to who was the first settler in this place, some claiming that George Pogue was; but I have evidence beyond dispute that Pogue did not come until the latter part of March of that year.

It was Mrs. McCormick that my father and others saved from falling into the hands of a desperate Indian, that I referred to on another page.

THE HARDING BROTHERS.

The Widow Harding and several sons came to this place in the spring of 1820. Her cabin stood on the bank of the river, on the north side of the ravine, near where the woolen factory of Merritt & Coughlen now stands.

Eleakem, Samuel, Israel, and Laban, were single, and lived with their mother. Robert was married, and lived on the bluff bank, just north of the east end of the National Road bridge. Ede Harding did not come to this place for several years after the rest.

Robert Harding's second son, Mordecai, was the first white child born on the Donation, and is still living four miles west of town, on the National Road.

The elder Hardings are all dead, except Ede and Samuel. Samuel lives at his old homestead, about a mile north-west of the Insane Asylum, on Eagle Creek.

The Hardings were all industrious and energetic farmers, having the opportunity as they did of selecting the best land in the New Purchase, and improved their farms in fine style.

Noah, the eldest and only other son of Robert Harding, lives about three miles west of the city, and is one of our most respectable farmers.

Laban, the son of Ede, owns and lives on one of the best

farms in the county, about six miles from town, north of the Crawfordsville State Road.

It was Samuel Harding who gave the writer his first lesson in horsemanship, allowing him to ride one of his plowhorses to and from the corn-field, morning, noon and evening.

Samuel and Israel Harding were brothers-in-law as well as brothers, having married two sisters, daughters of Jeremiah Johnson, and sisters of Jerry, spoken of on another page.

ISAAC WILSON.

This good old Samaritan came to this city in the spring of 1820, and built his double cabin on the northwest corner of the State House Square, the first house of any kind built on the original town plat. He built the first grist mill on Fall Creek, in the years 1821-22; he removed his family to his farm near the mill.

He was one of the most charitable and benevolent men I ever knew, and did as much for the poor during the four or five years he lived after the first settlement of the place as any person here. His house was the place for holding religious meetings and preaching as long as he lived in town, as it was also the stopping place for preachers of all denominations.

Mr. Wilson had been married twice. His first wife's children lived for many years on White Lick, about ten miles west of town, but those that are yet living have moved further west. He had four children by his last wife—the two boys, Lorenzo Dow and Wesley, are both dead; his two daughters are yet living. Patty is the wife of Samuel J. Patterson, and lives on her father's old farm; Elizabeth is the widow of Isaac Harris, and lives near her sister. They are the oldest settlers living near the town, while the writer claims to be the oldest living within the city limits.

Mr. Wilson was very kind to my father and mother, and

assisted us a great deal, which will be kindly remembered by the writer as long as he lives. He presented us with a cow and calf, ours having died a few days after my father's death.

SPRING OF 1821.

The spring of 1821 brought out a great many persons from the "settlement," for the purpose of raising a "crap," preparatory to moving their families in the fall.

The undergrowth of a large field was cleared in common by almost the entire population. The south side of the field only was fenced (with a brush fence); the north side and east and west ends were left open, as there was no stock that would be likely to disturb the growing crop. Indeed, the first and second years there were very few cattle and hogs, and they grazed on the south side of the field, where the fence was. The few horses were kept in the plow during the week, and on Sundays were taken to the island just across the river from the old city cemetery to graze. This island abounded with peavine and other fine pasture. The animals were generally "spanceled," or hobbled, by tying a rope around the forelegs, between the pastern-joint and hoof; and their owners watched them through the day, to prevent them being stolen by the Indians. The poor animals got very little to eat except spice boughs through the week. It was a great treat to them to have the fine pasture of the island on Sunday. I have often heard the settlers remark that their horses would do twice more work on Monday than any other day of the week.

A great many persons that were here for the purpose of raising a crop, were deterred from bringing their families in the fall, in consequence of the sickness of that summer. For a while there was scarcely one person able to hand another a drink of water.

Spring of 1821.

During the spring and summer there were many valuable and permanent accessions to the population, among which were Alexander W. Russell, Dr. Samuel G. Mitchell, Dr. Livingston Dunlap, Dr. Isaac Coe, our present and venerable fellow-citizen James Blake, Daniel Yandes, Samuel Morrow, of Georgetown, Kentucky (there being two Samuel Morrows,) Calvin Fletcher, Samuel Henderson, Thomas Chinn, Thomas Anderson, John Givan, James Givan, James Paxton, and many others, who proved to be valuable citizens; also the commissioner, Christopher Harrison, and surveyor, Alexander Ralston, to commence the survey of the new capital of Indiana.

In February of this year, my father had returned to Kentucky, and induced a man named Elisha Herndon to join him in the purchase of a keel-boat, and load it with flour, bacon, whisky, and such articles as might be necessary during the coming summer, in view of the survey of the town being made. The late Col. A. W. Russell, then a very young man, was prevailed upon to take charge of the boat as supercargo, and bring it from Frankfort, Kentucky, to this place, where he arrived about the first of May. The Kentucky and Ohio Rivers were descended without any difficulty, the rivers being high. The Wabash and White Rivers were ascended by what is called "cord-elling," or tying a rope to a tree some distance above the boat, and then pulling the boat up to the point; and sometimes poling or pushing the boat by means of poles. In this way, they were about six weeks in ascending the Wabash and White Rivers. This was the first boat that ever ascended the river this far; and the first Fourth of July was celebrated (by all who were not too sick) by a trip on this boat to Anderson's Spring, which was about one and a half miles above the settlement, on the west side of the river, near where the Crawfordsville State Road now crosses. The cargo of this boat was sold at a great loss, owing to the great expense incurred by the hire of hands necessary to bring it up the Wabash and White Rivers.

One or two other keel-boats, also ladened with provisions, arrived; their cargoes were in a damaged condition, the flour damp and musty; indeed, sweet flour was the exception, and damaged flour had to be used, and from this cause some thought the most of the sickness of that year arose.

The hands that were engaged to bring those boats here found ready employment by the surveying party as axe-men, chain-carriers, etc.

As I have said elsewhere, the historical events will be found in the biographical sketches I shall hereafter introduce.

ALEXANDER WILSON RUSSELL

Was born in Franklin County, Kentucky, on Benson Creek, about three miles from Frankfort, the capital of the State. His father, James Russell, was one of the most respectable farmers of that section of country; and was also the father of Captain John Russell (recently deceased), well known as one of the first and most efficient steamboat captains on the Ohio and Mississippi Rivers.

Alexander W. Russell, as stated in another sketch, came to Indianapolis in May, 1821, being the first white man that had ascended White River thus far in a keel-boat. It was not Mr. Russell's intention, for some time after he came here, to make it his permanent place of residence; but he immediately found employment in assisting to lay off the town. After that was completed he returned to Kentucky, and during the next winter concluded to make this place his residence. At that time he was quite young, and with but little experience, but had a very popular manner and way of making every person like him. In addition to this, he was a very fine performer on the "*fiddle*," which added greatly to his usefulness in a new country, as no log-rolling, house-raising or quilting, could well afford to dispense with the services of Aleck Russell (for he was not yet known as Major or Colonel, as he afterwards was). He was always on hand at Helrey's, on the school section, or old Jim McCoy's, near Broad Ripple; and no "gathering" of any kind would be complete until he had "entered an appearance." The first office, I believe, he was a candidate for and elected to, was that of "Major," which title he was called by for several years; then after the retirement of Mr. Harvey Bates, he was elected second sheriff of the county, which office he held the constitutional limit (two terms), and held the same office several times afterwards. He was elected to the office of Militia Colonel, and continued as such until the office died out for want of military spirit in the people to keep it up.

Colonel Russell was commissioned by Governor Noah Noble, the latter part of May, 1832, to raise three hundred volunteer militia, and proceed without delay to the seat of the Black Hawk or Indian War of that year, which he did; and the very fact that Russell was to be the commander-in-chief induced many to join that *bloody expedition* who otherwise would have remained at home. This expedition, it will be remembered, was composed of the best citizens of this and adjoining counties, who were to arm and equip themselves—horses, rifles and camp equipage—all at their own expense, and report in companies to Colonel Russell as soon as full. This was accomplished in a few days, and all ready for marching orders. Their camp or rendezvous was on the high ground just beyond West, and on the right side of Washington street.

Well do I remember the Sunday morning their long train of three hundred mounted men, reaching from their encampment to the corner of Pennsylvania street (where they turned north), wound their way along Washington; the many tears that were shed by loving wives and disconsolate mothers, as they took (as they supposed) a last long look at their friends, who were rushing to meet the "bloody Injuns," and offer their lives as a sacrifice upon the altar of their country. Well do I remember the tin-horn, about six feet in length, out of which was blown the most doleful noise that ever reached the ears of man; the only wonder to me was that the man, instead of blowing such a noise out of the horn, had not blown his own brains out.

Most conspicuous among this self-sacrificing band of patriots, if not martyrs, was General James P. Drake, Arthur St. Clair, Stoughton A. Fletcher, Judge Elisha M. Huntington, S. V. B. Noel, General Robert Hanna, John Tracy, Capt. John Wishard, Matthias T. Nowland, Capt. Alexander Wiley, Robert McPherson; and last, though by no means least, was Colonel Russell himself, and his worthy superior officer, Gov. Noble.

This expedition lasted just three weeks, and terminated on the third of July; on the fourth they were tendered and accepted a public dinner given by the citizens at Washington Hall. Out of the thirteen named above there are but five living, and I have no doubt they often recur to the many pleasing and amusing incidents of that campaign of the "bloody three hundred."

Colonel Russell was for many years a successful business man and merchant—was a stockholder in and director of the Branch Bank, also in Washington Hall. He was appointed Postmaster under General Taylor's administration, and died while in that office, in 1852.

There are many anecdotes of the Colonel extant. His clerks used to say of him that he would sell a man a pound of tobacco, and before the man would leave the counter ask him for a chew; such was his habit, he would ask for it when he really did not want it. No man ever lived in Marion

County that enjoyed the confidence of the people more than he did, and none ever died more regretted. He was of a cheerful and hopeful disposition, and his every act showed his kindness of heart and devotion to his friends.

Mr. Russell was an ardent and enthusiastic Whig of the old school—a warm personal friend of the late John J. Crittenden, of Kentucky; indeed, as he was of every person to whom he was attached. Like many others, he had one fault—he never learned how to use the word "No," and consequently injured himself by security, although he owned at the time of his death considerable property.

He left several children, all of whom seem to inherit his many good qualities of both head and heart.

As Colonel Russell's name is identified with the history of Indianapolis for the first thirty-two years, I shall have occasion to refer to it often.

JERRY JOHNSON.

This singular and eccentric individual came from the White Water country, with his father's family, in the winter of 1820-21. They settled on a piece of land they afterwards bought adjoining the Donation, on the north side, opposite "Camp Morton," the present Fair Ground.

A neighbor of theirs, "Old Billy Reagin," had two beautiful daughters (his only children), Miss Rachel, the eldest, and Miss Dovey, the younger. Young Jerry was not slow in discovering that "Miss Rachel was the purtiest critter his two eyes ever seed;" and, said Jerry, "I detarmined from the moment I first seed her, to have her, or die a-trying."

Jerry pressed his suit with all the ardor of his youthful passion, and soon won the heart and promise of the hand of the beautiful Rachel. There were other troubles to be surmounted of a more formidable nature—the county was not yet organized, and no person authorized to issue the necessary legal document to make the contract between him and Rachel binding, and consummate his happiness for life. The nearest point where the necessary license could be procured was Connersville, about sixty miles distant, and through an unbroken wilderness. Another circumstance made Mr. Johnson's trouble still greater; it was in the spring time of year, and his father could not spare him a horse from the plow. All these difficulties seemed to nerve rather than depress the spirits of Mr. Johnson. He well knew the danger of delay in such affairs, and fearful if he should wait for a horse, some other swain might woo and win the heart of the fair Rachel, which he wished to claim as quick as possible for his own, with a determination worthy of the cause in which he was engaged, he at once set out to "do or die," and started on foot, and barefoot at that, to make the journey alone. He accomplished his journey, and returned to find other difficulties, which if not so laborious, were equally disheartening, and calculated to make him believe that fate was against him. There was no magistrate yet appointed for the county, nor was there a minister authorized to tie the legal knot, and make them Mr. and Mrs. Johnson; so poor Jerry had to wait six long weeks, principally in the month of April, for a preacher to come and make him the happiest man in the New Purchase, and Rachel, as she was (like the goose that hung high), "altogether lovely." So ended the first courtship and wedding in or near Indianapolis.

There are many anecdotes of Mr. Johnson yet fresh in the minds of our old citizens. He was an ardent Whig, and took great interest in the elections during the existence of that party.

The first returns of a Presidential election received in this place by telegraph was in the year 1848, when Generals Taylor and Cass were the candidates. He remained in the telegraph office until a late hour of the night, to hear the dispatches read as they were severally received. Addressing himself to the writer, "Wall, John, has old Jerry lived to see the day when a streak of lightning can be made run along a clothes line, jist like some 'tarnal wild varmint 'long a worm fence, and carry nuse from one eend of the yearth to the tother? What would old Jim McCoy say if he wor here to see the nuse come in this way? He'd say, ''twiant slow for ten stops, boys; let's have something to drink. Landis, bring us some peach and honey. Whar's Russell, with his fiddle? and we'll have a reg'lar hoe down, *so we will.*'"

In the fall of 1847, there were several thousand persons assembled at the Madison depot to witness the arrival of the first locomotive and train of cars that ever came to Indianapolis. Mr. Johnson was standing on a pile of lumber, elevated above the rest of the crowd. As the locomotive hove in sight, he cried out, at the top of his voice, "Look out, boys; here she comes, h—ll on wheels." As the train stopped, he approached the locomotive; said he, "Well, well, who ever seed such a tarnal critter? It's wus nor anything I ever hearn on. Good Lord, John, what's this world gwine to come to?"

Mr. Johnson died about the year 1852. His wife survived him but a short time. His only child, a son, has since died. He was an upright, honest man, with many good traits of character. Although a rough, uncouth man in his manners, he possessed a kind and generous heart, ever ready to do a neighbor a kindness or favor. His house was always open to the unfortunate or wayfaring stranger, without money and without price. Such was Jerry Johnson, a fair specimen of the hospitality, generosity and frankness that characterized the early inhabitants of Indianapolis, when our selfish nature and the love of power and place had not assumed the entire control of our actions, and money was not the standard by which our characters were weighed.

There are many yet living that will attest the correctness and truthfulness (if not the elegance) of this short sketch of an "old settler."

DANIEL SHAFFER

Was a Pennsylvania Dutchman, and came direct from Cincinnati to this place in January, 1821. He brought the first merchandise of any kind to the New Purchase, or at least to this place, and was the first merchant of Indianapolis.

He built (with the assistance of the settlers) a double cabin south of Pogue's Creek, on the high ground, near the southern terminus of Meridian street. He was a large, stout man, about forty years of age, dark complexion, very black hair and eyes, and had the appearance of having been a laboring man; indeed, just such a person as would meet with a hearty welcome by all the settlers. He seemed to take hold of what was necessary to be done for the common good, with a will that showed great energy and industry. He was the first to call on the "new comers," and tender in behalf of the settlers such aid and assistance as they could and were able to render; was foremost at house-raisings and log-rollings, and at all times ready to make any sacrifice to help his neighbors.

The last time I remember to have seen him alive was about the tenth of August, at the raising of my father's second cabin. Being a stout man, he was always selected to "carry up a corner," which required great labor and bodily exertion. It was the labor of that day, I am told by Mr. Blake, that brought on the sickness that terminated in his death, about the eighteenth of the month.

There had been no event up to that time that was so disheartening to the entire community as the death of Daniel Shaffer. It seemed his loss could not be supplied by the accession of a dozen men or families; independent of his great services, every one looked upon him as a brother.

A few days before Shaffer's death, he, with Mr. Blake and my father, selected the site for the grave-yard, and was the first person buried in it. His grave stands immediately on the brow of the hill, near where the road ran until within a few years. A rude "sand-stone" marks the head, with his name and date of death engraved on it. A few days before my father's death, he requested to be laid by the side of Mr. Shaffer, which was done; and there, too, stands a similar stone, marked "Matthias R. Nowland, died November 11th, 1822." Could these two men, to-day, awake from their sleep of death of forty-eight years, what strange sights would meet their eyes; could they possibly believe this was the place they left?

Soon after Mr. Shaffer's death, his family, a wife and three children (two sons and a daughter), returned to Cincinnati, where I saw some of them but a few years since.

May the march of improvement and enterprise, now so busy in the immediate neighborhood of the sacred ground where rest the bodies of those two old settlers, never desecrate their graves, or lay unhallowed hands upon them; but may they be permitted there to lay, until that day when the graves shall be called on to give up their dead to appear before the Great Judge of the Universe.

ANDREW BYRNE,

Or "Uncle Andy," as he was known generally by both old and young, was the first tailor that came to and commenced the business in Indianapolis, in March, 1821, although he was here at the time the commissioners made the selection for the seat of government.

He was born in Frankfort, Kentucky, in the year 1800, and there learned the tailoring business, and was considered a "first rate workman." He was a small, spare-made man, black hair and eyes, and looked sharp enough to split a flaxseed in two pieces. You would hardly think he would weigh fifteen pounds, apothecaries' weight. He thought (especially if he had taken a little "bayou blue") he would weigh several ton, and felt as big as a two story house.

Uncle Andy could make a garment to suit the most fastidious dandy of that early day. He had the whole patronage of Indianapolis in that line; if any were disposed to grumble at prices, he would tell them they had better take their work to another shop. He was generally very independent in business matters, but was a very unobtrusive, quiet man, unless excited or irritated. His shop was about four feet square, in the corner of my father's cabin. Here the fashionable tailoring of Indianapolis was first done. One of the coats there manufactured would be worthy of Barnum's attention at this day. They were only equaled by the hats that were generally worn with them, and were manufactured by John Shunk, an account of which will be found in another sketch.

Uncle Andy made several trips to and from Kentucky, before he could make up his mind to make this place his permanent residence. He would sometimes drink a little too much, which always rendered him very happy as well as rich for the time being; he imagined he owned Indianapolis by the "right of discovery," and all the citizens were his "tenants at will."

For several years before his death, which was in April, 1851, his health was so impaired he was unable to follow his business, and made my mother's house his home.

He now lays in the family portion of the second cemetery, by the side of most of his relatives, who had gone before him. There are many who will see this short sketch, both in the city and throughout the State, who will remember "Uncle Andy Byrne." "May he rest in peace."

MATTHIAS T. NOWLAND

Was born in Frankfort, Kentucky, in 1807, and came with the family to this place. He was a fine English scholar, having enjoyed the benefit of the tutelage of the Hon. Amos Kendall. He possessed a great deal of native talent, and when grown up was a great wag, and enjoyed innocent sport, as will be seen before this sketch closes.

At the death of my father he was the only one of the children capable of rendering any assistance to my mother in the support of the family.

In the year 1823, he engaged with Messrs. Smith & Bolton, proprietors of the "Indianapolis Gazette," the first and only paper published here at that time, to learn the printing business, reserving the privilege of boarding at home. At the end of one year he was sufficiently advanced to earn, and did receive, half wages.

After he had obtained a pretty fair knowledge of the business, he went to Vincennes and took charge of an office, of which the Hon. John Ewing was proprietor and editor, often, in the absence of the editor, doing his duties.

After being in Vincennes one year (as he had engaged), he was persuaded by a printer to accompany him to New Orleans, which he did. The second day after their arrival there he stood upon his comrade's coffin to keep it under water while the dirt was being thrown on, he having died of yellow fever. This silent but impressive admonition caused him to return home as quick as possible, and he found work with Messrs. Douglass & Maguire, in the office of the "Journal."

About that time there was a kind of "Jack-legged lawyer" (as they were then called) here from Salvysa, Kentucky, named Eccles. This man was thrusting himself before the people on all occasions, for office. He talked so much about his former residence, and how he stood there, Mat gave him the soubriquet of "Salvysa."

Salvysa was a candidate for the Legislature, and Governor Ray a candidate for re-election. Mat, with his quick perception, soon discovered a fine opening for the enjoyment of his peculiar passion, and became a candidate against Salvysa. Knowing him to be a very irritable and passionate man, he set about getting up innocent charges against him. The first was that he thought it an insult to the people for a Kentucky lawyer, who, in his own State, was thought only fit for and did keep a "fancy horse," to offer himself to the intelligent citizens of Indiana, especially to those of the capital of the State, to represent them in the Legislature. This had the desired effect to irritate Salvysa, who, in a very excited manner, asked a suspension of opinion until he should have time to disprove "the vile slander." This gave Mat several weeks to enjoy this charge, for it took some time for Salvysa to send to Kentucky to get the necessary certificates; but in due time they came.

Salvysa, with great exultation, displayed a string of certificates three feet long to prove he was never known to be in any such employment while he lived in Kentucky, and that he (Salvysa) hoped that his opponent would publicly apologize for the "vile charge." This Mat did by saying he had been mistaken; it was not a horse, but a "Jackass" that Salvysa had kept in Kentucky, and that he defied the honorable Kentuckian, who had so insulted the people of Indiana, to disprove it. This was only the week before the election, and Salvysa knew he could not get a letter to Kentucky and an answer in less than three weeks, which excited him very much, and caused him to heap all kinds of imprecations upon the head of Mat.

While he had Salvysa going through the mill, he was not neglecting Governor Ray, but kept him busy clearing up charges. One charge against his Excellency was that, while traveling on a steamboat, he registered his name as "J. Brown Ray, Governor of the State of Indiana, and Commander-in-Chief of the Army and Navy thereof." Another was that, while on the steamboat, a servant placed a spittoon before him, and that the Governor told the servant if he did not take it away he would spit in it. The third charge was that the Governor, when he pardoned young Bridges at the falls of Fall Creek, for the murder of the Indians, commanded young Bridges to stand up, and then addressed him in this way: "Sir, do you know in whose presence you stand?" Being answered in the negative, "You are charged by a jury of your countrymen with the murder of several innocent Indians. There are but two powers known to the laws of your country that can save you from hanging by the neck until you are dead. One is God Almighty, the Great Ruler of the Universe; the other is James B. Ray—the latter stands before you." With these charges he kept his Excellency in hot water all the time of the canvass, and would occasionally follow him to adjoining counties.

Mat was one of the "bloody three hundred," and many anecdotes are told of him during that remarkable expedition. One of the company to which he belonged was very chivalrous, always expressing a wish to meet and encounter hostile Indians, and was very free to express the opinion that the most of the company were afraid that they would meet an enemy. When encamped on the Calumet, a false alarm was given that the hostile Indians were advancing upon them, and preparations made for action. Mat took particular pains to hunt this man up, and found him concealed under the baggage wagon, and charged it on him, which furnished sport for the entire command during the balance of the campaign.

Mat was the first to learn the "art preservative of all arts" in Indianapolis, and the first to learn how to make the composition roller, then so little used by printers. He was a fine pressman, a correct and quick compositor; in short, knew the whole routine of a printing office as well as any person of his day. He was a man of great vivacity and humor, ever ready for an innocent joke; very quick to detect and resent an intended insult or injury, and just as quick to forgive and forget it; was liberal and confiding to a fault.

He brought the first tame pigeons to this place, in 1824, which he carried on horseback from Frankfort, Kentucky, and from which sprung, no doubt, the myriads that now swarm and fly around the city.

No man ever cast a line in White River that was more successful as an angler. This taste he inherited from his father, who was the first to introduce that fascinating amusement here, in June, 1820, and caught about the first bass with hook and line, at the mouth of Fall Creek.

He was a ready writer, a fair speaker, and possessed the faculty of attracting the attention of the people. He had his faults, but they were rather of the head than the heart. He died suddenly on the fourth of October, 1834, leaving many friends, and, I believe, no enemies.

Thus passed away a generous-hearted young man, that might have been one of Indiana's brightest sons.

FISH, GAME AND SKUNKS.

At the time of which I am now writing (1821), White River abounded with fish of great variety and choice quality. Its waters were as clear as crystal, and the fish could be seen at the bottom in shoals, and a person could almost select from the number and capture any one desired. If a minnow was cast into the stream, a number of bass would dart at it at once. The people from "in yonder on White Water," came out in the fall when the weather began to get cool, with seines; and, provided with salt and barrels, would load their wagons in a short time with the finest—the refuse would be left upon the bank, or given to the settlers to feed their hogs.

The river abounded with a fish called gar, which was unfit for anything but feeding hogs. John McCormick, with a gig or spear, would load a canoe with them in a short time, sufficient to keep his hogs several days.

When the river was frozen over, people would supply themselves with fish, when they would find them up next to the ice, by striking on the ice over them, which would stun them until a hole could be cut and the fish taken out. After the day's work was over, my father often, with hook and line, would catch enough to supply our family for several days.

Fish were not the only game taken from White River at that day. The more substantial and valuable was the fine fat deer with which the forest abounded, and most generally taken at night in the river. The process was called "fire-hunting." In warm weather the deer would wade in the shallow water at night, to get the long grass and cool themselves, and could be approached very near, at least near enough to make sure of one of them. The bow of a canoe would be filled with dirt in such a way as to prevent any damage to the craft by the fire which would be made on it. The motive power would be a person in the stern of the canoe, who understood the business and the use of the paddle. The hunter would stand just behind the fire and completely hid from the view of the animal, which would be almost blinded by the light. In this way I have known two persons to take several in one night. Just opposite the mouth of Fall Creek was a great resort for deer, and they could be found there at almost any time of the night.

When the squirrels were emigrating, which was nearly every fall, they could be taken in the river without trouble. So the reader will see that White River furnished a bountiful supply of the finest game that was ever set before an epicure.

Nor was this all: the woods were filled with turkeys as "slick and fat" as Henry Clay's negroes (see his reply to Mendenhall). Although they were rather harder to capture than the deer in this way, yet they could always be taken by a hunter that understood the business; indeed, I have known the hunter to set behind a log and call them within ten steps, near enough to select the largest and finest of the number.

Among the most successful hunters was Mr. Nathaniel Cox, who never failed to have his larder and that of his friends well stored with the choicest game of the woods.

In the year 1825, and during the session of the Legislature, a fine turkey was shot from the top of Hawkins' Tavern. A flock had been scared in the north part of town, two lit on the house, one of which was killed. It was no uncommon thing, about the years 1846-47, for turkeys to be killed on the northern part of the Donation. About this time a bear was killed near where Camp Morton now is.

In 1837, a panther or catamount, measuring nine feet from the nose to the tip of its tail, was killed by Zachariah Collins on Fall Creek, near Millersville. In earlier years one frequented the island opposite the graveyard, and was often heard to halloo at night; that deterred some from pasturing their horses there on Sundays.

Another kind of game was plenty, but of no value to the white man—the porcupine. The quills with which its back was covered were very sharp; and I have often seen the mouths of the dogs that caught them filled full, which gave them great pain, and they had to be drawn out with tweezers or bullet-moulds. These quills the Indians valued highly, as they were useful to them for ornamenting their moccasins and other handiwork of the squaws.

There was another animal that the dogs never failed to let it be known when they met with them in the woods; although they were not so plenty as the others, a few of them would go a great ways, and generally supply the neighborhood with all they required, and when one was killed either by dogs or hunter, there was plenty to go around. This animal was known by the name of skunk, or generally, by the settlers, as pole-cat; and many was the laugh and jest at its expense. In the summer of 1821, a young man from Kentucky, named Mancher, visited his brother-in-law, Robert Wilmot. While in the woods he met one, and thought it a very pretty thing to take to Kentucky with him as a pet. He tried to capture it alive; but the first fire from the formidable battery of the animal convinced him it was useless to attempt to take him to Kentucky, unless he had a larger supply of *eau de Cologne* on hand than could be purchased in this market. He concluded to not cultivate the acquaintance of the pretty creature any further, although his friends well knew when he returned to the house he had made it.

Those persons who had not the time or inclination to hunt could procure game at almost nominal prices from the Indians. A saddle of venison for twenty-five cents; fine fat turkeys, of the largest kind, for twelve and a half cents, or three for a quarter; indeed, the Indians were not very close traders, and would take almost anything offered them, especially if it was paid in trinkets or brass jewelry of any kind.

Turkeys were often caught by means of pens constructed for the purpose—a small log pen, about eight feet in length and four wide, made of poles, something like a cabin, and covered tight. A trench was dug about fifteen feet long, and leading under the bottom log into the pen. This trench was of sufficient depth to admit the largest sized turkey. Corn or other grain was scattered along the trench and into the pen. The turkey would feed along with his head down until inside before he was aware of it. He would never think of going out the way he came in, but seek egress from the top. I have known five or six found in a pen at one time.

CHRISTOPHER HARRISON.

The only one of three commissioners appointed by the Legislature to superintend the laying out and survey of the town that appeared and acted. He was from Salem, Washington County; was a man about fifty years of age, and like the surveyor (Mr. Ralston), a bachelor. He stopped at the house of, and boarded with, my father. He had no more hair on his head than there was in the palm of his hand, and wore a wig. I shall never forget the fright he gave my younger brother, James. The morning after his arrival at our house, he was out at the well, washing, and had his wig off. James happened to discover the want of hair, and ran to my mother and told her "the Indians had scalped the man that came last night." This she did not understand fully until she stepped to the door and saw his bald head.

I think he was a Virginian by birth, but had been a resident of the territory and State for many years. He was a perfect gentleman in his manners and intercourse with his subordinates in this important work, and won their universal confidence and respect. He remained but a short time after his official duties were ended, and returned to his home.

I do not think he ever visited the place but once afterwards; that was during the first session of the Legislature, in 1825. He lived to a good old age, and died as he had lived, a bachelor.

DR. LIVINGSTON DUNLAP

Came to this place in July or August, 1821, a young physician, in search of a location to commence the practice of his profession. He was from Cherry Valley, New York, where I think he was born and raised.

When he first arrived in this place he stopped at the house of Dr. Samuel G. Mitchell, who lived on the southwest corner of Washington and Tennessee Streets, where the State offices now stand. The Doctor was not long here when he had the most indubitable evidence that this was a first-rate place for a physician. Not only the whole family with which he stayed were taken down with chills and fever, but himself, so bad he could neither render assistance to them nor they to him. In this situation my father found them one day when he called to see what he could do for them; although our own family were nearly all sick, Mr. Blake and himself were still able to wait on them. My father at once proposed to take the Doctor home with him. But how was he going to get him there? queried the Doctor. "Take you on my back," was the answer; which he did, something like the squaws carried their children or pappooses.

The Doctor remained an inmate of our house for some time. After he recovered, he rendered valuable service, not only to our family, but to those that were sick that fall. Physicians did not think their duty done when they merely had prescribed and given the necessary medicine (as now-a-days), but to their duties was added that of nurse. This portion the doctors performed well and cheerfully.

If I were writing only for the eye of those that knew him during his long career of usefulness in after years, it would be unnecessary to say he stood at the head of his profession. He was for many years the leading physician in this place, and there were very few doubtful or dangerous cases in which he was not consulted by his brothers in the profession.

He was councilman of his ward in 1834, and for several years after. He was physician for the Deaf and Dumb Asylum for several years; also, one of the commissioners of the Insane Asylum. He was appointed postmaster by President Polk in 1845, and held the office until April, 1849. All the duties of the different offices he held he discharged with credit to himself and to the entire satisfaction of the public, and his numerous friends of both political parties.

Dr. Dunlap was a man of very warm feelings and friendship, and would go any length to serve a friend; but if his displeasure was once incurred, and he had reason to believe his confidence had been misplaced, he would hardly ever forget it. Although he was not a revengeful man or bore malice, he would steer clear of those whom he thought had mistreated him.

He died in 1862, leaving a small family in very comfortable circumstances, with some fine city property. Of his three sons but one is now living, Dr. John Dunlap, of this city. James, his eldest son, and a portrait painter, died in 1865.

CONRAD BRUSSELL,

The first baker, was a low, thick, heavy-set Dutchman, nearly as thick as he was long. He was more generally known as "Old Coonrod." He came here in the fall of 1821, and built a small cabin on the north bank of the ravine (known at that time as the River Styx), just opposite where Kingan's pork-house now stands, and about one hundred yards above its junction with the river.

This cabin answered "Coonrod" for a residence as well as a bakery, as he was a bachelor and had no family, but his little dog "Boas." This dog resembled his owner very much in appearance, short, bow legs, thick, heavy body, and very good-natured, except when an Indian wished to enter the domicil. Coonrod said Boas could smell an Indian a mile; neither had the worthy baker a very exalted opinion of them, and preferred losing their custom to endangering his scalp. His oven was built on the east side of the cabin. Four posts were planted in the ground, about five feet apart, and formed a square. On the posts was made a platform of puncheons;

on the puncheons was dirt sufficient to prevent them from taking fire. The dirt was plastered to form the bottom of the oven. Then a kind of frame-work was built (the shape and size he wanted the oven), plastered and left a sufficient time to dry; a fire was kindled on the inside that burnt out the frame-work and left the oven. In this oven was baked the first rusk and ginger-cake in Indianapolis.

He was patronized by nearly all the inhabitants, his best customers being the travelers seeking locations in the New Purchase. Our family sent every time he baked (which was twice a week), to get some of his nice warm rusk; but a little circumstance occurred that lost him one customer. Coonrod was very much afflicted with sores on his arms; indeed, his whole appearance was rather *boilious* for a baker.

As usual, Saturday evening, I was sent to Coonrod's for the quarter's worth of rusk. I found the old man in rather a despondent mood; I saw in a moment that something was the matter; if Boas had died he could not have looked more woful. When I asked him for the rusk, "Oh, Johnny," said he, "I will have none for Sunday. Last Wednesday, when I baked, mixing the dough hurt me so much I have scarcely been free of pain since. The flour got into the sores on my arms, and I was not able to-day to mix the dough for the rusk." This simple but truthful tale was sufficient to induce our family to forego the use of his rusks from that time. Other customers found out the same thing, and he closed business for want of patronage. When, like the Moor of Venice, he found his occupation gone, he sought a home in other parts.

How different the first bakery of Indianapolis to those of the present day; how different from the last that has commenced business in this city—the establishment of G. W.

Caldwell & Co., where that beautiful and delicious acrated bread is manufactured, in any quantities the demand may require, from one to ten thousand loaves per day, and without the hand coming in contact with the dry flour or the dough. The flour is taken from the barrel with a shovel, and thrown into a sieve moved by machinery. This sieve will prevent the smallest particle of dirt passing through it. The flour passes into a reservoir or kneader, where it is mixed, and from the kneader passes into the pans for baking, and is never touched by the hand, until handling for delivery to customers. A visit to this establishment would induce the use of this kind of bread; if for no other reason, for cleanliness alone. You will see the utter impossibility of the smallest house fly passing through the sieve, to say nothing of the filthy cockroach often found in the middle of the loaf of bread manufactured in the ordinary way. I care not how careful and cleanly the baker or housewife may be, there will sometimes dirt or insects get mixed with the dough and not be discovered until it is baked.

In this establishment are two kneaders, one of which will mix a barrel, the other one and a half barrels of flour at a time; and in a few minutes from the time the flour is thrown into the sieve it is ready to bake.

In speaking of the above establishment, I do not wish to disparage the other fine bakeries of the city, in many ef which can be found as fine articles as in any similar bakeries in the United States.

In the houses of Nickum & Parrott, the Cincinnati Bakery, and Ball, of Illinois street, will be found every variety of cake; and they are in striking contrast with the first bakeries of Indianapolis.

The crackers of Mrs. Thompson have a reputation unsurpassed, if equaled, anywhere.

JOHN SHUNK.

John Shunk was the first man that ever attempted in this place to manufacture a "wild varmint" into something, and call it a "hat."

He built a log cabin on the bank of the river south of the ravine and woolen-mill, and near where Kingan's pork-house is now located.

His cabin was about fifteen by eighteen feet square, which served the energetic proprietor as parlor, kitchen, chamber, hall and shop. The kettle used for boiling or stewing the various kinds of skins into hats was placed on a stone furnace in the middle of the room, or dirt floor.

His bed stood in the northeast corner. The bedstead was made by boring two holes in the third log from the floor of the house, about seven feet apart. In these holes were driven two poles about four feet in length. The other ends of the poles were fastened to other poles about the same length, and, standing upright, thus formed the framework of the bedstead.

On this frame was laid lengthwise other poles, sufficient in number and size to form the bottom. On this structure was a bed-tick (the original color I can't tell) filled with a combination of leaves and straw. The "kivering" consisted of a very dirty horse or saddle-blanket, and a few dilapidated deer and other kinds of skins. On this couch Mr. Shunk could repose his weary limbs, and at the same time watch and feel the increase of his stock of fleas.

In the southwest corner of the cabin was the fireplace, which was made by building a stone wall on each side of the corner, about four feet high, to protect the logs from the fire. It was of a two-angle shape. A hole in the roof of the cabin was left for the escape of smoke. This, of course, was the culinary part of the establishment, where the potatoes were roasted, the venison broiled on the coals, wild turkeys stewed, fish fried, and spicewood tea boiled. Mr. Shunk (being a widower) was his own cook, and a cook is generally supposed to select such articles of diet and cook them as best suits his own taste.

In the northwest corner of the house was a broad table, about four feet high and six in length. Over this table, and suspended by a rope (fastened to the rib-pole above), hung a thing that looked something in shape like the bow of a base viol, only much larger. On this bow was a large cat gut string, which he would pull in such a way that it would strike and cut to pieces the combination of hair and fur.

The southeast, and last, corner of the cabin was used as a receptacle or depot for miscellaneous articles.

Mr. Shunk required his customers to furnish their own coon. He would receive them in animate or inanimate condition, as best suited the convenience of the customer, and was not slow in manufacturing them into something that looked more like the old-fashioned hollow-log bee-gums of that day than they would like one of Mr. Bamberger's fashionable hats of the present.

On one occasion Luke Walpole had employed Mr. Shunk to make him a hat. Whether Mr. W. furnished the coon or not I am not aware. However, the hat was finished and taken to the customer. On close examination Mr. W. thought the animal not quite dead, and wished to know of the worthy hatter if he thought there would be any danger of the hat disturbing his chickens.

In closing this description of the first hatter's shop in Indianapolis, I must say something of the close of the worthy proprietor. He was a large, fleshy man, would weigh over two hundred and twenty-five pounds, was very fond of grog, and often indulged to such an extent as to render him incapable of taking care of himself.

John Shunk. 51

He was found one morning in front of his furnace, completely baked brown. The skin was cracked open, and the grease or fat was oozing out.

All that could be done to alleviate his suffering (as recovery was impossible) was done by his neighbors and the citizens, but he was beyond the reach of human aid, and suffered a few days and closed his earthly as well as his *hatatorial* career. He was a relative of the late Governor Shunk, of Pennsylvania, and, I believe, otherwise highly connected in that State.

I will now pass from the first hatter-shop of Indianapolis, 1821, to that of Herman Bamberger, of 1870. A few days since I called in at Mr. B.'s, and was invited by the gentlemanly and polite proprietor to look through his extensive establishment. Although I had heard and read a great deal about his as well as other establishments of the kind in the city, I was entirely unprepared to see so large and extensive an assortment as he keeps on hand.

Although Mr. Bamberger is not an "old settler" in the strict senses of the word, or in the sense I generally use the term, yet he has been here sufficiently long, and his establishment is one of that kind I wish to use to draw a comparison between the first hatter of Indianapolis and those of the present day.

I can hardly realize that even the forty-eight years that have elapsed since the existence of the shop of which I have been writing could have brought such a change.

In Mr. B.'s store is found every conceivable shape, form, pattern, style and fashion that could be thought of, with perhaps the exception of John Shunk's style.

I am told by many of his patrons he never suffers a customer to leave his establishment dissatisfied in either price or quality.

Indeed, the very appearance of the store indicates success;

and success means fair dealing. I am told he has the bulk of the German trade, both in this and adjoining counties.

If a large stock, polite and gentlemanly bearing and accommodating disposition are requisite in trade, all those qualities will be found in Herman Bamberger. But I am digressing from my purpose to show the difference between the first hatter-shop of Indianapolis and those of the present. Could it be possible for John Shunk to awake from his forty-eight years' sleep on the banks of White River, and step into one of these fine establishments, he would hardly take it to be a *hatter's shop*, or that he, while in the flesh, was anything else than a hatter.

MATTHIAS R. NOWLAND

Was a native of Delaware, born at Dover, the capital, in the year 1787. When quite young, with the family of his father, he emigrated to Chillicothe, Ohio, where he remained until he had attained his majority. He then went to Frankfort, Kentucky, and shortly after his arrival there was married to Miss Elizabeth Byrne, in after years as well, if not more generally, known through Indiana than any lady in it. Who that ever visited Indianapolis, from its beginning to 1856, has not heard of Mrs. Nowland?

In Frankfort he engaged in active business, and was quite successful during his sojourn there, about fourteen years, and until his removal to this place, the "New Purchase," in 1820. He was a quiet, unobtrusive man, content to attend to his own business and let others do the same; was about the only person at the first settlement of this place who was not a candidate for office, although he was appointed by Mr. Bates, the sheriff, judge of the first election in the new county, that took place in 1822, the first and only office he ever held. In February he returned to Kentucky and induced several families to emigrate and help swell the population. In the meantime the two young men he had brought here were busy in clearing the common field, and preparing for a crop the coming season.

After his return from Kentucky he engaged in making sugar in an old Indian sugar camp at the southeast end of Virginia avenue. Many of the sugar-trees that he opened are yet standing. He and myself were there mostly alone, especially at night. That was a very fine season for the manufacture of sugar, the season lasting until April, which was very unusual, in after years. In the short time he attended to this business, he realized over six hundred pounds of beautiful sugar and a considerable quantity of the finest molasses;

> "Which showed he rightly understood
> The art, and in this Western wood
> He scooped the primal sugar-trough,
> And presided at the "*stirring off.*"
> He knew every labor, every joy,
> When quite alone with his rustic boy.
> He looked through winter, when March would bring
> The sugar-making and the spring."

The events of the summer of 1821 are already recorded in another chapter.

The agent of the State had set apart three outlots, of about three acres each, to sell to such persons as wished to make brick. One of these, situated at what was the then east end of Washington street, between East and Liberty and Washington and Market, he purchased; and here, in 1822, he made the first kiln of brick that was made in the new purchase, the *debris* of which may be seen at this time. Working very hard, and taking cold at this brickyard, caused the disease that terminated his life, on the 11th of November, 1822.

However much the stroke of death may be expected, it never comes without a violent shock to our feelings. I well remember

> "His farewell look, with Christian hope
> Shone as purely, calmly bright.
> Alas, when it vanished the night came down,
> And my poor lone heart no more might own
> A father's guiding light."

Before his death he had selected a warm, sunny knoll for his future resting place, and received the promise that the hand of affection should often render kind offices to his memory, and for thirty-two years was the pledge faithfully kept by the companion of his bosom.

He had purchased a number of lots at the sale, and had paid the first and second payments, which had to be forfeited in consequence of his death.

The expense incurred in the making of brick, and the loss on the keel-boat and produce speculation, had exhausted his means, which left his family in a quite helpless condition. But thanks to the old citizens who so generously aided us in our time of need, among whom were Calvin Fletcher, Jacob Landis, Isaac Wilson, Daniel Yandes, James Blake, and many others.

Although they, too, were poor, their countenance and advice to a family in our situation and without experience was valuable, and was remembered by my mother so long as she lived.

THE WHETZEL FAMILY.

Fifty years ago, I suppose, there was no family so well known throughout the entire west as that of the Whetzel family, consisting of five brothers, Martin, George, Lewis, Jacob and John. They, or most of them, were born in the Shenandoah valley, but with their father, John Whetzel, emigrated to Ohio County, Virginia, in the year 1769, and settled about twelve miles from Wheeling, and near where the Clay monument, which was erected by their cousin, Moses Shepherd, now stands,. It was here the Whetzels called home (although their home proper was the woods, or on the track of marauding bands of Indians); this, at least, was the residence of their families, and their place of meeting and rendezvous, where were planned their expeditions against the hostile savage. The different expeditions of Lewis, the third brother, and Jacob, the fourth, are pretty generally known to the reading world.

It is with Jacob, who settled on White Water River in the year 1811, and his son Cyrus, now living near this city, I shall confine what I have to say. During the time the white inhabitants of that part of Virginia, now known as Ohio County, were living in a fort, near Wheeling, a turkey was heard to call every morning, about daylight, across a ravine, and about two hundred yards from the fort. One of the men went out one morning and never returned, which created a suspicion in the mind of Mr. Whetzel that the turkey might be something else. He knew of a fissure in the rocks near where the sound of the turkey-call proceeded, and the next night informed his comrades that he was going to solve the turkey mystery. Accordingly in the night he secreted himself in this place, and awaited patiently the coming of day, as well as the call of the turkey. Just about daylight he heard the call, which proceeded from a tree-top just above where he was concealed, and within shooting distance. He patiently awaited the time when it should be sufficiently light for him to make no mistake of the kind of game he was seeking. After waiting about half an hour he plainly saw the form of a tall, well-proportioned Indian raise from his seat in the fork of the tree, and watching closely the path that led from the fort. Just at this time Mr. Whetzel took a sure and deadly aim, and down came the turkey in the shape of a large and athletic Indian, which he scalped as quickly as possible, and returned to the fort, lest the crack of his trusty rifle might bring the comrades of said turkey. Although this was not the last turkey in the woods, it had the effect to stop their gobbling for a while.

After Ohio County was organized he was elected a magistrate, and then, in turn, as was the custom and law that the oldest magistrate should be sheriff and collector of the revenue, he became sheriff, and, through dishonest deputies and other causes, became involved, and, eventually, quite poor. He resolved, in the year 1808, to emigrate farther west, and settled in Boone County, Kentucky, where he resided until 1811, when he settled near where Laurel, Franklin County, now is, living there until he settled near the Bluffs of White River.

In the year 1818 he visited the old Delaware chief, Anderson, at his village on White River, where Andersontown, Madison County, now stands, for the purpose of obtaining permission to cut a trace from his residence on White Water to the Bluffs of White River, which was granted. Accordingly he and his son Cyrus, with some hired hands, cut the trace that summer. The next spring, 1819, he and his son came out and raised a crop, moving his family in the fall to the farm his son now lives on. This trace commenced, as I said before, at his residence in Franklin County, crossed Flat Rock about seven miles below Rushville, Blue River about four miles above Shelbyville, and where a village called Marion now stands; and Sugar Creek near Boggstown; thence near where Greenwood now stands, to the Bluffs. This was the main thoroughfare for some time, to and from the settlement.

On this trace and near where it crossed Flat Rock, an Indian, named "Big Buffalo," was butchered by his comrades, in the summer of 1819. "Buffalo" had, twelve moons before, killed an Indian called "Old Solomon." The usual time of twelve moons was given him, to either pay one hundred dollars, one hundred buckskins, or forfeit his life. The band were encamped at this place when the time expired, and he was accordingly butchered and left lying in the trace, and was buried by some whites who found him.

The Whetzel Family.

In the fall of 1819 a party of Indians visited Mr. W. at his house, one of whom was a very large and powerful man, named "Nosey," from the fact he had lost a part of his nose. This Indian proposed shooting at a mark with Mr. W.'s son, Cyrus. The young man beat him very bad; but soon discovering that the Indian was very angry, and disposed to be quarrelsome about it, young Whetzel proposed to shoot again, letting the Indian beat him as badly as he had previously beaten the Indian, which had the effect of pacifying him, at least for a while. The Indians then left Mr. W.'s cabin, and had gone only about two miles, when "Nosey" killed one of his comrades. It was supposed the anger engendered by being beaten by Mr. W.'s son had not yet cooled. "Nosey" was also given the usual twelve moons to pay the price of life, which he failed to do, and in the fall of 1820 (about the time the writer of this came to Indianapolis, for I remember that the cruel manner of the butchery was talked about), "Nosey" was killed by the friends of the man he had murdered. At the expiration of the twelve moons he gave himself up. He was taken to a tree, his arms drawn up to a limb, his legs were parted, and ankles fastened to stakes driven in the ground, and then he was stabbed under the arms and in the groin with a butcher-knife, and tortured in other ways until life was extinct.

In the spring of 1820, the body of a man was found about one and a half miles above the Bluffs, and a man by the name of Ladd was suspected of the murder. He was arrested by a set of desperate men, who had banded together, styling themselves regulators; but he was soon released, as there was not a shadow of evidence against him. He then sued the men for false imprisonment, and they were taken to Connersville for trial. This was the first case of litigation in the New Purchase, and a very expensive one it proved, as the case occupied some time, resulting finally in the plaintiff getting nominal damages. This man, no doubt, was murdered by a desperate and notorious Delaware, named Hiram Lewis, as the Indian was in possession of his horse, saddle and bridle, pistol, and a red morocco pocket-book, containing some money on the Vincennes Steam-Mill Company.

In the Indianapolis "Journal," of the third of July, 1827, I find the death of Jacob Whetzel announced as taking place on the second instant. The "Journal" says:

"Captain Whetzel emigrated to the western part of Virginia when but a very small boy, and took a very active part in all the Indian wars in the west of Pennsylvania, Virginia, and what is now the State of Ohio, and carried many testimonials of his bravery, in the numerous wounds he received in the various combats with the savage foe.

"While in the army, under Generals Harrison and St. Clair, and several other commanders, he performed very laborious duties, and rendered signal service as a spy, which duties he preferred, and for which he was most admirably adapted by his former life."

He left a numerous and respectable family to mourn their loss. The writer, although young at the time of Mr. Whetzel's death, remembers him very distinctly as a square-built, broad-shouldered, muscular and powerful man, five feet eleven inches in height, about two hundred and fifty pounds in weight, without any surplus flesh, but a fair proportion for such a frame. He died at the age of sixty-three.

Of his seven children, five daughters and two sons, but two are living; his eldest son, Cyrus, and youngest daughter, Emily, now the wife of one of our most respected citizens, William H. Pinny, Esq. Cyrus Whetzel was born on the first day of December, 1800, in Ohio County, Virginia, and is now one of the few living that belonged to the eighteenth century. Before age began to tell on him he was as straight as an arrow, full six feet in height, hair as black as the raven, with an eye equally black and as keen as a hawk. As has been said before, he came to where he now resides (near Waverly, in Morgan County) with his father, in the spring of 1819, and has resided there, on his father's old farm, ever since. He has been very prosperous and has accumulated a fortune, not by speculation of any kind, but by industry and economy; in fact he literally dug it out of the ground, and now owns several of the finest cultivated as well as largest farms in the White River Valley.

I visited him a few days since at his farm, as has been my wont to do for near fifty years, and was shown in one pasture about fifty bullocks ready for the butcher's block, the lightest of which would weigh at least twelve hundred pounds; indeed, I do not think there is a better stocked farm, for its number of acres (about five hundred), in the State of Indiana, if in the entire great West.

He is a man of very general information, warm and devoted in his friendship, has represented his county in the lower branch of the legislature, was a good and efficient member, was an old line whig, and most sincerely devoted to the party and its measures, and, with the most of his associates in politics, when that party was disbanded, went into the Republican ranks, and during the rebellion was a strong Union man, and advocated the prosecution of the war with great warmth and zeal. The only one of his household capable of bearing arms was his son-in-law, the husband of his only daughter, Wm. N. McKenzie, who volunteered the first year, and served three years; was taken prisoner, and a portion of the time served in Libby Prison, at Richmond, Virginia. There is no man more respected among his numerous friends and acquaintances than Cyrus Whetzel. He is well known in this city, which has been his principal trading-place since the first log cabin trading-house was established here, in the winter of 1821. He is a man of great firmness and determination, and no person can mistake the ground he occupies on any subject, after conversing with him five minutes. He advocates his opinions with great earnestness and fervor, and is never at a loss for language to make himself distinctly understood.

His hospitality is as generally and favorably known as that of any man in the State; his house has been the stopping-place for public men and politicians of all parties, in their electioneering tours, for near fifty years, all of whom have received kind and courteous treatment at his hands, and from his estimable lady, now deceased. From his door no weary traveler was ever turned away hungry, no beggar empty-handed, no friend without an invitation to "call again."

As he is one of the links that connect the past with the present generation, so is he of many pleasing reminiscences connecting the past with the present. And when he shall be taken from among the living the country will have lost one of its best men, this city one of its most liberal patrons, his children a kind and indulgent father, and the writer, if living, a warm personal friend.

JAMES BLAKE.

When I come to write of this venerable and good man, I am carried back near half a century to my childhood's tender years, when he, as my Sabbath-school teacher, first taught me to lisp the A, B, C, at the school first organized and kept in Caleb Scudder's cabinet-shop, on the south side of the State House Square, in the year 1823. Mr. B. came to this place on the 25th day of July, 1821. A single man, but rather on the bachelor order, he soon became a great gallant of, and a favorite with, the young ladies and belles of the day. The late Calvin Fletcher told many anecdotes of his early gallantry.

He was an inmate of my father's family soon after his arrival here. The first year of his residence nearly every person was down with fever and ague. Indeed, in many families there was hardly one able to hand another a drink of water. It was a time just such a man as Mr. B. was useful, although shaking nearly every other day with ague himself. He would employ the well days in gathering the new corn and grating it on a horse-radish grater into meal to make mush for the convalescent. Indeed, our family, as well as others, would have suffered for food had it not been for his kind offices in this way, not only because the mush made from the new corn was more palatable, but the old could not be got, as there were no mills nearer than Good Landers, on the Whitewater River.

Mr. Blake has ever been hand in hand with Mr. James M. Ray, Dr. Isaac Cox, and others, in all the benevolent and charitable associations of the day, as well as such public enterprises as would be beneficial and calculated to add to the prosperity of the place. He was never ostentatious in his acts of charity, many of which were unknown to all save himself and the recipient.

I have known him to provide for the wife and family of an intemperate man (who had deserted them) for some time, until they were able to take care of and provide for themselves. This circumstance had slipped my memory entirely until reminded of it a few days since by the man himself.

During the time there was so much sickness in the summer of 1821, my father was suffering for water, and no one able to draw a bucket. He crept to the door of the cabin and saw a man passing. He beckoned to him and requested him to draw a bucket of water. "Where is your friend Blake," the man inquired. "He, too, was taken sick this morning," was the answer. "What on earth are the people to do now?" said the man. "God had spared him to take care of the people; they would now suffer as they never had before."

He acted upon the precepts of the Bible, and did good and dispensed his blessings as he went along. The first house of worship I ever attended in this place he was there, a young man in the pride and strength of manhood, and in the last (at this writing), where the Rev. Mr. Hammond was officiating, I saw him with his religious zeal unabated, although the frosts of forty-eight additional winters have fallen heavily upon and whitened his head. It was a silent but impressive rebuke to the writer of this humble tribute to his many virtues. It will require no flowers strewn upon his grave to make his memory fresh in the minds of his many friends, who will rather bedew it with their tears.

The late Calvin Fletcher told an anecdote of him. Mr. B. had employed a young lady, of the upper ten of that day, to make him a pair of pantaloons. They were finished and sent home. On examination they were found all right, except that the waistband buttons were sewed on the wrong side. He showed them to Mr. Fletcher, who told him the young lady intended he should wear them as "Paddy from Cork" did his coat, *i. e.*, buttoned up behind.

Mr. Blake was one of the company that built the first steam mill in this place. He brought the first piano and the first pleasure carriage. It was a two-horse barouche, with leather springs hung over steel, which he drove through from Baltimore with his bride the same year. He was the President of the first State Board of Agriculture, organized in 1835. Was a partner with Samuel Henderson in Washington Hall. He afterwards founded Blakesburg, in Putnam County. He established a factory for clarifying genseng, buying the article in different parts of the State, and shipping it east in large quantities. He was one of the foremost in establishing the present rolling-mill. He was the first to propose the celebration of the Fourth of July by the different Sunday schools, and was the marshal of the

different processions as long as the custom was kept up—
thirty years. Indeed, there are but few enterprises, either
public or private, that he is not identified with.

Although he has had a goodly share of earthly prosperity
he has never been avaricious, but used the means God placed
in his hands to accomplish good, thereby laying up treasure
where thieves could not reach it, nor moth nor rust destroy.

> "Thus to relieve the wretched was his pride,
> And e'en his failings leaned to virtue's side;
> But in his duty, prompt at every call,
> He watched, and wept, and prayed for all."

Mr. Blake's personal appearance would attract attention
quickly in any crowd. He is of a large, well-turned frame,
showing that in his younger days he possessed great physical
strength; very straight and erect in his carriage, with a step
as elastic as most men of thirty years of age, and, although
now in his eightieth year, is a man that would not be taken
for over sixty.

Mr. Blake is a man of great courage and resolution, and
does what he considers his duty without regard to consequences to himself.

> "Virtue is bold and goodness never fearful."

Such is James Blake, one of the first settlers of Indianapolis.

MAJOR THOMAS CARTER.

The reader will readily perceive that the first and "old
settlers" of Indianapolis were generally men of distinction,
if we should judge by the handle or title prefixed to their
names, especially in the military line. There were none of
the lower grades—but few less than a major; colonels and
generals we had without number, although military honors
were not so cheap as at the present day.

Major Carter was a major in every sense of the word. He was what John Givens calls a forty-gallon Baptist. He was more conscientious about every other vice than that of drinking, yet he did not indulge in the use of the ardent to excess himself. He thought it much more excusable in a person to take a "wee drap of the critter" now and then than it would be to dance, sing wordly songs, or play the fiddle. He had a perfect horror of fiddles, and thought the devil incarnate lay in the bowels of one. Under no circumstances would he allow one about his house.

Major Carter was about the first to start a tavern in Indianapolis. He built a double cabin on Berry's Trace early in 1821, and called it a tavern. This cabin lay between Washington and Market streets, just east of Illinois. Subsequently he built the "Rosebush," just in front of the log house on Washington street. The "Rosebush" was a one and a half story frame building, and, at that day, made a very imposing appearance. While at the "Rosebush" my father and mother took tea with the worthy Major and his lady. The old lady always had an apology ready for any deficiency of variety on the table. On this occasion she "was out of all kind of gardin sass except ham and eggs," and the only fruit she could get "was dried pumpkins."

Mr. Carter did not remain long at the "Rosebush," but built a third tavern on Washington street, opposite the Court House. Here he was very unfortunate. About two weeks after the Legislature convened, in January, 1825, this house burned. It took fire from a keg of ashes, about nine o'clock at night, and was burned entirely to the ground.

In the spring he purchased a two-story frame house of Jacob R. Crumbaugh, that stood on Washington street, west of the canal. This house he moved along Washington street to the site of the burnt building. The removal of this building occupied several weeks, and caused more stumps and logs to be burned and removed from the street than any thing that had yet happened. In this last house the Major continued some time, and seemed to prosper. This house in after years was, perhaps, the scene of more ludicrous incidents than any other house in town. After Carter left it, it was kept by persons of both high and low degree, among whom were John Hays, Jordan Vigus, Peter Newland, Pruett, and General Robert Hanna. It was at this house in which was held the first mechanics' ball in Indianapolis, and which created so much dissatisfaction at that time. There were no police officers then to keep down the uproarious, and on this occasion the dissatisfied parties behaved in a manner very detrimental to the furniture of the dining-room and glassware of the bar.

At this house, when kept by Carter, the first theatrical performance took place in this city, an account of which I wrote some years since, and which was published in several papers in the State. In order to show Mr. Carter's aversion to fiddles I will copy it at the close of this chapter. While Governor Ray kept this house he had painted on one side of the sign "Travelers' Ray House, Cheap." On the reverse was "Traveler's Ray House, Cash." It was while keeping this house the Governor made the prediction that there were then persons living who would see the State checkered with railroads in all directions. It was in this house he proposed a plan for building a railroad from Charleston, South Carolina, to the Northern lakes. It was from this house emanated many projects of State policy that were ridiculed at the time, but which were afterwards adopted and successfully carried out. It was then thought they were the production of a disorganized and demented brain. Although not more than thirty-five years have elapsed since these predictions were made, our State is truly checkered over with railroads, with eleven centering into this city, and direct railroad communication from Charleston, South Carolina, with the Northern lakes, although the Governor's plan was not carried out in the construction of the roads. One of his plans was to cut the tops of the trees off in the valleys to bring them on a level with the hills, and run the track over them to save grading and excavation.

While Mr. Carter kept this house, and "during the session of the Legislature, in the winter of 1825 to 1826, a strolling player by the name of Crampton visited this place for the purpose of giving the denizens of the Hoosier metropolis the benefit of his entertainments of legerdemain, hocus pocus, etc.

"As there was no public hall or room (as now) suitable for such an entertainment, he applied to the proprietor of the largest tavern in the place for the use of his dining-room.

"Mr. Carter had no kind of objection to his having his dining-room for the purpose. But the shows that usually came into the '*settlements*' always had music on the fiddle, and he could not think of suffering the fiddle to be played in his house.

"Mr. Crampton assured him that he (Crampton) was as much opposed to the fiddle as Carter could possibly be, and that the only music he required or ever tolerated was the *violin*, and under no circumstance should a fiddle be introduced at the performance. With this understanding Carter consented to let him have the room.

"Accordingly due notice was given that upon a certain evening Monsieur Crampton, just from Paris, would give a series of entertainments in the dining-room of Carter's Hotel.

"Nothing more was wanting to congregate the entire population of Indianapolis within the walls of that room, about twenty by thirty feet in size.

"All things being ready the doors were opened, whereupon a well-known character named 'Bill Bagwell' struck up the tune of 'Leather Breeches,' upon the fiddle.

"But suddenly the entertainment, that but a few moments

before bid so fair to go off without molestation, was brought to a dead halt. Mr. Carter appeared, cane in hand, and demanded that the music should be stopped; that it was the understanding between him and Monsieur Crampton that there should be no music except on the *violin*.

"Monsieur Crampton assured Mr. Carter that he was mistaken, as this was a *violin* he had brought with him from Paris.

"'No,' says Carter, 'I can't be mistaken, for Bill Bagwell can't play on anything else than a *fiddle*.'

"Bill, speaking, says, 'Major, just bring in a bottle of Bayou Blue and see how I'll play on it. You are mistaken, Major; this is nothing but a *violin*.'

"Major Carter for a while seemed inexorable, but finally consented that, inasmuch as the *congregation* had assembled, he would permit the performance to go on with the *fiddle* if they would play nothing but Psalm tunes. 'But,' says Carter, 'Bill Bagwell can't play Psalm tunes; he never heard one, much less played one.'

"Here he was again at fault, for Bill assured him he was raised at the 'Great Crossing,' in Kentucky, and that he then and there was a member in good standing in the Baptist Church, and learned many Psalm tunes, and as an evidence of the truth of his assertions struck up the tune of 'Jesus my all to Heaven is gone.'

"This, to Carter, was a clincher, and made all right. So the performance went on, and was closed with 'Yankee Doodle' from the *orchestra*, by request. All seemed well pleased with the entertainment, and none more so than Mr. Carter himself, especially with that part of it under the immediate charge of Professor Bagwell.

"Major Carter has long since been gathered to his fathers, and died in full hope of blessed reunion with his friends hereafter.

"The last the writer remembers to have seen of Bill Bagwell was on a coal boat at the Louisville wharf, playing the *violin.*"

CALEB REYNOLDS.

There was none that knew from whence he came, or whither he went; but he did go, and all were glad. What manner of man he was it was hard to tell; had not his size precluded the possibility, he might have been taken for a cross between a baboon and a skunk.

He had a cabin in Washington street, in front of Masonic Hall; he was a bricklayer by trade, but for three reasons did not follow the business. The first reason was, there was no brick to lay; second, if there had been he was too lazy to lay them; the third was, no person would employ him. His business was conceded to be foraging upon the neighboring smoke-houses, corn-cribs, and hen-roosts at night, and imposing upon the credulity of those that did not know him, in day time.

In his composition the animal rather predominated, as will be demonstrated by the following incident: Mr. Landis had received a barrel of fresh apple butter; Reynolds wished to make a bargain for what he could eat; Mr. Landis, knowing his customer, had none to sell him in that way; but a person present bet him the price of a gallon that he could not eat it at one sitting. Cale readily accepted the bet, and won it, costing the gentleman about two dollars, and, very nearly, the county the price of a coffin. Suffice it to say, for a while the smoke-houses could be left unlocked, the corn-cribs were unmolested, and the chickens roosted without interruption.

Cale wore a coat made from a saddle blanket, which he had colored with walnut hulls, giving it the color of a buffalo, this gave him the sobriquet of "Buffalo Cale," as there were two persons by the name of Caleb.

Caleb Reynolds.

A man called "Big Bije Smith," compelled him to get down on "all fours," he then fastened a bridle to his head, and put a saddle on his back, mounting it as he would a horse, and in this manner forced Reynolds to carry him into the grocery. Smith then addressed Mr. Landis in this style: "Landlord, take this brute animal of mine, put him in some deseparate apartment, give him some junutrals suitable for his frail body, and I will absurd you in the morning." Smith then took Cale by the back of the neck and seat of his pantaloons and threw him out of a window into the back yard. Cale used to say it did not require any of the letters of the alphabet to spell his name; he spelled it in this way:

"A frog ran down the hill with his tail up,
 Spelled Caleb;
Two whiskey jugs and funnels,
 Spelled Reynolds."

Shortly after this rough treatment of Smith's he was caught in a steel trap that was placed in the inside of a corn-crib, near where he was in the habit of thrusting his hand for the corn. The trap was chained inside to a log, and he was compelled to stand there with his hand in the trap until released by the owner of the corn, who found him about daylight standing by the crib. "Good morning Mr. Reynolds," said he, "wont you walk in?" "My dear friend," said Cale, "do let me go, and for the sake of my family say nothing about it." This led him to believe that the best thing he could do for Indianapolis and himself would be to emigrate, which he did without calling to bid his friends good bye. It is said that history repeats itself; if so, that portion of the history of Indianapolis, in which "Buffalo Cale" figured, I hope will be deferred until after my day.

This Abijah Smith was a very large, fleshy man, and very dissipated; always ready to attend log-rollings and house-raisings for the sake of the whisky. In the spring of 1829 he was at a log-rolling at old Mr. Kyle's, near Broad Ripple. After the day's work was over, he lay down by one of the burning piles of logs, and was found next morning, completely roasted. He was yet alive though insensible, and suffered a few days, when he died a most horrible death. This was the second man that had been burned to death while in a state of intoxication.

Two boys, sons of Lismund Basey and Samuel S. Rooker, had been burned to death, by their clothes taking fire, while playing around burning log piles.

BILLY TOWNSEND.

Or, Uncle Billy Townsend, as called by both young and old, was from Guilford County, North Carolina. How near he lived to Beard's hatter-shop, I am unable to tell, although I know that shop was in Guilford County. Uncle Billy arrived in Wayne County in the fall of 1820, left his family there, came out to this place and built a cabin preparatory to moving out in the spring. It was in this cabin we lived the first few days of our residence in this place.

Mr. Townsend was a short, thick, rotund man, pretty near as round as a pumpkin; he was a quaker, dressing in their style, and used their dialect. He was a very clever man, and an obliging neighbor, but sometimes very irritable, and could be as contrary as any person if he wished to, and often let his passion get the advantage of the mildness of the Quaker.

As has been said in another chapter, Uncle Billy's cabin happened to be where Kentucky avenue was afterward laid out, and the Agent of State, General John Carr, intimated to Mr. Townsend that he would have to remove the house; for the necessity of this Mr. T. could see no immediate cause, as it was all in the woods, and could not be used. This irritated the old man, and he got very angry with the agent while talking the matter over; he jerked off his coat and

Billy Townsend.

violently threw it to the ground, saying, "Lay there Quaker, until I administer to the 'gineral' a gentle chastisement." This the general politely declined to receive at his hands, and the matter was finally compromised. While living in this cabin one of Mr. Townsend's children died, and was buried close to the house; but after the graveyard was located, it was taken up and reburied there. This was the first white person that died in this place (not Mrs. Maxwell, as stated in Logan's history). This child died in May, 1821, from the effects of a burn she received while living in Wayne County.

Mr. Townsend then bought land on Lick Creek, four miles south of town, improved a farm, and built a mill; but subsequently, say about 1825, sold out and went to White Lick, in Hendricks County, where he also built a mill, and for many years furnished a good portion of the flour that was consumed in this place.

He afterward represented Hendricks County in the Legislature, and was the author and projector of the celebrated financial measure, known as "Billy Townsend's Bank Bill." This bill provided that the State Treasurer should find out the exact indebtedness of every adult citizen of the State, and cause a corresponding amount of bank paper to be issued and pay over to each individual an amount equivalent to his liabilities. Unfortunately for the success of the scheme, there was no means provided by this bill for the ultimate redemption of the paper. The discussion of the merits and demerits of this bill occupied several nights, toward the close of the session, when the members wished a little sport. The bill eventually passed both houses (as Mr. Townsend thought), while the bill was under consideration in the Senate. A resolution was offered and passed, admitting Mr. Townsend to a seat, and as a member of the Senate during the pending of his bill. A committee was appointed to conduct him to a seat, as Senator, *pro tem*.

After the passage of the bill in the Senate (which was late at night), Mr. Townsend, with others, was appointed by the chair as a committee to wait on the Governor and request his signature, that it might become a law. Mr. Townsend (with tears of joy in his eyes) presented the bill to Governor Whitcomb for his signature, and was not willing to take any denial or excuse until the Governor had to tell him he was the victim of a hoax.

Mr. Townsend died about fifteen years since (1854), at a good old age, leaving a large and respectable family living on White Lick, in Hendrick's County, all of whom are prosperous farmers and in good circumstances; and if this should meet their eye, I hope they will take no offence at my noting the part their father took in the early history of Indianapolis. With all his peculiarities he was an honest man and a good citizen, which is more than I could say of the person whose name stands at the head of the preceding chapter.

JOSEPH PRYOR DUVALL,

Father of the well-known detective of that name, came to this place about the year 1821. He was a Kentuckian in every sense of the word, and was from near the "Stamping Ground," in Scott County, a section of Kentucky noted for its "sharp-shooting rifles," fine horses, and pretty women. Mr. D. provided himself with one of each of the former before he left "Old Kentuck," but neglected to secure one of the latter. However, that deficiency he supplied soon after his arrival here, in the person of Miss Sally Wood, daughter of David Wood, Esq.

It was the custom of the country at the time he was married, to dance two or three days after a wedding, but Mr. Duvall's father-in-law belonged to a church the members of which had a "holy horror" of anything like dancing, but would not feel willing to consign a fellow mortal to endless punishment, if he would indulge in a "glass of old Bourbon;" so I believe the dancing was dispensed with in this case.

Mr. D. was a Clay Whig of the old school. With "latch-string outside the door," he was always glad to have his numerous friends call on him, and was ever ready to entertain them with an account of a Kentucky horse-race, a squirrell-hunt, a chew of tobacco, or a glass of whisky; or, if about the time of day, with a good, old-fashioned Kentucky dinner. He was constable of Center township from time immemorial. Their jurisdiction then was co-extensive with the county. It has been said of him that he would ride to the extreme limits of the county to see a person on official business, have his horse fed, take dinner, and return without mentioning business to his friend, lest in so doing he might injure his feelings. Like many others I have written of in this work, he was hardly ever at a loss for an anecdote to suit every occasion; if he should be, it would not require much mental labor to get up one to order.

There are many anecdotes of him extant, too numerous to mention in this short sketch. On the fourth of July, 1838 (I think it was), he invited several of his friends to a squirrel barbecue (the writer among the rest), which he had prepared in the creek-bottom just south of his house. After the solids were disposed of and the fluids began "flying fast and furious," and some of his invited guests had not yet entered an appearance, Mr. D. took a few bottles of "extracts" and hid them in a hollow log for the use of his absent friends, should they arrive. They not coming, he forgot them. His son tells me he found the bottles, their contents in a good state of preservation, long after his father's death.

Mr. Duvall lived on the Madison road, about what was, in his day, two miles from town, as a person would not be considered in town until he reached Washington street. His house was situated on the north or bluff bank of Pleasant Run.

One evening, as he was returning home from town, a tree fell across the horse on which he was seated, killing the horse instantly, smashing the saddle, and injuring Mr. Duvall severely, from which he never recovered, although he lived several years afterwards.

Mr. Duvall owned considerable property, and had he lived it would have made him quite wealthy. He was a man generally willing to take the world as he found it, and valued the friendships of his numerous acquaintances more than their money. He was a plain, off-hand man, free from intrigue or dissimulation, and a generous and kind neighbor. His death was regretted by all.

LISMOND BASYE

Came from Franklin County, Indiana, to this place late in the year 1821; and, like nearly all that came from that section at that time, he had a great thirst for office, and was willing to serve the people in any capacity they might wish. Like General Hanna, he only desired to be useful, and was a candidate for, and elected, magistrate.

While Mr. B. was a candidate, Mr. Nathaniel Cox wishing to vote understandingly, and for those he considered qualified, in order to satisfy himself on this point, propounded this question for the (would-be) esquire to answer: Said Cox, "Should you be elected, Mr. Basye, and a person was brought before you charged with burglary, and proved guilty beyond the shadow of a doubt, what would you do with him?" Basye studied a few moments, raised his spectacles, looked wise (as he was), and said: "I would fine him one hundred dollars and compel him to marry the woman." This answer was satisfactory to Mr. Cox, as he generally gave 'Squire Basye what business he had in after years. The 'Squire almost invariably decided in favor of the plaintiff, which had a tendency to secure him nearly the entire business of the village; and when defendants in former cases became plaintiffs in others, they always patronized 'Squire Basye, for two reasons: first, they were sure of success; and second, they would know the exact amount of judgment before the trial, which was considered in those days an advantage to a person bringing a suit. There were a great many amusing trials had before 'Squire Basye, that are yet fresh in my mind; but as the mention of them might not be agreeable to some of the parties yet living, I refrain from publishing them.

While the late Calvin Fletcher was prosecuting attorney, a person was arrested and taken before Mr. Basye, charged with stealing, and proved guilty. After hearing the evidence, the 'Squire examined the law and found the penalty to be not more than three, nor less than one year, in the penitentiary, and was about to pass sentence on the criminal for the shortest time, when he was informed by Mr. Fletcher that he could only recognize him to appear at court. The 'Squire thought the law very plain, and that he should at once be sent to the State Prison, thereby saving cost to the county and time to the criminal.

After the death of the 'Squire's wife, he, with the balance of his family, removed to Tippecanoe County, and settled just west of Lafayette, where he was shortly after married to quite a young woman, he being over sixty years of age. In due time after this marriage, Mrs. Basye presented her venerable husband with a pair of boys. The old gentleman was not slow in informing his old friend, Daniel Yandes, of his good fortune, and renewal of his youth, and that he had named his sons "Daniel Yandes Basye" and "Calvin Fletcher Basye." Mr. Yandes laid the facts before Mr. Fletcher, who proposed that they should jointly enter eighty acres of land in the name, and for the benefit of, the young Basyes, which was accordingly done; but the youngsters died in a few months, and the 'Squire, being the sole heir and legatee, became owner of the eighty acres of land so generously bestowed on his children by Messrs. Yandes and Fletcher.

DANIEL YANDES.

Mr. Yandes came to Indianapolis early in the spring of 1821. He was originally from Fayette County, Pennsylvania, where he was raised, but had stopped a short time at Connersville, in this State, before making this place his residence.

Mr. Y. was of German parentage, and was about the first citizen of this place who spoke that language. He is a large, stout man, and in his younger days there were but few his equal in strength. It was said, however, he did not like to waste that strength at house-raisings or log-rollings, but reserved it for other purposes more beneficial to the community.

Mr. Yandes, in connection with the late John Wilkins, established the first tan-yard in the place, in 1822, and has been interested in that business with several different partners pretty nearly ever since.

He has engaged in many business enterprises, and helped many young men in starting business in this as well as many other places; and there are many living, both here and elsewhere, who owe their success in life and business to Daniel Yandes

He has aided in building mills, and some of the largest manufacturing establishments, both in and adjoining the city; and was ever ready with money and countenance to aid in anything calculated to be beneficial to the county and city. He contributed liberally toward building the first church that was erected in Indianapolis—the First Presbyterian, a frame building erected in 1823—as he has to many different churches since. He was ever liberal to all benevolent and charitable institutions, contributing his portion for the general good. He is now, at his advanced age, connected with one of the largest engine and boiler manufacturing establishments in the city, and nearly every day visits it. He lost his wife, the companion of his youth, several years since, and has contented himself with gliding down the stream of time alone, thus far. I have known Mr. Yandes now nearly fifty years, and do not remember to have ever seen him show any anger whatever. He is a plain, common-sense man, and a Christian, without any ostentatious show of self-righteousness or bigotry. Although he has lived out his three-score years and ten, he seems by his universal good humor and fondness for an innocent joke, to be willing to enter upon another lease of life for the same lengthy term, should it please the Allwise Creator to grant it to him.

"He lives long, who lives well."

SIMON YANDES.

Were I to omit speaking of my old friend and school-mate, I would do great injustice to my own feelings and to the respect I entertain for him. Some forty-two years ago he was my antagonist in a pitched and warmly contested battle, caused by a question of territorial jurisdiction and the ownership of a head of cabbage. He then did not seem *so long* for this world as he does now, although four decades of time have passed away. This was the first and last difficulty we ever had, and was settled by a *pro tem.* magistrate in the presence of our parents. He studied law, and being diligent at his books and endowed with many good qualities, made a fair lawyer, and for several years successfully practiced his profession. He is at present, and has been for some years, engaged with J. H. McKernan in the real estate business, having quit the practice of law.

Mr. Yandes (like John Ewing, of Knox) has never met with a lady to whose keeping he felt willing to intrust himself, and is yet outside the pale of matrimony. He is plain and unpretending in his manners, regular and temperate in his habits, and has a pleasant smile and kind word for all with whom he meets, and his integrity is unimpeachable. Such is the eldest son of Daniel Yandes, a citizen that came to this city in the spring of 1821, when the subject of this sketch was but a child.

JOHN WILKINS.

Mr. Wilkins was from Hillsborough, Ohio. He came to this place in the summer of 1821, while the town was being laid out, and, in connection with Mr. Daniel Yandes, established the first tan yard, in 1822. During his long residence Mr. Wilkins was one of our most respected citizens; he was an honest man and an exemplary Christian. When he first came to this place, and for several years after, he was a single man; but finally returned to Ohio, and there married.

He brought the first one-horse carriage to this place, the wood-work of which he made himself. The bed of this carriage was set on wood springs running between the axles. There was no surplus iron or fancy work about it, although it was the most fashionable carriage in the place, and the young ladies would take it as a great compliment to be invited to take a ride in Johnny Wilkins' carriage. After Mr. Wilkins returned from Ohio with his bride, his carriage was not in so much demand, especially by the young ladies.

He was a plain, unpretending man, always disposed to attend to his own business in preference to that of his neighbor's. He died in 1868, without a struggle or a murmur, and his life went out like the flame of a candle that had burned until there was nothing left. Are we not led to believe by the manner of his death that there is something in being a *true Christian*, and that God has his own way of calling his chosen people home. As he lived so he died, without giving trouble to any one. May his children emulate the example of their father.

HENRY BRADLEY.

I have in a former sketch alluded to the fact that Mr. Bradley came to this place with my father's family, in the fall of 1820. After remaining here a few weeks, he returned to his home, near Frankfort, in Franklin County, Kentucky, and moved out in the spring. Mr. Bradley, in politics, was an old line Whig; in religion, a "hard shell" Baptist. He was for many years a magistrate of this township, and made a good and efficient officer. After his official career he was a successful merchant, and partner of Stoughton A. Fletcher in that business. Several years since he removed to his farm in Johnson county, on Sugar creek, and where the railroad and Madison State road cross that stream. He has now been dead about eleven years.

Mr. B. had but two children; James, the eldest, born in Kentucky, and William, born in this place. The latter died ere he had reached his majority. James, with his mother, still resides on their farm; they own some fine city property in this place. James is quite wealthy. He is a director of, and large stock-holder in, the Jeffersonville and Indianapolis Railroad Company; he was for some time President of, and stockholder in, the Jeffersonville bank. I have seen but little of him since boyhood, but am told he is possessed of fine business qualifications. He was fond of good cheer when a boy, and, to judge from his looks, is yet; and, like all other successful men, of course, *smart*.

ANDREW WILSON.

Twenty-five years ago, no name was more familiar to the people of Indianapolis than that which stands at the head of this sketch. Although he is yet living, he is not so well known to most of the present citizens of the city.

Mr. Wilson is a native of Pennsylvania, and raised, I think, near Union town. He came to this place in the summer of 1821, a young man, and some few years afterward was married to the eldest daughter of Obadiah Harris, who is one of our prominent and respectable farmers. Mr. Wilson was one of the proprietors of the establishment known as the Bayou Mills and Distillery, situated on the west side of White River, just beyond the old City Cemetery. It was at this distillery he manufactured to an alarming extent that delectable article of beverage, "Bayou Blue," which was sold to and drank by his thirsty customers a few days before it was a week old. This article has been referred to in another sketch.

Mr. Wilson was among the first litigants before Esquire Basye, and has been a liberal patron to the legal profession since that time. He has been a very energetic man, and has been engaged from time to time in various kinds of business; such as farming, merchandizing, contractor on the National road, the different railroads, built bridges, dug canals; indeed, did all kinds of public work; and, for a while, was a banker in connection with John Woolly.

Mr. Wilson resembles a lame tailor that lived here in early times, who, with one leg shorter than the other, used to say he had more ups and downs than any other person in the place. So has Mr. W. He has been considered rich several times, and as often *otherwise*. Whether he is now *otherwise* or not I have no means of knowing; but one thing I do know, I should never select him again to settle an estate that I was interested in. Time has fell heavily upon his head.

He looks as though he had lived out his three-score and ten years, and would ere long be called on to appear and render an account of his stewardship on earth. I hope he will be prepared and have his lamp trimmed. If he is not, I hope he Lord will be lenient with him.

CALEB SCUDDER

Was a native of New Jersey, but when quite young came to Dayton, Ohio. He was there married, and soon after removed to this place in the summer of 1821. He was the first cabinet-maker, and made the first coffin that summer that was made in the place. His shop was on the south side of the State House Square, and his dwelling opposite, across Washington street. His shop was a place of worship for some time, and there the first Sunday-school was established, in 1823.

Mr. S. was a Presbyterian, and for some years acted as clerk to the different ministers in giving out the hymn and starting the tune. He was afterward elected magistrate, and served as such for several years. He made a good and efficient officer, and his decisions were generally sustained by the higher court when appeals were taken, which was very seldom. While he was justice of the peace it became necessary for him to render a decision in a trivial matter against Joseph Buckhart, a blacksmith. Buckhart became very much enraged at the 'Squire, and as he left the office, remarked it should cost Mr. S. more than it had him. The 'Squire looked upon it as a mere passionate threat, and that he would soon get over it.

A few mornings afterwards Mr. S. missed his carriage out of his stable. It was found at the high banks of the river, with every spoke sawed out of the wheels and other portions thrown in the river. Mr. Scudder was satisfied in his own mind who the guilty parties were, but took no steps to have them arrested, fearful that other and more serious injury might be done him or his property.

This circumstance weighed heavily upon his mind and caused him some unhappy reflections, not that he thought he had done wrong, or rendered an erroneous decision, but that he should have made such an enemy in trying to render impartial justice.

Mr. Scudder was for several years connected with Mr. William Hannaman, in the drug business and oil mill. Had he lived to the time of the advent of Professor Black into this city, he might have had his voice improved considerably, as he used the nasal organ more than is fashionable at the present time; but I have no doubt he is where all voices are made perfect, and that he belongs to the great choir above.

He was a very peaceable and quiet man, and died without an enemy on earth, unless it might be the one above referred to (if living). He was strictly an honest and upright man, and died, deeply regretted by all who knew him, about the year 1866, leaving a wife, who has since deceased. He never had any children, but had raised several orphans that loved him as a father. Such was Caleb Scudder, the first cabinetmaker of Indianapolis.

SAMUEL S. ROOKER

Was the first person that ever painted a sign in this place. He came to Indianapolis in the fall of 1821, from Tennessee. At this time there was not a sign of any kind in the town. In addition to the joy felt at having gained a new citizen and neighbor, all were glad to have one qualified to announce their names and business in glowing letters. The first to order a sign from the painter was Caleb Scudder, cabinet maker. This Mr. Rooker painted on white ground with fiery red letters, and when finished it read, "Kalop Skodder, Kabbinet Maker."

Mr. R. soon received an order from Mr. Carter for a sign

for the "Rosebush," and one from Mr. Hawkins for the Eagle tavern. It was said that Mr. Hawkins' sign was that of a turkey, with a surname attached.

He afterwards painted one for Major Belles. The design was "General Lafayette in full uniform." This was a fine opportunity for the painter to show his skill in portrait painting. When he commenced, it was his intention to paint it full size, but after finishing the head and body he found there was not room for the legs full length; so he left out the section between the knee and ancle, and attached the feet to the knee joint, which gave the General the appearance of a very short legged man. This sign stood on the Michigan road, six miles south east of town, for many years.

In justice to Mr. R., I must say he improved very much in his profession in after years. He painted the portrait of the writer, which was complimentary to the subject and a great credit to the artist. Charlie Campbell thinks it was one of the most striking likenesses he ever saw. What became of it I do not know, but have no doubt it could be found in some of the New York art galleries.

He painted a sign for a man keeping tavern on the National road. The man had ordered a lion, full size, as the design. When it was finished he thought the good-natured painter had misunderstood him, and instead of painting a lion, as he wished, had painted a prairie wolf. Mr. Rooker had some trouble to convince the man that this was a *bona fide* African lion, and not a wolf. Mrs. Rooker was very indignant that the gentleman did not properly appreciate her husband's superior skill in painting. She thought that Sammy could paint as good a lion as any other person.

" The painter thought of his growing fame,
And the work that should bring him an endless name."

There are many yet living who remember Mr. Rooker's own sign, that stood on the north-east corner of Washington and

Illinois streets. It read, "Samuel S. Rooker, House and Sine Painter." It is proper to say that, although sign painting was not Mr. Rooker's *forte*, he was a good house painter, and generally rendered satisfaction to his customers in that line. Neither was he the only person that had not mastered Webster in the spelling book. A prominent merchant used to spell tobacco, "tobaker;" and bacon, "bakin."

Mr. Rooker yet lives in a neighboring town, but does not follow his profession as sign painter. He was an honest, upright man, an obliging neighbor and a good citizen.

JAMES PAXTON,

With his family, arrived here on the 9th of October, 1821. He bought a lot on Market street, near the canal, and lived there a few years. The house is yet standing, and is now the oldest in the city. It was a hewed log house, but has since been weather-boarded. He was a carpenter by trade, and about the first to follow the business. Soon after his arrival here he was elected colonel of the militia, which position he held until his death. In 1823 and 1824 he was elected to the Legislature, and was at Corydon during the last session in that place, and served the first session that it convened in Indianapolis.

In connection with John E. Baker, he was contractor for building the present old Court House, where the Legislature sat from 1825 to 1836; also, the Supreme and United States Courts. While building this house his partner (Mr. Baker), when intoxicated, rolled from the top of the cupola to the ground, striking nearly all the scaffolding in his descent, and to the surprise of all got up and walked home, a more sober if not a wiser man than he was a few moments before.

Colonel Paxton, after the Court House was finished, engaged in merchandizing and other pursuits until his death in the spring of 1829. No citizen enjoyed the respect and esteem of his neighbors to a greater extent than he did. He died, leaving a widow (but no children), who yet resides among us. She has lived to see this place, which she found with a half-dozen log cabins, a city of sixty thousand inhabitants.

Mrs. P. was one of the first to help organize a Methodist Church in this city. Her husband donated a lot to the Wesley Chapel congregation on Circle street for a parsonage. She was a member of that congregation when John W. Foudray, Billy Bay, Lismund Basye, Francis and William McLaughlin, and Jimmy Kittleman were among its members, and John Strange, James Armstrong, Edwin Ray, James Havens, Calvin W. Ruter, and Allen Wiley, were its preachers; all of whom have passed away.

Mrs. Paxton has yet in her possession a chair presented to her by the mother of the writer, when they first commenced housekeeping in this place, over forty-eight years ago. This was one of a set of split-bottomed chairs presented to my father by the keeper of the Kentucky Penitentiary, when we started to move to the New Purchase, in October, 1820. This chair Mrs. P. has kept for her own personal use ever since, and has had it re-bottomed but once.

She has a sister, the wife of William Hannaman, Esq., who resides in the city. There is an older sister now visiting her, that I remember to have seen at her house before the death of her husband, over forty years ago.

JIMMY KITTLEMAN.

This good old man came here at an early date, say 1821 or 1822. He was a shoemaker by trade, and lived many years on the south-east corner of Market and East streets. He was an honest but simple man, an ardent and enthusiastic Methodist, and most of his earthly joy consisted in meeting his brothers and sisters of the church in class-meeting or love-feast. He took great comfort in relating his experience and conversion to religion, and how it was brought about, the temptations and trials he was exposed to, and how the devil first appeared to him, and the offers he made to him.

He was attending to his father's sheep-fold late in the evening, he said, when the devil appeared to him and made offers equal to those he had made our Savior when on the mountain: the sheep and cattle upon a thousand hills, if he would worship him. He said he knew the "old sarpent" the moment he saw him; so he leaned his head upon a big "wether," and prayed the Lord to give him strength to resist the tempter. When he arose the devil had gone. He often appeared to him afterwards and renewed his offer, with the addition that he could go to all the dances and play the fiddle as much as he pleased. But he had as often sought the same old "wether" to lay his head against and pray for grace, and he as often found it. "Brethren," said he, "I feel this morning that I would rather be here and hear Sister Lydia Haws sing, 'We'll all meet together in the morning,' than to have all the sheep and cattle the old sinner had."

On one occasion, at a love-feast, the old man said "his sun had been behind a cloud for some days, and that he had not been in close communion with the Savior, but thanked God that this morning his sky was once more clear, and he could read 'his title clear to mansions in the skies,' and that he was able to raise his Ebenezer, and that the cloud had passed away, and that he was beyond the reach of the devil and all his cattle." On another occasion the old gentleman got very happy in class-meeting. He looked toward the roof of the house, extended his arms in an imploring manner, and said, "Do, Lord, come right down! Come right through the roof, right now! Do, Lord! Never mind the shingles, but come right down, Lord!" At this point the old man began flapping his arms up and down as wings, as if starting to meet the Savior. When he got in one of these ways the only remedy was to sing him down, and Sister Haws contributed a good portion, which generally elicited from the old man, after he became quieted, a "God bless Sister Haws."

In the sincerity and earnestness of Brother Kittleman there was none to doubt, but the old gentleman's zeal was sometimes greater than his common sense. He left this place many years since and removed to the far West, and no doubt is prepared to meet Sister Haws "in the morning," and "on the other side of Jordan."

BILLY BAY

Was the counterpart of Jimmy Kittleman, and his associate and brother in the first Methodist Church organized in Indianapolis. He was equally zealous in the good work, and never let anything keep him from the "Divine sanctuary." He too, like Brother Kittleman, had been very much tempted by the "old cloven-foot sarpent," and several times came very near yielding. Brother Bay was a man about five feet ten inches in height, rather spare made, a bald head, and about fifty years of age. He wore the old-style Methodist dress, round breasted or shad-belly coat. He was full of sighs on all occasions, and in church would add an amen to everything said, frequently out of place.

His main *forte* was in prayer. He had two stereotoyped upon his mind, and ever ready for use on any and all occasions; his morning prayer and his evening prayer. He sometimes (as Tom Harvey would say) "got the right prayer in the wrong place;" *i. e.*, he would use the morning prayer in the evening, and *vice versa*. I well remember his evening prayer, having heard it nearly every Thursday night for ten years. It ran thus:

"We desire to thank thee, O Lord, that we are once more permitted to assemble together under the roof of thy divine sanctuary, and that while many of our feller-critters, that are as good by nater and far better by practice, have sickened and died during the week that has passed and gone, and left these mundane shores, and gône to that house not made with hands, eternal in the heavens, we are still permitted to remain here as the spared monuments of thy amazing grace. And now, O Lord, in the close of our evening devotions draw feelingly and sensibly nigh unto us. Manifest thyself unto us as thou dost not unto the world, and grant that we may live as we shall wish we had when we come to die. And, finally, when we are called upon to put off this mortal and put on immortality, bring us to enjoy thyself and service; and all the glory we will ascribe to a triune God, world without end. Amen."

Brother Bay, too, sought a home on the distant prairies, and from his advanced age when he left has, no doubt, ere this, "put off this mortal and put on immortality," and has met his old classmate, Brother Kittleman, on the other side of the river, "where congregations ne'er break up, and Sabbaths never end."

DANIEL STEPHENS AND RICHARD GOOD.

In the character of Mr. Stephens there is very little to commend. He was more generally known by the name of "Sheep Stephens," than any other. An Irishman, named Richard Good, that had worked for him, charged him with being a "shape thafe," and that he had stolen VanBlaricum's ram, and when fearful of detection threw it into the well to hide it. He was, outside of the charges made by Mr. Good, considered the meanest man in the neighborhood, except "Buffalo Cale."

Mr. Stephens lost his wife. She was buried on Sunday, which fact brought out the entire population to the funeral. On his return from the grave he called at my mother's to ask her advice in regard to a suit of clothes for mourning. He wished to economize, and get such as would do to be married in, should he take a notion to; though he thought it very doubtful whether he would marry again, as he had looked around at the grave, and had seen none that he thought would fill Betsy's (his wife's) place. In justice to Mr. Stephen's judgment I must say, the variety of marriageable women was very small at that time.

Soon after his wife's death he returned to Kentucky, and soon found one he thought worthy to fill Betsy's place. He never returned to Indiana. The loss to Indianapolis in a citizen, it is to be hoped, was Mr. Stephens' gain.

Richard Good was the first Hibernian that ever made Indianapolis his home. He lived with Messrs. Henderson & Blake for several years, as ostler at Washington Hall, accumulated enough to buy him a quarter-section of land, which he improved and made a fine farm. He lived about two miles east of Greenwood, and there died a few years since, highly respected by his neighbors.

JAMES M. RAY

Was born in Caldwell, New Jersey, in the year 1800. Early in life he emigrated to the West. His first residence in Indiana was at Lawrenceburgh, in the year 1818, and afterwards at Connersville; in each of which places he was engaged as deputy clerk. He came to where Indianapolis now is early in the year 1821, and was clerk at the first sale of lots in October, of that year. At the first election, in 1822, he was elected Clerk of Marion County. Morris Morris was the principal opposing candidate, and it was a warmly contested election, Madison and Hamilton Counties being attached to Marion County for voting purposes. He was afterwards re-elected as clerk and elected as recorder, and held those offices until he resigned them at the time of the organization of the State Bank of Indiana, when he was elected cashier, which position he held during the existence of the bank. He was then appointed cashier of the "Bank of the State," which position he held until he was elected president of the same, which office he still holds.

Mr. Ray was active in the first Bible society, and helped to organize the first Sunday school; and has been the Treasurer of the Indianapolis Benevolent Society since its organization in the year 1836. He was secretary of the first temperance society, also of the Colonization Society; secretary of the first fire company, that of the Marion, organized in 1835, and one of the principal stockholders in the first steam-mill. He has ever been liberal in contributing to the erection of churches of all denominations. There has been but very few, if any, public enterprises undertaken in Indianapolis that he has not aided by money and countenance since the first settlement of the place. And even now, at his advanced age, he does not seem to have lost any of the zeal of his younger years for the public good. His public positions and private successes were well calculated to bring down upon him the envy and jealousy of those less fortunate, but the tongue of slander and vituperation has never been hurled at James M. Ray, or the defamation of his character ever attempted.

His great simplicity of character and manner; his wellknown and unostentatious piety, with a pleasant word and a smile for all that business or circumstances have brought him in contact with, have endeared him to all who know him. The duties of time and the reward of eternity seem to be his greatest pleasure on earth. In his family circle,

"His ready smile a parent's love expressed,
Their welfare pleased him, and their cares distressed,
To them his heart, his love, his griefs were given,
But all his serious thoughts had rest in heaven."

Mr. Ray is a small man, who would not weigh over one hundred and thirty pounds, but has prominent features, a mild black eye, and his whole contour at once denotes intelligence and an active mind. He was always very neat in his person and dress, even when engaged in the common avocations of life, but would never be taken for a fop.

In the late war he took an active interest in the cause of the Union, and was treasurer of the Indiana Branch of the Christian Commission, of the Indiana Freedman's Aid Commission, and also of the Indiana Soldiers and Sailors' Home. He also aided in selling the State bonds to procure means to arm and support our troops. He yet resides at the northwest corner of Meridian and Ohio streets, where has been his homestead for over thirty years. That antique, large and comfortable mansion, and beautifully laid out grounds, are the admiration of all who see them; and their whole appearance at once stamp the owner as a gentleman of culture, taste, and refinement. With one exception, this is the largest piece of very valuable property in the city, and long may the worthy proprietor and his estimable lady live to enjoy the comforts of such a home.

GEORGE SMITH

Was one of the proprietors of the Indianapolis "Gazette," the first newspaper and the first printing establishment of any kind in Indianapolis.

Mr. Smith was born in Lancaster, Pennsylvania, and learned his trade in the office of the Lexington "Observer," in Lexington, Kentucky. After his apprenticeship was out he went to Cincinnati and worked with Charlie Hammond, in the office of the Liberty Hall and Cincinnati "Gazette." He lived at several different places in Ohio as well as Indiana before he came to this place in December, 1821. In January, 1822, he, in connection with his step-son, Nathaniel Bolton, issued the first number of the "Gazette." Their office was in one corner of the cabin in which his family lived. This cabin was situated near by a row of cabins built by Wilmot, called Smoky Row, west of the Canal, and near Maryland street. From this cabin the "Gazette" was issued for the first year, then taken to a cabin on the northeast corner of the State House Square. This paper, after changing proprietors and editors, and name and location several times, we now have in the shape and name of the Indianapolis "Sentinel." Mr. Smith was the first to start a real estate agency in Indianapolis, as will be seen by his advertisement in the "Gazette" of 1827. He was afterwards elected associate judge and served two terms. He and Governor Ray were the only persons that wore their hair plaited and hanging down their back, in a cue.

The Judge had some difficulty with a lawyer named Gabriel J. Johnson. The lawyer got the Judge by the cue and for a while had him in chancery, but the Judge rallied his "strength" and administered to the lawyer a sound threshing. He was a man of warm feeling and devotion to his friends, and would go any length to serve and accommodate one. He cared nothing for money or property, further than to make himself and family comfortable. He had but one child, to which he was devotedly attached. She is now the wife of my nearest neighbor, Mr. William Martin. Her first husband, Samuel Goldsberry, is spoken of in another place.

After Mr. Smith had sold his interest in the "Gazette" and had quit the printing business, he bought the farm where the Insane Asylum now stands, and named it "Mount Jackson." He continued to live there with his wife until the time of his death, which was in April, 1836, at the age of fifty-two years. His numerous friends regretted his death. His loss was deeply felt by the poor, to whom he was ever liberal and kind, treating them with the greatest respect.

NATHANIEL BOLTON.

Reference has been made to Mr. Bolton's connection with the Indianapolis "Gazette," in the preceding sketch. He was born in Chillicothe, Ohio, and came to this place with his step-father and partner, George Smith, in December, 1821, when quite a young man. After Mr. Smith had retired from the "Gazette," Mr. Bolton continued the paper alone, and then with different partners for some time. In the meantime he was married to Miss Sarah T. Barrett, of Madison, now well known as one of Indiana's most gifted daughters. Although a very talented lady, she lost nothing in that way by her connection with Mr. B., but had a great deal to gain. For several of the first years of Mr. Bolton's residence in this place he was very much afflicted, so much so, that he was scarcely expected to live from one day to another; but for some years before his death his health had improved. He was a ready writer, and wrote most of the articles for the "Gazette," over fictitious signatures, beside writing the leading editorials. Several of the early articles I shall copy in this work, to show the style of writing in those days as well as the subject-matter.

About the second year of the administration of President Pierce he was appointed "Consul" to Geneva, and remained there until President Buchanan's administration, when he was compelled on account of his health to resign and return home. He arrived at home in May, and died the next November. In his social relations he was thought a great deal of. He possessed fine conversational powers and was ever entertaining to his auditors. He was a warm partizan, and expressed his views upon all and every occasion without stint or reserve, which may have made him some political enemies, but he had none personal. He left but two children, a son and daughter; his daughter, the wife of Mr. Frank Smith, of this city, has since deceased. She possessed, in addition to a large share of the native talent of her father and mother, fine accomplishments, and was one of the finest musicians of this city that abounds with talent of that particular kind.

ALEXANDER RALSTON.

In the Indiana "Journal" of January 9, 1827, I find the obituary notice of Mr. Ralston, the surveyor that laid out Indianapolis.

"Died in this place on Friday, the 5th instant, Alexander Ralston, Esq., aged fifty-six years." Mr. R. was a native of Scotland, but emigrated early in life to America. He lived many years at the city of Washington, then at Louisville, Kentucky, afterwards near Salem, in this State, and for the last five years in this place. His earliest and latest occupation in the United States was surveying, in which he was long employed by the Government at Washington, and his removal to this place was occasioned by his appointment to make the original survey of it. During the intervening period merchandise and agriculture engaged his attention.

"In the latter part of his life he was our county surveyor, and his leisure time was employed in attending to a neat garden, in which various useful and ornamental plants, fruit, etc., were carefully cultivated. Mr. Ralston was successful in his profession, honest in his dealings, gentlemanly in his deportment, a liberal and hospitable citizen, and a sincere and ardent friend. He had experienced much both of the pleasures and pains incident to human life. The respect and esteem of the generous and good were always awarded to him, and he found constant satisfaction in conferring favors, not only on his own species, but even on the humblest of the brute creation. He would not willingly set foot upon a worm. But his unsuspecting nature made him liable to imposition. His sanguine expectations were often disappointed; his independent spirit sometimes provoked opposition, and his extreme sensibility was frequently put to the severest trials. Though he stood alone among us in respect to family, his loss will be long lamented."

As has been intimated by the "Journal," he was an old bachelor. He had a colored woman named Chany Lively, as a house-keeper. She was the second colored person to live in this place. The first was a boy, brought by Dr. Mitchell, named Ephraim Ensaw.

Some years after Mr. Ralston's death, Chany married a well-known colored barber named John Britton, who yet lives here, and is one of our most respectable colored citizens.

ISAAC KINDER.

Among the citizens of Marion County that were prominent in early years was Mr. Kinder. He had bought a half section of land at the sale in Brookville in the year 1821, and in March, 1822, moved to and improved a farm located three miles north of town, on the east bank of Fall Creek, known now as the property of John Sutherland. While living on this farm he was county surveyor, and as such ran out the lines of the first farms that were improved in the county. About the year 1831 he sold this farm to the present owner, John Sutherland, and removed to town and engaged in merchandizing, and for about ten years successfully carried on that business.

Mr. Kinder's only son living at the time, Captain T. B. Kinder, raised a company of volunteers for the Second Indiana Regiment in the Mexican war, and fell at the head of his company during the battle of Buena Vista, on the 23d of February, 1847. In 1848 his father went to that distant and ill-fated battle-field and identified the body of his son, and brought it to this place, where it rests in one of the city cemeteries.

Isaac Kinder was a native of Delaware, having been born in Sussex County in 1792. When quite young he emigrated to Pickaway County, Ohio, and was there married in the year 1819, and at the time above mentioned became a citizen of Indiana. The death of his son sat heavily upon his mind, and greatly impaired his health, and hastened his death, which occurred in December, 1849.

His widow yet resides in this city, and though advanced in age is quite active, and may be seen attending to the ordinary duties of life as she did twenty-five years ago.

His six daughters, four of whom are married, yet reside in the city and vicinity. One is the wife of Mr. Clark, another of Martin Igo, a third of Mr. McLaughlin, and a fourth the wife of Mr. Trumbull. The two unmarried reside with their mother. The eldest daughter, now dead, was the wife of J. R. M. Bryant, of Williamsport, Warren County.

Mr. Kinder was an industrious and frugal man, and left his family in comfortable circumstances. They own some fine business property on East Washington Street, known as "Kinder's Block."

AMOS HANWAY, Sen.,

Came to this place early in the year 1821. He ascended White River in a flat-bottomed boat. He came directly from Vincennes to this place, and had come to Vincennes, in the year 1820, from Marietta, Ohio.

He was the first cooper, and made the first wash-tubs and and buckets, for which there was a demand from every new arrival of settlers. He brought the first barrel of whisky, although there had been large quantities brought here in smaller packages. He built a hewed log house on the north bank of the ravine, opposite to where Kingan's pork-house now stands. On this house he put a shingle roof (the shingles he made himself), the first roof the kind in the new purchase.

Mr. Hanway had several children, one of whom was then, and is yet, well known as a fisherman; then in pursuit of the finny tribe, now as a fisher of men. This was his eldest son, and took the name of his father.

Amos Hanway, Jun., although a great fisherman, would spend but seven days of the week in the profession, i. e., he would commence early on Monday morning (he was conscientious about beginning on Sunday), and would finish his week's work late Sunday evening. He knew the nest of nearly every bass between Lake's Ford and the high banks of the river below the graveyard. Some thought he was personally acquainted with each one of the fish. He had several ways of fishing, but his favorite was fire-fishing. He would build a platform on the bow of his canoe; on this he would build a fire, the reflection of which would show him the fish at the bottom of the deepest water.

Behind this fire he would stand, and select and spear or gig any fish he would wish. He was unerring in his aim, and hardly ever let a fish escape him. He was equally successful with hook and line, and his favorite bait was a worm which he called helgramte, which he procured under old logs. He sometimes, when he wished to make it a pecuniary object, used a seine, when he would take the fish by wagon loads and although they were very cheap compared with the prices now given, he would realize a considerable amount from one day's work.

Amos happened up town one evening, and wandered into a wheelwright shop which stood on the northeast corner of Pennsylvania and Market streets, where there was an old-fashioned Methodist prayer-meeting being held. It was here he first began to reflect upon the sin and wickedness of fishing on the Sabbath day, and resolved he would "go and sin no more" in that way, and joined the Methodist Church. After remaining in that church for some time he joined the "United Brethren," and is now a fisher of men in that most respectable religious organization, and if he is as successful in this kind of fishing as he was in the former, has no doubt caught many *scaly* fish as well as fat ones.

He was for years one of the presiding elders, and officiated for many years in different parts of the State in that capacity, and, I understand, is one of the best preachers of the denomination. His brother Samuel, well-known to our citizens, is also a member of the same church, and one of our reliable business men.

"There's a divinity that shapes our ends,
Rough hew them as we will."

JAMES JOHNSON, ESQ.

There were, in early days, three Esquire Johnsons in Marion County—Joseph, James W., and plain James. It is of the latter I write, who has, for over forty-five years, resided on the Crawfordsville State road, five miles west of the city.

He is a native of Grayson County, Virginia, and inherits many of the traits of character peculiar to the citizens of his native State. At an early age he came to Butler County, Ohio, and there lived until he came to this place in the year 1822. Since coming here he has held several offices of honor and emolument. For eleven years he was a justice of the peace in and for Wayne Township, at a time when the magistrates of the several townships, as a board, transacted the business of the county.

While the Hon. Jesse D. Bright was United States Marshal of the State, Mr. J. was his principal deputy. He was elected to represent the county in the Legislature in the years 1838 and 1839, and served two sessions. He was a good and efficient member, and attentive to the interests of his constituents.

Near fifty years since he purchased one hundred and sixty acres of land, lying on the Noblesville State road, about eight miles north of the city. There has never been a stick of timber cut off this land, unless stolen or unauthorized by the owner. This land is very heavily timbered, the majestic oaks and poplars still standing with all their native dignity. This fact indicates that he has never been hard-pressed for money. He owns several pieces of valuable city property in addition to his several fine and productive farms.

NATHANIEL COX

Was a native of Maryland, and born in Talbott County, but at an early age emigrated with his parents to Chillicothe, Ohio. After living at several different places he came to Jeffersonville, in this State, where he remained a short time. From the latter place he came to Indianapolis in the fall of 1821. He was a great hunter and fisherman, and for some time did but little except in that line. He would often dress himself in Indian costume, and hunt for several days without returning, camping out as an Indian. He was very fond of frightening those who had just come to the settlement, and who had not seen much of the Indians.

He was a great wag, and fond of playing pranks on the unsuspecting, to many of which I have been the victim. One of his best practical jokes was upon himself. Before the days of soda fountains, he requested Mr. Hannaman to prepare him two glasses, one containing carbonate acid, the other soda, as he wished to try the effect of the effervescence in the stomach. He first drank one draught and then the other. The experiment was satisfactory, at least so much so that he never wished to try it again. The fluid came from his eyes ears, mouth and nose in such a way that it alarmed the bystanders. I have often heard him say he thought the Falls of Niagara were running through and out of his head.

In the month of January, 1825, and while the Legislature was in session, he conceived the idea of serenading its members. There was a society, of which he was the head and master spirit. This organization Mr. Cox named the "Indianapolis Anarugian Society." They numbered about thirty persons, and their object was fun or amusement, in any shape whatever not injurious to the public.

One Pete Harmon was the proprietor of four yoke of oxen and two log-sleds, which he used for hauling saw-logs to the mill. The sleds Mr. Cox attached together in such a way that a platform was built on them to accommodate the whole society, who were dressed in all kinds of fantastic style that fancy or convenience might dictate, and with everything conceivable that would make a loud and disagreeable noise—strings of tin cups, horns, cow-bells, drums, tin pans and kettles—and to the sleds the four yoke of oxen were hitched. On the near steer of each yoke was a driver, dressed in a similar manner to the performers on the platform. In this way they left the store of Mr. Jacob Landis, about nine o'clock at night, and, after visiting the various hotels and boarding-houses, where members of the Legislature did mostly congregate, and performing at each place upon their instruments, returned to the place of starting, where a bountiful supply of Mr. Landis' staple article, "peach and honey," awaited them.

While Mr. Blake was supervisor of the roads, he had some men at work on Meridian street, in Pogue's Creek bottom, among whom was Mr. Cox. Mr. Blake, missing him from work, sought and found him sitting in the shade on the bank of the creek, with a sewing-thread and pin-hook, fishing for minnows.

Mr. Cox was a singular and erratic man, possessed a generous and kind heart, and was universally respected. He died about the year 1850, leaving a wife and a respectable family of children, all of whom yet reside in the city.

SAMUEL HENDERSON,

The first postmaster, was a Kentuckian. He came to this place in the fall of 1821. Like one or two other of the early settlers, his services were considered more valuable in any other way than at house-raisings or log-rollings. He was a large, fleshy man, and could not have been very serviceable in that way had he been so disposed.

He held the offie of postmaster until the summer of 1829, when he was removed by General Jackson, and Captain John Cain appointed as his successor.

Mr. Henderson, in connection with Mr. James Blake, built Washington Hall tavern, in 1824, and they kept it for some time as partners, Mr. Blake selling out to Mr. Henderson, who kept it as sole proprietor for many years. He, in 1835, sold it to the Washington Hall Company, who built additions to it, and it was kept many years by Mr. Edmund Browning, and was the principal hotel in the place. It then changed hands and name, and was kept by General Elliott as the Wright House. It was also kept by the late Henry Achy, and others, and was always a first-class hotel for Indianapolis. It has been remodeled, and is now known as "Glenn's Block," or "The New York Store."

He was the first Mayor of Indianapolis, and discharged the duties quite as well as any have since at much larger salaries than he received, and with quite as much dignity and satisfaction to the public.

Mr. Henderson owned and, for a time, lived on the quarter section of land a portion of which is now "Camp Morton," or the State Fair grounds. He also owned the residence of the late Judge McDonald.

About the time the various railroads that center to this

city were being built, Mr. Henderson became alarmed as to the future of Indianapolis, and sold the two pieces of property last named for less than one-tenth their present value.

I saw him in Washington City, en route for his present home, California. He expressed the opinion that the general railroad system being inaugurated would ruin this city; that the thousands of persons who passed through it would not stop long enough to get a drink of water, and that Indianapolis would retrograde, and become nothing but a way station.

Could the worthy old gentleman see it to-day, with its sixty thousand inhabitants, its two magnificent rolling mills, its eight or ten foundrys of different kinds, its various steam establishments, how quick he would see his error.

No man that ever lived in Indianapolis was more respected by the old citizens than Samuel Henderson, no man ever left it more regretted by his many friends, and no person would meet with a more joyous welcome than he should he visit us again.

He was a man of warm feelings for his friends, and strong prejudices against those he did not like. He was a most inveterate opponent of General Jackson, and the party that sprung up and supported the measures advocated by him. He was a time-honored patron of the two leading Whig newspapers of their day—the "National Intelligencer," of Washington City, and the "Liberty Hall and Cincinnati Gazette"—and would generally sacrifice any other pleasure for that of perusing these papers.

DR. JONATHAN COOL

Was a native of New Jersey, and a classmate of the late Judge Blackford, at Princeton College, where he graduated with high honors.

He studied medicine, and received a diploma at one of the Eastern institutions. He was, when very young, appointed a surgeon in the United States army, and was for some time stationed at the barracks in Newport, Kentucky.

Dr. Cool was a man of fine native as well as acquired abilities, but, like many others placed in similar situations, fell a victim to intemperance. The Doctor had descended too far in dissipation to practice after he came to this place. He lived with his mother, about three miles north east of the city. When Dr. Cool first came here, in 1821, Dr. Coe was the only physician well enough to practice, the the three other doctors, Mitchell, Dunlap and Scudder, being all sick and unable to render any assistance whatever. Dr. Cool soon made the discovery that Dr. Coe gave very large doses of medicine, and it was true. Dr. Coe went on the principle that if a "little was good, a great deal was better," and acted upon that hypothesis. This fact elicited from Dr. Cool this couplet:

"Oh, Doctor Coe, oh, Doctor Coe,
What makes you dose your patients so?"

There was no person better known to the citizens, from 1821 to 1840 (about the time of his death), than Doctor Jonathan Cool. He was very fond of quoting from the poets, and ever had a quotation at the end of his tongue to illustrate anything he said. He was, I suppose, one of the most gentlemanly drinking men we have ever had in the place, never using vulgar language under any circumstance. If he would borrow anything it would be with the understanding that it was never to be returned. His word he valued very highly, and on no occasion would he violate it. He went to a liquor store on a Saturday evening and asked for a bottle of whisky, which was given him, on condition that he would not open it until he reached his mother's spring. After arriving at the spring he cooled his mouth with water, and prepared for a "good jorum," as he expressed it, but found the bottle contained only water. After this he never went to that store again, and they lost his custom.

There was nothing they could have done to him that would make him so angry as to deceive him. He made it a point of honor never to deceive any person, no matter how much he needed a drink or anything else. Some persons, who stand high in the social scale, might have learned a lesson from him in that respect that would be valuable to them.

The old citizens will recognize in this one of his oft-repeated quotations:

> "Just like love is yonder rose,
> Heavenly fragrance round it glows,
> But underneath a briar grows—
>   Just like love."

DR. ISAAC COE.

The memory of this man should ever be revered by the early citizens of Indianapolis, especially by those who were here or had friends here in that ever memorable year of sickness and death, 1821. He came to this place in May of that year, and was the only physician able to render any assistance to the people during the two months of sickness, August and September.

The Doctor had brought a large supply of Peruvian bark and wine, which was the only thing with which he could conquer the fever and ague. Had it not been for his untiring services the mortality of that year would have been much greater. He could be seen at almost any time of night dodging through the woods (in his gig, and by the light of his lantern), from one cabin to another, administering to the sick in other ways as well as giving medicine.

After the sickness had abated he was prominent in forwarding and promoting the interests of the settlers in other ways. He was active with Messrs. Ray and Blake in organizing the first Sabbath-school, the first church and the first Bible society.

Dr. Coe was, for several years, one of the three fund commissioners of the State, in connection with the late Caleb B. Smith, and Samuel Hanna, of Fort Wayne.

He was a native of the State of New Jersey, and, as above stated, came to this place in May, 1821. He first settled on the bank of Fall Creek, just below where the Crawfordsville State road crosses that stream, and lived there several years. He then bought a lot, and built a house on Circle street, about equi-distant between the "Journal" buildings and Christ (Episcopal) Church, where he remained during his residence in this city.

Dr. Coe was ever active in all benevolent or charitable associations calculated to benefit the poor and unfortunate, without regard to their religion.

The few years previous to his death he spent in some portion of the West with his friends. His remains were brought to Indianapolis for interment, and now rest in Crown Hill Cemetery.

> "Here will I rest, until the day declines,
> A voiceless pilgrim toward the land of song,
> And, like a sentinel, the herald signs
> Of him whose coming hath been stayed too long."

MORRIS MORRIS

Was from Carlisle, Nicholas County, Kentucky. He and his eldest son, Austin, had come to the bluffs of White River in 1821, and put in a crop of four acres of corn.

At the sale of land in Brookville, in July, he purchased a quarter section that lay about a mile from the donation, and adjoining the sixteenth section that had been reserved for school purposes, and on the west side of the river.

To this land he moved his family about the first of October, and a few days before the first sale of lots. Soon after he settled in his new home his whole family were taken sick with chills and fever. This discouraged him very much, so much so that he wished to return to Kentucky, and would have done so had not Mrs. Morris opposed it, and to her Indianapolis is indebted for what afterwards turned out to be several of its most valuable citizens. Mr. Morris brought the corn he had raised at the bluffs to within a mile of his house in a boat.

He was a candidate for clerk of the county at the first election, held in April, 1822, and was defeated by the "in yonder on Whitewater" vote, which outnumbered that of the Kentuckians.

He represented this county several years in the Legislature, and was afterwards elected Auditor of State, and served two or three terms. He made a very efficient and popular officer.

His family consisted of six children when he first came to the new purchase, four sons, Austin, Milton, Thomas and John, and two daughters, Amanda and Julia, to which was added, after they came here, Elizabeth and William.

Austin was for many years, and up to the time of his death, in 1851, a leading man and a successful politician, and enjoyed the confidence of his (Whig) party to a great extent. I believe his first office was that of colonel of militia. He represented the county several times in the Legislature. He was an enthusiastic member of the Methodist Church, and a devoted Christian.

Milton was for several years a clerk for the late Nicholas McCarty, and then engaged in the mercantile business at Covington, Fountain County, and was quite successful. He died in the South many years since, where he had gone with several boats laden with produce.

The third son we have now in the person of Gen. Thomas A. Morris, one of our most prominent men. He was a graduate of West Point, but resigned to follow pursuits more congenial to his taste. While he was in the army he was considered one of the best disciplinarians in it, as he is now one of the most skillful of civil engineers. He was for many years employed on the public works of the State, was chief engineer on the Cincinnati and Indianapolis Railroad, and has had some connection with nearly all the roads centering to this city, and is at this time President of the Indianapolis and St. Louis Railway, which is being constructed under his supervision. In the early part of the rebellion he rendered signal service in Western Virginia for which others got the credit. He was tendered a prominent position in the army but declined (as I understand), because the Government had not properly appreciated his services already rendered.

John D. Morris, the fourth son, has for several years been engaged in the freight office of the Cincinnati and Indianapolis Railroad, and to him the writer is indebted for having stood by him at a very trying time, and he takes this occasion to return him thanks, after twenty-nine years, for the prompt manner in which he performed his part. True, he made a slight mistake at the altar in handing the minister the money instead of the legal document.

Amanda was the wife of one of our leading physicians, Dr. John L. Mothershead. She has been dead several years, and so has William, the youngest child.

Julia is the wife of Mr. Ross, formerly superintendent of the Cincinnati Railroad, but now engaged in one of the departments at Washington.

Elizabeth is the wife of John D. Defrees, for several years Superintendent of Public Printing at Washington, and for many years editor of the Indianapolis "Journal," and a leading Whig politician of Indiana. It is to John D. Defrees that the present Vice President of the United States is indebted for his high position, and, as the New York "Tribune" remarked in regard to Grant and Rawlings, so with Colfax and Defrees: had there been no John D. Defrees there would have been no Vice President Colfax.

Mr. Morris had the faculty of holding on to the city property which he bought at an early day, and which now constitutes the finest business property in the city. He owned the entire square north of and adjoining the Union Depot, which made his heirs quite wealthy.

When Mr. Morris first came to Indianapolis our parents were known only as "dad and mam," or "pap and mammy," but we soon learned to call them "pa and ma," from Mr. M.'s children.

His house was ever the home of ministers of all denominations, among whom was numbered, as the particular friend of Mr. M., the late James Havens. Mr. and Mrs. Morris were, from time immemorial, called, by both old and young, Pa and Ma Morris. At the time of Mrs. Morris' death, which occurred in 1864, they lacked but one month of having lived together sixty years—an ordinary lifetime. He died in 1867, at the ripe age of eighty-three.

> "Howe'er it be, it seems to me,
> 'Tis only noble to be good;
> Kind hearts are more than coronets,
> And simple faith than Norman blood."

DR. SAMUEL G. MITCHELL

Was the first physician who came to Indianapolis, in April, 1821. He was from Paris, Kentucky. He first built a hewed log house on the southwest corner of Washington and Tennessee streets, where the State offices now stand. He then bought the lot, and built a frame house, on the northwest corner of Washington and Meridian streets, where the "Bee Hive" store now stands. At the latter place he lost his wife and only child. This bereavement he never got over until his death. He was a large, fleshy man, and, like that kind of men generally, was very good-natured. He possessed many fine traits of character, and was noted for his hospitality and liberality. I do not think he was considered as good a physician as either of the other three physicians of that time.

He brought with him the first colored person that came to Indianapolis, a boy about fifteen years old, named Ephraim Ensaw. This boy took advantage of the Doctor's good nature and kindness, and became so bad that the Doctor had to get rid of him.

The Doctor had a stroke of palsy, and became paralyzed. He was taken by his friends to Ohio, and there died about the year 1837. He was a brother-in-law of Samuel Henderson, the first postmaster, and father-in-law of Henry Porter, a prominent merchant of his day.

JERRY COLLINS,

Or "Uncle Jerry," as he was familiarly called by the lovers of the ardent, and especially by his immediate customers, kept a small whisky-shop on the southwest corner of Washington and Meridian streets. He also kept other refreshments for his lady customers, such as ginger cakes, smoked herring and spruce beer.

Uncle Jerry was not permitted by law to sell whisky in a less quantity than a quart, and that not to be drank upon his premises. Being a law-abiding man, and to accommodate his many customers, and more especially those from Waterloo, he had a pump placed on Meridian street, just around the corner from his front door, which could not be construed to be upon his premises.

For the information of those who were not acquainted with Indianapolis at that time, I would say that Waterloo was that portion of the county and river bottom lying between the bluff road and the river, commencing about three miles from town and extending about five miles south.

In Waterloo there were about twenty adult male inhabitants, viz: the Mundys, Snows, Tharps, Fanchers, Paddocks, Pressers, and last, but by no means least, were the Stephenses, among whom was "Rip-Roaring Bob," as he called himself.

When Waterloo came to town their headquarters was Uncle Jerry's pump. Soon after their arrival you would see one of them go into the shop, and soon return to join his comrades with a quart measure (filled with whisky, the price of which was twelve and a-half cents) in one hand and a small tin cup in the other. The quart cup would make the trip to the shop and return about every half hour, and continue until each and every one had accompanied it at least once, by which time each one would have drank his quart of whisky and contributed his shilling. On public occasions the trips were made in more rapid succession, and about two to each person, when the quantity drank and the money expended would be doubled. It is proper here to say that while the quart measure is making the various trips to and from the shop, if feminine Waterloo should be in town, they would be seated in the shade of the house regaling themselves with ginger cakes, smoked herring and spruce beer.

Then would begin their gymnastic and other performances, under the direction of their leader, "Rip Roaring Bob," and they were generally kept up until the small boys would return from school, and the young men had quit their several avocations for the day. Waterloo would then be invited to leave town, and were generally accompanied on their forced march down Meridian street to the limits of town, and often some distance south of "Pogue's Creek." To accelerate their movement and to assist them along, eggs, brickbats, boulders and other missles were brought into requisition by the assailing party. When the eggs began to fly "fast and furious," and the boulders fell like hail around them, they would retire in a very disorganized and demoralized condition. "Rip Roaring Bob" was generally in the rear keeping back the assailing party, and covering the retreat of his comrades, while Garrett Presser would be far in advance of his retreating friends, going at the rate of "two-forty" on his little black mare, and Jonathan Paddock would be close at his heels, with his umbrella hoisted to keep off the flying missiles. On one occasion a young man of the town party was some distance in advance of his friends (who had stopped pursuit). "Rip Roaring Bob" was some distance behind his party, and, with his quick perceptibility, soon saw the true situation, and "made for" the young man, who barely escaped Bob's clutches, receiving in his back on his retreat some of the same missiles thrown by his own party at Waterloo.

"Rip Roaring Bob" moved from Waterloo to Hamilton County, and became a respectable man, and accumulated a considerable property. The balance of Waterloo has been scattered upon the broad prairies of Missouri, Iowa and Illinois, and have no doubt often related to their neighbors their many hair-breadth escapes from, and daring adventures with, the early settlers of Indianapolis.

Jerry Collins and Cader Carter dug the grave of Daniel Shaffer, the first person buried in the old graveyard, in August, 1821.

Uncle Jerry died of cholera in 1852, and left a fine property to be divided between his nephews and other relatives, he being an old bachelor.

HUGH O'NEAL.

When I attempt to write a short sketch of the career of this noble and generous-hearted young man, and my early schoolmate, the involuntary tear drops on the paper. I am carried back many years to our schoolboy days and childish sports, before our selfish natures had assumed entire control of our actions, and when, if we had a vein of good feeling running through our thought it would not be crushed out by what society would think of our action if we took some fallen young man by the hand and gave him an encouraging word. How many young and promising men have been ruined and lost for the want of some such friend, who undeterred from doing their duty by what society would think of them, instead of frowning upon them for their offense and shunning them as they would a leper, would "condemn the fault and not the actor of it," and thereby let them know 'twas their fault and not their person they shunned.

Could they only know the heart and secret workings of the tortured mind of those they condemn, how different would they act.

Hugh O'Neal came to this place when a boy, in the year 1821. His father, Thomas O'Neal, lived on and owned the first eighty acres of land north of and adjoining "Camp Morton," where are now the State Fair grounds. He was poor, and could do but little toward the education of his children.

Hugh, being industrious and very energetic, managed to acquire a fair English education, studied law and rose to a respectable position in his profession. No young man in the State bid fairer to rise to eminence and distinction than he did. When the California mania was raging, in 1849, his ambition prompted him to risk his chances for fortune in that golden region, and it was there he fell a victim to that destroying demon (intemperance) that annihilates all that is good and virtuous in our natures, and sends us to an early grave unhonored and unsung. After his return from California he did but little business. True, he was successful in some very important cases intrusted to his care, but the love of drink and a disappointed ambition brought him to an early grave, with but few relatives, though many friends, to drop the sympathetic tear upon his coffin.

In his case I would reverse the quotation so often used from Mark Anthony's oration over the dead body of Cæsar, which reads: "The evil men do lives after them; the good is oft interred with their bones." I would say, "The good men do lives after them; the evil is oft interred with their bones." So let it be with Hugh.

Some of the new and present citizens of Indianapolis may ask who was Hugh O'Neal? To such I would say, he was the peer in social standing and superior in talent to many who now stand upon the top round of the ladder in this refined society. He was very irritable, and frequently let his passion get the better of his judgment, and would often make harsh and uncalled for expressions to those he had intercourse with, but was always ready, when the momentary ebullitions of passion were over, to make reparation for anything said or done.

On one occasion he and the late Governor Wallace were opposing counsel. The Governor rather got the advantage of Hugh, which made him very angry, and he was quite abusive, to which the Governor paid no attention, knowing that it would soon be over. After court adjourned, the Governor was passing by the door of a saloon. Hugh was some distance behind. He called out to the Governor to stop. After Hugh came up he said, "Let's take a drink." "Certainly," said the Governor; "that is the only sensible remark I have heard you make to-day." And all was as well with them as though nothing had happened.

> "The social glass I saw him seize,
> The more with festive wit to please.
> Daily increased his love of cheer;
> Ah, little thought he death was near.
> Gradual indulgence on him stole;
> Frequent became the midnight bowl.

> 'Twas in that bowl the headache placed,
> Which, with the juice, his lips embraced.
> Despair next mingled with the draught;
> Indignantly he drank and laughed."

JOHN VAN BLARICUM.

This brawny son of Vulcan was the first in Indianapolis to lay a plow, steel an ax, make a grubbing-hoe, or shoe a horse. He might have been the same that forged the bolts of Jove. He had a will to dare do anything. He was as much a terror to the children in an early day as Dave Buckhart was in after years to the "colored society."

The old man was very clever if you would get on the right side of him, but very few had the good fortune to do so. He claimed the same right for his hogs, geese and cattle that he did for himself, *i. e.*, to do as they pleased.

He had an apprentice boy named Jim Shannon. This boy he whipped with an iron nailrod, as he said it was the only thing that would reach the quick. He said his skin was like an alligator's, and when he struck him with an iron rod the scales would fly off. Perhaps he meant the scales of iron from the rod.

On one occasion his geese had got into trouble. He wished for the power of King Herod for twenty-four hours. He said he would slay every boy in the settlement of the age of six years and under. He would commence with John Nowland, and when he got to the Carter boys would take the old man with them.

Captain John Cain had a very fine dog, which he kept chained in his yard. Mr. Van Blaricum became very suspicious that this dog was kept for protection against his hogs. He took his gun and went down to the Captain's house and shot the dog in the presence of the family, and while the dog was chained. Out of this transaction grew a suit for damages. It commenced in the circuit court, and, I think, ended in the supreme court. It cost Van Blaricum several hundred dollars. It was during this suit that it was proved his hogs had been seen in the second story of Hawkins' Hotel.

A gentleman went to his shop to have some work done, which he needed very much. Van Blaricum told him he would not stop to make a nail for his coffin.

Mr. Van B. owned the lot, and had his shop, on the southeast corner of Washington and Meridian streets, where Blackford's block now stands. He also owned and lived on the lot immediately back of it, fronting on Meridian street. He sold them and removed to a farm four miles from town, on the Crawfordsville road.

It was John Van Blaricum who whipped the captain of the steamboat "The General Hanna," and cleared the boat of the balance of the crew in 1831, an account of which will be found on another page.

He died at his residence in the year 1850. Like every person else, he had *many traits of character*—some were bad and some were very bad.

"In yonder on Whitewater," near Brookville, furnished us with John Van Blaricum, in the year 1821. He had several sons, some of whom will be mentioned in another sketch.

"The smith, a mighty man is he, with large and sinewy hands;
The muscles of his brawny arms are strong as iron bands.
Thus, at the flaming forge of life our fortunes must be wrought;
Thus, on the sounding anvil shaped, each burning deed and thought."

OLD HELVEY

Lived on the school section (No. 16), west of Eagle Creek, and near what was called the "big raspberry patch." His house was the headquarters for dances and sprees of all kinds. He made it a point to invite all the "new comers," on first sight, to visit him.

He made the acquaintance of the late Colonel A. W. Russell soon after the arrival of the latter to the "new settlement." He invited him to come over and become acquainted with his family. Said he, "Thar's no such gals in the settlement as Old Helvey's; thar's Bash, and Vine, and Tantrabogus, and the like o' that.

"I'll tell ye, stranger, that Bash is a hoss. I would like you to come over and take a rassell with her. She throwed Ole 'Likum Harding, best two in three; 'tother was a dog fall, but Bash soon turned him and got on top on him.

"Vine ain't slow for ten steps, as Ole Jim McCoy sez. She flirted Cader Carter every lick. Cader wanted to spark her, but the gal thought she seed nigger in his eye. It wouldn't do, stranger. Vine's clear grit, as Jerry Johnson sez.

"Now, you are from Kaintuck; you watch Cader's eye; see if thar ain't nigger thar.

"I'll tell you, stranger, that gal Bash killed the biggest buck that's been killed in the new purchase. She shot offhand, seventy-five yards. He was a real three-specker, no mistake.

"There's a lame schoolmaster, from Jarsey, arter Bash, and the gal, I b'leve, has a kind of hankering arter him. He can't dance much, but he's an awful sight of book larnin'. He used to keep school in Jarsey. He's mighty nice kin folks; he's kin to them new comers, Johnsons and Cools. You know that Doctor Cool; he degraded in college. The school teacher aint far ahind him. So, stranger, come over and see what kind of gals Old Helvey's are, anyhow."

Mr. Russell accepted Mr. Helvey's invitation, and was frequently a guest at his house, and when he came all had to stand back, even the lame schoolmaster. He became a great favorite with the family generally. The old lady said "he was the only man in the new purchase that could play Yankee Doodle or Leather Breeches right on the fiddle," and after that dancing never commenced until " Young Kaintuck" had arrived.

The lame schoolmaster was successful, and won the hand as well as the heart of Miss Bashaby. Young Kaintuck was master of ceremonies on the occasion of the wedding. There are many of the guests yet living, among whom is Jacob Landis.

After the bride and groom had retired, the whisky gave out. There was no way of getting more of it except at Mr. Landis' grocery. He was present, but there was no pen, pencil or paper with which an order could be sent to his clerk. Old Helvey suggested that Mr. Landis should send his knife, which would be recognized by the young man, and would certainly bring the whisky. This was done, and the whisky came, to the great joy of all present.

Mr. Helvey thought the bride and groom must be dry by this time, so he took the jug to them and made them drink to the health of the guests.

Miss Viney soon followed her sister, and became the wife of Champion Helvey, her cousin. At this wedding there was a grand serenade by Nathaniel Cox's minstrels, which was under his direction. The principal musical instrument was a horse-fiddle.

Old Helvey distinguished himself in many hotly-contested battles at Jerry Collins' grocery, and never failed to vanquish his adversary, and fairly won the trophies of war, which were, generally, an eye, a piece of an ear, a part of a finger, or a slice of flesh from some exposed part of his antagonist's person. In Mr. Helvey's house could be found a great variety of munitions of war, such as rifles, shot-guns, muskets, tomahawks, scalping and butcher-knives. In his yard were all kinds of dogs, from the surly bull-dog to the half-wolf or "ingin dog." In his pound or stable was a variety of Indian ponies. In his second cabin, used for a kitchen,

> "Dried pumpkins over head were strung,
> Where venison hams in plenty hung."

After the treaty with the Miamis of the Wabash, at the mouth of Little River, in the year 1832, Mr. Helvey moved to the treaty ground, and there died.

His only son and right bower, Tantrabogus, was drowned in Eel River. The last the writer ever saw of Bashaby she was a dashing widow, and could out dance the world.

JOHN GIVAN.

Among the great variety of characters I have met with in writing these reminiscences, the counterpart, or anything that approximates to that of Mr. Givan, cannot be found. He is a man of as much general information on commonplace subjects as can be found anywhere.

He has an acquaintance throughout this as well as nearly all the Western States. Indeed, there is scarcely a town but what he can tell you the name of some person living there, or had lived there, or intended to, or had come from there, or something in regard to it. He has an uncommon memory, and is possessed of more incidents connected with the early history of this city than any person now living, and, although I profess to know something of this city myself, I am compelled to yield the palm in that particular.

His mind, from some cause, took an unfortunate turn some years since, from which resulted the loss of his property, or he might be to-day, as he once was, one of the prominent men of this city.

Mr. Givan's store was a perfect curiosity shop. In it could be found any article that utility or necessity might demand. A gentleman once inquired (in sport) for goose yokes, and to his surprise they were produced by dozens.

In the early settlement of Boone County large quantities of wild honey was taken and brought to this market for sale. Mr. Given was the purchaser of the honey as well as the beeswax. The honey was brought to market in this way: Two hickory poles were attached together like shafts, the ends resting on the ground. On these poles the barrel of honey was fastened by pins. In front of the barrel boards were placed, on which the beeswax was carried. When the roads were bad two horses were necessary to pull the load; in that case one horse was hitched in front of the other, or tandem fashion.

About the year 1826 a man named Whaley sold Mr. Givan a barrel of honey, and a large cake of beeswax that had been molded in a sugar-kettle, and, although very large, Mr. Givan thought it very heavy for the size. He told Whaley that it was too large to pack in a barrel, as he did for shipping, and proposed that Whaley should help him break it open. For this purpose he took a fro (an article used for splitting boards), and had Whaley hold it across the cake while he struck it with a maul. The cake opened and disclosed a rock as large as a man's head, which broke the fro. Mr. Givan not only charged Whaley with the rock, but the profit he would have made on it had it have been wax. He also charged him with the fro. Nor was that all; he told his customer that he kept an account of what was stolen from him, and that whenever he detected any person in rascality he made him pay this account; all of which Whaley paid, and seemed glad to get off in that way.

James Givan, the father of John, and for many years his partner, lived on his farm at what is now the east end of Washington street, and near where Col. John W. Ray now resides. He there died in the summer of 1834.

Since this sketch was written, and in the month of May, 1870, Mrs. Margaret Givan, the second wife of James Givan, has died. No woman, since the first settlement of Indianapolis, has been connected with so many benevolent and charitable institutions.

John Givan, the last of his father's children living, yet resides here, and looks as though his sands of life were well nigh spent, and is a fit subject for the charity of the few old settlers of Indianapolis, most of whom have grown wealthy, while he is quite poor. I hope this suggestion will not be disregarded by those who could render him assistance without feeling any poorer in consequence, and thereby do an act of kindness for one who, in his better and prosperous days, did many acts of charity for the poor and unfortunate.

ROBERT PATTERSON

Was among those who came to this place in the year 1821. He was directly from Jennings County, where he had lived a short time prior to his coming here. He was originally from Cynthiana, Harrison County, Kentucky.

Mr. Patterson had a large family of children (about ten) when he first came, with the addition of several after he came to this place. Those of his children that are yet living still remain in the city and neighborhood.

Samuel J. Patterson, the eldest son, lives on his farm adjoining the city, where he has lived for the last thirty-five years, and near his old mill, where he carried on milling for many years. This mill was originally built by his father-in-law, Isaac Wilson, and was the first built in the new purchase. It has been abandoned for some years, and the water power, which was so valuable, turned and used in the mill near the west end of Washington street.

Elliott M. Patterson, the second son, and as noble hearted a man as ever lived, was killed in Green County, in 1851, by being thrown from a wagon while the horses were running away. He lived but a few hours after being found.

Madison, the third son, is the present engineer and surveyor for the city. He has been engaged in this business for nearly thirty years, and is very proficient in that line.

James M. Patterson, the fourth son, was, for many years, engaged in the livery business. In the year 1862 he fell from his chair and expired in a few moments. He was sitting at his stable door, apparently in good health. It was thought he died of apoplexy. There are two of Robert Patterson's daughters yet living, one the wife of the Hon. David Macy, President of the Peru and Indianapolis Railroad, and one of our most enterprising citizens. The other is the wife of James L. Southard, secretary of the company above referred to.

Robert Patterson was for many years Probate and Associate Judge of the county. He has done a great deal of work on the National road and canals. He also had the contract for delivering the laws to the different county seats. This was before we had railroads, and wagons were brought into requisition. He brought the first pair of mill-stones that came to the new purchase, in 1821, for the mill built by Isaac Wilson, and owned by his son, Samuel J. Patterson, for several years.

CALVIN FLETCHER.

The first lawyer that came to this place, about the middle of August, 1821. He was a native of Vermont, and there educated. His first residence in the West was at Urbana, Ohio, where he taught school, and studied law with James Cooley, an eminent and distinguished lawyer of that place, and for whom he named his first child, James Cooley Fletcher, who is the present Consul to Brazil.

Mr. Fletcher and his young wife came by way of Winchester and down White river in a small two-horse wagon that contained all his worldly goods. There was a cabin stood near my father's, a man named Winslow had raised and covered, but no floor was made; a door was cut out, and a place for a chimney. My father advised him to take possession of it, as it was not likely the owner would ever use it, it being understood he had declined moving to the place since it had proved so sickly. This cabin was situated about the middle of the square between the Canal and West street, and Washington and Maryland streets. It was here Mr. Fletcher lived the first year of his residence in Indianapolis, and until Mr. Blake had built a small one-story frame house (the first in the place) about the middle of the square on the south side of Washington, between Illinois and Tennessee streets; in this house his first two children, James and Elijah, were born.

After the death of my father Mr. Fletcher borrowed of my mother a horse for the purpose of attending court at Pendleton. While in his possession the animal foundered so bad that he died. Mr. F. bought of Mr. Blake the only horse in the settlement, that was for sale, to replace the one that had died. This was not so good a horse as the one he had got of my mother. Said he, "When your daughter is old enough, and is married, I may be able to give her a better horse and (pointing to the babe in my mother's lap,) when she is married I will give her one also." Both of those pledges he faithfully kept, the latter twenty-five years after it was made, thus giving three horses for one.

Mr. Fletcher was the first Prosecuting Attorney for this Judicial Circuit, and when practicing before magistrates had frequently to explain the law both for and against his client as was the case I have referred to on another page, where Esquire Basey was in favor of sending a horse-thief direct to the penitentiary without troubling the higher court with the case.

Mr. F. was elected senator for the district composed of the counties of Marion, Madison, and Hamilton; and it was while a senator he first met in that body that irritable old bachelor and Irishman, "John Ewing, of Knox."

Mr. Fletcher was quick to discover the weak points in Mr. Ewing's character, and amused himself and the Senate often by attacking them. Mr. Ewing was one of the most talented men of the Senate, and had been very overbearing toward his associates, but had never met his match in wit and sarcasm until he met the "Yankee poney," as he called Mr. Fletcher.

Many a practical joke did he play upon his associates at the bar while traveling the circuit. On one occasion himself, Harvey Gregg and Hiram Brown were going to attend the Johnson Circuit Court; Mr. Brown wore a very high-crowned hat, which Mr. Fletcher said resembled a North Carolina tar bucket. At or near Greenwood Mr. Brown stopped a few minutes, while Messrs. Fletcher and Gregg rode on. They had not gone far when they met a traveler; said Mr. Fletcher to him, "you will meet a man riding a white horse, tell him we have found the tar bucket;" and so he told every person they met between that and Franklin, and by the time Mr. Brown reached the latter place he had been told at least a dozen times that they had found the tar bucket, which annoyed him very much.

Mr. Fletcher was a successful practitioner of the law for about thirty years. His unequalled success was as much the result of his close application and attention to the business intrusted to his care as to his talent; he was, during nearly the whole time he practiced, the collecting lawyer for Eastern merchants throughout the State. This great business he got through the influence of his friend, the late Nicholas McCarty.

At the time Mr. F. first came to Indianapolis there was a strong prejudice existing among the people against the Yankees (as all Eastern people were called), but he soon overcame this by his disposition to suit himself to the times, and taking a deep interest in the welfare and success of all the settlers, and his attention to them in that trying time, when nearly every family was helpless by sickness.

As I have said before, he was worth but little in property when he first came to this place, but he brought with him that which afterwards made him a fortune, and one for all his numerous family, *i. e.*, perseverance, industry and economy. At the time of his death, 1867, he owned and managed some of the finest farms in this and the adjoining counties, and I have been told that the immediate cause of his death was over-exertion on one of them. One of Mr. F.'s maxims, and by which he was governed, was never to leave until to-morrow that which could be done to-day.

The first night he spent in Indianapolis was under my father's roof; and he was for many years after the death of my father the friendly adviser of our family.

About the time of his death it was said that he came to this place a laborer; this was not true; to my certain knowledge he never did a day's work for any other person but himself, save in a professional way, or assisting at house-raisings or log-rollings, after he came to this place.

Mr. F. has several sons residing in the city and county, all of whom inherit the leading traits of their father's character.

He was a contributor to, and for, the erection of nearly every church built in the city, from the beginning up to the time of his death. He ever took great interest in Sunday Schools, and was for many years the Superintendent of one. Such was Calvin Fletcher.

ANDREW SMITH.

Among the early settlers of Indianapolis, and one of those entitled to notice, is Andy Smith. He came here in 1822, a mere boy, in search of work. His father, at that time, lived on White River, north of this place, and near the residence of the Conners. He afterwards removed to near the bluffs, and adjoining his old Whitewater neighbor, Jacob Whetzel, where he resided many years before his death. His son Robert now owns his homestead, and lives there, and is a near neighbor of Cyrus Whetzel.

Andy did not make his father's house his home much after they came to the "New Purchase." His first work in Indianapolis was for Thomas M. Smith, and then, for several years, he lived with and worked for General Hanna. It was during this time, and on the third of July, 1830 (the fourth being Sunday), while firing the cannon, that he lost his left arm by a premature discharge. Mr. Smith had admonished those engaged with him that the gun was becoming too hot, and in five minutes after, and while General Hanna was standing on the table, singing his favorite song, "The Liberty Tree," and which he used to sing on all public occasions, the discharge took place that robbed him of an arm.

Andy afterwards married the niece of the General and daughter of Mr. John Hanna, of this county. He was for many years, nearly a quarter of a century, a deputy sheriff, sometimes buying the business from the sheriff elect.

Twenty-five years ago Andy might have been seen at almost any hour of the day on Washington street, with his book under his arm, filled with divers writs, summons, executions and all kinds of legal documents that pertain to a sheriff's duties, and calculated to intimidate debtors as well as culprits, and there were but few that cared to meet Andy, lest he might have something for them.

Although he had but one arm and a half and but one hand, he did not seem afraid to arrest the most daring criminal; and with this one hand he could use the ax as dexterously as most persons could with two.

Andy is now one of our prosperous farmers of Lawrence township, in the north part of the county, near the Peru railroad.

SAMUEL DUKE

Was among those citizens that came to this place in the winter of 1821-22, and the second cabinet maker that cast his lot with the hardy pioneers of Indianapolis. He was an Irishman by birth, and the second one of his countrymen to make this place his home, and an honest, upright man, and in his every-day deportment seemed that he would rather suffer a wrong himself than do a neighbor an injury.

Mr. Duke was fond of fun and enjoyed a joke. It was he that induced the *blessed* Ingins to pay a visit to the tonsorial establishment of "Fancy Tom," an account of which will be found in a subsequent sketch.

He brought the first "hearse" to this place in 1824. To describe this vehicle is entirely out of my power; like a gentleman of Lafayette, my friend E. J. Peck tells of, in a similar situation, for the want of language to describe something he had seen, he said that "there was not language in the whole English '*vocbuluary*' to give an idea of it;" I never saw anything like it before nor since; it was enough to give a well man a sinking chill to see Mr. Duke, with his old grey horse in the thills, on the way to the grave-yard. Perhaps the worthy undertaker had an increase of business in view when he purchased it, as an experiment of the effect it would have upon the mortality of the people.

Mr. Duke died several years since. He has several children yet residing in the city; one is the wife of David Lang, a well known carpenter and builder, who has also been a citizen of the city near forty years. He is an honest, upright Scotchman, content to attend to his own business and let others do the same.

Forty-five years have come and passed away since the first hearse was brought to this place, and now we have in its stead those elegant vehicles of that kind of Messrs. Weaver, Long and Williams, which look as though they intended that our last ride, though a silent, should be a stylish one.

In the undertakers' establishments of the gentlemen above named the most fastidious, who wish to "shuffle off this mortal coil," can be suited and fitted, for in them

"Coffins stand round like open presses
That show the dead in their last dresses."

INCIDENTS OF 1821 AND 1822.

The first dance of any kind that came off in Indianapolis with perhaps the exception of that of the war or scalp dance of the tawny Delaware or dusky Pottawattamie, was at the double cabin of John Wyant, in December, 1821, on the bank of White River, near where Kingan's pork house no stands.

Mr. Wyant had invited the entire dancing population of the "new settlement," men, women and children. The father and mother of the writer were there, as well as himself. Indeed there was but little of a public nature in Indianapolis at that early day that I did not see, although there were many private transactions that I did not witness for the want of an invitation, but I have heard considerable about them since.

There was a charge of twenty-five cents admittance for each male adult that attended this "gathering;" this charge was to furnish the fluids, which was the only costly article used on those occasions.

The guests had began to arrive, and while the landlord was in "t'other house," as the second cabin was called, my father (having been educated in a different school of etiquette from that of Mr. Wyant) thought it but politeness to invite Mrs. Wyant with him to open and put the ball in motion, which she gracefully accepted, and they were, with others, going it in fine style when the landlord returned. He at once commanded the music (which was being drawn from the bowels of a dilapidated looking fiddle by the late Colonel A. W. Russell) to stop, which order was instantly obeyed.

Mr. Wyant said, that "as far as himself and wife were concerned, they were capable of and able to do their own dancing, and that he thought it would look better for every man to dance with his own wife; those that had no wife could dance with the 'gals.'" This order, as far as Mr. and Mrs. Wyant were concerned, was strictly adhered to and faithfully carried out the balance of the night. When the guests were ready to leave, at dawn of day, Mr. and Mrs. Wyant were still "bobbing around" together, oblivious to surrounding circumstances, and seemed highly delighted with each other's society.

The second marriage in the "new purchase" was early in the year 1822, that of Uriah Gates to Miss Patsy Chinn, daughter of Thomas Chinn, Esq. Mr. Chinn lived on the north bank of Pogue's creek, near the residence of the late Governor Noble; he lived in a "double cabin," one of which was very large, the other was of the ordinary size, about eighteen by twenty feet square. In the latter room was a dirt floor; in this room the dinner table was made the day preceding the wedding. The table was made by driving forked poles into the ground of sufficient height and number; on these upright poles others were laid the length of the room; on these last poles puncheons were laid crosswise, which constituted the table.

The invited guests began to arrive on the morning of the wedding about nine o'clock; the large cabin was being pretty well filled; the elder ladies came for the purpose of assisting Mrs. Chinn in the culinary department, the younger ones for dancing, so soon as the marriage ceremony should be performed. As the two rooms were already occupied, the bride had to make her toilet in the smoke house, where she received the bridegroom and his retinue.

About half past ten o'clock they were seen winding their way up the bank of Pogue's creek, and met the bride and her next friend in the house indicated above.

About eleven o'clock, and after it was known that the 'Squire had arrived, they came forth from the smoke house and went to the large cabin, where they were made man and wife with the shortest number of words the 'Squire had at his command to perform the ceremony.

Then the older guests and the bride and groom were invited to the dinner cabin. As I was more deeply interested in this part of the programme I went along as a spectator and to reconnoiter, and to take a peep at the good things in store for me at the proper time.

On either end of the table was a large, fat wild turkey, still hot and smoking as when taken from the clay oven in which they were roasted; in the middle of the table and midway between the turkeys was a fine saddle of venison, part of a buck killed the day before by Mr. Chinn expressly for the occasion. The spaces between the turkeys and venison were filled with pumpkin, chicken and various other kinds of pies; from the side-table or puncheon Mrs. Chinn, assisted by the old ladies, was issuing coffee, which was taken from a large sugar-kettle that was hanging over the fire; by the side of the tin coffee pot on this side table was a large tin pan filled with maple sugar, and a gallon pitcher of delicious cream.

Although there was no great display of silver or China ware on that rude table, there was all that the most fastidious appetite could desire, and even at this day it might be considered "a dainty dish to set before a king." The dessert and pastry was got up without the aid of a "French cook." Such was the first fashionable wedding-dinner in Indianapolis.

While the first party invited to the table were engaged in stowing away its contents and complimenting the bride and groom, those in the marriage room were "tripping the light fantastic toe" to the tune of "Leather Breeches."

After the bride and groom had left the table they were invited to join in (as Beau Hickman would say) the festivities of the occasion. The bridegroom excused himself, as he had no "ear for music or foot for dancing, but was ready for fun in any other shape that might be offered."

The dancing was continued for two days and nights after the wedding. I remember that my father and mother came home after daylight the second day, slept until the afternoon, then went back and put in another night.

It may be proper to say that farmer Tom Johnson was conspicuous among the guests at this wedding, and never did his curls that hung down on his cheeks, and his white linen pantaloons with black ribbon drawstrings at the bottom, tied in a bow knot, appear to a better advantage than they did on this occasion; although Tom had not yet seen a "*Purranner*," he seemed to enjoy the music and dancing.

Mr. Gates died but a few years since; he was the father of Mr. John Gates, the well known and popular blacksmith of our city.

On the morning of the fourth of July, 1822, my father's family was aroused before daylight by persons hallooing in front of our door. It turned out to be Captain James Richey, who lived near the Bluffs, and a young man and lady that had placed themselves under the Captain's charge and ran away from obdurate parents for the purpose of being married. Mr. Richey was not slow in making known to my father what they wanted, and intimated that, "what it were well to do, 'twere well it were done quickly." He and my father soon found the county clerk (the venerable James M. Ray) at Carter's Rosebush Tavern, and procured the necessary legal document, and the services of Judge Wm. W. Wick, and before breakfast the two were made one.

They had scarcely arose from the breakfast table before the young lady was confronted by her angry father. Captain Richey informed him that he was just a few minutes too late, and that he had not lost "a darter," as he supposed, but had gained a son, and that when old Jim Richey undertook to do anything, he did it with all his might, and accomplished his object.

The parties were reconciled and invited to attend the barbecue and ball that was to take place that day, which they did.

This was the first fourth of July celebration in Indianapolis; the barbecue was in the middle of Washington street, just west of the Canal. A fine buck had been killed the day before by Robert Harding, and was roasted whole, and was partaken of by the entire population of the town and surrounding country.

After dinner the people were entertained by a teamster from Dayton, Ohio, who dressed himself in fantastic or clownish style, singing comic songs and in various other ways amusing the people. This was the first clown that performed in public in this place, although we have had them by hundreds since in our legislative halls, courts of justice, and political conventions.

Soon after the clown was through with his performance the dancing commenced in a large, unfinished frame building on the north side of Washington street, near where the barbecue was, and continued until some time on the fifth. This was the first public dinner and ball in Indianapolis.

In writing these incidents my object is to show the great difference, and contrast the customs of the early citizens of this place with those of the present day, and the variety of character found among the early citizens.

I have recurred so often lately to those early scenes in the history of this city, that it has led me to ask myself the question and inquire where was there contentment and true happiness found if not in the pioneers of Indianapolis?

There was no finely decorated halls then as now, no cornet or fine string bands to pour fourth their melodious strains of music, no fine carriages, with drivers in livery, to take the ladies to the dance, no kid gloves or paper-collared gentlemen to help them in and out of the carriage, no white-aproned servants to hand them the iced custards and creams.

They were content then to dance in the log cabin, on a puncheon floor; were glad of an opportunity of listening to the musical strains of Champ Helvey, drawn from a three-string fiddle; were happy to be able to walk to the place barefoot and save their shoes for dancing; they were rejoiced to meet Tom Johnson there with his beautiful curls and white pants; and when they were hungry were able to help themselves to the chicken pie or roast venison.

Then, when merry autumn came with its profusion of mellow richness, its luxuriant and happy associations, and above all, the bountiful supply of the productions of the soil to gladden the hearts of man and beast, would the hardy pioneers assemble together, and, with their families, celebrate the end of the summer's toil and labor in the manner described in this sketch.

These cabins were scattered over a radius of two miles, and their location was only known to the weary traveler as he journeyed along the lonely Indian trace, by the slowly and lazily rising wreaths of blue smoke that here and there curled above the trees of the dense forests that once stood where now stands this beautiful city. This was all that marked the presence of man.

I would ask the "old settlers" of Indianapolis, especially those that were here at the time I am writing of, were not these primitive their happiest days in this city?

Since I commenced writing these sketches I have been, in

imagination, carried back so often to those days that I have wished myself a boy again.

> "When bright dreams of my childhood, fair scenes of my youth,
> So laden with visions of friendship and truth;
> And when come the dark hours of sadness and pain,
> There memory illumes my pathway again."

WILKES REAGAN

Was the first man that essayed to carry on the butchering business in Indianapolis, or to offer fresh meat for sale in a public market. His slaughter house was on the bank of Pogue's Creek, between New Jersey and East streets; it was without floor, roof, or sides, and consisted of two posts, about twelve feet long, planted upright in the ground, and about seven feet apart; two others running from the top of the first to the ground, slanting or obliquely; between these posts he would kill the bullock or beef, and when ready for hoisting, with the aid of two forked poles and his neighbors, would push it up the slanting poles for cooling preparatory for market.

Mr. Reagan slaughtered but once a week, and in the summer time would have to select very small animals, lest a portion should remain on hand, after the market was supplied, and spoil; the hide and tallow was the only portion that would command cash; the fore quarter was sold at from one to one and a half cents, and the hind quarter at from one and a half to two cents per pound on credit, and the way those bills were paid was in stock for slaughter, such as the customer might have to dispose of; for instance, if a bill should be seventy-five cents or one dollar, it would require a sheep to liquidate the debt; if from one fifty to two dollars and fifty cents, it would take a good sized, fat hog; if from three to four dollars, a young steer or heifer; and if it should have run up to six or eight dollars, a large cow or bullock "would fill the bill."

In this way did Mr. Reagan carry on the butchering business for several years, using less money in one year than either H. D. Davis, of the Union Meat Market, Andy Gass, Richard Essick, or the Messrs. Roos would in one day at the present time.

In the winter season he would have shooting matches. The beef would be put up at so much a shot for first choice of the quarters, there being five quarters to a beef, the hide and tallow constituting the fifth, and always the first choice. A winner would often put up the same quarter to be shot for again, unless it should be the fifth; and not unfrequently after shooting all day for a beef, the butcher would have the largest portion of it at night ready for the morning market, and would appear with it at his shed on the northwest corner of Washington and Delaware streets, with his books, ready to supply his customers on credit, at prices and payable as above stated.

In after years the worthy butcher added to his business that of magistrate, and dispensed justice with as much alacrity as he ever dispatched a bullock, never failing to find so much for plaintiff, and costs, as was the wont and practice of our early justices of the peace, thereby increasing litigation and business for themselves—unlike my Teuton friend and magistrate, Charles Coulon, in assault and battery cases fine both parties, and costs accordingly.

Mr. Reagan removed from this place to Evansville, where some of his children yet reside.

JOHN W. REDDING

Was a large, fine-looking man, and a pompous Kentuckian, full of braggadocio, frequently using language that neither himself nor any one else understood the application he intended, although found in the English "vocabulary."

He was a candidate for clerk of the county at the first election in 1822, and was a standing candidate for years for any office that might be to fill by the people; he was a member of the Baptist church, and would not think he was violating any of his religious obligations if, on public occasions, he should take "a drop too much," and would frequently do so when the occasion was not so public.

Doctor L. Dunlap had a patient at his house, which was directly at the south-east end of Virginia avenue. The Doctor had visited his patient late in the evening and had almost despaired of his recovery, but requested Mr. Redding to call at his office in the morning and let him know how his patient was.

Accordingly, Mr. Redding called at the Doctor's office the next morning and said that "after he left the evening before the patient threw up from the concavity of his stomach a concave three inches in length, and from that moment he relapsed and was much better, and that his body congealed sweat until the bed was wet with the water that was exhausted from his system."

Mr. Redding was among the first to volunteer in the defense of his country in that terrible campaign of the "bloody three hundred" in 1832, and afforded a great deal of fun for his comrades by his high-flown language in military parlance.

As far as the acquaintances of Mr. Redding were concerned they were willing to bury his faults with him; they were rather of the head than the heart, and there were none to harbor malice against him after death.

After his death, which occurred about the year 1836, his family returned to Kentucky. The farm he owned has lately been sold for near one thousand dollars per acre, which was purchased by Wm. S. Hubbard and others, with the intention of making an addition to the city.

OBED FOOTE.

This eccentric gentleman was a native of the State of Delaware, a lawyer by profession, though he did but little in that line after he came to this place, except as a justice of the peace. He became a citizen of Indianapolis late in the fall of 1821. He was then a single man, but on the bachelor order, and kept "Bachelor's Hall" for some years. He resided on the north side of Washington, east of the alley, between Delaware and Pennsylvania streets.

Soon after he was eligible he was elected a magistrate, which office he held until he died, September, 1833.

On one occasion he was ploughing in his corn field, in the north part of the donation, when a couple came to him and wished him to go to his office for the purpose of uniting them in marriage. He inquired if they had the license with them, and being answered in the affirmative, he called a man who was ploughing in an adjoining field as a witness; he then ordered the bride and groom to stand up in the fence corner, and there he performed the ceremony; after which he gave instructions to the groom more pointed than classic.

Mr. Foote was a man of more than ordinary native, as well as acquired ability, and possessed a large fund of general information.

His first wife was the eldest daughter of Luke Walpole; they had one child, a son, who is named for the father; he now resides in Paris, Illinois. His second wife was a widow Davis. They also had one child, a daughter, who is now the wife of Mr. Frederick Baggs, a gentleman well known in the business and social circles of this city.

Mrs. Baggs is the half or step-sister of Mrs. McCready, wife of James McCready, once the Mayor of this city.

Mr. Foote died in the prime of life, and long before this city assumed to be anything more than a country village.

HON. WILLIAM W. WICK,

The first judge of the Fifth (this) Judicial Circuit, was a Pennsylvanian by birth and education, but had lived a short time at Connersville, in Fayette County, previous to coming to this place in February, 1822.

Judge Wick was a tall, fine-looking man in his younger days, as straight as an arrow, firm, elastic step, large, full eye, hair as black as a raven, dark complexion, very neat in his dress, his whole contour was that of a gentleman, and denoted intelligence of a superior order.

As a judge he was popular with the bar, and they are supposed to be the proper judges of that qualification. As a lawyer he also stood high; and as a man, was respected by his neighbors and acquaintances.

He served several years as judge of this district, during which time he was elected Brigadier General of the State Militia, then Prosecuting Attorney, one term as Secretary of State, and to represent this Congressional District in 1840, and it was during the delivery of a speech while a member of this Congress he pledged himself to eat a horse should Indiana vote for General Harrison—this pledge he never kept, as the writer of these sketches won a fancy horse on that election and tendered the judge for the purpose of redeeming his pledge; but he declined, as the kind I offered was not intended by him, being rather tough.

He was also a member of Congress during the last two years of Mr. Polk's administration, and Postmaster of this city during the entire term of President Pierce, which I think was the last official position he held. The last few years of his life he resided with his daughter at Franklin, in Johnson County, where he died in the year 1868. He left many friends throughout the entire State, and no enemies. In all the relations of life Judge Wick was kind and affable.

HARVEY BATES,

The first Sheriff of Marion County, was a native of Cincinnati, Ohio, born in that place when it was called Fort Washington, in the year 1795. His father was "Master of Transportation," during the Indian War, under Generals Wayne and Harmar, and chiefly engaged in forwarding provisions and munitions of war from the frontier posts to the army in the wilderness.

At that time it was an unbroken wilderness from "Old Fort Washington" (now Cincinnati) to Detroit, in Michigan Territory.

When Mr. Bates was quite young, not more than five or six years of age, he lost his mother; his father married again' and he, failing (as most children do) to find a true one in the person of the step-mother, left the paternal roof and launched his bark npon the broad ocean of life, as it were, without sail or rudder.

At the age of six years he went to Lebanon, Warren County, Ohio, where he met with friends and received a fair English education, at least sufficient to fit and qualify him for the ordinary pursuits of life at that early day.

About the time that he had attained his majority he came to Brookville, Franklin County, where he met with and was married to Miss Sidney Sedgwick, a cousin of General James Noble, United States Senator, and the late Governor Noah Noble, and thus far, like John Anderson and his worthy spouse, have have glided down the stream of time together. At Brookville, in 1816, he cast his first vote for a delegate to form a constitution for the new State of Indiana.

Soon after Mr. B.'s marriage he removed to Connersville, where he remained until February, 1822, when he came to where this city now stands.

Jonathan Jennings, who was the first Governor after the

State was admitted into the Union, had appointed William W. Wick President Judge of this (the fifth) Judicial District, and Harvey Bates Sheriff of Marion County, which then embraced several of the surrounding counties for judicial purposes, investing Mr. Bates with the power of putting the necessary legal machinery of the county in motion.

This he did by issuing a proclamation for an election to be held on the first day of April for the purpose of electing a clerk of the court and other county officers, which was the first election of any kind held in the "new purchase."

At the October election Mr. Bates was chosen and elected sheriff for the regular term of two years, after which he refused to be a candidate again. He did not seem to partake of the love of office, or had not the taste for public preferment thas was peculiar to others hailing from the same section he did.

After the term of office for which he was elected expired, he entered into mercantile and other pursuits more congenial to his feelings. In all his business enterprises he brought great energy and industry, which is very nearly always rewarded by success, as was the case with him. He seemed to think with Richelieu, and acted upon the principle that "In the bright lexicon of youth there was no such word as fail." He possessed in an eminent degree the main springs to prosperity and success—integrity, industry and economy—without which but few succeed.

Mr. Bates was the first and for ten years President of the "Branch of the State Bank," located in this place, and no institution of the kind, either in or out of the State, was more successful, not only for the bank, but beneficial to the business and trading part of the community while under his management. Indeed it was through the help and assistance of the Bank that most of the surplus produce of this and several of the adjoining counties was able to reach a market. I have known that bank to withhold discounts from our merchants and best business men of the city that they might be the more able to accommodate the produce dealers, and thereby assist the farmer, keep the money in the hands of our own citizens and benefit the whole country. This wise and judicious course of the bank, of which he was the principal, was a lasting benefit to the producers of the county, which should long be remembered by them.

He was instrumental in getting up the first insurance company, a stockholder in the first hotel built by a company, the first railroad that was finished to this place, the first and only gas light and coke company, and indeed nearly every public enterprise of the city.

In 1852 he commenced, and afterwards finished, that large and palatial hotel, the "Bates House," at that time one of the finest in the West. This house was built at a cost of sixty thousand dollars, subsequent improvements making the whole cost seventy-five thousand dollars, and could not be built at this time for much less than double that amount.

There are many other business and private buildings scattered throughout the city that own their existence to the energy and means of Mr. Bates.

He has ever been a liberal contributor to our religious and benevolent institutions; was a warm friend of Henry Ward Beecher during his residence in this city and in his less prosperous days.

He is now in the seventy-fifth year of his age, and is yet quite active for one of his years, retaining a great deal of his youthful vivacity and sprightliness, and manifests a disposition to make all about him feel the same way.

A few months since he and his estimable lady celebrated the fiftieth anniversary of their marriage, or "Golden Wedding;" may they live to celebrate the seventy-fifth, or "Diamond Wedding," is the sincere wish of their numerous friends and acquaintances, and "may I be there to see" them, like John Anderson and his worthy lady.

> "Now we maun tother down, John, but hand in hand we'll go,
> And we'll sleep thegither at the foot, John Anderson, my Jo."

DOUGLASS MAGUIRE,

In connection with Harvey Gregg, started the second newspaper in this place, in March, 1823. He had come out from Kentucky the year before, and in the spring the first number of the "Western Censor and Emigrant's Guide" was issued from a house belonging to Mr. Gregg, on the west side of the alley on the north side of Washington, between Meridian and Pennsylvania streets.

This paper has been continued ever since under different names and by many different editors, until now we have it as the "Indianapolis Daily Journal," with a large circulation throughout the State.

It started out in opposition to the election of General Jackson to the Presidency in 1824, and has strictly adhered to the opposition of the political party that sprung out of his administration ever since.

Mr. Maguire was long the manager and editor of the Journal, but during his editorial and newspaper career the business was not so profitable as at the present time; indeed there was but little money in the country to transact business with, and people, very foolishly, did without newspapers and advertising rather than to incur the expense.

After he quit the "Journal" he held several offices of profit and emolument, both in the gift of the people and the legislature; was Representative in the Legislature, Auditor of State, a member of the Constitutional Convention in 1850 that framed the present State Constitution—all of which he filled to the entire satisfaction of his constituents.

In personal appearance Mr. Maguire was very much like

his personal and political friend Henry Clay, tall and slender, with a quick, nervous temperament, and quite excitable.

In the summer of 1844, and during the Presidential contest between Henry Clay and James K. Polk, Mr. Maguire was one of a fishing party of ladies and gentlemen enroute for "Broad Ripple," on Bob Earl's canal boat; he and the late George Chapman, at that time one of the editors of the "Sentinel," got into a controversy in regard to the approaching election, and both of them became very much excited. Mr. Maguire while gesticulating and stepping back went into the canal up to his chin. He was dressed in light, linen clothes, which stuck close to his person, and when he was taken on board presented a very ludicrous appearance. He remarked that Democrats had a right to laugh, but he did not think that the Whigs should.

This coolness in the manner of Mr. Maguire, which was so unusual and unexpected in him, caused a roar of laughter in which he joined himself, but did not like to have the circumstances referred to after the first burst of laughter was over, though there was many a silent titter by both Whigs and Democrats unperceived by him.

Mr. Maguire took great pleasure in attending Democratic meetings, and managing to have Governor Ray called on by some of the faithful for a speech, well knowing that gentleman's gift of continuance on such occasions, and that he would occupy the whole time of the meeting if left alone, such was his love of fun.

He was a kind-hearted and hospitable man, and died in 1857, regretted by many new friends and all the old settlers of this city. He is still represented here in the person of his son, who bears his father's name.

HARVEY GREGG.

I have, in the preceding sketch, referred to Mr. Gregg's connection with Mr. Maguire in founding the second newspaper in this place, in 1823. He was from New Castle, Henry County, Kentucky, a waggish lawyer that stood high in his profession. He was the second attorney to make Indianapolis his home.

Mr. Gregg's first visit to this place was at the first sale of town lots, on the ninth of October, 1821. He brought considerable money with him, principally in gold and silver. After he had paid the first payment on the property he had bought he had about two hundred dollars in gold left; this he carried in his pocket wrapped in paper.

One morning he missed his money; it could not be found; as he did not remember having it the night before, he came to the conclusion that he had dropped it somewhere in the woods, as he had been looking at different pieces of property he had bought; he borrowed money to pay his expenses and returned home, not dreaming of ever finding the lost money or hearing of it again. The following spring my mother was taking up the rag carpet in the room in which Mr. Gregg had slept; her attention was attracted by something bright in the corner where he had slept on the floor; on examination it turned out to be the gold Mr. Gregg had lost nearly six months before; the paper in which it was wrapped had been worn away, and there was the entire amount, somewhat scattered by being slept on during the time it had been lost.

My father wrote immediately to Mr. Gregg informing him that the money had been found, and where, and received an answer that Mr. G. then remembered, for the first time, having placed it under the edge of the carpet when he lay down at night, and that he would never have thought again what he did with it had it not been brought to his mind by the manner in which it was found. Although the house, and, indeed, the whole woods, was thronged with strangers, there was not the least suspicion that any person had taken it improperly, or had even found it. Mr. Blake tells me there were seventeen persons who slept in that cabin, three in each of the three beds, and eight on the floor, with their saddles for pillows.

I introduce this incident to show the difference in the morals of the people then and now. The first thing Mr. Oregg would do at this day would be to have the man who slept next to him arrested as a pick pocket, and with, perhaps, circumstances to sustain the charge.

Then we had no bars or bolts to our doors and windows, no "guardian *angels*" (with blue coats and brass buttons that shine so beautiful under the gas light at night, and glitter in the sun by day) to watch our persons and property. Were not these the days of true happiness and contentment, the good old days of Adam and Eve:

> "When no noise was heard but the birds a singing,
> Except sometimes a cow-bell ringing:
> With a tree here and there for the cattle to get under
> Out of the way of lightning and thunder."

JACOB LANDIS.

When I come to speak of my personal friend of forty-seven years, and one of my first employers as a store-boy, I am reminded of many incidents connected with his long residence in this city that would be interesting to the reader, if the space would allow and I was able to depict them as they occurred.

Mr. Landis came to this place early in the spring of 1822, a young as well as single man. He built a cabin on the south side of the State House Square, near Mississippi street, and there for a year or two dealt out his *wet* as well as dryware of different kinds to the dry and thirsty citizens of the "new purchase."

His house was the scene of many practical jokes, many of which have been referred to in other places in this work; and sometimes the joke turned upon him, as in this case:

He had a customer who lived in Urbana, Ohio, a painter by trade. This man had managed to get into Mr. Landis' debt for solids and liquids to the amount of about ten dollars; he wished to return home for the purpose of seeing friends and raising the wherewith to liquidate that for which he had already liquored. In order to raise the ways and means he proposed to Mr. L. that if he would furnish him ten dollars more he would leave in pledge for the whole amount of indebtedness his box of tools, including his diamond used for cutting glass, all of which were very valuable. This proposition Mr. L. readily acceded to, as it would secure what was already due. The honest painter brought the box, neatly packed and nailed, with two brushes on the outside. Mr. L. advanced the money, and in a few days the painter was enjoying the society of kindred and friends.

Some weeks after a well known citizen, Willis A. Reed, wanted to use some sash-tools that could not be had in the stores, and knowing that this man had had them, got permission of Mr. Landis to open the box and use them. When the box was opened a few copies of the "Indianapolis Gazette" came first in view, and then about a half-bushel of as fine a specimen of White River corn as could be found in the settlement, but no painter's tools.

Mr. Landis afterward met him in Cincinnati and charged him with the trick. He again turned the joke on him by denying his identity, and saying Mr. Landis was mistaken in the man.

Mr. Landis has held many lucrative and responsible offices within the gift of the people of the county—such as sheriff and collector, county treasurer, etc., and enjoyed the confidence of the masses to a considerable extent; and, indeed, on several occasions has had a fortune within his grasp had he looked more to money than to what was just and right; in fact, he never learned to use the adverb which Webster defines to mean denial. I have known him, while county treasurer, to advance the taxes of his friends, and those that were unable to pay, to save their property from sale, and, consequently, additional costs, which would come into his pocket. How unlike the officers of the present day. Sheriffs then could not build a four-story block on the fees of a single term.

The writer was for several years employed as a clerk in his store, and has known him to let the poor have goods when he certainly must have known they were unable, or would be, to pay for them; the consequence is he has yet to continue to labor, and does so as much as he did forty-seven years ago; and while many have accumulated wealth by grinding and oppressing the poor, Jake Landis has ever been their friend, and has carried out the injunction of the Bible more by practice than by profession or precept, "Remember the poor."

Such is our old and esteemed citizen whose name heads this sketch.

THOMAS JOHNSON.

We had two Tom Johnsons in early times, farmer Tom and tinner Tom—it is the farmer of whom I now write. He came with his father in the year 1820, and settled on the quarter-section of land adjoining to and east of Camp Morton, or the State Fair grounds, and there remained until his death, which occurred but a few years ago.

Tom was one of the leading beaux and gallants of the young ladies. He dressed very exquisitely, especially when arrayed for church, a dance, or a quilting party. He wore his hair curled in front and hanging down on the sides of his face. In summer he wore white linen pantaloons with a black ribbon drawstring at the bottom, tied with a bow knot. He imagined himself very handsome as well as very smart, and was the first to call on the young ladies when they arrived, and never failed to let them know that he was the favorite with all that had already been here for sometime.

He called to see a family of several young ladies that had arrived, and tried to make himself very agreeable in the way of asking questions as well as informing them who were the "purtiest and smartest gals in the settlement." Among other questions he asked them to let him see their "purranner, as he had hern they had one, and that he had never seed one of the critters in his whole life." Being informed that it was a mistake, and that they did not bring one, he was very much disappointed. He said he would like to see a "purranner," that "thar was a show come to the settlement, in yonder on Whitewater, that had an orging and made nice music."

Mr. Johnson finally found a young lady, in the person of Miss Rody Parr, that suited him and he married her. He was for many years one of our most prosperous farmers, and lived to see "purranners" manufactured in our city and his farm worth five hundred dollars per acre. He was a younger brother of Jerry Johnson, and although they were "Tom and Jerry," they took their liquor plain.

LUKE WALPOLE AND FAMILY.

The father of the late Thomas D. and Robert L. Walpole was from Zanesville, Ohio. He had descended the Muskingum and Ohio Rivers to the mouth of the Wabash, and then ascended that stream and White River to this place in a keel boat, arriving here in the summer of 1822.

His family consisted of fourteen persons, himself and wife, four sons and six daughters, a nephew and colored servant, Belle; in addition to his family and household furniture he brought on this boat a stock of goods.

He first lived on the northwest corner of the State House

Square, in a house built by Isaac Wilson, and referred to in another sketch, in a cabin, near which he had his store.

Mr. Walpole having several daughters in the heyday of life, caused a considerable sensation with the young bucks of the settlement. It was those ladies Tom Johnson called on and requested to see their "purranner."

The old gentleman was a small, spare-made man, not weighing over one hundred pounds apothecaries' weight, if that; he dressed in the old English style, short pants, long stockings, and silver shoe buckles, and a coat to suit this style of dress.

The old lady was not any taller than her liege lord, but was considerably larger, and would weigh at least two hundred and fifty pounds avoirdupois; their joint weight would not be more than that of two ordinary persons, but it was so unequally divided that it would attract attention and sometimes draw forth a jocular comment when they would take their usual evening walk together.

The old gentleman enjoyed a joke, even should it be at his own expense; his friends often twitted him with the disparity in size between himself and wife; he replied, that in selecting a wife he was like he was in buying goods, that when he found a good article he wanted a plenty of it.

Of the fourteen persons that constituted Mr. Walpole's family when he first came to this place, but four are living: Miss Susan, the second daughter, still resides in this place; Mrs. Harriett Quarles is living in Kansas City, Missouri; Mrs. Elizabeth Colerick, the fifth, lives in Fort Wayne; the colored woman, Belle, still lives with Miss Susan.

The elder daughter, Miss Ann, was the first wife of Obed Foote, Esq. She died many years since, leaving one child that bears the father's name, and now lives in Paris, Illinois.

The third daughter was the wife of Wm. Quarles, an eminent and early lawyer of this place. Mr. Quarles died in the winter of 1849, and although twenty years have elapsed since his death, she yet mourns his loss as if of but a few days—a rare thing in women.

Miss Mary, the fourth, died some three or four years since. Miss Elizabeth, the fifth, is the present wife of the Hon. David Colerick, of Fort Wayne.

The sixth daughter, named—I think—Margaret, died a few years after they came to this place.

Edward, the oldest son, went south about the year 1824, and there remained. He at one time was very wealthy, but I understand he lost the most of it before his death, which occurred several years since.

Thomas D. Walpole, the second son, and at present remembered by most of the citizens of this city, was a most extraordinary man. With nothing more than a common English education, he studied law with his brother-in-law, Wm. Quarles, Esq. Mr. Quarles informed us that, before he had half finished his studies, he went to Greenfield, Hancock County, and there commenced the practice. He at once became popular as a man and quite successful as a lawyer. He has often told me that he would never let a judge try a case when he could get a Hancock jury; "then," said he, "I cared not who was the opposing counsel."

He was State Senator from the counties of Hancock and Madison several years, also, Representative from Hancock; indeed, in those counties he was invincible before the people.

In 1840 he was an ardent and enthusiastic Whig, and rendered great service to the Whig party, and contributed largely to the success of General Harrison. It was during this canvass that Tom gave to the Democratic party their emblem, which they have claimed ever since, the chicken cock, or rooster. George Patterson, then editing the Democratic paper, wrote, just before the August election of that year, to Joseph Chapman, of Greenfield, that the Democratic party would be beat, and that there was no hope, but, said he, "crow,

Chapman, crow." By some means Tom got possession of the letter and exposed it. A year or two subsequent to this circumstance Messrs. George and Page Chapman became proprietors and editors of the Democratic paper and placed a rooster at the head of their paper, and from that circumstance it was generally supposed that they were the persons to whom the letter was addressed and the original crowers; but such is not the case. It is to Tom Walpole the Democratic party is indebted for the emblem of the rooster.

Tom was a great wag, and many was the prank he played upon his friends as well as enemies. During the Mexican war he procured a blank colonel's commission by some means from the War Department at Washington. This he caused to be filled up with the name of Joseph Chapman, of Hancock County (the same Chapman referred to above), with instructions to raise a regiment of volunteers and proceed direct to the seat of war in Mexico. This he caused to be mailed to "Colonel Joseph Chapman, Greenfield, Indiana." Immediately on receipt of this Mr. Chapman mounted his horse (there were no railroads then) and came to Indianapolis and direct to Governor Whitcomb for instructions how to proceed. After the Governor had examined the commission and instructions, he remarked to Mr. Chapman that he thought he was the victim of a playful hoax. "Yes," said Mr. Chapman. "It is that Tom Walpole; can I ever get rid of that fellow, he has dogged me since he first got hold of that crowing letter."

Nor was Mr. Chapman the only one that had received a commission in this way. Colonel Nineveh Berry, of Anderson, also received one with similar instructions.

Colonel Berry, I understand, at once established recruiting headquarters, with the United States flag unfurled, and drum and fife constantly playing at the door, and had actually received some volunteers, and did not find out the joke

Luke Walpole and Family.

until it was discovered by Mr. Chapman. Were I to attempt to give half the jokes and pranks of Tom, it would fill this volume.

He was a man of great native ability, a fine speaker, and set out in life with an ambition and determination worthy of a brilliant career and sequel. He had plucked the flower, but threw it withered at his feet.

Tom was my early school-mate and ever my personal friend, and in this sketch I have endeavored to do him, as well as his father's family, justice; if I have failed it is an error of my head, and not of my heart.

The third son of the family, Robert L. Walpole, died about two years since, an old bachelor. In his early life he had followed merchandizing with but little success, and after that studied law and practiced with success, at least so far as the accumulation of property was concerned. His ability as a lawyer consisted in his ever watching the mistakes of the opposing counsel, the quirks and turns of law, and any advantage that might be thrown in his way. These are my own opinions, and I think the most of the present bar of Indianapolis will sustain me in them.

John, the fourth son, and last of the family that I notice, was a young man of more than ordinary promise. When quite young he went to Fort Wayne and there finished the study of the law that he had commenced in this place with his brother-in-law, William Quarles, and then commenced with a fine prospect of success in the profession, but was stricken down by death quite young, before his early promise had ripened, and ere he had reached the meridian of life.

As a family there was none ever lived in Indianapolis that was more respected, nor none that ever came to the place that created at the time such a sensation as the Walpoles. They had brought a large, old-fashioned sideboard, which was boxed up in such a way as might be readily taken for a piano. The late Calvin Fletcher, knowing the great curiosity of the people, especially the young men, to know everything pertaining to the "new comers," and seeing an opportunity to have some fun, informed the young men that they certainly had a piano, as there was no other kind of furniture that would require a box of that shape. All the young men were quick to call on the young ladies and tried to get a peep at the instrument; none, however, made their business known except farmer Tom Johnson, who had never "seed a purranner."

The great verdancy on the part of the "young bucks" caused the young ladies a great deal of merriment, and they gave each a fancy name, a few only of which I now remember. "Oyster Tongs," "Tallow Face," "Mutton Head," "Simon Shears," and "Sleepy Hollow," the latter was named (like all our original names) by circumstances. He had called to spend the evening, or may be, to look at and hear the "purranner," and went to sleep, and they gave him the name above indicated.

There are but two of the persons above named that are living. "Tallow Face" is a prominent citizen of the city. "Mutton Head" lives in the suburbs.

Mr. Walpole's family were connections of the Hon. Thomas Ewing, of Ohio.

GEORGE NORWOOD,

The first wagon maker, came to Indianapolis in March, 1822, from Middle Tennessee. He carried on the wagon making business for several years on Illinois street, opposite where the Bates House now stands. He was successful, and possessed the faculty of holding on to what he made, and laid it out in property, which he held until it made him quite wealthy; indeed, he yet holds a good portion of what was then in the city.

He has four children living. His eldest son, G. W. Norwood, lives in Putnam County, and is a prosperous farmer; his other son, Elbert, lives on his father's old farm, four miles south of the city, on the "Bluff road." His eldest daughter is the wife of Abram Bird; a second is married to Mr. Jesse Jones. These two gentlemen are well known as enterprising business men, and are residents of the city. Mr. Norwood and his estimable lady are yet living, although advanced in years.

JOSEPH PENCE

Was among the first settlers of Wayne Township. He tells me he took the first grubs from the ground in his immediate neighborhood. He came to his present residence in the year 1822. He had been raised near Germantown, Montgomery County, Ohio.

Mr. Pence is now one of the prosperous farmers of the county, and looks as though he will yet live many years to enjoy the prosperity that he has contributed a great deal to produce. He is one of our staid and substantial citizens, and enjoys the confidence and respect of all who know him.

ARCHIBALD C. REID

Was an early and prominent farmer of Marion County, having removed to this place from Connersville, Fayette County, in the year 1822, and settled about one-half mile east of the southeast corner of the donation, on Pleasant Run, and there farmed successfully until the time of his death, which occurred, I think, in the spring of 1835.

Mr. Reid took a very active part in politics, held several county and township offices, and at one time was the Jackson candidate for representative of the county in the State Legislature; he was defeated, although he outran the party ticket.

He was a member of the Baptist Church, and one of its

most prominent supporters, financially as well as in other respects. He was a charitable and benevolent man, and threw all his influence on the side of morality and religion.

His widow yet lives in the vicinity of the old homestead, and although advanced in years is yet quite sprightly.

Mr. Reid's old farm became very valuable, and is worth at the present time one thousand dollars per acre. It was divided among his heirs, who yet retain a large portion of it.

John Wesley, the eldest son living, who is well known to the citizens of Indianapolis, still resides on a portion of the land that fell to his share, as also does Erastus. The younger brother, J. B. E. Reid, is too well known to the citizens of Indianapolis to require any commendation from me; suffice it to say, that he is one of the firm in that popular wholesale and retail boot and shoe establishment doing business at No. 25 West Washington street, under the name and firm of William R. Hogshire & Co.

A daughter is the wife of George Drum, a jovial and fun-loving man, and ever ready to *spin a yarn* for the amusement of his friends. I will never forget George as one of the "Wild Oats of Indianapolis," that went to the Tippecanoe Battle Ground in May, 1840. George could sing as loud as the loudest,

"Come all ye log cabin boys, we're g'wine to have a raisin,
We've got a job on hand, and you'll think it will be plasen."

He also fought for the stars and stripes during the late war.

ISAAC N. PHIPPS

Came to this place in June, 1823, and was connected with Conner and Tyner in merchandizing. He was for many years one of the prominent merchants of the place. Mr. Phipps is well acquainted with the early history of this place and very near all the old settlers.

Isaac N. Phipps.

When he first came here, and for many years after, it was customary for merchants to keep whisky for their customers, and all that wished to could drink without money and without price. An empty whisky barrel was set up on end in front of the counter, with a hole in the upper head for the drainage of the glasses. On this barrel was set a half gallon bottle filled with whisky, a bowl of maple sugar, and a pitcher of water, and often in winter a tumbler of ground ginger; this was intended as an invitation to all who came into the store to help themselves, regardless whether they purchased or not. In these country stores could be found anything, from a log-chain to a cambric needle, from a grubbing-hoe to to a silk shawl, from a sack of coffee to a barrel of whisky. How different from those splendid, fashionable establishments, the New York Store, the Trade Palace, the Bee Hive, the Farmers' Store, and many others; how the fancy clerks of these fashionable marts of merchandise would giggle and laugh was it possible for old Jim McCoy to visit his old "stamping ground" again and stumble into one of these stores and tell them their "bottles wanted filling up," or that he wished an ounce of indigo, a quarter of a pound of madder, or that the "old 'oman wanted to know if they were gwine to have any more Leghorn bonnets with two crowns, as her and the oldest gal wanted one."

It was customary for the merchants, in those days, to bring bonnets in this way, take the back part of one and sew it to the odd crown, and make a second bonnet.

Mr. Phipps has lived to see this great change in the manner of doing business in Indianapolis, in his own as well as other branches of business. He has raised a large and respectable family of children. Two of his sons and a son-in-law are engaged in the jewelry business. Another son-in-law, P. G. C. Hunt, is a prominent dentist; another is a merchant, and yet another is a prominent lawyer.

Mr. P. has long since retired from active business, and seems content to attend to his little suburban farm, and worship according to the dictates of his own conscience.

ALFRED HARRISON.

This gentleman made his first appearance in this place in the month of June, 1823, as clerk for John Conner, in his country store. He was from one of the Whitewater towns.

He was for several years a well known and successful merchant, and is at this time engaged in banking, in connection with his son-in-law, John C. S. Harrison, Esq.

Mr. Harrison is opposed to any innovations upon the primitive customs that prevailed at the time he first arrived in this place; to illustrate—he seems to be in favor of the old fashioned way of going to mill, *i. e.*, by placing a stone in one end of the bag and the grain in the other.

I understand he opposes the introduction of organs and other instruments into church music; he also is opposed to the renting of pews or seats in the house of God. He favors separating the male from the female portion of the congregation, *i. e.*, the goats from the lambs.

He is a kind of negative man in many things, especially in banking, and primitive in nearly all things. It seems, by some fortuitous circumstance, that he has been placed two or three generations behind the time he should have been upon these mundane shores.

ROBERT CULBERTSON

Was from Georgetown, Kentucky, and became a citizen of Indianapolis in the year 1823. He was a great beau and gallant of the young ladies, and a general favorite with them; he wore a wig, and had managed to keep it a profound secret from the female portion of the village.

He was a clever, whole-souled kind of a man, liberal to a

fault, and would stop at neither labor nor expense to accommodate a friend or display his gallantry.

He had invited the elder sister of the writer (now Mrs. S. H. Patterson, of Jeffersonville) and another young lady to take a ride in his carriage to the plumb orchard at the old Delaware village of Bruettstown, about twelve miles north on White River; the writer, as usual, was on hand a horse-back. On the return from the orchard the horse he was driving stopped, or balked, in the middle of the river at Broad Ripple, and could not be induced to move. Mr. Culbertson stepped out of the carriage on a large stone that stood close by, and while flourishing his whip to strike the horse knocked his hat, and with it his wig, into the swift water at his feet; with an oath he exclaimed that his "hat, head, wig and all were gone;" he jumped into the water, and with difficulty recovered it and placed it on his head dripping wet; he got on my horse and left me with the balky one to get out as best I could, which in due time, and by the help of a passer-by, I did. He was a very sensitive man, and so deeply was he mortified that I could not induce him to get in the carriage again that evening. Soon after this occurred he left the country.

I saw him in New Orleans in the year 1840, some fifteen years after this incident, and he referred to it with tears in his eyes as being the ruin of him, and causing him to become dissipated. This incident shows what trivial circumstances sometimes seals a person's destiny for life.

JAMES SULGROVE

Was one of the early settlers of Decatur Township, having come from Montgomery County, Ohio, and settled there in the year 1822.

After living in the country for seven or eight years, he and a younger brother, Joseph, engaged with Christopher Kellum to learn the saddle and harness making business. After having finished their trade they commenced business jointly on their own account, and were for several years the leading saddlers of the city, and were very successful. After that Joseph left the firm and engaged in farming, and at this time is one of the best farmers of the county. James continued to carry on the business of their trade, and has been longer in the same business than any person of the city, and has now the largest saddlery and harness hardware establishment in the State.

James Sulgrove is the father of Berry R. Sulgrove, who is, perhaps, as well and favorably known as any man in the State, and respected for his profound learning and native talent, as well as for his great generosity and kindness of heart.

Berry was educated at Bethany College, Virginia, while that institution was under the presidency of Alexander Campbell. He there graduated with the highest honors.

He was for many years the leading and political editor of the "Indianapolis Journal," and during the long career of that popular paper he was numbered among its ablest writers.

It has been our fortune to know Berry from his earliest boyhood, and we have yet to hear a harsh or unkind word spoken of him.

NICHOLAS McCARTY.

After writing the name above, I have to lay down my pen to think of language befitting to give the reader an idea of the many good qualities and characteristics of this man.

He was many years a prominent and popular merchant of this place, and during that time did the largest business of any person in it. He became a citizen in the fall of 1823, and early manifested a deep interest in the place and all its citizens, especially the young men, many of whom he assisted and started in business.

Mr. McCarty was never known to oppress any person he

thought was honest and intended to act so with him, and during his whole career (thirty-one years) he enjoyed the confidence of the people at large and the respect of his neighbors as much as any person of the county.

He was my friendly adviser from my boyhood to the time of his death, and never did I have cause of regret, unless it was when I did not heed it; and often do I think of his friendly salutation when we met, "how do you do, Johnny?" Although I never had occasion to ask pecuniary aid of him, I had that which was more valuable, his friendship and advice. He was a plain, unassuming, practical, common-sense man, with as warm and generous a heart as ever beat in the bosom of a human being; no duplicity or deceit was found there.

In 1852 he was the Whig candidate for Governor of the State, and the last one that party ever ran. Although beaten by Joseph A. Wright, he made a very energetic and vigorous canvass, and kept his honorable opponent quite busy to answer some of his plain, off-hand and sensible speeches in defense ef his party and its measures. His efforts had been almost uniformly successful, but in this he was doomed to defeat.

Mr. McCarty died in May, 1854, beloved by his family, respected by his neighbors, and well satisfied with the fortunes he had experienced in life. He left a son bearing his name, who is still a resident of this city, and two or three daughters, one of whom is the wife of the Rev. Doctor Day, pastor of the First Baptist Church, and another the wife of John C. S. Harrison, a prominent banker.

Reader, when you pass the grave of Nicholas McCarty, you can truthfully say, there lies "an honest man, the noblest work of God."

> "Like dews of morning, he was given
> To shine on earth, then rise to heaven."

DAVID WILLIAMS,

Or Cousin David, as he was familiarly called by all, young and old, when he first came to this place, which was soon after Mr. McCarty, who was his cousin, was chief clerk in Mr. McCarty's store for several years, and in the absence of the proprietor was the Major Domo of the establishment. After being with Mr. McCarty several years he became a partner in merchandising and appeared to prosper during the entire time of this partnership.

In after years he had other partners, but I do not think he was so successful. He has several connections by marriage still living in this city. He and the late John Wilkins married sisters and were brothers-in-law of the Rev. John and Andrew Brouse.

The best evidence of Mr. Williams' strict integrity and honesty was, that he had the entire confidence of his friend and cousin, Nicholas McCarty, to have which, in his day, was a "carte blanche." He survived his friend but a short time, having died several years since.

HIRAM BROWN.

During his residence of thirty years in and adjoining this city, there was no man more generally or favorably known than he. He was the fourth lawyer to make this place his home, having come here in November, 1823. He was a native of Brownsville, Pennsylvania; his father was the proprietor of that town, hence its name.

At an early day he came to Lebanon, Ohio, and entered the law office of that distinguished lawyer and statesman, the late Thomas Corwin. Mr. Brown proved himself a worthy student of his talented preceptor, and soon occupied a high position in this judicial circuit as a lawyer, and from the day he first came to this city up to the time of his death was never without clients in abundance, especially in criminal cases. No man, in his day, in the State, ranked higher as a criminal lawyer than Hiram Brown. There are many of our old citizens who will remember his defense of Major John Jamison in a case where a woman was the prosecuting witness.

In wit and repartee he was unequalled in the State, and was never vanquished in a war of words.

Mr. Brown has a son and several daughters residents of the city. One of his daughters is the wife of that well known lawyer, Albert G. Porter; another the wife of Jas. C. Yohn; and a third is the wife of Samuel Delzell.

GEORGE TAFFE, SR.

This worthy farmer was among the early settlers of Marion County. He improved and owned the farm now belonging to Calvin Fletcher, Jr., about one and a half miles from the donation line, on the Pendleton Pike. He was, during his life, as well known in this city as any farmer in the county, and one whose word was considered his bond. He was the father of the present Marshal of this city, George Taffe, and his brother, Hannibal Taffe, the well known and efficient policeman, who does his duty without any unnecessary show of authority and blustering, common to officials of small caliber.

The grandfather of these two last named gentlemen, and father of the former also, lived here in an early day. He had been a revolutionary soldier, and took great pride in talking of and recounting the scenes of his early years and the days that tried men's patriotism.

There also lived in Mr. Taffe's immediate neighborhood an old man named North, who claimed that he, too, had been a revolutionary soldier. The two old men whose heads had been whitened by the frosts of three score and ten winters, were from the same part of North Carolina.

Mr. Taffe charged that North was a tory and gave aid and comfort to the royalists and enemies of the country. This

North denied; but Mr. Taffe's opinions were founded upon personal knowledge and observation, and could not be changed.

At that time there lived in this county ten or twelve of the old patriots of the revolution of '76, and who always headed the procession at the celebration of the anniversary of our natal independence; but whenever Mr. North undertook to take a place with them Mr. Taffe would drive him out, even should it require physical force to do so; nor would he allow North to sit down and eat with them at the same time, but after they were done dinner he would hunt up North and see that he got his rations.

Those scenes were sure to occur on every public occasion n which the revolutionary soldiers took part, so long as both of these old men lived and were able to attend them. They are, no doubt, fresh in the minds of those citizens who were living here during the first decade of the settlement of this city.

DAVID MALLORY.

This half-breed "American citizen of African descent," come to this place at an early day, about the year 1824. He was from that part of the "settlement" known as Brookville, Franklin County, which furnished this place with more great men than any other locality at that day.

Mr. Mallory was a broad-shouldered, square-built, muscular man, about five feet ten inches in height; his complexion was copper or saddle-color; with a large, bushy head, the compound of hair and wool standing on end; a very large mouth—when open might be taken for a Pennsylvania hillside barn door; to see nothing but his head you would be reminded of Dan Rice's grizzly or Rocky Mountain bear.

He was a very good-natured man, except when irritated. It was asserted by Tom Johnson that he heard him laugh at the distance of one mile. He was possessed of a large fund of anecdotes, which he related with great gusto and self-satisfaction, and was never at a loss for listeners. He enjoyed to a high degree the confidence and respect of his colored fellow citizens, and was often referred to by them to settle points of honor, or other disputes that might arise in their intercourse with each other. He was always ready to give his friends good advice; they were generally more disposed to follow his practice and example than his precepts.

He kept a shop in Judge Stevens' row on the south side of Washington, about midway between Pennsylvania and Delaware streets, where he shaved his customers with very dull razors in day time, and low white men with very keen cards at night; and often the passer by late at night would hear his sonorous voice demanding "Tom" to ante, as he had put up last, or that it was his deal, or that he was entitled to the last shuffle, or, if any one should refer to Hoyle, offer to bet a V that Hoyle said nothing about poker in his work on games; or if a dispute should arise as to where and when draw poker originated, he was willing to bet that it was at the mouth of White River, Arkansas, it originated, and that Bowie first introduced it as well as the Bowie Knife hand. This was a new hand to the worthy barber, and he said he did not care about learning it. While playing he kept his money in his mouth, it held just twenty dollars in silver; his usual "bluff" was a mouthful, which he emptied from his mouth on to the table.

A citizen returning home late one night heard loud and boisterous talking in the shop of Mr. Mallory; supposing the usual game of poker or seven up was going on, stopped to see if he could recognize any of the voices.

It turned out to be a one-armed Italian organ-grinder and the proprietor disputing about the nativity of Christopher Columbus. The organ grinder asserted that Columbus was a native of *Virginny*, born and raised in old Richmond, for he knew him well.

The shaver was astonished at the Italian's ignorance; for although he was not personally acquainted with Columbus, he had read and "herne" a great deal about him; he was certainly born and raised in Liverpool. How the dispute was settled we have no means of knowing, but are inclined to the opinion that Mr. Mallory would have backed his judgment to any amount at his command.

In justice to this tonsorial artist, I must add that he was not the only citizen of Indianapolis that cut deep and shaved clean at that day. Some used financial razors that cut both ways, and after one or two operations were performed upon the same person they would hardly be worth shaving afterwards.

Mr. Mallory claimed that his wife had descended from the true native American (Indian) race, and did not like the attention of the "niggers," and said his daughters should not associate with them, but were for the society of T. J. and other white gentlemen of his acquaintance.

He has closed his game and handed in his checks several years since, but he is well represented, both in appearance and practice, by his only son, who rejoices in the name of David Mallory, Jun.

"For wheresoever the carcass is there will the Eagles (buzzards) be gathered together."

INCIDENTS OF 1823-24-25-26.

In the year 1823 the people began to look forward to the time when the barrier that cut them off from the balance of of the "world and the rest of mankind" would be removed; the mails began to arrive semi-monthly; the Centerville mail was carried on horseback by a lame fiddler named "Amos Dilly;" his arrival was looked forward to with rather more interest than the others, and was generally celebrated by a dance, as he furnished the music. The Brookville, or "settlement mail," was carried by Samuel Frazier, now a promineut temperance lecturer. The Madison or Berry's Trace mail was carried by an old man named Metcalf; he was more familiarly known as "Old Madcap." These mail carriers frequently had to swim all the streams on their respective routes, and were often several days behind time in consequence of high waters; the mails were often damaged by water. I have frequently seen Mr. Henderson, our worthy Postmaster, spreading them out in the sun for the purpose of drying.

In the spring of 1824 the murder of the Indians eight miles east of Pendleton, in Madison County, occurred. They were encamped on the bank of a small stream for the purpose of hunting and trapping. Four men and a boy went to their camp pretending to be hunting horses, but for no other purpose really than to kill and rob them. The names of the murderers were Harper, Hudson, Sawyer and Bridges and his son, a boy about eighteen years of age. Harper made his escape with the whole of the booty acquired. Hudson and the others were arrested, tried and three hung.

Hudson was first tried, in the fall of 1824, and sentenced to be hung in January. He managed to escape a short time before the day of his execution, and lay in the woods and got his feet frozen so badly that he was unable to travel, and in this condition he was retaken, and hung on the day appointed by the court.

The other three were tried at the spring term of the court and sentenced to be hanged in June, 1825. The writer had obtained the consent of a young man to ride behind him on the same horse to witness the execution, as he did.

It was generally understood that, in consequence of the age of young Bridges (he being a mere boy), and the fact that he had been induced to engage in the crime by his father and Sawyer, who was his uncle, Governor Ray would pardon him.

Up to ten o'clock of the day of execution neither the Govenor nor a pardon had arrived. The three criminals were taken from the palisade prison to the place of execution, about two hundred yards above the Falls of Fall Creek, on the west side; a wagon was drawn up on the side of the hill with the wheels on planks, so they would move easy and quickly, a post was placed on the side of the hill just above the wagon; to this post the wagon was fastened by a rope, so that when the rope was cut the wagon would run down the hill without aid. The two old men were placed in the tail of the wagon, the ropes adjusted, the white caps drawn over their faces, and at a given signal the rope was cut and the wagon quickly run from under the unfortunate men. Sawyer broke his arms loose that were pinioned behind; he caught the rope by which he was hanging and raised himself about eighteen inches; the sheriff (Corry) quickly caught him by the ankles, gave a sudden jerk, which brought the body down, and he died without another struggle.

After they had hung about thirty minutes they were taken down and placed in their coffins at the foot of the gallows. The young man, who had witnessed the scene, was then placed in the wagon (which had been re-adjusted on the hillside) with the intention of waiting until the last moment for Governor Ray or a pardon. He had not been in this situation long before the Governor made his appearance (which created a shout from all present) on a large "fancy grey" horse. He rode directly up to the gallows, where the young man was seated on a rough coffin in the wagon. The Governor handed the reins of the bridle to a bystander, commanding the prisoner to stand up: "Sir," said the Governor, "do you know in whose presence you stand?" being answered in the negative, the Governor continued: "There are but two powers known to the law that can save you from hanging by the neck until you are dead, dead, dead; one is the great God of the Universe, the other is J. Brown Ray, Governor of the State of Indiana; the latter stands before you (handing the young man the written pardon), you are pardoned." The Governor received the thanks of all present for this act of clemency.

The whole scene was witnessed by about twenty Indians, said to be relatives of those murdered. They seemed well satisfied that the death of their friends had been avenged, and it restored confidence throughout the "new purchase" that there was no danger to be apprehended from the Indians in consequence of this murder.

In the fall of 1824 the court house was approaching completion ready for the legislature, which was to convene in this place for the first time, on the first Monday in January, 1825, The seat of government had been fixed by law to remain at Corydon. Until 1825 the Legislature had convened on the first Monday in December of each year; the members had become very much dissatisfied with the treatment they had received at the hands of the citizens of Corydon and determined to get the seat of government from there one year earlier. In the Legislature that expired in the winter of 1824, a resolution was introduced and passed that "when the Legislature adjourn it would meet at Indianapolis on the first Monday in January, 1825."

In the fall of 1824 the State offices were removed to Indianapolis. It brought several good and permanent citizens —Samuel Merrill, as Treasurer of State, Dr. Wm. H. Lilly, as Auditor—the time of the Secretary of State expired that winter and he did not remove his family—John Douglass, as State Printer, also came that fall.

At the appointed time the Legislature met, but the fondest hopes of the people were not realized; neither the advantages nor pleasure they had looked forward to with so much anxiety were experienced:

> "But pleasures are like poppies spread,
> You seize the flower, its bloom is shed.
> Or like the snow falls in the river,
> A moment white, then melts forever.

> Or like the borealis' race,
> That flit ere you can point their place.
> Or like the rainbow's lovely form,
> Evanishing amid the storm."

The members of the Legislature were huddled together, six generally in a cabin, and paid from two to three dollars per week board.

Among the prominent members of this session of the Legislature were John Ewing, of Knox, Daniel Gross, of Spencer, Samuel Chambers, of Orange, Benjamin Irwin, of Bartholomew, Milton Stapp, of Jefferson, Calvin Fletcher, of Marion and Hamilton, George Boon, of Sullivan, John H. Thompson, of Clark.

The members came on horseback; their horses were kept by the farmers, who were anxious to have them at from fifty to seventy-five cents per week. For many years after the Legislature first met here all debts were made payable at the close of the next session, as more money was distributed among the people at that than any other time of the year.

When the next Legislature met (at the usual time, the first Monday in December) considerable improvement had been made for their accommodation. The mother of the writer had built a brick house, in addition to her cabins, and was enabled to furnish board for twelve men. Henderson and Blake and John Hawkins had also made additions which enabled them to accommodate more persons and in better style than the previous year. In after years, when the price of board was increased, the members began to threaten the citizens that they had once removed the seat of government from Corydon on account of the extortions of its citizens, and they would do so again; but this was only boasting, for they well knew they could not, it being out of their power, as the four sections of land on which Indianapolis stands was donated by the general government for a permanent seat of government, and that when the Legislature accepted the grant the capital was fixed for all time to come.

FANCY TOM

Was one of the citizens we gained when the capital was removed to this place. Tom had been connected with the seat of government at Corydon from the birth of the State, and considered himself one of its institutions, and his presence indispensable at its capital.

Thomas Bennett, which was his proper name before he came to Indianapolis, was a professor of the "tonsorial art," practically he was a better cook. The way in which he got the prefix to his name was this: He was living with Governor Ray and the Governor sent him to his neighbor, Mr. Wilkins, to borrow a basket of corn; Tom asked for fancy corn, as he wanted it to feed the Governor's horse. From that day he was known as "Fancy Tom." His complexion was a dark mahogany, or horse chestnut; he wore his wool plaited quite around his head, the plaits about two inches in length, and resembled very much the "pigtail" tobacco so much used at that time. He had a very effeminate voice, and were you to hear without seeing him, you would take it to be a female's.

Tom had a barber shop on Washington street, north side, between Pennsylvania street and the alley west. One morning one of his old legislative customers that represented one of the Ohio river counties, named "Tadlock," called in to be shaved; after Tom had complimented his customer, as was his wont to do on all occasions, he invited him to be seated in his tonsorial chair—this man had one leg off above the knee, which was supplied by a block of wood fastened with a leather strip, which, for the convenience of Tom and the comfort of himself, he took off while the professor was operating upon his phiz.

Tom was very much afraid of Indians and his customer had

no very high opinion of them himself. Tom had shaved one side of his face and had come round to the other side, so that his back was to the front door, and while he was flourishing his brush over the man's face in fine tonsorial style, very much engaged in conversation, dilating upon the future of the new capital, four or five Indians, unobserved either by him or his customer, come to the door, (an Indian hardly ever passes an open door without looking in). A large and finely painted Indian put his hands on each side of the door, the others were peeping under his arms; Tom was between them and his customer, and in order to see what he was doing the big one gave one of their peculiar ughs. Tom turned round, and as soon as he saw the Indians dropped his professional tools and cried out, "oh, blessed ingins," he made a spring for and through the back window, crying as he went "oh, blessed ingins." The Indians not understanding his movements followed to the window to see what he intended. Mr. Tadlock began to think he was in no very enviable situation, alone in the room with the Indians; he made a spring in the direction of his wooden leg, as he could not get out of the way without it; in this jump he fell to the floor, which caused his nose to bleed profusely, but he got hold of his leg and hobbled into the street, crying "ingins" and "murder" at every step. The blood on his face and the presence of the Indians alarmed those that were attracted to the place. The noise and cry of murder had attracted all the whites in the neighborhood and several more Indians, that happened to be in town, to the place, all of whom were alarmed until the frightened legislator became composed enough to explain. In the meantime Tom had jumped over the fence and ran down the alley west until he came to Mr. Ungles' yard near Mr. Hawkins' tavern; he ran into Mr. Ungles' house, crying murder and "ingins" at every step. Mrs. Ungles had a pan of breakfast dishes in her hands at the time Tom entered, and his abrupt enterance so frightened her that she dropped the pan and broke all her dishes. After things became more quiet a search was made for Tom, but he was no where to be found. Mr. Hawkins had an attic room that he did not often use; that night it was necessary to put some strangers up there to sleep; when they went into the room Tom stuck his head out from under the bed, and inquired if the "ingins had killed many people."

Tom lived to see many Indians after that, and died in 1850. He was found sitting in the kitchen of the Capital House with a boot in one hand and shoe-brush in the other.

HENRY BRADY.

The name of Mr. Brady has been a household word in Marion County for forty-seven years. He is a native of Pennsylvania, but emigrated to this State when quite young. His first residence in Indiana was in Jackson County, from whence he came to this county and settled six miles east of town, in Warren Township, in 1822, where he yet resides. He went, as all others did, into the woods, and now, by his own labor principally, has one of the finest farms in that neighborhood.

He was for many years a magistrate of that township. He has represented the county at different times in both branches of the legislature, and was ever popular with the people; the county has nearly always been opposed to the political party to which he belongs, yet when he was a candidate before them the people seemed to forget for awhile their party allegiance; indeed, he has been successful over some of the most popular leaders of the opposite party. He came to this county a Jackson man, and has strictly adhered to the political party that sprung from the administration of the old hero.

I have before me an "Indianapolis Gazette," printed in the year 1827. In this he offers his services to the people as a surveyor at two dollars per diem.

The old gentleman has moved on in the even tenor of his

way ever since. He has lately renewed his youth by taking to himself a young wife, and it is to be hoped by his many friends he will get a renewal of the lease of life.

It is quite unnecessary to say that Esquire Brady is one of the solid farmers of Marion County, and is universally respected as far as known.

HUMPHREY GRIFFITH,

The first watch maker to make this city his home, came here from Centerville, Wayne County, in 1825; though there had been one or two itinerant workmen of that kind, there was none to stay any length of time.

Mr. Griffith is a native of Wales, but came to the United States when quite young. He, like many others, made his money by the increase in value of real estate, and possessed the faculty of making a little money go a great ways.

Some ten years since, when those magnificent steamers, the Jacob Strader and Telegraph, were the mail line between Cincinnati and Louisville, there was an opposition evening line put upon the route; the mail company, in order to run the opposition out of the trade, put the fare down to one dollar between the two points.

At that time Mr. G. was visiting Cincinnati for pleasure and sight-seeing, and was paying first-class hotel bills, which was more than double the daily board on those steamers. He took a state room on the Strader and remained about two weeks, paying his fare every day to the next port. The clerk thought there must be something wrong, and approached him on the subject. Mr. G. gave a shrill whistle; said he, "don't you know me, I am Humphrey Griffith, of Indianapolis; I've been watching the manner in which you have managed this boat, and have made up my mind to buy it." After Mr. G. was perfectly satisfied of the good accommodations on the Strader, the superior liquors kept in the bar, and, above all, the polite and gentlemanly captain, he left the boat well satisfied with himself and the balance of mankind.

I am sorry to hear that at this time Mr. Griffith's health is very bad, and that he is unable to leave his house. I fear at his advanced age there is but little hopes of his recovery. Such is Humphrey Griffith, a citizen of this place for forty-four years.

ROBERT TAYLOR,

For many years one of the most respected citizens and industrious mechanics of this city, came to this place from Harrison County, Kentucky, early in the year 1826.

He was one of the founders and leading members of the Christian Church in this place, a worthy man, and was valued for his plain and unassuming manners, unostentatious purity, and his benevolent and charitable acts and sympathy with the poor and laboring classes. He died several years since, leaving a family of several children.

His eldest son, Napoleon B. Taylor, Esq., is one of the prominent lawyers of the city, who is also respected as a man of strict integrity and upright deportment, as a lawyer for his legal knowledge and fidelity to the interest of his clients, and as a neighbor, for his social and genial qualities.

SAMUEL McGEORGE.

I had forgot in the proper place, 1821, to notice Mr. McGeorge as one of the prominent citizens of that year. He lived on the river bank just below where the National road bridge crosses. Like every person else, he kept a "tavern." As there were no hotels at that time, they were all "taverns," or "private entertainments."

He was a tall, fine-looking man, with light hair and complexion. He had six or seven daughters that inherited the father's good looks.

He moved from this place to an Indian reserve on Wild Cat, in Tippecanoe County, near where Dayton now stands. He became a contractor with the government for furnishing provisions, horses, &c., for the Indian treaties and payments; he finally bought of Chief Rickardville the reservation of the six sections on which he lived, and managed to get a special act of Congress passed granting him a patent; this made him quite wealthy.

The writer spent a month at his house in the fall of 1828, when he was surrounded by his friends, the dusky Pottawatamies and Miamis, and many a ramble have I had with his beautiful daughters in visiting the many Indian graves and procuring the remnants of silver jewelry yet to be found, one of which was in a log; a slab was split from the top of the log the proper length, then the log was dug out sufficient in depth to hold the corpse, and the slab replaced; in this grave there was nothing but the bones and the remnants of jewelry.

Mr. McGeorge was a liberal, whole-souled man, and such a one that if he made money would do it at a single dash (as he did); he had no idea of saving and making it in dribs. He died many years since, at his farm on the reservation referred to.

His eldest daughter, Emily, was the wife of a Mr. Holloway, the first merchant in Lafayette; another married a Methodist preacher, named Tarkington; another Ezra Bush, the son of a neighboring farmer; Nancy was the wife of Doctor Lank and owns her father's old farm, one of the finest on Wild Cat prairie. I have no knowledge who the others married, but am sure their good looks secured them good husbands, although sometimes the reverse is the case.

I hope my fair companions that I have referred to, nor myself, by obtaining those antiquities, will ever be charged with robbing "Lo, the poor Indian," or a grave, for pecuniary benefit.

JOHN W. FOUDRAY,

Or brother Foudray, as he was generally called by young and old, came from Champaign County, Ohio, in the fall of 1824. His son John showed me a silver Mexican dollar, bearing the date of that year, which his mother had kept as a memento of their arrival here.

Brother Foudray was very active in organizing the church, and one of the founders of Methodism in this place. He was the compeer in the church of Billy Ray, Jimmy Kittleman and Francis and William McLaughlin, and was a class-leader from the organization of the church to the time of his death, in 1850.

His family consisted of himself, wife and three children, Milton, John, and his daughter Jane; all are now dead with the exception of John.

John E. Foudray was many years a constable, then sheriff of the county; he is now engaged in farming and the livery business.

I often meet him on the street, and am reminded by him of a circumstance that occurred between Christmas and New Year, 1836.

His brother Milton was clerking in a store at Bloomington; my sister, afterwards Mrs. Rousseau, was there at school and the sleighing was very fine; he and myself rigged out a cutter with a fine pair of horses, well decked out with sleigh-bells, in order to pay our relatives a visit; we invited a young man (yet a resident of the city) to accompany us. We started about dark with the intention to, and did, drive all night. The great noise made by our bells brought the inmates of the cabins along our route to their doors, often only to hear us in the distance after passing. Just after daylight next morning we reached the Bean Blossom Hills, about seven miles from our place of destination. As we were ascending one of those hills we saw a man just before us on horseback, and heard cries of "wo, Bally! wo, Bally! wo!" Before we could check up our horses and stop the noise that had evidently frightened his, the man, with a gun in his hand, was thrown into the deep snow on one side of the road, and a dead hog, which he was carrying before him on the horse, on the other side, his horse keeping straight forward as fast as his legs would carry him. When we came up the man was on his feet, brushing the snow from his clothes.

"Wal, stranger," said he, "what tarnal things ar' them you're got thar?" They are organs, replied John quickly. "Orgings, orgings," said the man; "what ar' tha?" "They are a kind of music they have in churches;" answered Mr. Foudray. "Churches," said the man; "do you mean meeting houses?" "Yes," was the answer, "meeting houses." "Wal, stranger, my house is jest on this road, if you'll gather up my hog I'll show you whar I live. I would like the ole 'oman and the youngsters to see these 'ere orgings."

We took them, *i. e.*, the man and hog, as well as gun, in our sleigh, and soon landed them at the cabin door, where the "ole 'oman and youngsters" were awaiting us, attracted by the unexpected and unceremonious arrival of Bally, as well as the noise of our bells. "Ole 'oman," said he, "these fellers have got orgings, and they ring um in metin' houses."

John gave his horses a turn in the road to give them another tune on the organs.

"Now, stranger," said the man, "as you're so kine as to haul my hog in your sled, you must wait til the ole 'oman cooks some of it for breakfast, and I'll gin your horses some fodder; I'll skin away a place on the hine leg and we'll soon have some on't fried." This invitation to breakfast we respectfully declined, as the animal heat was still in the hog, and it was yet smoking.

This man had only done what was customary in the country

at that time. *i. e.*, when they were out of meat they would go to the woods and kill any unmarked or wild hog they found.

After our arrival at Bloomington, and we had met our friends, we were invited to spend the evening at the house where my sister boarded, and where there were several young ladies. While one of them was performing on the piano a loud noise was heard as an accompaniment to the music, which was found to proceed from the nasal organ of the young man who had accompanied us; he sat in the corner fast asleep, and had to be roused up when we left. This incident he yet hears of when he chances to meet Mr. Foudray or myself.

DAVID BURKHART.

About the time of which I am now writing, 1824, there came to this place a man that became renowned in after years for fighting, and a terror to the colored population; indeed, they would tremble in their boots at the mention of his name. He was a stout-built, stoop-shouldered man, about five feet eight inches in height, with an arm as muscular as a bear, red hair, sandy whiskers, and a florid complexion; when drinking he was a very dangerous man, and seemed crazed from the effect of the liquor. When he took a liking to a person he would do anything for them in his power; at least I found it so until I incurred his displeasure; when sober he was a very good-hearted man, and liberal in money matters.

He kept a grocery on the southwest corner of New York and Tennessee streets and Indiana avenue. This place he called "The first and last Grocery," *i. e.*, it was the first in coming into town on Indiana avenue, and the last in going out.

Dave was a man of considerable influence with a certain class that were in the habit of congregating at "The first and last." Out of this class he formed what he called the "chain gang," of which he was the leader. This gang was formed to take care of any son of Ham that should be so unfortunate as to incur the displeasure of the leader or any of his party, and wo be unto any of them that should get the "chain gang" after them. Any mandate issued by the gang, or their leader, was faithfully obeyed by the colored society.

There was a negro, called Colonel Hunter, that lived in a cabin on the back part of my mother's lot; he became troublesome on account of the free use he made of our chickens, wood, &c. My eldest brother had loaded a log of wood with a charge of powder that had no other effect than to cover the colonel's floor with hot ashes and coals. This only made him more careful to leave all logs he found with a plug in them alone. My brother then tried the Dave Burkhart remedy, and it produced the desired effect.

One evening my brother addressed him in this way: "Colonel, what is the difficulty between you and Dave Burkhart?" "Why, has massa Burkhart got anything agin me, massa Mat?" "I don't know," said my brother; "I heard him and one of the chain gang talking; they said you had better move to where the white people were not so thickly settled."

The colonel requested my brother to see "massa Burkhart," and tell him he would leave as soon as he could get a cabin to go into; and in a few days we were rid of our neighbor.

In September, 1836, there was a camp meeting, under the direction of the late Rev. James Havens, on the military ground, just west of the canal, between Market and Ohio streets. For some weeks before the meeting was to take place there was a great deal of talk as to the course Burkhart would probably take in regard to it.

Finally, Dave was heard from. He said, "Ole Sorrel (as Mr. Havens was sometimes called) should get a whipping on the occasion, and he, himself would do it." The meeting was progressing very quietly, and nothing was seen of Dave until Saturday afternoon.

David Burkhart. 179

I was sitting on the end of one of the seats next to the main aisle. Mr. Havens had given out the hymn, and the congregation had kneeled in prayer; he then left the preacher's stand, and, as he passed me, gave me to understand that he wished to see me outside of the congregation.

At the edge of the encampment he said to me that "Dave Burkhart was on the ground raising a disturbance, and that he was going to take him before Esquire Stevens; and," said Mr. Havens, "when I take him by the right arm I wish you to take him by the left." We came up rather behind Dave, and had him as above indicated before he saw either of us. When he saw Mr. Havens, "Ah," said he, "Ole Sorrel, I've got you, han't I?" "No," said Mr. Havens, "we've got you, Davy, and you must go to 'Squire Stevens' with us."

He floundered around for awhile, but soon became convinced that he had to go. Mr. Havens was a stout, athletic and determined man, just in the pride of manhood and strength, and I considered myself rather on the double-jointed order at that time. We had no difficulty in getting him before the 'Squire, who fined him very light and sent him to jail for two or three days, and until the meeting should be over. Mr. Havens managed to have him released on Monday morning, Dave promising not to disturb the meeting again, which promise he honorably kept.

Ever after this circumstance, when Dave was drinking, he would have something to say about John Nowland, although quite friendly when sober. In 1843, seven years after the incident above narrated (and when I was at my store seventeen miles from town), he got into a fight with an Irishman in front of the Palmer House; the Irishman was rather too heavy for him, and had the best of the fight. When Dave arose from the gutter, and had wiped the blood and dirt from his face, he jumped up and cracked his heels together, and made a request of me, which, although I was not present, I do not think I should have complied with had I been there. All the old citizens, and many of the new ones, will understand what I refer to. As this was the second time he had been conquered, he supposed I had something to do with it. Dave has some children yet living in the city, who are quite respectable people. Mr. Burkhart has long since been able to exclaim with the poet,

"My race is run, my warfare's o'er,
The solemn hour has come."

JOSEPH BEELER

Was born in a "Block House," situated in what is now Ohio County, West Virginia, about twelve miles from Wheeling, in the year 1797; his father, being in command of the station established for the protection of the people, as well as a place of refuge for the settlers when attacked by the Indians, which was frequently the case. This Block house was called "Beeler's Station," and up to the present time it still retains the name.

He, with his mother's family, descended the Ohio River in a kind of "dug out," called a pirogue, in the year 1818 or 1819. The latter year he visited where this city now stands, before there was a cabin of a white man in it.

In the year 1820 he, with his mother and brother (George H. Beeler, who was the first clerk of Morgan County), settled near what was then, and is yet, known as the bluffs of White River.

In the rear 1822 he was married to Miss Hannah Matthews, the daughter of one of their neighbors, and settled, with his young wife, in Marion County, about seven miles southwest of this city, on the west side of White River, in Decatur township, where he resided up to the time of his death. Mr. Beeler underwent all the privations and trials incident to a pioneer or backwoods life.

Joseph Beeler.

He was for many years a justice of the peace—in fact as long as he would consent to serve. He was often solicited to become a candidate for higher positions, but always declined. He ever advised his neighbors, as well as others, against litigation, and was a peacemaker as far as his mild and persuasive manner could accomplish that end.

Mr. Beeler was a man of untiring perseverance and industry, and considered his vocation, that of a farmer, of the highest respectability, and had a great ambition to excel in his calling.

He was one of the first farmers of the county to import improved breeds of stock. His cattle, sheep and hogs early gained the reputation of being the best in the county, as the records of the first agricultural societies of the county and State will show by the premiums awarded.

He also took a deep interest in horticulture and the cultivation of improved varieties of fruits. Were I writing for the eye only of those who knew Joseph Beeler, it would be unnecessary to say he was a man of the strictest integrity, and one whose word was as good as his bond, and was never questioned.

He was at the time of his death, and for many years prior, a member of the Christian Church. He died on the 12th of July, 1851, well satisfied with his experience in life, and in the full vigor and strength of manhood; and when his days of toil and hardships were over, he found the forest had given place to cultivated fields, the log cabin to stately mansions, the unpretending log churches of our city to those magnificent temples of worship we now have.

Mrs. Beeler still survives him, and makes her home with her son, who will be the subject of my next sketch.

FIELDING BEELER

Was the first-born, and is the eldest son of the worthy gentleman I have noticed in the preceding sketch. He is one of the oldest native born citizens of Marion County, having made his first appearance upon the stage of action on the 30th day of March, 1823.

At the time he received his education the opportunities were very limited for the rudiments of a common English education; for a portion of what he did receive he walked three miles in winter, most of the way through the woods to the log school house, where his young ideas were first taught to shoot, frequently on his way seeing deer and flocks of wild turkeys, with which the woods abounded at that time.

Mr. Beeler tells me his earliest recollection was seeing Indians passing his father's cabin, hearing the wolves howl at night, and their killing all the sheep his father had, ten or twelve in number, and that his mother considered it a great calamity, as she did not know how her family was to be provided with the necessary winter clothing. She dressed and spun flax and wove linen for summer clothes; and for a Sunday suit, and to be worn on special occasions, she would generally stripe it.

At the age of twenty-one years (not being willing to lose much time) he was married and settled on a farm just west of Eagle Creek, on the Mooresville road, three and a half miles from town, where he yet resides.

Although, like his father, very decided in his political views, and frank to express them, he has never taken a very active part in politics. He cast his first vote for a Presidential candidate for Henry Clay in 1844.

In the year 1850 he was nominated by the Whig convention as its candidate for Representative of the county in the Legislature, and though he got the full vote of his party was defeated, the Democrats having the ascendancy in the county at that time.

During the existence of the Marion County Agricultural Society, from 1852 to 1860, he was a member, five years a director, and two years its president.

He was nominated by the Republican party, and elected a member of the House of Representatives in October, 1868, and served in the regular and special sessions; was chairman of the Committee on Agriculture, and took an active part in all questions relating to it, as well as the interests of his immediate constituents and the general welfare of the State, and introduced a bill for the appointment of a State Geologist and a geological survey of the State, which was about the only bill of general importance that became a law at the first session of that legislature.

After the death of A. J. Holmes, Mr. Beeler was appointed his successor as "Secretary of the State Board of Agriculture," and has passed through one of the most successful fairs of the West with entire satisfaction to the public and credit to all its officers.

As Fielding is rather good-looking, I hope he will excuse me if I attempt to give the reader an idea of his personal appearance.

As will be seen by his age, he is just in the prime of life, about five feet eight inches in height, rotund form, light hair, florid complexion, a blue eye and smiling countenance, and inherits all the candor and frankness of his father.

SAMUEL MERRILL

Was one of the good men, substantial and permanent citizens Indianapolis gained when the seat of government was removed to it. He was a native of one of the Yankee States, I think Vermont, but came to the West when a young as well as single man. His first residence in Indiana was at Vevay, where he was married. He then practiced law for a short time. In the winter of 1822-23 he was elected Treasurer of State, and in the spring removed to Corydon, then the capital of the State.

In the fall of 1824, when the State offices were removed to this place, he, with his family, made this place their home. He held the office of Treasurer of State until the State Bank of Indiana was chartered in 1834, when he was, by the legislature, chosen its president, and organized it, as well as the different branches, throughout the State. This position he held about ten years. He was then chosen President of the Madison and Indianapolis Railroad. It was while he had the supervision of this road its stock was worth from twenty-five to thirty per cent. premium.

While Mr. Merrill held these public positions he was ever active in private pursuits and enterprises. The first summer he was here we had no person that was qualified or willing to teach school; he was induced to do so, and kept school in the log Methodist Church on Maryland street, between Illinois and Meridian. Some years afterward he engaged in merchandising, and then, in connection with Mr. Yandes, built the mills on Fall Creek, known now as Bretts' Mill. He was ever active in all benevolent and charitable institutions, and during his entire residence was superintendent or teacher of a Sunday school. While he was president of the Benevolent Society he kept such clothing as was donated for that purpose in a room in the State Bank, adjoining his office. He had just bought himself a fine cloth cloak, such an one as was fashionable at that day, and very costly. One morning he entered his office through that room, and had thrown his cloak off on the pile of clothing left for distribution to the poor; a few moments afterward an old man, that lived upon the charities of the people, came to Mr. M. for clothing; he told him to go into the room and help himself to such as were there, which he did, and among other articles took the fine cloak.

When Mr. Merrill was ready to go to dinner his cloak was no where to be found. As it was a cold, disagreeable day, he certainly had worn it to the office; he could not think what had become of it. On his way home he met old man Wilson (the person referred to as having come for clothing) promenading Washington street with it on.

Mr. Merrill was one of the first to join the Second Presbyterian Church when first organized by Henry Ward Beecher, and was a warm personal friend of that eminent divine during his residence in Indianapolis.

During the thirty years he was a resident of this city, no person enjoyed the confidence and respect of its citizens to a greater degree than Samuel Merrill.

He has several children yet living in the city. His eldest daughter is now the widow of the late John L. Ketchum; a son, bearing the father's name, is a prominent bookseller and stationer, and there is no sign now in the city whose name is more familiar to the writer than that of Samuel Merrill.

JOHN DOUGLASS

Was the "State Printer," and came to this place when the other State officers came, in 1824. He immediately became connected with Douglass Maguire in the "Western Censor and Emigrant's Guide," by the purchase of Mr. Gregg's interest, and changed the name to the "Indiana Journal." He was connected with the paper several years, for sometime as sole proprietor, and then with S. V. B. Noel as a partner. He was a practical printer, and a very industrious man.

Mr. Douglass was an honest, upright man, and, as I have said of another in these sketches, would rather suffer a wrong himself than knowingly do another an injury; and were he living at this time he would hardly be considered qualified to superintend a printing establishment, when their advocacy of a measure is sometimes procured by selfish motives or a pecuniary reward.

The writer was well acquainted with him during his twenty-six years' residence in this place, and has never heard a harsh or unkind word spoken of him.

He has several children yet living in the city. His eldest daughter is the present wife of Mr. Alfred Harrison, a prominent banker. Three of his sons are living, Samuel, James and George. Samuel and James are partners in one of the largest printing establishments in the State, the "Indianapolis Daily Journal," that had descended from their father's paper. Mr. Douglass died about the year 1850, respected by all who knew him, and his death much regretted.

ARCHIBALD LINGENFELTER.

Were I to omit speaking of Archy, as he was thirty years ago, it would be passing over the name of one who contributed in his way a great deal to the merriment of the fun-loving citizens of Indianapolis.

Archy came to this place in 1826, a red-hot, full-blooded Kentuckian, and for several years pursued his avocation, that of plastering, until he was finally overtaken by a too fond indulgence in the use of ardent spirits, and which for several years rendered him useless to his family and a burthen to himself. When drinking he seemed to think he was commander-in-chief of the army; he would dress himself in the United States uniform and with a martial air parade the streets, and has often declared the town under martial law.

He would sometimes call all the ends of the earth to come unto him, never omitting, however, to except one, who had incurred his displeasure, this one he would assign to a country or place said to be rather warm than pleasant.

About this time he went to Doctor Mears and told the Doctor he wished he would give him something to kill him. The Doctor gave him a large dose of tartar emetic in a glass of brandy, which he drank without ever making a wry face. (See sketch of Dr. Mears).

When Archy first came to Indianapolis he boarded at one of the "taverns" of the place. On one occasion several of the boarders of the other taverns and boarding-houses were speaking of the fare their different landlords gave them. Archy said he thought that his landlady gave her boarders the greatest variety of any tavern in the town. He said they had three kinds of meat, ram, sheep and mutton; three kinds of vegetables, boiled potatoes with the skins on, boiled potatoes with the skins off, and fried potatoes; two kinds of bread, corn bread baked in a skillet, and corn bread baked on a griddle; two kinds of milk, buttermilk and sour milk; he said they had but one kind of fruit pie, and that was pumpkin pie.

Archy has about lived out the three score and ten years generally allotted to man, and I think is indebted to Doctor Mears for having lived the last twenty-five years of it.

NATHAN DAVIS.

About the time of which I am now writing, 1826, there lived in Indianapolis a hatter known to the citizens as "Honest Nathan." His shop, as well as his residence, was on the north side of Washington, between Meridian and Illinois streets.

"Honest Nathan" was not overstocked with either energy or industry, and was content if he could transform coon skins enough, into something he called hats, to provide for the daily demands and comforts of his family. In one of his hats there would be material enough to make a dozen of Ike Davis' fashionable hats of the present day; and like his predecessor, John Shunk, sometimes required his customers to furnish their own coon, which were generally caught the night before they were needed by the hatter.

Before he made this place his residence he had lived on Blue River, about twenty-five miles east of this. One day, just before noon, two of his old neighbors and friends from his latter residence called, and were invited to have their horses fed and stay to dinner; which invitation they readily accepted. The worthy hatter brought out his bottle of "bayou blue," at the same time remarking that his neighbor, Doctor Scudder, had some very fine Madeira wine, and as it had been sometime since they had taken a "jorum" together he would step in and get some. The Doctor not being at his shop, Mr. Davis took the liberty to hunt up his wine bottle, which he found, but did not notice on the label the abreviation of "anti" going before wine.

From this bottle his friends and himself drank pretty freely. After dinner, and before resuming their journey, the three took a parting drink together, the travelers speaking in the highest terms of the Doctor's Madeira. They had crossed the river at the grave yard ford, and found themselves so sick they could neither proceed on their journey or retrace their steps to their friends' house. They laid down under a tree anI left their horses to graze at pleasure.

A farmer passing by on his way to town, they sent word to the worthy hatter that they were "pizened," and to come and bring the Doctor as quick as possible, for they would certainly die if they did not soon have relief. When the messenger arrived at Mr. Davis' he found him in the same situation, "heaving and pitching," and crying to the Doctor (who had just returned) for help, or he would surely die.

The Doctor inquired what they had eat or drank. "We only drank some of your wine." On examination of the bottle, he told him they had drank enough to start Mount Vesuvius. He hurried to the travelers to give them the only help and consolation in his power, that in due time the Madeira would *work* OUT all well, and that they would be better before they could possibly be much worse. The hatter lived here many years after this occurrence, but never outlived hearing of it from his neighbors.

CHARLES C. CAMPBELL.

Charles has been so long in this city that he has almost become a part of it, at least as much so as the State House, or the Governor's Circle.

Mr. C. first came to this place as an apprentice to the tailoring business. After his apprenticeship was out he carried on the business for a short time, long enough, however, to learn that it could not be carried on without work, and arrived at the conclusion that it was about as easy for a needle to go through the eye of a camel as it was for a Campbell to sit cross-legged all day on a broad board and pull a needle through tammy cloth, with nothing but a goose (tailor's) for a companion.

Charles has held several offices of trust and emolument, such as sheriff, deputy sheriff and receiver of public moneys. He made a good and efficient officer, and was never known to unnecessarily oppress or put to trouble those with whom he had official business.

Although he is not a professional juryman, he has served his country in that capacity a great deal, hardly ever being objected to, unless some unfortunate descendant of Ham should be engaged in a suit with a white man; his well known preference for his own race and color might be urged as an objection.

Mr. Campbell is, perhaps, as well acquainted with the early history of this city as any gentleman now living; indeed, he knows a great deal his modesty would prevent his telling.

He has been an honorary member of all the political conventions of both parties for forty-five years, always honoring them with his presence, and is possessed of many anecdotes in regard to them; he, also, has considerable legislative experience as a lobby member.

He has managed to glide down the stream of time without over taxing his physical energies; he lives "at peace with all the world and the rest of mankind," in the full enjoyment of extraordinary good health, and a conscience reasonably clear.

In his business career I had forgotten to mention that for a short time he engaged in the banking business with Kilby Ferguson to the amount of fifteen hundred dollars; if not a silent partner, Charley says he would like it kept as silent as possible.

Although he has no pretensions to aristocracy, he owns property and lives in the midst of that class of citizens on North Meridian street.

The writer cannot close this sketch without acknowledging his obligations to Mr. C. for the privilege of looking at the first elephant that ever came to Indianapolis, although he has seen several *elephants* since that cost him more money.

"He is well paid, that is well satisfied."

CORNELIUS W. VAN HOUTEN

Is a native of the city of New York. He, with his father's family, emigrated to the West in 1816, and settled in Dearborn County, Indiana.

In the fall of 1827 he visited Indianapolis on a tour of inspection, and seeking a home for himself and family.

In the month of April, 1828, with his family, including his mother (now 87 years of age), he came to and made this county his home. He settled on eighty acres of land about one mile south of the donation line, on what is now the Shelbyville pike, and immediately on the bank of Bean Creek.

Here he lived for many years, and was one of our most prosperous farmers.

About the year 1845 he engaged with his brother, Captain Isaac B. Van Houten, and built that splendid steamer, Eudora, which they ran between St. Louis and New Orleans. Captain Van Houten died in March, 1847; then Cornelius took charge of and commanded the boat until 1848, when the steamer, with twenty-six others, was burned at the St. Louis wharf.

In June, 1847, my wife and self visited St. Louis, and were very hospitably entertained by Mr. Van Houten on board the Eudora, and invited to take a trip with him to New Orleans, and return.

By the burning of this steamer he lost a considerable sum, and was satisfied with steamboating, at least enough to quit it and return to his farm.

He has several children living in the city. A daughter is the wife of Mr. J. J. Graham, one of the business men of the city; another, younger, the child of his second wife, lives with her sister; and a son, a young man, who resides with his father and grandmother, Mr. Van Houten being a widower the second time. His first wife was the sister of our venerable fellow-citizen, James M. Ray, Esq.

SAMUEL V. B. NOEL.

The name that stands at the head of this sketch has been as familiar to the writer, for forty-four years, as that of any person now living, and his acquaintance, like wine, has improved by time.

Vance Noel, as he is generally known to the old citizens of this city, is a native of Bath County, Virginia. At the age of three years his parents removed to Harrodsburgh, Mercer County, Kentucky, and from the latter place they came to Indianapolis in the fall of 1825.

In 1828 Vance engaged with Messrs. Douglass & Maguire

to learn the printing business, in the office of the "Indiana Journal." He continued in that office, boy and man, apprentice and journeyman, foreman, partner, and finally sole proprietor, for nearly twenty years.

It was while he was engaged in the "Journal" office he earned and acquired the reputation he is so justly entitled to for integrity, industry and perseverance.

After he retired from the printing business he engaged in merchandising and the produce business, and owing to his too confiding nature and disposition he lost heavily. He shipped a large quantity of grain to a firm that failed, owing him several thousand dollars. Nothing daunted, he still persevered, and never seemed to lose any of his youthful energy, being always ready to "pick his flint and try again."

Vance was one of the "bloody three hundred" that went forth in 1832 to fight the bloody "Ingeans," and returned with a record as bright as any that were engaged in that memorable campaign, and unstained with blood.

He was, also, one of the seventeen "Wild Oats of Indianapolis" that journeyed to Tippecanoe Battle Ground in May, 1840, and shouted as loud as the loudest for "Tippecanoe and Tyler too;" and the few of that seventeen now living will remember the first night out at Eagle Village, where we met that veteran dancer *Ezikel* Benjamin, who danced in the rain to the tune of

"We'll dance all night, till broad day light, &c."

Then, in 1844, Vance, with the Clay Glee Club, sang—

"The moon was shining silver bright,
The stars with glory crowned the night;
High on a limb that 'same old coon,'
Was singing to himself this tune—
Get out of the way, you're all unlucky,
Polk can't come it with old Kentucky."

In 1841 he was married to Miss Elizabeth L. Browning, who was one of the belle's of Indianapolis, and daughter of

Edmund Browning, Esq., one of our most respectable citizens.

Mr. and Mrs. Noel have thus far floated down the stream of time together, and their hearth-stone has been ever cheered by the voices of little ones. "A babe in a house is a wellspring of joy," and they have had their full share of joy in this way.

When I say there is no man in Indianapolis more respected by the old citizens than Samuel V. B. Noel, I but say what everybody knows that is acquainted with him.

GENERAL ROBERT HANNA

Was a native of South Carolina, but, with his father's family and a number of brothers, came to Brookville, Franklin County, at an early day in the history of the Territory.

He was a member of the Constitutional Convention in 1816, that framed the Constitution with which the Territory was admitted into the Union in that year.

From Brookville he came to this place as Register of the Land Office in 1826; this office he held until the election of General Jackson as President, when he was removed by the old hero in the spring of 1829.

Old Bob, as he was familiarly called, was quite fond of office, and was not backward in offering his services to the people of Marion County in any capacity, they might be useful; as he used to say, "he cared not for his own aggrandizement, he only wanted to be useful to the people."

If not always successful and popular it was no fault of his, for no man ever tried harder to be so than he did; he was always ready to lend a helping hand at a log rolling, house-raising, or go a friend's security, and on public occasions sing a patriotic song; his favorite one I well remember, "The Liberty Tree," having heard him sing it at several fourth of July celebrations.

Although a southerner by birth, he had an innate prejudice against slavery and slaveholders—peculiar to those who live in the south that are not owners of slaves themselves; those prejudices he was very careful in speaking of in his day, as the time " had not yet come " when they were popular.

At the time of the alleged murder of Morgan by the Masons, the General felt the public pulse on the subject of anti-masonry, but it did not vibrate very strong in the direction he wished.

The General, like most backwoods politicians of that day, wanted a hobby, and determined, if there was a possibility, to have one. Just at that time there sprung up a prejudice in the country against the people of the town; this hobby-horse he rode until its life was extinct. I have before me a speech he made against the village aristocrats that sat on store-boxes concocting plans to oppress the honest farmer.

One of General Hanna's fatal errors was, he calculated too much upon the credulity of the people. He was a man of considerable electioneering tact, and at last managed, with a small capital of talent, to reach the Senate of the United States.

Senator General James Noble had died; General Hanna and Governor Ray had some business transactions in regard to that well known tavern, "The Traveler's Ray House Cheap," "Traveler's Ray House Cash," which the General kept awhile. The Governor appointed him to fill the vacancy in the Senate until the Legislature should elect one, which they did in the person of General John Tipton a few days after they met. General Hanna was a United States Senator some two weeks, which was long enough, however, to secure the honor, which is considerable, and the mileage, which at that time was a more substantial item.

The General was considerable of a military man, and took great pride in arraying the corn-stalk and hoop-pole militia in line. I have seen him with the entire militia force of this and one or two adjoining counties on parade, when there was not a dozen guns among them, mounted on his little, bald-faced pacing poney, dressed in the continental uniform of a Major General, cocked hat, buff pants and vest, and high top boots; his whole contour would remind you of the cheap pictures we see of General Washington at the head of his army, or crossing the Delaware.

To Robert Hanna belongs the credit of first navigating White River to this point with a steamboat, bearing the name of "The General Hanna." She arrived at her dock at the Indianapolis wharf and steamboat landing in April, 1831, amid the shouts and greetings of the entire population of the village. As she was the first, so she was the last, seen here, with the exception of the "Governor Morton," whose history was a brief one, and is yet fresh in the minds of the people.

I have taken Robert Hanna as a fair specimen of the early politicians and military men of the country. He was a man of good common sense, very democratic in his dress and habits, made no pretensions to be more than what he was, an honest and upright man, plain and frank in his intercourse with his neighbors.

General Hanna was killed by a train of cars on the Peru railroad in the winter of 1858, while coming from his residence to the city.

He has five sons living, V. C. Hanna, Robert B., William, Thomas and John. The latter has been deputy sheriff of this county for about three years.

His only daughter, Catharine, is the wife of a Mr. Hughes, a worthy and respectable farmer, who lives near McCordsville, in Hancock County.

RILEY B. HOGSHIRE.

With Mr. Hogshire the writer was intimately acquainted for the full length of time he was a citizen of Marion County, thirty-three years, and during that time never heard a harsh or unkind word spoken of Riley B. Hogshire; and in writing of him our imagination wanders to the days of by-gone years, when the joyful gladness of youthful days shed its enlivening radiance on the hearts of the young.

"Pleased with the present, full of glorious hope,"

he lived to see his children grown up around him, and the fondest hope of his youthful days realized, in a great measure. But he has gone from the hum of the busy world and solved the great problem of life.

He was born in Worcester County, Maryland, in the year 1798, and there remained until he had attained his eighteenth year, when he settled near Lawrenceburg, Dearborn County, in the year 1826; he emigrated from the latter place to Marion County, and settled in Pike township, seven miles northwest of Indianapolis, in the midst of his political friends; his heart untainted by any desire to injure any one, he soon built up a host of personal friends.

Like most others who settled here at that time, he possessed but little of worldly goods, but he had that which was more valuable—integrity, industry and perseverance—and which always brings its reward.

The first spring he was in this county he helped twenty-eight families to roll logs, burn brush and clear a garden, or "truck patch," as it was commonly called, where cabbage, potatoes and other "garden sass," as old Mrs. Carter would say, was raised.

A garden spot was generally the first improvement made after the settler had raised his cabin, and many is the time we have have heard the housewife directing her liege lord where and how to prepare it.

He had an extensive acquaintance throughout this and the adjoining counties, and perhaps exercised as much influence, politically, as any person in his township. He served as justice of the peace for about fifteen years, often officiating as peacemaker and settling difficulties between his neighbors without their resorting to law or litigation.

He was among the number of Pike township that in the year 1828 cast their ballot for the "Sage of the Hermitage," and, throughout his entire life, was a Democrat of the Jackson school, and adhered strictly to its political faith.

He moved to Morgan County in the year 1837, and there died in the fifty-sixth year of his age. He had lived to see "the wilderness blossom as the rose," and transformed into happy homes for his many friends. He died with a full hope of a reunion hereafter with his kindred and friends.

"He is the happy man, whose life e'en now,
Shows somewhat of the happier life to come."

WILLIAM R. HOGSHIRE.

Riley B. Hogshire is represented in this city in the person of his son, whose name heads this sketch, and who inherits a great many of the father's fine traits of character, and is considered one of the true business men of the city.

William R. Hogshire was selected and appointed Steward of the Deaf and Dumb Asylum in the year 1858. This position he held for several years, and then, in connection with another of Pike township's good-looking young men, John F. Council, as a partner, bought out the retail grocery establishment of J. J. Bradshaw.

After keeping this store sometime they in turn sold out, and it was during the time that they were out of business that Mr. Hogshire received the nomination of the Democratic convention for County Auditor, and received the full strength of the party vote against General McGinnis, the candidate of the opposing party. After this he and his old partner, in connection with another old citizen, J. B. E. Reid, commenced the wholesale and retail boot and shoe business, at their old stand, No. 25 West Washington street.

While writing of this locality, I am reminded of an incident that occurred there over thirty years ago. At that time there stood on that ground a small one-story building, in one of the back rooms of which was a tiger's lair, kept by two enterprising and well known citizens. At that time this animal many fought but few conquered.

A prominent Wabash merchant, en route to Cincinnati for the purchase of goods, stopped over night in the city. This merchant was fond of excitement of any kind, especially that kind that pertains to the feeding of this animal. He stepped into this place to pass an hour and meet old friends and acquaintances. The animal happened to be hungry and voracious, so much so that the gentleman found it unnecessary the next morning to pursue his journey farther east, and returned home.

I hope my three friends that are there engaged in business may be as lucky as these two old sharks were in former days, and while they are fortunate, it does not necessarily follow that any should be the poorer, but, on the other hand, all who give them a call will be benefited, for in

> That establishment they will find
> Boots and shoes of every kind:
> Stocky boots for rainy weather,
> And lighter shoes of finer leather.

There they will also find those three native-born citizens of Marion County, whose genial countenances are as familiar to the eyes of the people of Indianapolis as the tune of "Old Hundred" is to the ears of our church-going people. In this sketch I have noticed the sons of three of this county's old and most respectable citizens, and may they, like their fathers, retain the good name they now enjoy.

JOHN SMOCK.

Among the early and prominent farmers of the county was Mr. Smock. I remember seeing him early in the spring of 1821, when he was hunting a location preparatory to purchasing at the sale that was to come off at Brookville the ensuing summer.

At that time nothing but gold and silver coin was received by the government in payment for land. He had traveled all over the new purchase with a considerable amount of money, carried on a horse that was ridden by his eldest son, Peter. They never entertained any fear of being robbed.

I doubt very much if they were to start out of the city at this time, in a similar way, and it was known that they had such an amount with them, that they would travel five miles without being robbed, and perhaps murdered, such has been the progress in this branch of the *industrial* art as well as others.

Mr. Smock bought the land and made the farm west of Pleasant run, on the Madison State road (now owned by John Hœfgen), and there died many years since.

His two only sons, Peter and Richard, are well known citizens of the city, and reside in the southeastern portion. Most of his daughters are dead.

JAMES B. RAY

Was one of the remarkable public men of his day. He held the office of chief executive of the State for seven years, one year by virtue of the office of lieutenant governor, which he held when Governor Hendricks was elected to the United States Senate, in 1825, and was twice elected for a full term of three years each.

At the time he first became Governor he was a widower, and quite a showy and dressy man, good-looking, with the exception that he had one cross eye. He was of a tall and commanding form, straight as an arrow, wore his hair plaited or wrapped, and hanging down his back in a cue. He walked with, or rather carried, a cane, which he flourished in a way that denoted he knew and felt the importance of his position and the authority vested in him.

In 1826 he was appointed, in connection with Generals Tipton and Cass, a commissioner to treat with the Pottawatamies and Miamis of the Wabash and Eel Rivers for certain of their lands on these rivers. It was through the influence of Governor Ray that a donation was obtained from the Indians to the State of a section of land for every mile of a road one hundred feet wide from Lake Michigan, via Indianapolis, to a point on the Ohio River, to be designated by the legislature.

The location of the southern terminus of this road was legislated upon for several years, and was finally located at Madison, via Greensburg, and is known as the Michigan road.

Governor Ray was considered a very visionary man, and some of his predictions were ridiculed that have since been verified, one of which is the present railroad facilities of the State and country.

Governor Ray was the owner of that tavern, known in its day as the "Travelers' Ray House Cheap," and "Travelers' Ray House Cash," and which sometimes brought his excellency into personal combats with his tenants.

At one time this house was kept by James Forsee, Esq., attorney and counsellor at law, and who I have spoken of in another sketch. He and the Governor had an altercation; Forsee got the Governor by the cue, and, for awhile, had him in a very disagreeable position; but the Governor rallied his whole strength, got loose from his antagonist, and struck him a severe blow over the nose that made it bleed profusely; just then a traveler rode up on horseback with the intention of "putting up." Mr. Forsee, anxious to secure a customer, left the Governor, and running toward the traveler with his face bloody, exclaimed, "d—n him, I'll kill him!" The traveler, thinking he was after him, put spurs to his horse, and Mr. Forsee lost his customer.

In the year 1840, at one of the Whig conventions, Isaac Naylor, who had been in the battle of Tippecanoe, made some allusions to Governor Ray which were distasteful to his excellency, and which he, at the next Democratic meeting, in speaking of the battle of Tippecanoe, said, where " Owen, Warren, Spencer and Davis fell," and after a pause of a minute or more, "and Isaac Naylor lived," which seemed to imply that Mr. Naylor had kept himself out of danger. The Governor's manner convulsed the house with laughter.

While Governor of the State he registered his name at hotels and on steamboats as " J. Brown Ray, Governor of the State of Indiana, and commander-in-chief of the army and navy thereof."

A short time before his death he advertised for sale a farm near Augusta, in this county, his tavern stand in the city, and a proposition to build a railroad from Charleston, South Carolina, through this place to the northern lakes, all in one article. The farm and tavern have been sold, and the railroad built, although the latter is not exactly on the plan he proposed. Governor Ray was a man of ability, but, like every one else, had some weak points, which would sometimes intrude themselves upon the public to his injury, and cause him to be ridiculed. Such was Indiana's third State Governor. He died about the year 1850.

NOAH NOBLE,

The fourth Governor of Indiana, was born on the banks of the Shenandoah River, in Frederick County, Virginia. When his father removed to Kentucky he sold his plantation to a Mr. Swearengin, who was afterward the father-in-law of his son.

Noah Noble returned to Virginia in the year 1819, and was married in the same house in which he was born. At an early day he removed to Brookville, thence to Indianapolis in the year 1826. Governor Noble's father-in-law visited him several times at this place. We remember him as a fine specimen of the "Old Virginia gentleman."

Lazarus Noble, brother of Noah, had been receiver of public moneys at Brookville, and when the land offices were ordered to be removed to this place, started to remove with his family, and ere he had reached the Franklin county line was taken sick and died at the house of his friend Judge Mount.

Noah was then appointed the successor of his brother, and immediately entered upon the duties of the office, and removed his family to this place.

In 1829 he was among the first removals made by General Jackson, and James P. Drake appointed in his stead. After this he engaged in farming near the city; a portion of his farm now forms an important part of the eastern portion of the city north of Washington street.

In 1831 he was selected as the Clay candidate, and ran against James G. Reed for Governor, and although the Jackson party was largely in the majority his great popularity with people not only crowned him with success, but also Milton Stapp, who was on the ticket for lieutenant-governor. The office of chief magistrate of the State he held for two terms of three years each, and although he had attained the highest office in the gift of the people directly, his ambition was not yet satisfied; he aspired to the United States Senate, a place so long and ably filled by his elder brother, General James Noble. In this he was doomed to disappointment, intriguing and less scrupulous politicians outmanaging him.

He held several other important offices, and came out of the political arena with an unsullied reputation as a public man, never yielding to anything that might be construed into selfishness, or bring reproach upon him as a public officer.

In his friendship he was warm and devoted, and confiding to a fault. He had a mild and benevolent countenance, and a smile for all that either business or circumstances brought him in contact with. He died in the winter of 1844.

Governor Noble left a widow and two children, a son and daughter. The daughter was the wife of the late A. H. Davidson; she died in the summer of 1851, leaving several children who yet live in or near the city. The son, W. P. Noble, and his mother, yet reside on a portion of the old farm, and near the city.

"When by a good man's grave I muse alone,
Methinks an angel sits upon the stone."

HENRY P. COBURN

Was one of the estimable citizens Indianapolis gained when the capital was removed to it. He, with his family, came to this place in December, 1824, only a few weeks previous to the time the first legislature convened.

He had been a citizen of the State since its first admission into the Union in 1816, and was clerk of the Supreme Court, and as such came to this city and remained in office for several years.

Mr. Coburn was a native of Massachusetts, born and raised in the village of Dracut, but as an adventurer in search of a home and a fortune, he first settled in this State, at Corydon, at the time above stated.

Mr. Coburn was one of the most conscientious men we have ever known, honest in his dealings with his neighbors, and punctual in everything he undertook.

He ever took an active part in the cause of education in the city and throughout the State, and did, perhaps, more than any other person toward bringing into existence the present free school system which is such a blessing, especially to the poorer classes and laborers of the country, and is educating their children along with those of the wealthy and more favored citizens.

He also took a lively interest in agriculture and horticulture, and State and county fairs, and was always, from the time they were first introduced in the State and county, among the exhibitors of fruits, flowers, etc., that had been cultivated by his personal labor.

Although a lawyer of fine attainments he did but little in the practice of his profession after he came to this place, but contented himself with attending to the duties of his office and his large and splendid garden of four acres, which he took great pains in cultivating. This garden spot is now almost in the center of the city, and a large portion of it is yet owned by his son, the Hon. John Coburn, member of Congress from the Capital District.

Mr. Coburn was a very unobtrusive and retiring man, never trying to force his opinions, either religious or political, upon others, though firm and decided in them himself. His manner had in it the affability and social qualities calculated to make all feel easy and at home in his society; was ever ready to contribute anything in his power to promote the happiness of his friends. He was for many years one of the leading members of the Second Presbyterian Church, and died in 1854, regretted by all who knew him.

Mr. Coburn's eldest son, Augustus, was drowned in Lake Superior a few years since. His second son, Hon. John Coburn, raised and commanded the 33d Indiana Regiment in the war for the preservation of the Union. He has since been twice elected to Congress, and it is to his exertions and influence the people of this city are mostly indebted for the present free delivery system, by which they receive their mail matter at their doors.

A third son, Henry, is engaged in the lumber business in connection with his father-in-law, Mr. William H. Jones, another old citizen.

In the death of Mr. Coburn Indianapolis lost one of its best citizens, the church one of its most active members, and the poor a sympathizing friend.

> "The dead are like the stars by day,
> Withdrawn from mortal eye;
> But not extinct; they hold their sway
> In glory through the sky."

SAMUEL GOLDSBERRY

Was from Berkley County, Virginia, and came to this place a young man in 1824. He was a carpenter, and followed his business up to the time of his death, which occurred in 1847. He had accumulated considerable city property, and left his young family in good circumstances.

Soon after he came to this place he was married to Miss Elizabeth, daughter and only child of George Smith, Esq., one of the proprietors and editors of the "Indianapolis Gazette."

He left a family of ten children—six sons and four daughters—nearly all of whom are still living in the city. His second daughter is the wife of Thomas Cottrell, Esq., Councilman from the Seventh Ward, and one of the enterprising business men of the city.

His widow was married several years after his death to Mr. William Martin, one of the respectable farmers of the county, but now a citizen of the town.

Mr. Goldsberry was esteemed as an honest, upright and industrious man; he was for many years a member of the Methodist Church, and died lamented by all who knew him.

JOSEPH WINGATE

Became a resident of this city early in January, 1826. He was from Falmouth, Kentucky, and inherited that liberal, kind and obliging disposition peculiar to that generous-hearted people.

The second year after Mr. Wingate became a citizen of this place, he was induced by the Rev. Edwin Ray (then the traveling preacher who visited the place every four weeks) to go with him one evening to the old log church on Maryland street. The next evening the reverend gentleman was surprised to find his new-made acquaintance and friend as one of his hearers, and yet more astonished when he invited persons who wished to become members of the church, to see Mr. Wingate come up and give them his hand as such. He lived for seven years afterwards, and died an exemplary member of the Methodist Church.

Mr. Wingate was a bricklayer by trade, but did not follow the business long. He was elected a justice of the peace, and the fact that there were but very few appeals from his docket, was evidence that he generally gave satisfaction in his decisions. He died in December, 1834.

His wife survived him several years, and became the wife of Joshua Black, another old and respectable citizen.

Mr. Wingate has several children yet living in the city. His eldest son living, William, studied law, but never practiced to any great extent. J. F. Wingate is one of the live business men of the city. The youngest, Edwin, named in honor of, and for the gentleman under whose ministration Mr. Wingate joined the church, is also a citizen.

Mr. Wingate's sons, like their father, enjoy the confidence and esteem of all who know them.

JOSHUA STEVENS.

Of Judge Stevens I am somewhat at a loss how and what to say, that the reader may get anything like a definite idea of the character and peculiarities of the man.

He was a shoemaeer by trade, and followed the business for several years after taking up his residence in this place, which was about the year 1824.

He was elected, and for several years served, as associate judge of the county. In this field of public service there was but little opportunity for the exercise of his legal ability. Wishing for a more extended field, he sought for and was elected a justice of the peace, and served as such until or about the time of his death.

That he understood his own docket, and particularly the amount of costs due him, no one will pretend to deny; but I have never seen any one else that pretended to understand it. He was prompt in making his decisions, and they were generally in accordance to the law and evidence in the case.

Judge Stevens, like his old and personal friend, Humphrey Griffith, of whom I have already written, early acquired the happy faculty of making a little money go a great ways, and as his costs accumulated on his hands he laid the money out in real estate that was then near the city, and has since become a part of it.

A great portion of this property lay between Virginia avenue and New Jersey street, and extended to the southern boundary of the donation, and now forms a very important part of the city, which made his heirs quite wealthy.

He also owned some fine Washington street property. On one of those lots, the northwest corner of Washington and Delaware streets, he built a three-story brick house, the windows of which were fifteen light eight by ten glass; the doors were plain batton. The house is still standing, but the windows and doors have been modernized.

His turnout, in which he took his Sunday morning airing, was a natural, or rather an unnatural, curiosity; the whole rig and horse would not to-day, if put up at auction in Washington street, bring fifteen dollars. The writer was once so unfortunate as to have a similar one, and passing one of the back streets was beckoned by a waggish gentleman on the sidewalk to stop; coming up he congratulated me, and said that he had not until that moment known that I was one of the heirs of Judge Stevens. Upon my asking why he should make such a mistake, he pointed to the horse and vehicle and said, "that certainly once was Judge Stevens' family carriage."

Judge Stevens was a native of Vermont, and brother of Thaddeus Stevens, of Pennsylvania, that figured so conspicuously in national politics during the rebellion.

He was a man of more than ordinary ability, and possessed a great fund of humor and wit, and was, at times, very sarcastic and bitter toward those whose opinions did not run in the same channel with his. His speech was short but generally to the point, and told upon those it was intended for. Out of a large family of children but two survive him, his son, Doctor Thaddeus M. Stevens, and a daughter, the wife of Mr. Coffman, who occupies the old homestead near the southern terminus of New Jersey street.

Judge Stevens was always kind to the poor, and ever shared his sympathy with them as well as his means. He died in 1858, regretted by a large circle of acquaintances.

CAPTAIN JOHN CAIN

Was a native of the "Old Dominion," born in Culpepper County in the year 1805. He there learned the book-binding business, but ere he had attained his majority came West, and for a short time worked at his trade in Hamilton, Butler County, Ohio.

In the year 1826 he came to Indianapolis, when its whole population did not exceed eight hundred souls. He immediately commenced, and opened the first book-bindery in the place. In 1832 he published a book of miscellaneous poems the first book of any kind, with the exception of the laws of the State, published in the place; he also opened the first bookstore about that time.

Shortly after his arrival here he wooed and won the hand of Miss Eliza Jenison, the only daughter of the late Rufus Jenison, one of the prominent farmers of the county; she at that time, although a child in years, was one of the reigning belles of the city.

At the time Mr. C. first came to this place there were very few men that supported the claims of General Jackson to the Presidency. Of the two newspapers then here both opposed the Old Hero, and supported Henry Clay He immediately became known as a warm Jackson man, and was ever found in any assemblage of that kind.

After the election of General Jackson, and in the spring of 1829, he was appointed Postmaster, which position he held through his eight years administration, and four years of Mr. Van Buren's, always taking an active part in political meetings and elections, and he was so violent a partisan that in that ever memorable year, 1840, brought down upon himself the displeasure of some of our best and leading citizens, for whatsoever his hand found to do in a political way he did with all his might. Shortly after the inauguration of General Harrison, in 1841, he resigned, but after the disaffection of President Tyler, from the Whig party, he was replaced in the post office, but held it a short time only.

It was during the time he was postmaster, and through his

exertions, that this was made a distributing office, and also the express mail from Washington and Baltimore via the National Road through this place was established by Amos Kendall, then Postmaster General.

After he had quit the post office the second time he engaged in merchandising, but, owing to dishonest clerks and a temperament not suited to the business, he was not successful.

At that time he owned some very valuable city property, as well as the farm now owned by Calvin Fletcher, Jr., adjoining the city on the Pendleton road; he also owned the ground where that elegant dry goods mart, Trade Palace, is located, and many other pieces of city property, which would now make him very wealthy.

About the year 1847 he sold out his entire property and removed to one of the lower Ohio River counties in Kentucky, bought a farm and mill, and commenced merchandising again. His farm was stocked with negroes, and although he was raised in a slave State he did not understand the managing of them; he thought, in order to keep them under subjection, it was necessary to flog them occasoinally, whether they needed it or not, to give them a proper appreciation of their true situation and his authority. In consequence of this rigorous course the negroes set fire to his mill and store, and almost burned him out of house and home. He then, with his family, returned to Indianapolis, and for awhile kept the Capital House, which was noted for its fine table, for he had ever been a good liver and a bountiful provider for the culinary department of his family; in living he never exercised any economy.

In 1853 he was appointed by President Pierce Indian Agent for Washington Territory, and with his eldest son, Andrew J. Cain, went there and remained some years, and somewhat recuperated his damaged fortune, and returned to his family and remained until his death in 1867. He died very suddenly and unexpected to his family.

John Cain was a generous, warm-hearted man, devoted in his friendship, but equally bitter to his enemies; there was no duplicity or deceit in his composition; there was no mistaking his position on any subject; he never practiced dissimulation in any way; this, if a fault, was his greatest one, and he sometimes made an enemy by his plain, blunt manner of speaking.

As a husband and father he was ever kind and indulgent, and a bountiful provider for the various wants of a family. When I say no more hospitable man in his house ever lived or died in this city, I speak of personal experience of forty-one years, and of which many of the recipients yet living will testify.

He had a very good command of language, and possessed fine conversational powers. In person he was about five feet eight inches in height, a rotund form, inclined to corpulency, and a florid complexion; in movement very quick and active for a person of his build.

Mrs. Cain is yet living, and a resident of the city, and, unlike most ladies, thinks the place of her husband can never be filled on this side the grave. As she was ever a devoted wife, so she is a weeping widow.

JAMES M. SMITH

Was a tailor by trade, a very clever man, but when drinking was quite overbearing and quarrelsome. He was a large, powerful man, without any surplus flesh. Mr. Smith was fond of a fight, but it was intimated that he liked to select his antagonist. When drinking he stood upon his dignity, and sometimes refused to recognize his best and most intimate friends, unless there was a chance for a quarrel.

About the year 1835 there was a Kentuckian, named Nathaniel Vice, who lived a few miles south of town. He was not so large a man as Smith, but more active; he was built like, and as fleet of foot as a deer; he was never beat in a foot race, was never thrown in a wrestle, nor was he ever whipped in a fight. His success in the latter amusement was attributable as much to his activity as to his strength. He used a great deal of language found in the Kentucky vocabulary only; in disposition he was something like Smith, *i. e.*, quarrelsome when drinking, but, unlike him, he was willing to fight any person and under any circumstances.

One evening those two gentlemen met in front of Morely's saloon, that stood opposite the Court House, on Washington street. "Good evening, Mr. Smith," said Vice. "I don't know you," said Smith. "Ah, sir, you don't know Nat Vice, the great boa constrictor of the Universe; then I will introduce you to him." Simultaneous with these words Nat knocked him into the gutter, and then helped him up, took him into the saloon and they drank together as acquaintances, and Mr. Smith always recognized him as such afterwards.

In the year 1844 Mr. Smith went from his shop to his residence at the usual time in the evening, in apparent very good health, and died within half an hour after he reached his house, supposed to be of disease of the heart.

The last I ever saw or heard of Nat Vice was on the levee at New Orleans. He was offering to bet he could out run, throw down, or whip any man in the Mississippi Valley, and I believe he would have won his bet.

JAMES MORRISON.

It is when I attempt to write a fitting tribute to the memory of such a man as Judge Morrison, that I feel the magnitude of the task I have undertaken, and my incompetency to hand down to posterity and future generations, that they may have a proper appreciation of his great legal ability, and his many moral and social virtues.

My acquaintance with Judge Morrison began when I was a

boy, and before he had reached the noonday of life. Forty years ago I was often his fishing companion upon the banks of White River and Fall Creek, he angling for the fine black bass with which those streams abounded at that time, and I for the tiny minnow he used for bait.

He was a great smoker, and carried a tinder-box for the purpose of lighting his cigars (this was before such a thing as locofoco matches was thought of). I have often been attracted to his place of concealment on the banks of these streams by the clatter of his tinder-box, or the curling smoke from his fragrant Havana, rising above the bushes. This was when the vanities and sorry conceits of the world were strangers to me, and when my youthful spirit had known but little of the evils of this inconstant world. It was upon the banks of these streams that I learned much of the true dignity of character he possessed, and before either of us thought we would ever bear the relation of attorney and client to each other, which we did for years afterwards.

Although my hair is now silvered o'er, and my brow bears the marks of time, I have not outlived the memory of those happy days in the early history of this city; the days of so much enjoyment that I passed when a boy, and the reflection of whose pleasures linger with me yet.

In the "Indianapolis Journal" of the 22d of March, 1869, I find the following announcement of his demise:

"The early settlers of the State, and the founders of our city, are dropping off in such close succession that we are warned of the near approach of the time when all shall have passed away, and the birth of Indianapolis have ceased to be a memory to any, and faded into history. Since the beginning of the year two have left us, and in the last decade they far outnumber the years. We cannot think but with profound sorrow of the inevitable hours when all the names so long identified with our prosperity and honored as the links that still bind the present to the past, have ceased to speak a living presence, and to offer a living example of beauty, of goodness, and a well spent life.

"Among all that have left such sad vacancies, no one has filled a more prominent place than the Hon. James Morrison; though for some years his failing strength and feeble health have secluded him from active life, his presence has been felt, his existence has been an influence, and his death is not so much the end of a flickering light as the extinguishment of a gleam that leaves darkness in its place.

"He died on Saturday evening, the 20th Instant, of pneumonia, after an illness of several days."

From the "Indianapolis Sentinel," of the same date, I copy as follows:

"Judge Morrison was born in Ayrshire, Scotland, the birth place of Robert Burns, in the year 1796. His parents came to this country when he was quite young, and settled at Bath, in Western New York. He studied his profession with Judge William B. Rochester, a distinguished jurist of that State, and when admitted to the bar he emigrated to Indiana and located in Charleston, Clark County, where he practiced law for many years with the late Judge Dewey, who was one of the truly great men of the nation.

"He remained in Charleston about ten years, and a gentleman who knew him during his residence there, says his devotion to his family (he was the oldest son) was most remarkable, and that he was their main reliance.

"In the winter of 1828-29, he was elected Secretary of State by the Legislature, and removed to this city, then a town of 1,100 inhabitants, January 1st, 1829. Subsequently he filled the offices of Judge of this Judicial Circuit, President of the State Bank for ten years, succeeding Samuel Merrill, Esq., Attorney General, the first to fill that office, and other trusts of less importance. So high an appreciation had the members of the bar for his qualifications for the judgeship, that they presented him with five hundred dollars to induce him to take it.

"Of the Clark County bar he leaves but two survivors, we believe, Judge Thompson, now in the city, and Judge Naylor, of Crawfordsville.

"Of the Indianapolis bar of 1829, the year he became connected with it, he was, as we recollect, the last, not one now left. Harvey Gregg, William Quarles, Hiram Brown, Henry P. Coburn, B. F. Morris, Andrew Ingram, Samuel Merrill, Calvin Fletcher and William W. Wick, who were his associates then, all passed away before he was called to his final rest.

"As we call the familiar names of those so prominent in the early history of the bar of Indianapolis, the convulsive throbs of many hearts will attest their worth and the appreciation with which their memories are still cherished. Yet the sadness with which we recur to the ties of early associations, and the early friendship of the past thus severed, will give place to the cheering thought that those endearing ties will be renewed, refined and strengthened in the new life upon which they have already entered.

"Judge Morrison was also identified with the history of the church in this city; he was one of the first class that was confirmed here about thirty years ago, and the rite was administered by the now venerable Bishop Kemper, of Wisconsin, who was then Missionary Bishop of the Northwest. For twenty-five years he was Senior Warden of Christ Church, in this city, and since the organization of St. Paul's Church he has filled the same office in that parish. He was educated a Presbyterian, but became a Churchman after thorough investigation, and remained so with steadfastness through life.

"Judge Morrison was a man of decided convictions, strong prejudices, with fixed habits that only physical inability could change or overcome. He had opinions upon all subjects and questions to which his attention was directed, and, as would be expected from his peculiar mental organization, they were always positive even to ultraism. He was thoroughly a lawyer. His eminent talents and active mind were peculiarly adapted to the profession in which he attained such high reputation, only yielding active participation in it when compelled to surrender to the great enemy of man. He was learned and profound, and had thoroughly mastered the science of law.

"As a husband and father Judge Morrison was affectionate, devoted and indulgent, and he leaves a wife, sons and daughters who will, through life, cherish the memory of his many virtues and unfailing affection and kindness."

I cannot add more than I have said in the beginning of this sketch, and what is said in these extracts from the "Journal" and "Sentinel," announcing his death.

> "Friend after friend departs;
> Who hath not lost a friend?
> There is no union here of hearts
> That finds not here an end."

WILLIAM H. MORRISON,

The younger and only survivor of three brothers so prominent in the early history of this city, was born in the city of New York. When a boy he came with his elder brother, the late Judge James Morrison (who was the subject of the preceding sketch), to Charleston, Indiana, where he remained until his brother's election as Secretary of State and removal to this place in the year 1829. He was then quite young and a single man, and has remained a citizen since that time.

His first business, after acting for some time as his brother's clerk in the office of Secretary of State, was that of merchandising in connection with John G. Brown, then one of our prominent and wealthy citizens. Their house of business was on the northwest corner of Washington and Pennsylvania streets, where for several years he was a successful and popular merchant, enjoying the confidence of all who knew him. During this time he was a stockholder in and a director of the branch of the State Bank of Indiana in this city.

He possesses many of the fine traits of character so conspicuous in his brother, Judge Morrison. Warm and devoted in his friendship; and when the citadel of his heart is once gained and possessed by a friend, no effort of enemies can change it. He is also strong in his prejudices; but if he finds himself in the wrong he is quick to make the amende honorable, and set himself aright. He never suffers selfish or groveling feelings to mar the cordiality of affection or interfere with motives so upright and honorable.

Like his brother, he has contributed liberally, and without stint, of his means for the erection of churches of all denominations, and especially for the construction of those two beautiful temples of worship, Christ's and St. Paul's Episcopal Churches. I understand his house has been the home and stopping-place for ministers for several years.

Mr. Morrison has also contributed to the growth and prosperity of the city by the erection of a fine residence on Circle street. He also built that splendid business house on the northeast corner of Maryland and Meridian streets, known as "Morrison's Opera House," at a cost of $65,000; but this fine building was doomed to destruction, and it was entirely destroyed by fire on the evening of January 17th, 1870, taking fire about 9 o'clock, and while John B. Gough was lecturing to a large and fashionable audience within its walls.

The smoke had scarcely disappeared from the smouldering debris before he had, with his accustomed energy, contracted for the rebuilding on the same site another fine business house. He is now President of the "Indiana Banking Company." I called at the bank a few days since and found him at his desk, giving to his business the same attention as was his wont to do some thirty years ago, and with the same dignified and courteous deportment so characteristic of him.

MAJOR ALEXANDER F. MORRISON,

The brother of Judge and William H. Morrison, was born in New York city, but with his brothers came to Charleston, Indiana, in the year 1818. He there learned the printing business. In the Legislature that convened on the first Monday of December, 1830, he represented Clark County, and while here made arrangements to commence in the spring the publication of a weekly paper, to be called the "Indiana Democrat." In accordance with this arrangement Mr. Morrison, with his family, removed to this place early in the spring of 1831.

The "Democrat" was started in the interest of and supported General Jackson for re-election to the Presidency. Mr. Morrison was a ready political writer, and made the "Democrat" a spicy paper. Its editorials would compare favorably with those of the city papers of the present day. He was very bitter toward his opponents, and his articles sometimes read as though he had dipped his pen in gall.

He was engaged from time to time in various kinds of business here during his life. He was one of the "bloody three hundred" that in 1832 went out to meet Black Hawk, but all returned without any other than their own scalps.

During the Mexican war he was a quartermaster in the army, and it was while there his already feeble constitution was greatly impaired. I do not think he ever experienced a well day after his return. His eyes, that were naturally weak, were almost entirely destroyed.

Mr. Morrison was a very kind, generous-hearted man to his friends, but very bitter to his enemies, or those he had reason to believe were such. In his social relations and intercourse with his neighbors, he was deservedly popular, and a very hospitable man. As a husband and father, he was devoted and indulgent, anticipating every want of his family.

Mr. Morrison leaves two sons, Will. Alex. and Charles, and also two daughters, Mrs. Allison and Mrs. Murphy, who, together with their mother, yet reside in the city.

Major Morrison died in December, 1857, at the age of fifty-four, regretted by many old friends and acquaintance.

> "Unfading hope, when life's last embers burn,
> When soul to soul, and dust to dust return."

EBENEZER SHARPE.

To this worthy old gentleman the writer is indebted for the most of what little education he has got. After the venerable James Blake had learned him the A B C's at Sunday school, in Caleb Scudder's cabinet shop, Mr. Sharpe learned him to put them and the balance of the alphabet together and make the b-a ba's, b-i bi's, b-o bo's and b-u bu's, and afterwards to spell b-a-k-e-r baker, c-i-d-e-r cider. Although I could spell the latter we got none of it, as Mr. Sharpe was by practice, as well as precept, a strict temperance man.

He came from Paris, Bourbon County, Kentucky, to this place in the year 1826. Shortly after he came he opened a school in the back part or school-room of the old Presbyterian Church, on the alley that runs north and south between Pennsylvania and Circle streets, north of Market.

Mr. Sharpe was a man of a fine, classical education, and was peculiarly adapted by nature and disposition for the profession of a teacher, mild and genial in his manners, and believed more in moral suasion to gain the respect and obedience of his pupils than he did in the rod, although he sometimes made a gentle application of the latter, never, however, without prefacing its use with a lecture.

He owned and carried an old-fashioned, repeater gold watch that struck the time very musically, by using a spring in the handle; this he was frequently in the habit of sending to his friend, Humphrey Griffith, to compare the time, or to have it regulated; by watching the boys he selected to carry it he found out they were in the habit of starting it to striking as soon as they had reached the outside of the school-house door. He watched the writer, who was also watching him, and did not touch the spring until out of his hearing; consequently he was always after that selected to carry the watch, but was always very careful never to touch the spring within a reasonable distance of the school-house, but enjoyed its musical strains when distant. Mr. Thomas H. Sharpe tells me that he still has this watch.

Among Mr. Sharpe's pupils were Thomas A. and John D. Morris, Hugh O'Neal, Thomas D. and Robert L. Walpole. The former has risen to distinction in his profession, that of civil engineer; the three latter might in theirs, had they paid that attention they should have done to the example and precept of their worthy tutor.

I doubt whether there is a person in the State to-day connected with the cause of education, and our general system of free schools, that understands the practical part of a teacher, or that of the head of an institution of learning, as well as did Mr. Sharpe.

He was ever diligent at his books; his studies were often carried for into the silent watches of the night. He was one of the finest readers we have ever heard, his pronunciation loud, clear and distinct; his emphasis imparted great force to the language. Nor can I forget his daily moral and religious instructions to his pupils, by which he gained their love and the esteem of their parents. It was evident, from the pains that he took in the instruction of his scholars, that he indulged the hope that their parents would some day reap the reward of his honorable labors in the prosperity of their children.

Often in the absence of a minister was he called upon by the congregation to read a sermon, which he would do, and impart to it quite as much interest as though it was original and the first time delivered.

He was Agent of State for the town of Indianapolis for several years before his death, and was then succeeded by his son, Thomas H. Sharpe, Esq., now one of the prominent bankers of this city.

When I recur to the scenes in the old school-house, where I spent a short portion of life's early years, I delight in taking a retrospective view of those days when our never-to-be-forgotten teacher tried so hard to inspire us with the love of knowledge and literature.

Mr. Sharpe brought with him to this place a large family, but few of which are now living. He died in the fall of 1835, at the age of fifty-six,

"Pleased with the present, and full of glorious hope."

His was the largest funeral that had ever been seen in Indianapolis at that time. I do not think there was a vehicle in the place that was not in the procession.

THOMAS H. SHARPE,

The oldest surviving son of the worthy gentleman who was the subject of the preceding sketch, came to this place with his father a mere boy, yet in his teens, but well qualified to assist his father, as he did, in training "the young idea how to shoot."

About the year 1831, he engaged with Arthur St. Clair as a clerk in the Land Office, and had almost entire charge of the immense sales of land in this district; it was then his business qualifications were first developed.

After his father's death he was appointed Agent of State for the town of Indianapolis, a position previously held by his father.

He was appointed teller in the branch of the State Bank of Indiana, and after the retirement of Judge Morris as its cashier, Mr. Sharpe was appointed his successor, and held the place until the affairs of the bank were wound up.

He then engaged with the late Calvin Fletcher in a private bank, and, although Mr. Fletcher is dead, he requested that the business of the bank should be continued by Mr. Sharpe, and without change, the same as if he was yet living.

This is one of the highest encomiums that could be paid to his integrity, worth and merit; for no person knew him so well as Mr. Fletcher; they had been associated in business near twenty years.

It is unnecessary to say that he now has the entire charge of one of the prominent banks in the city, and does quite as large a business as any of them.

Mr. Sharpe has quite a large family of children; in the person of one of them he has brought down to the present time the good name of his father in full, and I hope it will be continued to future generations.

When he first came to this place he was a very active young man, and prided himself on his fleetness of foot, and many was the race he ran with the young men of the place, and was never beaten. He yet steps with an elasticity that leads me to believe he would be hard to beat.

JOHN G. BROWN

Came from Paris, Bourbon County, Kentucky, to this place in 1828. He had been used to negro slavery all his life, but was anxious to rid himself of the negroes as well as slavery, and for that purpose he emancipated his entire stock, both old and young.

But the negroes did not wish to part with Mr. Brown. He was scarcely settled in his new home in this city before several families of his former slaves were his nearest neighbors.

This circumstance speaks volumes in his favor as being a kind-hearted man and a christian, and requires no commendation from my pen.

He purchased of Harvey Gregg property on North Meridian street, where his son James and a daughter still reside. Another daughter is the wife of Stephen D. Tomlinson, another old and respected citizen.

Mr. Brown was a member of the First Presbyterian Church, and during his residence in this city the associate of Mr. Jas. Blake and James M. Ray in many benevolent and charitable organizations, and contributed liberally of his means for those purposes.

He was a man of unostentatious piety, unobtrusive and retiring in his manners, and enjoyed the confidence and respect of all who knew him. He has been dead many years, but his memory still lives fresh in the hearts and minds of his many friends, and his goodness leaves a fragrance behind.

REV. EDWIN RAY.

This talented young minister, in connection with Constant B. Jones, was assigned to the Indianapolis Circuit in the fall of 1826. The circuit then embraced several of the adjoining counties, and it took two weeks to make the round, so that one of them was here every Sunday, and the same one every other Sunday.

They preached in the old log church on the south side of Maryland, on the corner of the alley between Meridian and Illinois streets. It is a well known fact that young ministers have, from time immemorial, possessed the faculty of gathering into their congregations the young ladies of all denominations, as well as those outside the pale of any church.

It is not surprising, then, that the young minister above named should exercise a similar influence, as he was young, talented and good-looking, and just at that period of life when ministers, as well as worldly people, are supposed to be looking for a partner for life.

Suffice it to say that every other Sunday, at least, the beauty and fashion, as well as those that were not the beauty and fashion, of Indianapolis, were assembled in that log church; old maids primped their mouths, and young ones cast their glances and sly looks.

The old maids and mothers were not slow in discovering that the young minister was frequently found accompanying one of the young ladies home who was not a member of the flock, and, oh, what solicitude for the safety of the church, and the cause of our blessed Redeemer, was felt and manifested by them.

There was a family of five of those church and moral guardians more exercised than the rest; they thought that should the young minister bestow his affections outside the church Methodism would suffer beyond redemption.

The consequence was, that great preparations were made for the young minister when he should have accomplished his semi-monthly round; invitations were showered upon him to dine, take tea, etc. Many a yellow-legged chicken's head paid the penalty for the young minister's indiscretions.

Those old maids last referred to usually dressed very plain, in the good old Methodist style; now, it was noticed that a curl sometimes hung down behind the ear, supposed to be intended for the minister's eye, as he was pouring forth the word of God to his devout congregation.

At last one of them, more solicitous for the welfare of the church than the others, ventured to approach him on the subject, and wanted to know if he was aware that the young lady to whom he was paying attention danced: "Yes, she dances," said she; "Oh my, my, my, brother Ray, she dances; how can people be so wicked and sinful!" The only reply she elicited, and comfort she got in her interview with the minister. was, "the wilder the colt the tamer the horse."

The young minister married outside the church, the church survived the shock, and now, instead of the old log church we have eight or ten magnificent Methodist Churches inside of the city limits, and at least two hundred within the territory that then composed his circuit.

Edwin Ray was a man of marked ability, perseverance and industry. He studied and mastered the Latin and Greek languages on horseback, traveling from one appointment to another, and had he lived even to the meridian of life, would have ranked among the first theologians of the country.

He fell a victim to his industry and zeal in the cause in which he was engaged, and died at the house of a friend on the Otter Creek Prairie, in Vigo County, on the 15th day of September, 1831, in the 29th year of his age.

He was born in Montgomery County, Kentucky, near Mt. Sterling, and there entered the ministry, but soon came to Indiana, where there was a wider field for usefulness.

He had but two children, a son and daughter; the daughter has deceased several years since; the son, John W. Ray, is the present Commissioner in Bankruptcy of Indiana, and a resident of this city.

T. R. FLETCHER

Came to Indianapolis a boy in July, 1836, and engaged as a clerk in the dry goods store of Fletcher & Bradley. After the dissolution of partnership of this firm, his uncle, Stoughton A. Fletcher, being the successor, he continued with him as clerk, and then as partner, for several years, and since with his uncle sometime in the banking business. He was successful in the accumulation of money while he was with his uncle, and made this city his home.

He left this place some few years since. For awhile he resided at Chicago; now, I believe, he is at Dayton, Ohio.

About the year 1845 the name of Dick Fletcher, as well as that of Horace Fletcher, William Stewart, Ben and Henry Horn, were as familiar as household words to the people of Indianapolis.

Mr. Fletcher was considered a first-class business man, and possessed more than an ordinary financial ability, and with his strict integrity won the confidence and respect of all who knew him.

BAZIL BROWN,

Like many others I have sketched in this work, would have to be seen to be properly appreciated in personal appearance. I have never seen anything that resembled him, except the English caricature of John Bull; indeed, he possessed many of the qualities claimed for that amiable gentleman by his admirers; his weight would be at least three hundred pounds avoirdupois.

He was a very active man. I have seen him jump from the floor of his bar-room and kick the ceiling, which was of the ordinary height.

He was an extraordinary man in many particulars. He did not know a letter in the alphabet, yet he was well informed on most all subjects, especially political. He was blessed with a very retentive memory, and when he once learned anything it was indelibly stamped upon his mind, and after his wife had read to him from the "Cincinnati Inquirer," "Washington Globe," or "New York Herald," he would quote from them more correct than many persons who had read for themselves; he would speak of what he had seen in them, and used language that would lead a stranger to believe he was a finely educated man, when, in fact, he would not know his own name if he should see it in print.

I was an inmate of the same house with him one year, and have often read the papers to him, and in five minutes after would hear him telling what he had seen in them.

He came to this place from Princeton in the fall of 1829, and kept for many years the principal hotel in the place, which was the Democratic headquarters of the city, as well as that of members of the Legislature.

It was his custom to retire early in the evening, and was the first to rise in the morning. His clerk, Charles Stevens, before closing the house at night, would make out the bills of such travelers as were to leave early in the morning, and Mr. Brown would collect them.

One morning he handed a stranger his bill; the man said "read it to me." Says Mr. B., "I would rather you would read it for yourself." "No," said the man, "you had better read it." Mr. B., shaking his head, said, "I have never read my customers' bills for them." "Well, I can't read," said the man. "Neither can I," said Brown. A bystander had to be called to read it for them.

Mr. Brown was very fond of the society of ladies, and when he wished to spend an evening with them had a very good excuse to furnish the old lady, in the fact that he was a Mason, and was going to the lodge.

While myself and wife were boarding at the same house with him, we often called in his room to see Mrs. Brown. One evening, while we were there, the old gentleman came to the door; addressing his wife, he said: "Well, mother, when you get ready you can retire, I am going to the lodge." "Well, well," said she, "when you get through at the lodge come home." After the old man had left, she addressed my wife, looking me in the eye, "Melie, when you get old and ugly like grandma, Johnny will be going to the lodge, too."

I am happy to say that, although Mr. Brown was very

assiduous in his attendance upon the lodge, it never created any unpleasantness between him and the old lady.

Their greatest trouble was the lack of children of their own. They were very fond of them, but Providence had so decreed that no little Browns should cheer their fireside.

When Mr. Brown kept hotel he made his bar-room a very interesting place to his guests, and others that might call, by his inexhaustible fund of anecdotes, which he told with a gusto, and never failed to amuse his auditory.

He died on the 2d of February, 1849, and his remains lie in one of the city cemeteries.

STEPHEN PITTS

Came to the vicinity of this place in the year 1827, and soon rose to distinction in his profession—that of trapper and hunter; indeed, there were but few coons within twenty miles of this place but knew him by reputation, and none wished to extend it to a personal acquaintance; or if they knew of his intention to call on them, would make it convenient to be from home, or, like the ladies of the present day, have him told so; or, if he should come upon them unexpectedly, they would, like Captain Scott's coon, *come down* and surrender, sometimes without a struggle.

He was familiar with every "otter slide," or musk rat hole, between Strawtown and the bluffs of White River, and many an unsuspecting mink fell a victim to his *deep laid* schemes.

Mr. Pitts was a man that minded his own business, paid his debts, voted the unterrified Democratic ticket, and worshipped God according to his own conscience; he was a back-woodsman in every sense of the word. He died many years since.

His only surviving son, George W. Pitts, yet resides in the city, and is one of the *coolest* men, in his business transactions, we have ever known: however, he is not willing to confine his coolness to himself, but is anxious to keep his neighbors *cool*, also, at the rate of twenty-five cents per hundred weight: where his father once speared the salmon, trapped the otter and shot the musk rat, George now cuts and gathers his beautiful crystal ice.

He also has a daughter, the wife of John L. McCormick. one of our most enterprising and industrious master carpenters, who is the nephew of John McCormick, who built the first log cabin in Indianapolis.

THOMAS McOUAT

Was born and raised in Falkirk, Scotland, and came to the United States and settled in Lexington in the year 1816; in 1818 he was married to the daughter of George Lockerbie, another of Scotia's sons, whose sketch will follow this.

Mr. McOuat first visited Indianapolis in the fall of 1821, in attendance upon the sale of lots that occurred on the 10th of October of that year. He purchased several lots, some of which are yet owned by his heirs. He did not move to this place until the fall of 1830.

In the spring of 1831 he bought a stock of goods at Louisville, Kentucky, and shipped them for this port " on that elegant double-decker, lower-cabin, fast-sailing steamer 'The General Hanna,'" and took a first-class passage himself. It was four weeks from the time the noble steamer entered the mouth of White River until she entered this port. Mr. McOuat's family not hearing from him after they left Louisville until their arrival here, were very uneasy about him. Nor was his situation a pleasant one. As the steamer wound her way along the meanderings of the river, I have no doubt he often thought of the land of the thistle, "Ye banks and braes of bonny doon," and other beautiful streams of his native land; he had time, and the circumstances were calculated to inspire meditation. As he was the only person that ever traveled as a steamboat passenger from Louisville to this place, I hope the reader will pardon a digression from the main subject, and should I get somewhat poetical when writing of our own beautiful White River, I would still ask forbearance, as 'tis but seldom anything of the kind drops from the point of my pen.

As the beautiful river winds its serpentine course through the south-western portion of the State, its waters are covered from either bank with various hanging wood and vines, calculated to inspire the solitary passenger with thoughts of the great Creator and the majesty of his works. But by the stroke of the woodman's ax those beautiful scenes have been removed and have disappeared, as well as all hope of navigating White River successfully by steam; and its placid waters have ever been undisturbed by the paddles of a steamer, with the exception of those of the late "Governor Morton."

And now, instead of the scenery I have described, we have in their place those beautiful farms extending from this city to the mouth of the river, which show that the hardy pioneer had been there and brought with him a liberal share of intelligence and industry, and has made the wilderness the happy homes of thousands yet unborn. But enough of this.

Mr. McOuat was a man devoted to his family and the enjoyment of home, and the society of friends. With the Scotch poet, he might well exclaim:

> "I view with mair than kingly pride
> My hearth a heaven: O, rapture,
> My Mary's hand in mine will glide
> As Jockie reads the chapter."

Mr. McOuat died in the fall of 1838, a year long to be remembered for sickness and mortality. He left a wife and a family of several children.

George, the eldest son—what shall I say of George, farther than that he is one of the wheel-horses that drew the Democratic wagon, and has never tired, even when the load was heavy and the feed was light, but ever ready at his post; and when the wagon got in the mud (as it has sometimes), he put his herculean strength to it and did all in his power to get it out. He is one of the business men of the city, owns some fine property, and enjoys the unbounded confidence and respect of all who know him.

Robert L. and Andrew are engaged in the wholesale and retail stove, tin ware and house-furnishing business, and are much respected for their probity and their universal kind and accommodating disposition to their customers, and liberality to the church and benevolent institutions.

The eldest daughter, Elizabeth, is the wife of Ovid Butler, Esq., a retired lawyer, and one of our most exemplary Christians and worthy citizens. Another daughter is the wife of Obed Foote, of Paris, Illinois, son of Obed Foote, Esq., one of the early citizens of this city.

> "Dear to my spirit, Scotland, hast thou been,
> Since infant years, in all thy glens of green.
> Land of my birth, where every sound and sight
> Comes in soft melody, or melts in light.
> Land of the green wood, by the silver rill,
> The heather and the daisy of the hill.
> The guardian thistle to the foeman stern.
> The wild rose, hawthorn, and the lady fern."

GEORGE LOCKERBIE.

This Birkie "old Scotch gentleman" was born and raised in Dumfries, South of Scotland. He came to the United States in the year 1809, and for several years lived in Philadelphia. He then migrated to Lexington, Kentucky, and there resided until the year 1831, when he removed to this place.

Mr. Lockerbie was a man of more than ordinary native talent, well read and conversant with Scottish authors, particularly with the writings and poems of Robert Burns, his favorite author.

He had a quotation on the tip of his tongue for most all

occasions. How oft have we heard the old gentleman quoting this—

> "Some books are lies fra end to end,
> And some great lies were never penned.
> E'en ministers, they ha been ken'd
> In holy rapture,
> A rousing whid at times to vend
> And nair twa Scripture."

I have often seen him and his old friend, the late Judge Morrison, together talking of the father-land, and relating anecdotes and incidents connected with it. He was a man of great vivacity and life, and his society was almost a sure antidote for hypocondria; his very appearance indicated goodness of heart, honesty of purpose and cheerfulness and contentment of mind, a smile and playful remark for all. The old man was fond of a glass of Scotch ale or beer, and would accompany his glass with this sentiment:

> "We are na fon, we're na that's fon
> But just a droppie in our ee;
> The cock may craw, the day may daw
> But aye, we'll taste barley brie."

In height he was about five feet eight or nine inches, quite fleshy, round, smooth features, a florid complexion, full, ruddy cheeks that hung down, and when he laughed his whole body seemed to enjoy it.

Mr. Lockerbie was invested with a certain dignity, sufficient to produce a respect that would have been denied an ordinary man, and always commanded it from the high as well as low, either of whom he treated with the same courtesy and gentlemanly demeanor.

He was proud of his nativity, and loved to talk of the land of the thistle. He possessed much of the agility of youth, with a considerable degree of strength for one of his advanced age.

He has a daughter, Mrs. McOuat, and several grand children living in the city, of whom I have spoken in the preceding sketch. He died in the year 1856, regretted by all who knew him, and is worthy this epitaph, written by his favorite author:

> "An honest man here lies at rest,
> As e'er God with his image blest.
> The friend of man, the friend of truth,
> The friend of age, and guide of youth.
> Few hearts like his with virtue warmed;
> Few heads with knowledge so informed.
> If there's another world he lives in bliss;
> If there is none, he made the best of this."

JOSEPH LOFTON,

The father of Doctors Sample and Alman Lofton, and Joseph, was a native of Davidson County, North Carolina. He came to Marion County, and lived awhile in Pike township, in the year 1827; he then returned to his native State for a short time, but again came to Indiana, and lived a short time in Lawrence County, but was not satisfied until he was again a citizen of Pike township, where he died.

Mr. Lofton was a Jackson man, and a warm supporter of the old hero in all his campaigns for the Presidency, and afterward a strong and warm friend and member of the Democratic party. He is well represented in that particular by his three sons above alluded to.

Joseph is one of the wheel-horses of the party in Pike township, and 'tis said can make as long and as strong a pull, when the load is heavy and roads are bad, as any one; though he is a poor horse to go down hill, he can't be made to back and wants to go as fast as possible; neither does he ever look back or balk, but always keeps his collar warm and dislikes to pull with a cold one. He is one of the prosperous farmers of the county, and trades a great deal in stock of all kinds.

Dr. Sample Lofton is also a farmer, of Wayne township, and trader, and furnished the government with many fine horses during the war.

Dr. Alman Lofton is a practicing physician of Augusta, in the northwest portion of the county, and is universally respected as a man as well as a physician.

Neither of the M. D.'s will allow Joseph to outdo them in their devotion to the old party and its principles, although it forms a considerable portion of his religion.

The three brothers are large, fine-looking men, and in their personal appearance indicate that they are in the enjoyment of a goodly share of this word's goods, with philosophy enough to enjoy life as they go along, and in the possession of cheerful dispositions, casting a glow of good feelings around them, and Joseph's smiling countenance "smiles to the smiling morrow," and with his social qualities and large fund of anecdotes which he relates to his numerous friends, renders him a very interesting personage.

JOHN F. HILL

Came to Indianapolis a mere boy in May, 1830, from near Urbana, Champaign County, Ohio, where he was born on the 24th of October, 1812. Mr. Hill became a pupil of Thomas D. Gregg, who at that time taught school on the corner of Market and Delaware streets, where "the young idea was taught to *fire*."

He then engaged with the Steam Mill Company as a clerk in their store for three years, at a salary of thirty dollars for the first year, to be doubled every year until the expiration of the term of his engagement; for the entire three years' services he received two hundred and ten dollars, less than some clerks in Indianapolis now get for one month.

After a short respite he re-engaged with the same company, which was composed of James Blake, James M. Ray, Nicholas McCarty and Joseph M. Moore, and remained with them until the year 1848. He was then offered and accepted a partnership with Daniel and James Yandes. They, as partners, did business three years; then, as partner of Isaac N. Phipps & Co., afterwards with W. W. Wright & Co., then as Hill & Wright. Finding that close confinement was impairing his health, he quit the mercantile business and engaged in the manufacture of brick with S. V. B. Noel as a partner; in 1850 changed partners, engaged with Levi Rogers in the same business, and in 1856 was a partner of the late James J. Drum in the wholesale grocery business. Of the many partners that Mr. Hill has had, from time to time, all are living with the exception of his brother-in-law, Mr. Drum; and of the many persons he did business for but two have passed away, viz., Mr. McCarty and Joseph M. Moore.

Mr. Hill is now engaged in the nursery business in the eastern confines of the city, where he owns many acres, for which he has been offered one thousand dollars per acre. He owns a fine private residence on North Alabama, between Market and Ohio streets; so the reader will readily perceive he has not slept away the forty years he has been a resident of Indianapolis.

He is the brother of the first wife of the late Calvin Fletcher, likewise a brother of that staid old farmer, Mr. James Hill, who, also, resides near the city, and looks as though he had a common lifetime yet before him.

Another brother, William, yet lives in the vicinity, but the writer for the past few years has lost track of him, but has no doubt that where e'er he be he is trying to "turn an honest penny," as was ever his wont to do.

In the "Indianapolis Gazette" of December 25, 1827, I find this allegory. It was supposed at the time to have been written by the editor, Mr. N. Bolton, and that he intended it (although figuratively) to apply to his uncle, Mr. Nathaniel Cox.

AN ALLEGORY.

"Truth under fiction I impart,
To weed out folly from the heart."—MOORE.

December spread her frosts around,
  And with her whitest snows she dressed
The rich, black earth; the frozen ground;
  Dame nature's cold and chilly breast.
To sweat, and cure my ague chills,
  I took my morning's early race;
It led me through thickets, over hills
  Where nature wore a "blue-cold" face.
Seated upon a walnut log,
  I gnawed upon my morning prog.
    The trees cracked quite o'er me
    To Boreas' loud blast,
    The sun shined before me;
    The stream is froze fast.
When lo! I saw a human form
  Shivering before me stand,
Clad quite too light to stand a storm,
  He held to me his hand.
His robe was hanging on his back,
  His hat a great raccoon-skin cap,
His eye mocked ebony; so black
  And scowling deep that eye did snap.
Such features, and afraid to run,
  In true Dutch rage I cried,
Good, sir. don't shoot me with that gun
  "Mistake me not," the man replied;
"I am, bold sir, a *hunter* brave;
  My house is in yon morass fair,
But hunting lodges still I have,
  All thro' the woods as well as there.

An Allegory.

O'er bluff and brook; o'er stump and stick,
    Thro' this great wild I roam around;
I have a blind at every lick,
    High or low; on tree or ground.
Apart from human creatures I
    Have lived e'er since I was a boy;
I shoot the wild geese soaring high;
    Come see me squirrel nests destroy;
Go where deep Pogue creek's waters dash,
    And o'er old sodden logs down pour,
'Twas I that peeled that big swamp ash,
    I burnt that hollow sycamore.
I mustered many a dog and pup,
    I gave command; a fox they chased;
I ripped, when caught, his bowels up;
    'Twas I that gave to each a taste.
A ground hog ran up sapling tall,
    At him I took a deadly aim;
By bullet then I made him fall,
    By death his carcass lay quite tame.
Possums all have feared my dogs,
    E'er since one rainy day,
In hollow trees and hollow logs,
    Full forty they did slay;
Or since we watched the pigeon roost,
    Or eke the turkey's nest;
By night they made some bite the dust,
    By day I shot the rest.
These shall suffice:—yet I could name
    A thousand muskrats I have skinned;
A thousand more now dread my fame,
    Their ranks, like me, no man e'er thinn'd.
'Tis thus I sway the small beasts' hearts,
But yet I act much nobler parts;
Old bear and cub, or sick or sound
I rule the world of bears around;
From tree top down to brush heap low,
I ever stand of bears the foe,
In corn field or asleep in den,
Robbing a garden or hog pen,

I hold a weapon that can send
His ursine soul to its last end.
Soon as he grows big enough
To run abroad and growl quite gruff,
Upon his track I send a hound;
I chase him 'till I run him down;
I seize him, weary, by the tail
If every other hold should fail.
'Tis then with joy I smile to see
Him strive to get away from me.
Next then if he get in a passion
His back I quickly lay the lash on;
I teach him all obedience,
Or else I learn him impudence;
Then thro' his various after ages,
Whether peace or war he wages,
I am"— "Bow wow," a voice spoke now,
"Bow wow bow wow wow wow wow wow."
I looked and saw, of skin and bone,
A starving dog came barking on;
Impetuously I broke and run,
Determined man and dog to shun;
I turned about; they both were gone,
I turned again and toddled on.

PHILO PHILIATROS.

In the "Indianapolis Gazette," of February 20, 1826, I find this ballad, and re-publish it as a specimen of old style literature.

A PATHETIC BALLAD.

A lady gay once *pensive* sat
All under a willow tree,
And, "Oh," said she, "for a wealthy man
To come and marry me."

Then up stepped Abner Tompkins bold,
"Oh lady gay," said he,
"I am a rich and handsome man,
And I will marry thee."

A Pathetic Ballad.

Then out he took a heavy purse,
And chink'd it in his hands,
"All this is mine," said he, "and more
In houses and in lands."

The lady's heart was then subdued;
"Oh, Abner dear," said she,
"Receive my plight, thou handsome man,
All under this willow tree."

And so he did, but oh, how soon
Do earthly prospects crash,
And sad the fate of ladies gay
Who sell their hearts for cash.
Too soon she found his boastful talk
A base, deceitful lure;
And he who seemed so very rich
Now turned out very poor.

The purse he chink'd held borrowed cash
(Oh vile, perfidious lover),
And all his houses and his lands
Were mortgaged four times over.

Ah, fate, how busy wilt thou be
Rudely our fortunes moulding.
That lady never more took tea,
But took to rum and scolding.

And Abner Tompkins had his due
For all his lying speeches;
She clawed his visage black and blue,
And ragged went his breeches.

And nightly to the pond he'd go
And sit among the bushes,
And hear the bull-frogs sullen plunge,
And crouch among the rushes.

One night as he sat there, he saw
A sight that made him shudder;
'Twas Mrs. Tompkins floating down
Without a sail or rudder.

"My dear," said he, "you've drown'd yourself
All in this pond of water,
And soon as ever I can strip
I'll in and follow after."

So off he takes his coat and shirt,
And eke his ragged breeches;
He plunges in—the night wind moans,
He sinks, the screech-owl screeches.

Now all ye handsome gentlemen,
Boast not of borrowed cash so;
And ladies gay sell not your hearts,
Lest your bright hopes may crash so.

DEATH OF THE POTTAWATAMIE PROPHET.

The Pottawatamie prophet died suddenly during the winter of 1825-26, and, as usual, his death was attributed to witchcraft. The surviving relatives determined who was the witch and resolved to avenge his death. The unfortunate woman (who they selected as their victim), with her husband, was at the house of a trader, when two brothers and a nephew of the prophet arrived and avowed their determination to kill her. They told the family of the trader not to be under any apprehension, as no injury would be done them.

They then directed the unfortunate woman to sit down, and one of them struck her a violent blow on the head, another gave her a second blow, and the third cut her throat.

They then dug a grave and buried her. The husband was a spectator to these proceedings, and after they terminated was compelled to pass over the grave, that she might not return, and was then made to run around a tree and depart as though he had escaped without their permission.

The last manœuver was to prevent the return of the prophet to reproach them for sparing the life of the husband.

This was not the Shawnee prophet, and brother of Tecumseh, that commanded at the battle of Tippecanoe.

The killing of this woman occurred on Eel River, above Logansport. We have had the place pointed out to us frequently.

JAMES FORSEE.

In the "Indianapolis Gazette," of the 27th of November, 1827, we find this advertisement:

JAMES FORSEE,
ATTORNEY AT LAW,

Having recommenced his professional labors, offers his services to his friends generally. He will attend the several Courts within the Fifth Judicial Circuit, and may be found at his office in the second story of Paxton & Bates' brick building, in the town of Indianapolis, at any hour, except whilst on the circuit. Such business as may be entrusted to his care, in the Marion circuit, except in criminal cases, will meet with the joint services of James Whitcomb. Indianapolis, January 4, 1827.

Mr. Forsee was from Elkhorn, Franklin County, Kentucky. He professed to be a lawyer, but knew as little about it as any person we ever knew, to make as much profession as he did. He was full of bombast, and used language that he nor any one else understood the meaning of.

To hear him talk you would think him wealthy, and that he lived in magnificent style. His household furniture consisted of one or two old bedsteads, a few chairs, a puncheon table, and a few half-starved dogs.

He wore a cap of coon skin made by drawing the ends of the skin together, so that when the cap was on his head that part of the skin that covered the animal's nose protruded over his, and the tail hanging down his back, the skin retained the original shape. The body that contained the head and brains of the profound attorney presented a rather bulged appearance, and he might be thought to be carrying a large-sized coon upon his head.

He was a large man, with blood-red hair, his face as red as a turkey's nose. His team was a pair of small steers, both of which were not as heavy as a common-sized cow. Before the steers he hitched an old grey mare, that most likely resembled "Tam O'Shanter's" mare Meg. With this team he would haul about a third of a cord of wood to town, for which he would receive twenty-five or thirty-one cents. He was fond of boasting of his rise in the world, and of being an entirely self-made man, and what a man might make of himself with perseverance and industry, and how he had rose from obscurity to his high position as a lawyer. He lived on the donation line just north of where the "Blind Asylum" now stands. He and his son Peter were plowing in a field near his house, when the following instructions he was giving Peter were overheard:

"Peter," said he, "take an object and plow direct to it, then your furrows will be straight. Just so in life, Peter, you must take an object and plow straight to it. It was so with me, my son; I took the law for an object, I plowed straight, and my furrows were even. You see, Peter, what I have made of myself. I now stand at the head of the legal profession in the capital of Indiana, and next to me stands my law partner, James Whitcomb, Esq., of Monroe County. Peter, you have advantages that but few young men enjoy, and you should improve them."

Mr. Forsee's daughter, Mary Jane, partook a great deal of her father's pride as well as looks. Her hair was as red as that of her father. She wore it in a water-fall on the top of her head. Her face was the color of a turkey egg, but rather more speckled. She had a great passion for jewelry, which was gratified by her indulgent father.

She said "it was very difficult to get such articles of jewelry here as her father wished her to wear; her father had sent to 'Sinsinnaty,' by Mr. McCarty, and bought her a pure silver ring; it cost him three quarters of a dollar."

Mary Jane was invited to a quilting and log-rolling at Judge McIlvain's. As soon as she was seated at the quilt she began to apologize for her lack of jewelry. She said "she had broke her ring; that dad had a large log to load on the *slide*, and she, in helping him, had broken her ring, and that dad had taken it to the *dentists* to have it fixed, but it could not be fixed in time for her to wear it to the quilting."

She said "in Kaintuck, whar they come from, 'twarn't fashionable to war jewelry, but she reckoned 'twas case they hadn't got none. Dad said nobody wurn't nothin' here that didn't ware no jewelry, so he got me that nice ring."

Mr. Forsee moved from this place to the Indian Reserve, thence to California, where he, no doubt, stands high in his profession, and can indulge his daughter in her admiration for jewelry, and where no doubt Peter has taken an object and plows his furrows straight.

"O wad some power the giftie gie us
To see oursels as others see us;
It wad frae monie a blunder free us,
And foolish notion."

THE HOOSIER NEST.

Forty years ago this morning (January 1st, 1870) the carriers of the "Indiana Journal" handed their patrons and the citizens of Indianapolis the following lines as their "New Year's Address."

It was republished at the time throughout Europe and America, and is worthy of being perpetuated as a graphic sketch of Hoosier life.

It was written by John Finley, a tanner of Richmond, Indiana, at that time a member of the Legislature:

Untaught the language of the schools,
Nor versed in scientific rules,

The humble bard may not presume
The Literati to illume;
Or classic cadences indite
Attuned "to tickle ears polite;"
Contented if his strains may pass
The ordeal of the common mass,
And raise an anti-critic smile,
The brow of labor to beguile.

But ever as his mind delights
To follow Fancy's airy flights,
Some object of terrestrial mien
Uncourteously obtrudes between,
And rudely scatters to the winds
The tangled threads of thought he spins.
Yet why invoke imagination
To picture out a new creation,
When nature, with a lavish hand,
Has formed a more than Fairy land
For us. An Eldorado real,
Surpassing even the ideal.

Then who can view the glorious West,
   With all her hopes for coming time,
And hoard his feelings unexpressed
   In poetry, or prose, or rhyme.
What mind and matter unrevealed
   Shall unborn ages here disclose;
What latent treasures long concealed
   Be disinterred from dark repose.
Here science shall impel her car
   O'er blended valley, hill and plain;
While Liberty's bright, natal star
   Shines twinkling on her own domain.
Yes, land of the West, thou art happy and free,
And thus ever more may thy hardy sons be;
Whilst thy ocean-like prairies are spread far and wide,
Or a tree of thy forest shall tower in pride.

Blest Indiana, in thy soil
Are found the sure rewards of toil;

The Hoosier Nest.

Where harvest, purity and worth
May make a paradise on earth.
With feelings proud we contemplate
The rising glory of our State,
Nor take offense, by application,
Of its good-natured appellation.
Our hardy yeomanry can smile
At tourists of the "sea-girt isle;"
Or wits who traveled at the gallop,
Like Basil Hall, or Mrs. Trollope;
'Tis true, among the crowds that roam
To seek for fortune or a home,
It happens that we often find
Empiricism of every kind.

A strutting fop, who boasts of knowledge
Acquired at some far Eastern college,
Expects to take us by surprise,
And dazzle our astonished eyes;
He boasts of learning, skill and talents,
Which, in the scale, would Andes balance;
Cuts widening swaths from day to day,
And in a month he runs away.
Not thus the honest son of toil
Who settles here to till the soil,
And, with intentions just and good,
Acquires an ample livelihood;
He is (and not the little great)
The bone and sinew of the State:
With six-horse team, to one-horse cart,
We hail them here from every part.
And some you'll see *sans* shoes or socks on,
With snakepole and a yoke of oxen;
Others with pack-horse, dog and rifle,
Make emigration quite a trifle.

The emigrant is soon located,
In Hoosier life initiated;
Erects a cabin in the woods,
Wherein he stows his household goods.

At first round logs and clap-board roof,
With puncheon floor, quite carpet proof,
And paper windows, oiled and neat,
His edifice is then complete.
When four clay balls, in form of plummet,
Adorn his wooden chimney's summit;
Ensconced in this, let those who can
Find out a truly happier man.
The little youngsters rise around him,
So numerous they quite astound him;
Each with an ax, or wheel in hand,
And instinct to subdue the land.

Ere long the cabin disappears;
A spacious mansion next he rears.
His fields seem widening by stealth,
An index of increasing wealth.
And when the hives of Hoosiers swarm
To each is given a noble farm.
These are the seedlings of the State,
The stamina to make it great.
'Tis true, her population various
Finds avocations multifarious.
But having said so much, 'twould seem
No derogation to my theme
Were I to circumscribe the space
To picture but a single case;
And if my muse be not seraphic,
I trust you'll find her somewhat graphic.

I'm told, in riding somewhere West,
A stranger found a *Hoosier's Nest*.
In other words, a Buckeye cabin,
Just big enough to hold Queen Mab in;
Its situation low, but airy,
Was on the borders of a prairie,
And fearing that he might be benighted
He hailed the house, and then alighted.
The Hoosier met him at the door,
Their salutations soon were o'er.

The Hoosier Nest.

He took the stranger's horse aside
And to a sturdy sapling tied;
Then having stripped the saddle off,
He fed him in a sugar trough.
The stranger stooped to enter in,
The entrance closing with a pin,
And manifested strong desire
To seat him by the log-heap fire,
Where half a dozen Hoosieroons,
With mush and milk, tin cups and spoons,
White heads, bare feet and dirty faces,
Seemed much inclined to keep their places.
But madam, anxious to display
Her rough but undisputed sway,
Her offspring to the ladder led
And cuffed the youngsters up to bed.

Invited, shortly, to partake
Of venison, milk and Johnny cake,
The stranger made a hearty meal
And glances round the room would steal.
One side was lined with divers garments,
The other spread with skins of *varmints*,
Dried pumpkins over head were strung,
Where venison hams in plenty hung.
Two rifles placed above the door,
Three dogs lay stretched upon the floor.
In short the domicil was rife
With specimens of Hoosier life.
The host, who centered his affections
On game, and *range* and quarter sections,
Discoursed his weary guest for hours,
Till Somnus' all-composing powers
Of sublunary cares bereft 'em,
And then I came away and left 'em.
No matter how the story ended,
The application I intended
Is from the famous Scottish poet,
Who seemed to feel, as well as know it,
That burly chiels and clever hizzies
Are bred in sic a way as this is.

JOHN W. HOLLAND.

This worthy gentleman was one of four brothers that, with their father, came to this city at an early day—George, John, David and Johnson. Their father, John Holland, Sr., came about the year 1826, and for many years kept a family grocery.

John W. Holland came in the year 1830; since which time he has been engaged in active business. For some years he was a clerk in the dry goods store of Conner & Harrison, and then as a partner of the late A. W. Russell. I suppose he has cut as much tape, measured as many six yards of calico (at that time a dress pattern), weighed as many half dollars' worth of coffee, and taken in exchange therefor as many pounds of butter, dozens of eggs, yards of flax and tow linen, and pounds of maple sugar, as any person now living in the city. He is now the business and active partner in that large and popular wholesale grocery establishment of Holland & Ostermeyer, on the south side of Maryland, between Pennsylvania and Meridian streets.

Mr. Holland has long been one of the leading members of the Methodist Church in this city. We remember him, near forty years since, leading the Thursday evening prayer meeting that worshipped in the first brick church built in Indianapolis, and situated where the "Sentinel" office now stands.

Johnson, his youngest brother, died many years ago; George only about six months since. John is the only one of the original family that came here that is living in the city.

His son, Theodore F. Holland, is the book-keeper in the establishment of his father, a worthy young man. If all would do as he did, and expressed himself that others should do, *i. e.*, that all who were born in this city should subscribe for this book, my humble efforts would at least be a *financial* success. I take this opportunity to thank him for his timely remark.

Theodore married the only daughter of Thomas M. Smith, another of the old citizens of this city, but at present, and for a few years past, a resident of Louisville, Kentucky.

STOUGHTON A. FLETCHER, Sr.

Mr. Fletcher is one of the citizens that came in the second decade of the settlement of the city. He came here in October, 1831, a young man, unencumbered with wife or any other valuables, but with a robust and healthy constitution an ambitious disposition, industrious and temperate habits, and a temperament that suited itself to the surrounding circumstances. Such was Mr. F. when we first made his acquaintance.

He did not engage immediately in active business, but made his home with his brother, the late Calvin Fletcher.

In the mean time, June, 1832, a call was made by Governor Noble for three hundred good and trusty riflemen, who were willing to peril their lives, gird on their armor and march against the bloody "Ingins" in defense of the frontier settlements and the defenseless women and children.

Mr. Fletcher was among the first to volunteer and arm himself with a long-range rifle, a tomahawk, scalping knife, a camp kettle, coffee pot, a wallet of hard tack, and went forth to meet the dusky Black Hawk, in that ever memorable campaign, as one of the "Bloody Three Hundred," which lasted just three weeks. None distinguished themselves more, or returned with brighter laurels to the fireside of kindred and friends, than did Mr. Fletcher. This expedition was something like that of the king of France,

"Who with all his men
Marched up the hill, and then down again."

Soon after his return from the "Black Hawk War," he engaged in merchandising in connection with the late Henry Bradly, and then with different partners, and alone, and was a successful and popular merchant for several years. Indeed he prospered in everything he undertook, which would lead a person to think that there was something more than luck in success. I hardly know what it is, or what to call it, unless it is " true grit."

He was the first to start as a private banker in the city, and is now, and has been for years, one of the leading bankers of the place. I understand that he, as well as his brother Calvin, rendered material and substantial aid to the Government during the rebellion, by advancing funds to pay bounties and encourage enlistments; indeed more was to be done in this way than by shouldering the musket and enlisting themselves.

Mr. Fletcher owns some of the finest farms in White River valley, and has them worked and conducted in such a way as to make them remunerative to him as well as beneficial to the country, furnishing employment to a large number of laborers, and bread and comfortable homes for their families. Should I say that fifty families received their support from the farms of Mr. Fletcher, I do not think it would be an exaggeration.

That he is entirely free from the envy of others less fortunate than himself, I will not pretend to say, for there are many

> "Men that make
> Envy and crooked malice nourishment,
> Dare bite the best."

In thirty-nine years of an acquaintance with Mr. Fletcher, we have got to hear the first person say that he violated any contract with them, either written or verbal, but lived up to it to the letter; prompt in all his engagements, he expects others to be so with him.

He is a man of warm personal feelings, and if he becomes attached to a person will go any length to serve or accommodate him. It was but recently a business man of this city told me had it not been for Mr. F.'s friendship for him during the war, his family would have been turned out of their home and he bankrupt.

A prominent business man of the city, that has transacted business with him for several years, says he has often went to him when in great need of money, but was never charged more than the regular rate of interest; indeed, if he accommodates a person at all it will be at the regular rates; he never takes advantage of the necessities of his customers.

He is a man of considerable vivacity and life, and now, as well as in his younger days, enjoys a joke, many of which we have heard pass between him and his old friend Peck, when we were all inmates of the same house several years ago,

> "Wi merry songs an' friendly cracks
> I wat they did not weary,
> An' unco tales, and funnie jokes
> Their sports were cheap and cheery."

He is not ostentatious in his display of favors, and as far as he is concerned it is kept within his own bosom. He is a contributor to nearly all the benevolent and charitable institutions, although his name seldom stands conspicuous on the subscription list.

He is, also, a man of great firmness and decision, and after weighing a matter well in his mind, and coming to a conclusion, he is as immovable as a mountain, and his conclusions are generally correct, which is one of the great secrets of his unprecedented success in business. He is well versed in human nature, and it does not take him long to make up his mind of those that circumstances or business brings him in contact with.

I know several young men that owe all they are and have to Mr. Fletcher's aid and liberality, and are now on the high road to wealth, if it has not already been attained.

He has done, and is yet doing, a great deal for the country at large with the means God has placed in his hands; I see evidences of it pass my door daily. In conclusion, I would merely say, in the language of Rip Van Winkle's favorite toast, "May he live long and prosper."

EDWIN J. PECK,

Like his old and particular friend, the subject of the preceding sketch, came to Indianapolis unburthened with the cares of a family, and a stranger to its pleasures.

He came from near New Haven, Connecticut, to this place, in May, 1833. He was the superintendent of the masonry and brick work of the State House.

It was not Mr. Peck's intention to make a home in the West when he first came to it, but after being here some two years in the capacity above stated, he became so much attached to western customs and manners that he concluded to cast his lot with his new-made friends and acquaintances, and make Indianapolis his permanent home.

After the State House was finished (which was in the fall of 1836), he had the superintendency and contract for building several important houses in different parts of the State—among which were the Branch Bank buildings at Madison, Terre Haute, Lafayette and South Bend.

He was for sometime, during its prosperous days, a director of the Madison and Indianapolis Railroad Company, during which time its stock was worth from twenty-five to thirty per cent. premium.

He was foremost in getting up the Indianapolis and Terre Haute Railroad Company, and accompanied the engineers along the route when it was being surveyed and located, taking a lively interest in its beginning and then in its completion. He was the first treasurer of the company and remained as such for several years after its completion; then its president and a large stockholder. There is no person to whom the friends of this popular road are more indebted for making it what it is to-day—one of the best paying roads in the West, and its high and enviable reputation as a well-conducted thoroughfare—than they are to Edwin J. Peck.

He has been connected with the management of the road from its beginning (now nineteen years) up to the present time, being a portion of that time its president. He was, also, president of the Union Railway and Depot Company, the tracks of which are used by the several railroad companies in entering and leaving the Union Depot.

The by-laws of the latter company required that the president of it should be selected from the presidents of the different railroad companies that ran into it; but when Mr. Peck resigned the presidency of the Terre Haute and Indianapolis Company, such was the appreciation of his services that they changed their by-laws, and he is yet the Superintendent of the Depot and the several tracks that run into it.

I understand that it is to Mr. Peck the citizens of this city, as well as the traveling public, are indebted for having a Union Depot at all, most of the citizens thinking it would be an injury to the city, and make it nothing more than a way station where the passenger would merely pass through without even a look at the interior of any of the business houses. In this particular especially has his great foresight and wisdom been manifest and beneficial to the city as well as to all who travel through it.

He has, perhaps, done as much toward making the city of his adoption what it is to-day, as any person either living or dead; being liberal and public spirited, he has always aided with money, as well as countenance, any enterprise calculated to benefit the city and redound to its future prosperity, and its social as well as religious and educational advantages.

He is one of the largest contributors for the erection of that beautiful temple of worship, the Second Presbyterian

Church, of which he has been an honored member and elder for many years.

He was president of the Indianapolis Gas Light and Coke Company for many years, which position he resigned much against the wishes of the stockholders, but his two other presidencies made his labor too much for his physical abilities. The Gas Light and Coke Company flourished under his supervision, like every other institution he has had the management of, and he left it in a high state of prosperity.

He was, also, for sometime one of the directors of the State Insane Asylum, a very responsible but poor paying position, and such a one as persons are sought to fill who are well paid by the self-satisfaction of alleviating the misfortunes of that unhappy class of our citizens.

He also, in connection with Messrs. Blake and Ray, in 1852, laid out an addition to the City Cemetery, a want so much needed and called for at that time.

Were I to stop at his public services and liberality it would be doing him but partial justice, and the object I have in sketching him as a character that should be emulated. He has never been known to turn a deaf ear to the poor or those less fortunate than himself, but has acted upon the scriptural principle that "He that giveth to the poor lendeth to the Lord."

He has assisted many persons in business; and though he has never been the person to speak of it himself, we came in possession of the fact from the beneficiaries themselves.

He has furnished means for the erection and carrying on of several manufacturing establishments in this city, as well as other places, in which his name does not appear to the public. He has dispensed his liberality in such manner as he will be enabled to witness the good he has done as he passes along, and without waiting, as too many do, to let others do it for him, and without, perhaps, carrying out one of his wishes, and without any regard for them.

With temperate habits, a good constitution and a clear conscience, he has managed to get himself a wife, a handsome income, and the universal respect and friendship of his many acquaintances throughout the State. The writer was one of the first acquaintances he made in this city, and we have never heard an unkind word spoken of Edwin J. Peck.

His genial manners, universal good humor, kind and obliging disposition, has won him hosts of friends. There is none that enjoys an innocent joke more than he does, and although but a Peck in name he is a bushel in humor.

> "I readily and freely grant,
> He downa see a poor man want;
> What's na his ain, he winna take it,
> What once he says, he winna break it."

May he live long to enjoy the prosperity he has done so much to produce, is the sincere wish of the writer of this brief but truthful tribute to his many virtues.

HON. DANIEL D. PRATT.

This distinguished gentleman, who has within the past year been called by the Legislature to surrender one high position to accept that of another still higher in the National Legislature, was for about two years and a half a citizen of this place. While here he won the respect of all who knew him.

I have before me a letter from him in answer to one I had written, which portrays in every line the true character of the man. Although it was not intended by him for publication, I will take the liberty of so doing, as it contains very interesting reminiscences of his stay in the city.

Mr. Pratt is a man of fine legal ability, and, as a lawyer, is devoted to his profession, and in his character fills that

> "Column of true majesty in man,"

talent, honesty and kindness of heart; and I am not surprised that he feels out of place in the United States Senate, as now constituted, for he is a stranger to the scheming intrigue and corruption of professional politicians, and will not lend himself nor influence to aid them in their own nefarious and selfish purposes to the injury of the country.

Twenty years ago that Senate would have been more congenial to him, when Henry Clay, Daniel Webster, Lewis Cass, and Stephen A. Douglas were its prominent members; but it is now composed of a far different class of men.

Mr. Pratt's great success as a lawyer is attributable to his untiring industry and perseverance in studying his profession. His tall and strongly built form, keen eyes and dark hair, and other decided casts in his features, gives him a noble and commanding air, and displays in his personal appearance the native power of his mind to a considerable extent. His record in life is one worthy to be read and remembered fresh in our minds.

The mock marriage Mr. Pratt alludes to may need some explanation. At the time he boarded with the mother of the writer there was a kind of half-witted fellow working about the house, as fire-maker, water-carrier, etc., named Henry Wilson. He was about twenty-two years of age, large and fleshy, with a considerable share of laziness.

Henry became very much enamored with one of the servant girls, and was teasing her at every opportunity to marry him. This fact reaching the ears of Mr. Pratt and an Episcopal minister, who was a member of the Legislature, they induced the girl to accept the proposition to marry him, and set the wedding for a certain evening, and they would get her out of the scrape, and at the same time rid her of his importunities.

This she did, and set the time for the consummation of the nuptials. Henry wished to start immediately to White Lick, in the neighboorhood of Mooresville, and invite his friends;

but the affianced bride would not consent to have any but the inmates of the house invited.

Mr. Granville Young was to personate the bride, and the clergyman was to perform the ceremony free of charge. Up to this time Mr. Pratt had acted as general superintendent and next friend to the groom; he also attended to the making the toilet of the bride.

At the last moment the minister thought he might be going too far, and declined to perform the ceremony; it then devolved upon Mr. Pratt to solemnize the nuptials, which he did with all the gravity and composure with which he afterwards charged a jury.

After the happy groom had received the gratulations of the company, and before proceeding to the bridal chamber, Mr. Pratt prepared him a glass of wine, in which was put a copious dose of aloes, the effect of which disconcerted the groom in a short time.

The reader will remember this was when the distinguished Senator was quite young, and before he had reached his twenty-first year. Although thirty-six years have passed away, and with them many of the actors in the scene, Mr. Pratt yet enjoys the narration of the ludicrous incident.

LOGANSPORT, IND., Oct. 19, 1869.

Mr. J. H. B. Nowland:

DEAR SIR:—My occupation in court has prevented me until this moment from sitting down and giving you the brief sketch you request.

Born in Palmer, Maine, on the 26th of October, 1813. My father emigrated to central New York when I was but a year old, so that I have considered myself a son of the Empire State.

My father was a country physician and I was raised on a farm, and until sent off to school was accustomed to farm labor. After leaving college I turned my face westward, in the spring of 1832, when eighteen years of age. For fifteen months I taught school in Lawrenceburg and Rising Sun, and in the fall of 1833 went to Indianapolis and entered the law office of Calvin Fletcher, and took board with your excellent mother. I made her house my home most of the time I lived in your city. It was a village then, and a very unpretending one, with a population of about 2,500 souls.

When my school earnings were expended, and they did not last very long, I obtained odd jobs of writing; during the legislative sessions wrote in the office of Secretary of State; was appointed Quartermaster-General by Governor Noble with a salary of fifty dollars a year, and from these sources, and the aid I was able to render Mr. Fletcher, eked out an economical living and laid by fifty dollars, which I invested in forty acres of wild land. The law knowledge I gleaned while a resident of Indianapolis, was very scanty, since most of my time was occupied in providing the ways and means of living. But, scanty as it was, the friendship of Judge Wick secured me a license to practice law, and on March 1st, 1836, I came here, where I have ever since remained.

I recall with peculiar pleasure the period I was a member of your mother's family. She was a favorite with the boarders. Her table was always bountifully supplied, and she had a kind word for all. To me, young and inexperienced, and a stranger, she was more than commonly kind.

I can recall the names and faces of but few of her many boarders—Boyd, Webster, Peck, Dumont, Young, Garret and Ramsey occur to me, and a tall man, a printer, whose name has escaped me.

The State House was being built at that time, and many of the workmen and two of the contractors, Messrs. Levermore and Peck, boarded with her. During the legislative sessions many of the members took rooms at your house.

I remember the mock marriage to which you allude. It was during the session; the bridegroom was decked out with the coat of one, the boots of another, and the watch of a third. The dining-room was filled with spectators. A waggish clergyman, a member of the House, was to have officiated, but at the last moment took a serious view of the matter and backed out. Then it fell upon me to join the couple in marriage and conduct them to the bridal chamber. It was Young, I believe, who personated the female. Never was bridegroom more eager or deeply in earnest than poor Henry. To him it did not seem out of order that the false bride should be deeply veiled. That foolish prank came near costing me my life, for when the defrauded bridegroom had recovered from the severe effects of the purgative administered, he sought the earliest opportunity of attacking me in the dining-room with the carving knife. While his system was undergoing depletion he was nursing schemes of revenge against the author of his shame.

During that period the Athenæum was organized; it was in the nature of a Lyceum. We had written lectures and it was well patronized. We also had mock legislatures and mock courts. The social condition of Indianapolis was excellent at this early period of its history. All well-behaved persons had the entree to good society. During the winter social parties were common. Governor Noble was a very hospitable man, and fond of seeing his friends at his house. Morris Morris, Mr. McClure and N. B. Palmer gave fine parties.

There were no railroads and canals in those days in the State; the three leading thoroughfares radiating from Indianapolis were the Michigan road, running north to the lakes and south to Madison; the National road, then in process of construction, and the road to Lawrenceburg; the latter was the direct road to Cincinnati and was much traveled.

During the late fall and early winter this road was lined

with droves of hogs on their way to market. All the roads at this season, and, indeed, during the winter, were execrable. I remember being upwards of three days in reaching Cincinnati, on horseback, in the fall of 1835. But others will speak of these matters with better recollection and authority than myself.

I left Indianapolis on March 1st, 1836, for this place, seventy miles distant, and by hard traveling reached here in two days. Logansport, at that time, contained about 800 white inhabitants. The Pottawatamie and Miami tribes of Indians afforded the principal trade which the town then had. The merchants were nearly all Indian traders; Cyrus Taber and George W. Ewing were the largest and most influential. Their stores were crowded with Indians. All contracts among the whites for the payment of money were made payable at the next annuity. The "Indian payments," so called, were general settlement days. Silver coin was paid by the Government and constituted the principal currency.

It was a poor time for lawyers in those days, but I found several here. I think my earnings for the first year amounted to three or four hundred dollars.

But if the demand for professional labor was little, there was no lack of occupation in the pursuit of pleasure, which, I take it, is, after all, the substantial and sensible business of life. The surrounding forests were grand, filled with game, and the red men; the rivers and lakes were alive with fish, and their capture by hook, spear and net was the business of the sportsman and idle man, who supplied his necessities, and careless of the future grand hunts were organized. When the Indians were removed west of the Mississippi, in the fall of 1837, nearly all the young men were drafted into the service of the government to aid in the removal.

Kansas was their "*terre incognita*," and many vacant hours

was spent on the return of the party in telling and hearing their wonderful experiences.

I forgot that you desired simply a personal sketch. Well, I have but little to say of myself. My business, as a lawyer, increased by degrees, and journeying on horseback from one county to another during the sessions of court, I practiced law in what are now the counties of Cass, Miami, Wabash, Huntington, Allen, Grant, Howard, Carroll, White, Pulaski, Jasper, Marshall, Fulton and Kosciusko.

Sometimes I would be absent on the circuit for five weeks, continuously, before returning home. Content with my profession I had very little aspiration for political honors. But, in 1847, having been nominated for Congress by the Whig party, I canvassed the old Ninth District with Mr. Cathcart, and was defeated, his majority being about four hundred. The next year, being a candidate for District Elector, I canvassed the same district with Dr. Fitch. In 1850, and again in 1853, I was a member of the Legislature. In 1856, again a candidate for District Elector, I canvassed a portion of the Ninth District in the interest of the Fremont ticket.

But political life was never agreeable to my tastes. Whatever may have been my success at the bar, and of that it does not become me to speak, I am satisfied that I have entered the arena of politics too late in life to render myself useful in any high degree to the country.

The large and varied interests of a great and growing nation like ours, require comprehensive study and practical statesmanship. Familiarity with State interests and State legislation is one thing, while a comprehensive knowledge of the agricultural, manufacturing, money, commercial and shipping interests of the country at large, and its relations, diplomatic and commercial, with foreign countries, is another, and quite a different thing.

Late in November, 1837, I was married at Rising Sun, to

Colonel Pinkney James' daughter. She had been my pupil six years before while I taught school in her native town. By her I have four children, two only of whom are living. My oldest son fell in the war.

In the spring of 1865 I was married a second time, to Mrs. Warren.

This is all that it occurs to me to say. I regard the most useful and honorable part of my life that engaged in teaching, not to speak of the period above alluded to, while engaged solely in that business. I have educated in my law office twenty-five or thirty students, most of whom have succeeded well in their profession. Experiencing when a poor young man great kindness while studying my profession, I have made it a point never to charge any student for the use of my office and books and such instruction as I could impart. In this I have endeavored to do by others as was done to me.

Yours respectfully,
D. D. PRATT.

THOMAS W. COUNCIL.

This gentleman is at present a citizen of Columbus, Bartholomew County, but was for many years a resident of this county, a portion of the time living in the city, and then in Pike township. He was among the first to join the Christian Church when it was first organized in this place, about the year 1833, at which time he was married.

Mr. Council was a native of North Carolina, born near Fayetteville in the year 1810, where he lived until 1831, when he went to Camden, South Carolina, and was living there at the time the celebrated proclamation of General Jackson was made in regard to nullification in 1832, which was the cause of the greatest excitement among the people of that city he had ever before witnessed, and caused the shedding of blood between the friends of the "old hero" and those of nullification.

In the year 1832 he became a citizen of this city, and then a resident of Pike township; assisted his neighbors and friends in rolling logs, burning brush, raising cabins, and contributed largely in labor and means in making that beautiful township of land what it is to-day.

Mr. Council is a man of considerable ability and a fair political speaker, and during his residence in this county was an active politician of the Jackson school, and was ever ready to contribute his time and money with profuse liberality to secure the success of his party; he was at one time its candidate for Representative of the county in the State Legislature.

About the year 1842, a man named Carter, who had been living near Allisonville, in the north part of this county, moved to the southwest part of the State of Missouri. He hired a well known mulatto man, named Eli Terry, to drive his team, and engaged to work for him one year. At the expiration of the year Carter proposed to Terry to return with him to Indiana, and sold him a horse, saddle and bridle in pay for his labor, which Terry was to travel on. Instead of taking the north-eastern direction, as he should have done to reach this State, Carter struck toward Arkansas and to the interior and wilderness portion of Texas. That State had not yet become a portion of and one of the United States. Carter induced Terry to acknowledge himself a slave to avoid being interrupted, as he alleged, as a free negro, the laws being strict in regard to free persons of color. After Terry had made this acknowledgment publicly Carter sold him into slavery for six hundred dollars, and he was kept in that condition for seven long years, when he was released through the agency of Mr. Council and two other gentlemen, Mr. Ryman, of Lawrenceburg, as a lawyer, and Mr. Harrison, of Hamilton County.

The Quakers in and near Westfield, Hamilton County, learning the facts of Terry's abduction and sale into slavery, raised a sufficient sum of money to employ a lawyer and defray the expense of witnesses, and sent and had Terry released and brought home.

Mr. Council, who had known Terry's father to be a free man in North Carolina, and Terry himself here, was induced to go as a witness in the cause of freedom, that boon so dear to us all.

I have before me a pamphlet written by Mr. Council, and in very good style and language, giving an account of their travels and perils, both by land and water, to that distant land, and the danger that threatened them after they had found the object of their journey of several thousand miles. They were pointed to a tree and told that there had already been six abolitionists hanged on it, and that if they persisted in trying to establish the man's freedom, they would add three to the number.

Although Mr. Council had never sympathized with political abolitionism, he wished justice to prevail though the heavens should fall, and persevered in doing what he conceived to be his duty to God and an unfortunate and injured fellow creature. About five years since he removed to Columbus, where he now resides.

His son, John F. Council, to whom I am indebted for these facts in his father's history, is a resident of this city, and is engaged with his old school and play mate, William R. Hogshire and J. B. E. Reid, in the wholesale and retail boot and shoe business, and, like his two partners, is esteemed as an upright business man, and a genial gentleman.

In the short space in which I am compelled to confine myself in these sketches, it is very difficult to do full justice to two such persons as the father and the son, the subjects of this sketch.

HENRY TUTEWILER

Has been a citizen of Indianapolis since 1834. He was from Lancaster, Ohio, and like most others that settled here at an early day, had but little of worldly goods. He had a good trade, industrious habits and a healthy and robust constitution.

He engaged as a partner with William Lingenfelter in the plastering business, and the fact that two such singular names should be associated together as partners, "Tutewiler & Lingenfelter," often caused a laugh from the "new comers," or Yankees that might chance to settle in our city.

Mr. Tutewiler was, and is yet, one of the most energetic mechanics, of any kind, in this place. See him when you will he is in a hurry, driving his work instead of its driving him. We have often met him in different parts of the city, within the same hour, overseeing his different jobs of work; and although able to live without work, I do not see any abatement of his youthful zeal and industry.

Soon after he made this place his residence he connected himself with the Methodist Church, and has ever bore the name of a true and consistent Christian, as much by practice as precept. He was a member of the Wesley Chapel congregation when it was the only Methodist congregation in the city, and there often listened to those eminent and old-fashioned ministers, such as James Havens, Allen Wiley, Calvin W. Ruter, with many others of less notoriety, and has there often met brother Jimmy Kittleman and Francis McLaughlin, and heard their loud amens, accompanied by a clap of their hands that would ring through the ears of the congregation.

Mr. Tutewiler has looked forward through the vista of years to his sons as the pride of his old age, and who, as the representatives of his family, were to carry down to succeeding

generations its respectability, and credit and good name of
their father, who has not wasted time

> "In dropping buckets into empty wells,
> And growing old in drawing nothing up,"

but has accumulated sufficient to start his sons in a lucrative
and respectable business, while he yet remained on earth to
assist them by his counsel as well as his means.

Tutewiler Bros. are the proprietors of one of, if not the
largest, stove stores in the city, where all kinds of copper,
tin, japanned and pressed wares are kept and sold; also, nearly
all kinds of house-furnishing goods, table cutlery, furniture,
grates, marble and metal mantels—in short, all kinds of hardware used by house-keepers.

It is seldom we see such an establishment as theirs even in
larger cities. How different from the first tinning establishment of this place, that of Mr. Davis, up stairs, on the northwest corner of Washington and Pennsylvania streets, and
when one small room answered for shop, parlor, kitchen and
hall; or how different from the stove store of Aaron Grover,
on the southeast corner of Washington and Meridian streets.
Could it be possible for these two early proprietors to be
called from the spirit land, would they not be astonished at
the improvement made in their branch of business. To please
their customers seems to be a specialty with Tutewiler Bros.,
and their pleasant and affable clerk, David W. Brouse, whose
genial countenance is generally met at the threshhold of the
establishment, as the customers enter.

WILLIAM H. H. PINNEY.

Major Pinney is a native of Thetford, Windsor County,
Vermont, and inherited a considerable of the true Yankee
character—industry, enterprise and perseverance. He was
blessed with a good English education, such as is obtained in
the common and high schools of Yankeeland.

At the age of nineteen he engaged as a guard at the State Prison of his native State; served about four years as guard and shopkeeper, then as deputy warden, and had entire control and management of the prison; then as clerk in a large manufacturing establishment, and early earned the reputation of a good business man. He was then appointed aid-de-camp in the State militia, and there acquired the title and rank of major, which is not bogus; and to be a major in Yankeedom meant something.

In 1828 Major Pinney first visited Indianapolis as the traveling agent of the "American Hydraulic Company," in order to try to sell to the town, or its citizens, a fire engine. He saw most of the leading and business men of the place, and they concluded that the people were not able to purchase one at that time. He had traveled over his native State, New Hampshire, New York, Pennsylvania, Ohio, Upper Canada, Michigan, West Virginia, Indiana, Kentucky, Tennessee, Alabama and Missouri, and visited all the towns of note in those several States, and found no place that cared as little about an engine as Indianapolis. What a change forty years have wrought!

Now our five steam fire engines are considered inadequate for the safety of property, and on occasions powerless for awhile to control the devouring element.

Mr. Pinney, after remaining here a few days, left for Madison, and was three days, hard traveling through mud and mire, in reaching it, thence homeward.

He returned to Indiana in 1831 and settled at the bluffs of White River, where he engaged in merchandising, and followed it for several years; in the mean time he married Miss Emily, youngest daughter of Jacob Whetzell. He was appointed postmaster at that place by General Jackson, more as a punishment for being a Clay Whig than the good-will of the old hero. This he held until the office was removed to Waverly, a new town that had sprung up within a mile of his place.

Major Pinney is a very pleasant and agreeable man, and is disposed to look on the bright side of sublunary affairs, and sees more of sunshine than shade in the lot of man generally. Although during the rebellion a strong Union man, he did nothing towards furnishing soldiers bearing his name, neither could wives be found for them in his family. The writer hopes he may yet live to see his hearth-stone surrounded by many little Pinneys.

CARY H. BOATRIGHT.

I notice this man for the purpose of bringing before the public the singular fact that he is now living with his tenth wife.

He came to this place in 1831 a widower, having lost his third wife. He soon supplied the last vacancy with a Miss Pugh. She also, in turn, died. Then he married Miss Sally Cool, his fifth wife. They had not lived long together when she applied for and obtained a divorce. As I am not sketching "Early Indiana Trials," I shall not go into the details of this one. He then wooed and won the heart and hand of a Miss Hinsley, a lady of large *proportions* and *size*. She bore him one son, and, like her predecessors, left her liege lord again free to make the seventh selection, which he did in due course of time, and he has continued in selecting and his wives dying until he has now the tenth, and from what I learn of his robust health and constitution, although he has lived out the time generally allotted to man, he may yet enjoy the society of his fifteenth wife. This is one of the singular facts and incidents that I have selected to assist me in showing the great variety of character and men found in the early history of Indianapolis.

If Mr. Boatright was unfortunate in losing his wives, he

was very fortunate in not having more than one in his house at the same time.

> "I kissed her lips sae rosy red,
> While the tears stood blinken in her e'e;
> I said, my lassie, dinna cry,
> For ye ay, shall mak' the bed to me."

WILLIAM SHEETS

Is a native of the "Old Dominion," having been born near Martinsburg, in Berkley County. When quite young, in the year 1817, came to Madison, Jefferson County, Indiana. He there studied law, and for a few years practiced the profession.

In the winter 1830-31, he was elected one of the clerks of the House of Representatives of the Indiana Legislature, an office he was peculiarly fitted for, being a fine reader as well as penman.

In 1832 he was elected by the Legislature Secretary of State, and then commenced his residence in Indianapolis. During this term of office he was married to Miss Randolph, formerly of Virginia, a relative of the distinguished statesman of that State, "John Randolph, of Roanoke," and adopted daughter of President William Henry Harrison.

When the canal was finished between Broad Ripple and this place, about the year 1838, he erected a large Paper Mill (the first in the city), and manufactured large quantities, and every variety, and furnished nearly all the paper used in the western part of this State and the eastern portion of Illinois. We have frequently met his wagons in the interior of the latter State.

In 1840 he was again elected to his former position (Secretary of State) and served another term of four years. Since which time he has been engaged in attending to his private business.

He owns some very fine business as well as private property. He still resides at his old homestead, where he has lived for near thirty-five years.

In politics Mr. Sheets was an old line Henry Clay Whig, and followed the fortunes of that party from its first organization, in 1832, until its disrupture after the defeat of its candidate (General Scott) for President in 1852; he then, and has since, acted with the Republicans.

In religion he is a Presbyterian, being a member of the First Church very nearly the whole time since his first residence in this city.

As an official, he was unexceptionable; as a man, kind and courteous in his intercourse with others, and possessed a great deal of native dignity, and, withal, a hospitable man.

He has a family of several children, all of whom reside in or near the city. Such is William Sheets, one of our most respected citizens.

DOCTOR GEORGE W. MEARS.

> "A man in many a country town you know
> Professes openly with death to wrestle;
> Entering the field against the grimly foe,
> Armed with a mortar and a pestle."

The worthy Doctor, whose name heads this sketch, came to Indianapolis in February, 1834, fully armed as above quoted, and entered immediately upon the practice of his profession, and has continued it up to the present time.

Doctor Mears was originally from Philadelphia, but was direct from Vincennes to this place. At the latter place he had lived a few years, and was there married to Miss Caroline Ewing, a daughter of one of its most respected citizens, and a pioneer of the West.

The Doctor is, at this time, the veteran practicing physician of the place, and has, perhaps, stood by the sick and dying bedside of as many poor and unpaying patients as any physician in the State, and with that class of people is universally popular, as well as with the wealthy.

In the Doctor's extensive practice if he should, like the "New Castle Apothecary," have

> "Hurled a few score mortals from the world,"

Like him, too, he has

> "Made amends by bringing others into it."

He has enjoyed the confidence and respect of the citizens of this county and city as a man as well as a physician, and no person stands higher in either respect. And in his shop. like that of Dr. Hornbook's, will be found all kinds

> "O' doctors saws and whettles
> Of a' dimensions, shapes and mettles,
> A' kind o' boxes, mugs and bottles,
>   He's sure to hae;
> Their Latin names as fast he rattles
>   As A, B, C.

When he first came to Indianapolis it was the custom of physicians to keep in their shops different kinds of liquors for medicinal purposes. One of the "dead beats" of the place gave the Doctor considerable trouble in that way when he could not procure the article at the groceries.

One morning he called and told the Doctor if he would not let him have any spirits, that, for God's sake, let him have something that would kill him, as he was tired of living, at any rate.

The Doctor told him he would give him something, he would think, would kill him before he got through with it.

He mixed a large dose of tartar emetic with some brandy, which the patient swallowed with evident self-satisfaction. In the course of an hour or so the Doctor was riding near the old graveyard, where he found, or rather heard, him in a corn field, heaving and pitching, and calling for help. The Dr.

informed him that he was in no kind of danger, and would certainly be better before he could possibly be much worse.

About that time he quit drinking, and he told us a few days since that he had not tasted spiritous liquor for twenty-five years.

This man I have referred to was in the habit, when under the influence of liquor, of calling "all the ends of the earth to come unto him;" if he ever should again he will probably not forget the worthy Doctor.

Although the Doctor has ever had an extensive practice, he has never sought to lay up wealth by oppressing his patients and debtors, and I have no doubt can show as many unpaid bills upon his books as any physician in the city.

Unlike the "New Castle Apothecary," his fame has more than

> "Six miles a'round the country ran,
> And all the old women call him a fine man."

He at an early day built himself a fine mansion on Meridian street, where he yet resides. At the time it was built it was the largest family residence in the place, as well as the finest. He owns the largest piece of very valuable property of any person in the city, over the quarter of a square, in the most fashionable neighborhood.

In religion he is an Episcopalian, and was prominent in organizing the first congregation of that denomination in the city, and yet worships at Christ Church, and was for years one of its vestrymen.

In politics he was an ardent and enthusiastic member of that good old National Whig party, now defunct and numbered among the dead.

He was appointed by the Legislature one of the Board of Trustees to direct the organization and management of the Institution for the Education of the Blind, and subsequently to superintend the application of the fund appropriated by the Legislature for that purpose.

He was for years President of the Board of Health of the city and county, as well as City Physician, all of which he filled with entire satisfaction to the public and credit to himself.

Doctor George W. Mears is one of the leading physicians of Indianapolis, and is, perhaps, oftener called in consultation with his co-workers in the healing art than any other in the place. Long may he live to enjoy his enviable reputation, both as a man and as a physician.

FIRST FIRE, FIRST BURGLARY AND FIRST HOMICIDE IN INDIANAPOLIS.

It is a fact that should not be overlooked, and one worthy of note, that for the first fifteen years after the settlement of Indianapolis we had neither fire engines nor police officers, and during that entire time there was but one fire, one burglary, and one homicide.

The fire was that of Carter's tavern, in January, 1825, and did its work very effectually, burning down the entire building, leaving many members of the Legislature without a place to lay their heads.

The burglary was that of Jacob Landis's grocery, by an old man named Redman and his son-in-law, Warner. Suspicion pointed to them, and a search warrant issued to sheriff Russell to search their house. The missing articles were all found there, with the exception of a bolt of brown sheeting. The sheriff had noticed that Mrs. Warner was much larger in front and more rotund in person than she was but a few days before, and suspicioned that there was "something more than meal" concealed there, and asked for an examination. She was very indignant, that a gentleman should wish to examine a lady in her condition; but the sheriff could not be put off; he had seen too many women in that situation, and never knew one to assume so large proportions in so short a time. The examination disclosed the missing goods. The burglars were promptly tried, convicted and sent to the penitentiary for several years.

The homicide was the drowning of William McPherson by Michael Van Blaricum, on the 8th of May, 1833.

It had been known for some time that Van Blaricum entertained no very good feelings toward McPherson, and had, on several occasions, manifested a disposition to ridicule and make sport of him.

McPherson was employed by William H. Wernwag as a clerk and time-keeper, while the White River bridge was being built.

Van Blaricum was going to cross from the east to the west side of the river in a canoe, and McPherson requested the privilege of crossing with him, which was granted. Van Blaricum had some augers in his hand which he fastened to the bow of the canoe with the rope used for fastening the boat, observing at the same time that he intended to drown McPherson. When about the middle of the river he turned the canoe over, and when in the water grappled McPherson, they sank together, and McPherson never rose until brought out a corpse.

At the coroner's inquest finger marks were found on the throat of McPherson, which the examining physicians said were made before life was extinct.

Van Blaricum was tried for manslaughter, convicted and sent to the penitentiary for a few years.

Although he had said he would drown McPherson, and did, there were none who believed that he intended to do so, but only to scare him, and went farther than he intended; indeed he told the writer so himself after he had paid the penalty of his crime, and could have had no inducement to lie.

The jury must have been of the same opinion, hence the verdict, which was for a shorter time than the burglars above spoken of, and less than a person would now be sent for the larceny of a ten dollar watch.

HON. NATHAN B. PALMER.

This venerable old citizen and worthy gentleman is perhaps as generally and favorably known throughout the State of Indiana as any person now living. He has been a citizen of the State half a century, and a great portion of the time in active public life.

No person who was a citizen of the State from 1840 to 1843, can forget the large, bold signature of "N. B. Palmer" affixed to the "State scrip" that was authorized by the Legislature to be issued by the Treasurer of State in payment of its indebtedness to contractors on the public works.

The name of N. B. Palmer, if not in the mouth of every citizen in the State, was in the pockets of many of them. His signature was affixed to the two classes of scrip, the old, dated in 1840, bearing six per cent. interest, the new, or green, as it was it was called, dated 1841, bearing the fourth of one per cent. interest. These two kinds of scrip formed for several years the principal circulating medium of the State as a representative of money.

Mr. Palmer was born in Stonington, Connecticut, on the 27th of August, 1790, and at this writing is some months over seventy-nine years of age. In his tenth year, 1800, with his mother (his father having died) removed to the State of New York, where he remained until 1812, when he, with his family, emigrated to Pennsylvania, having, in the meantime, been married to Miss Chloe Sacket, who is yet his comfort in his declining years, and a helpmate worthy of emulation by the young ladies of the present day.

Mrs. Palmer has ever manifested a disposition to take the

world as she found it, and not try to remodel the order of nature, to conform to her own peculiar views and personal convenience; of this the writer can speak understandingly, as he was an inmate of her house for one year.

In Pennsylvania, his new home, Mr. Palmer was soon called into public life. The few years he resided there he held many offices of trust and emolument, all of which he filled with honor to himself, satisfaction of the public, and the benefit of the State.

In the year 1819 he removed to Indiana and settled in Jefferson County, where he resided fourteen years and held many offices of importance; he was a Representative of that county in the Legislature, and was elected Speaker of the House of Representatives for the session of 1833-4.

He was a prompt and efficient presiding officer, at all times commanding the respect of his associates for his knowledge of parliamentary rules and an impartial application of them to cases that might arise.

At the ensuing session of the Legislature of 1834-5, he was elected Treasurer of State, and immediately entered upon its duties and removed his family to this place in the spring of 1835; this position he held for several years, and retired from it without the tongue of vituperation or slander ever reaching his public acts, which is a very uncommon thing with persons who have charge of large amounts of public moneys and their disbursement.

In 1841, after he had retired from the office of Treasurer of State, he was selected by the Legislature to examine the State Bank and the different branches, and report their financial condition to the next annual session of that body.

In that office was a great opportunity for corruption and speculation, had it been placed in the hands of a person susceptible of bribery, or could even be approached on the subject; such was Mr. P.'s character I doubt whether such a thing was ever thought of, although at the Terre Haute branch a deception was attempted by the cashier which was quickly discovered by Mr. Palmer, and the author of it rebuked in such a manner that he would never attempt anything of the kind again, at least with Mr. Palmer.

When Mr. P. had made his business known to the officers of the bank, he was cordially received and invited to proceed in his examination in his own way and at his leisure.

After the examination of the books of the bank, and counting the office or business paper and bank notes on hand, he found a deficit of about twenty thousand dollars; this the cashier told him would be accounted for in the retired paper, or bills too much worn for circulation, and were tied up in five hundred dollar packages and laid away in the vault of the bank, to be exchanged with the mother bank for new paper.

About ten thousand dollars of this kind of money was handed Mr. P., which he counted and returned to the cashier. This money had laid in the damp vault of the bank so long that the notes adhered to each other, and in counting the ends were loosened.

After Mr. Palmer had returned the packages above named, the cashier wished to be excused from proceeding any farther with the counting that day, as he had company at his house and invited Mr. Palmer to tea. Mr. P. granted the request, but declined the invitation to tea.

When the counting was resumed the next day, Mr. Palmer was surprised to find the same packages he had counted the day before presented to him again to be counted, although an attempt had been made to disguise them by tying the packages with a different colored ribbon from those they were tied with when he first handled them. There were other marks too familiar to the penetrating eye of Mr. Palmer for him to be deceived. Without mentioning his discovery to the cashier, he expressed a wish to that functionary to have the directors called together, which was complied with by the very accommodating cashier.

After the directors had assembled, Mr. Palmer said to them that "he had been received and treated very kindly by the cashier, for which he felt grateful to that gentleman, but that he relied too much upon his credulity or want of business capacity, by presenting him those (pointing to the packages) retired bills to be counted again and credited to the bank.

The cashier at once acknowledged the attempted deception. Although the directors must have known the true amount, the cashier was promptly dismissed by them, and he left the State.

Mr. Palmer was afterwards canal commissioner, councilman from his ward, and held several other minor offices.

When Mr. Palmer held the most important offices was before the incumbents were selected because of their national politics, but alone for their strict integrity and qualifications for the position; at that time when a man's views as to the expediency or inexpediency of certain national measures were neither a qualification or disqualification for State or county offices, as in the canvass for Governor of the State in 1837, both candidates were Whigs, divided on local issues or State policy.

The first gubernatorial election in Indiana that turned upon national politics was that of the ever-memorable canvass between Samuel Bigger and General Tighlman A. Howard, in the year 1840. Governor Noble, although a Clay Whig, was elected over James G. Reed when the State voted for Jackson.

Mr. Palmer's whole public life, as well as his private, seemed to be without reproach or fault; and while he was highly appreciated as a public man, he was no less esteemed as a gentleman and a citizen.

He built, and yet owns, that fine hotel that bears his name, and has built and owns other important buildings in different parts of the city, and is, also, the owner of a fine farm about half a mile west of the city on the National road.

He kept the Palmer House in person from 1844 to 1851, and none that ever sat at its hospitable board can forget the superabundance of every thing upon it, and the superior style in which it was gotten up; without ostentatious display of fine table furniture that could not be consumed, the eye met on every hand something far more interesting to the empty stomach of the weary traveler. Very little ever went on that table but had been subjected to the strict scrutiny of Mrs. Palmer.

The writer can never forget the great change he experiencd in the transition from that house to that of a Washington City fashionable boarding-house. None can realize it but those who have tried the latter.

In religion Mr. Palmer claims the right to worship God according to the dictates of his own conscience, and is willing that others should enjoy the same high prerogative, and "render unto Cæsar the things that are Cæsar's, and unto God the things that are God's."

In politics he is an old school Democrat in the strictest sense of the term, and thinks that, in a political point of view, "there is yet a God in Israel."

He is one of the few links in the chain that connect the eighteenth and nineteenth centuries, and when he is called hence the world will have lost an honest man, and this city one of its best citizens.

PHILIP SWEETSER

Was a native of the State of New Hampshire, born in the village of Morrow, in the year 1795. He was educated at the same college, and in the same graduating class with that eminent Massachusetts lawyer, Hon. Rufus Choate, and had he lived to the age that gentleman did, I have no doubt he would have stood equally high in his profession.

Mr. Sweetser, for a short time, was a teacher in the Academy at Charlotte Hall, Maryland, and it was there, in that capacity, he made the acquaintance of our townsman, Esquire William Sullivan.

From the latter place he came to Indiana, and for a short time practiced law in Madison, and from there to Columbus, where he resided many years and was one of the most popular and successful lawyers in the Fifth Judicial Circuit.

While at Columbus he became the law partner of General James Noble, at that time a United States Senator, and afterwards the father-in-law of Mr. Sweetser. They were the principal lawyers in conducting the prosecution against the murderers of the Indians at the falls of Fall Creek in the year 1824, and it was the opening speech in that prosecution, made by Mr. Sweetzer, that first attracted the attention of the people, and the members of the bar particularly, to the Yankee lawyer, although his *forte* in criminal cases was defense, where he was more at home on the side of mercy; indeed, he was a man of too noble and generous feelings for a successful prosecutor, and he has told me himself that nothing gave him more pain than to prosecute a criminal.

In the month of June, or July, 1833, the writer happened to be in Columbus on the day that a man named Jones was to be hung. A large concourse of people had assembled to witness the execution. Among them were many friends and neighbors of the man that Jones had murdered, all eager to see the law enforced, and the unfortunate man launched into eternity.

It was known that Mr. Sweetser, as the criminal's lawyer, had started to Indianapolis (on horseback) only the evening before to try and have the execution postponed and the criminal respited, in order that he might get the case before the Supreme Court. There was great excitement and various threats made against Mr Sweetser if he should be successful.

About the last hour he arrived, and had been successful. Learning of the great excitement and threats against him, he caused the people to be collected together, when he made a short speech to them that had the desired effect and allayed all bad feelings against himself; he convinced the excited people that he had done only what his oath, as a lawyer, and fidelity to the interest and life of his client required.

They found that, amid their own departure from the rules of propriety and sober life, he was immovable and determined to do his duty regardless of the consequences to himself.

Although Mr. Sweetser delayed the execution, his client was subsequently hung; he had the satisfaction of knowing that he had done his duty to his client and his God.

As a lawyer and an advocate, it was remarked of Mr. Sweetser that he never allowed his dignity to be lowered by vulgar or ungentlemanly remarks to the opposing counsel or of their clients; neither did he ever use any of the "slang phrases" too common at the present day, but at the bar, as in the parlor, was governed by the same rules of propriety that stamped him the gentleman.

Although a fluent speaker, his main strength before a court or jury was found in his strong and convincing arguments, which he presented with such force as to readily carry conviction to the minds of his auditors.

Mr. Sweetser had been a constant attendant of the different courts that were held in this city from the time he first came to the State up to the time of his death, which occurred in the summer of 1843.

He removed his family to Indianapolis in the year 1837. He has two sons who are among our well known citizens; the eldest, James Noble, who possesses a great many of the father's traits of character, and, as a lawyer, considerable legal ability. Another, George, has been connected for many years with the city post office, and is well known to our old as well as new citizens. The younger portion of the family still live with their mother, who yet makes her home among the many friends of her departed husband.

JOHN M. TALBOTT

Was born in Bourbon County, Kentucky, in September, 1811, and, with his parents, removed to Charleston, Clark County, Indiana, in the year 1818, where he resided and spent the most of his boyhood days, except two years he worked in the printing office of Shadrick Penn, in Louisville, Kentucky.

Mr. Talbott came to Indianapolis with his brother-in-law, the late Major Alexander F. Morrison, in the spring of 1830, and entered the printing office of Messrs. Morrison & Bolton as a journeyman printer. He there continued until that old pioneer printer, George Smith, commenced the publication of the "Farmer," when he and Matthias T. Nowland (a brother of the writer) undertook to do the entire work of publishing that paper, doing the compositor's as well as the pressman's work, the latter on an old "Ramage Press," and at the same time publishing an Almanac for Butler K. Smith.

When the publication of the "Farmer" was suspended, Mr. Talbott quit the printing business and engaged in the employment of the Government, with a corps of engineers, in laying out the National road, which was then being located through the State, and the entire route from Richmond to this place lay through a dense forest. He remained in that employment until 1835, when he commenced the mercantile business, and continued in it till 1847. He was then elected Treasurer of Marion County, which he held for one term, and then again resumed the retail dry goods business, and prosecuted it successfully for two years, when, in 1853, he commenced the wholesale dry goods business, which was about the first house of the kind in Indianapolis, and the only one at that time. It was then considered a rather hazardous undertaking, but instead of a failure, as nearly all predicted, he built up a fine business, drawing a considerable trade from different parts of the State that hitherto had patronized Madison and Cincinnati.

Mr. Talbott was appointed postmaster in this city by President Buchanan in 1857, which position, with others, he filled to the entire satisfaction ef the public.

He has done considerable toward the improvement of the city; he has a splendid private residence at the corner of Ohio and Tennessee streets, and some fine business houses on North Illinois street which he has lately improved in a very substantial manner.

Mr. Talbott was married in the year 1840 to a niece of the late Philip Sweetser, who is yet alive to enjoy his prosperity and success in the journey of life.

Mr. Talbott is a member of St. Paul's Episcopal Church and a contributor for the erection of that beautiful temple of worship. He is a liberal and hospitable man, and enjoys the entire respect and confidence of all who know him. He has a large family of relatives, most of them living in the city, to whom he is devotedly attached, and is a kind and generous brother.

WILLIAM H. TALBOTT

Came from Charleston, Clark County, to this place in the year 1833, and is another that lost nothing by becoming a citizen of Indianapolis. He was a mere boy, and lived with his brother-in-law, the late Major Alexander F. Morrison.

Soon after he came here he engaged with Daniel A. Webb to learn the trade or business of a jeweler. When Mr. Webb sold out and left the place Mr. Talbott continued with his successor, Elliott K. Foster, until he finished or perfected the trade. He then, for several years, carried on the business of jeweler, which also embraced that of watch repairing. He was attentive and assiduous to his duties, and did a larger portion in that branch of business than any one in the city, and by that means, and others, was enabled to retire with a competency.

He has on several occasions been a delegate at large from this State in the Democrat conventions, was for some yeaars chairman of the Democratic State Central Committee, and considered an efficient officer, a good political tactician and wire-worker for the party.

In 1863 he was elected by the Legislature president of the Sinking Fund, and held the office for several years. He is not now engaged in any particular business farther than the attention to his private property, which is considerable. He has a fine private residence at the southwest corner of Ohio and Meridian streets, one of the most fashionable portions of the city.

Mr. Talbott was for several years one of the leading beaux of the capital, and thought by some to be given over to bachelorism, but by a fortunate circumstance he met with a daughter of the late Captain Tinker, then of Cincinnati, and surrendered to her charms a "prisoner at will."

JAMES C. YOHN.

Shakspeare, or some other speare, once wrote something like this, that there "is a tide in the affairs of men which, if taken with the flood, leads on to fortune." Mr. Yohn must have have fallen into that tide, as he has floated gently on until he has reached the port spoken of by the distinguished writer.

James C. Yohn, with his mother, two sisters and a bachelor uncle (James Gore), came to this place from Baltimore County, Maryland, in November, 1834. The elder sister was soon married to a Mr. Walker, then of Danville, Illinois, afterwards a United States Senator from the State of Wisconsin. The younger sister died in this place several years since, unmarried.

Mr. Yohn, when but a mere boy, engaged as store-boy, then as clerk, with one of the leading merchants of this place, afterwards a partner, and finally engaged in the mercantile business on his own account, and was a successful merchant, and in the meantime he was married to a daughter of Hiram Brown, a distinguished attorney of this place.

During the war he was appointed a Paymaster in the United States service, with the rank of Major. This position was uncongenial to his feelings, and he resigned sometime before his services were not required.

He owns some fine private as well as business property in the city. The elegant block, known by his name, on the corner of Washington and Meridian streets, he built and owns. He is considered a good man, upright and punctual in all his dealings, and remarkably quiet and retiring in his habits. He has been a consistent member of the Methodist Church since his boyhood.

His mother and uncle yet reside with him on North Delaware street. Of the five in family when they came to Indianapolis, thirty-six years ago, three are yet living.

HENRY H. NELSON.

In writing this short sketch of Mr. Nelson, I am at a loss what to say that every person does not know that has lived in this city for the last thirty years.

Mr. Nelson, like his friend Charles C. Campbell, has honored with his presence nearly every political convention that has assembled from time to time in this city for the last quarter of a century, and like him, too, has considerable experience in legislation as a lobby member.

I think Mr. Campbell has served his country, as a juror, oftener than has Henry; yet his willingness to serve his fellow citizens in that way has never been doubted by his many friends.

He was born in Washington County, East Tennessee, and inherits a considerable share of the Jackson Democracy so peculiar to those who reside in the vicinity of the old hero's late residence.

He came to Indianapolis in the fall of 1833, and has continued to reside he resince that time, having changed one to and added several to the name of Nelson.

Henry is an upright, honest and jovial man, with a smile and pleasant word for all, a frown for none, and is universally respected by all who know him.

BENJAMIN EMERSON

Was generally called "Uncle Ben" by all who enjoyed the benefit of his acquaintance and friendship. He was from the "Great Crossings," Scott County, Kentucky, a locality noted for horse-racing as well as swapping. Uncle Ben understood both branches of the business to perfection, but before leaving Kentucky he had joined the Christian Church and left off racing; se he came to Indianapolis a regenerated man.

He was a smooth-talking, oily tongued man, calculated to win the confidence of almost any person, more especially the young and unsuspecting, and would generally compass his object upon first trial, but after that it was very difficult to have a second transaction with the same person.

When he met an acquaintance he would extend both hands, and tell them he was just that moment thinking of them, and ask them if there was anything he could do for them. He would often remark to the writer, that it did him so much good to do a kindness for a friend; "true religion," he would say, "consists in acts of kindness to our neighbors."

Uncle Ben's store was adjoining the residence of the writer's mother. One morning I stepped into his store quite early. He met me with his usual bland manner, both hands extended; "Johnny," said he, "I was thinking of you just this moment. Johnny, do you know (in a low tone of voice) that the horse you got of Boyer, I mean one of the blacks, is taking the glanders?" I answered in the negative, and was surprised to hear him say so. Said he, "he certainly is, although as yet it is hard to discover."

"Johnny," said he, "you know old Joe Pratt treated you very bad in the horse trade you made with him, I wish you to get even with him, and I'll tell you how we'll do it; I'll give you that bob-tail grey of mine and fifty dollars for your blacks; I can put them on to old Joe, and then the laugh will be on him."

Nothing more was wanting than Uncle Ben's word, and the trade was made; the horses were changed from one stable (which were adjoining) to the other before my friends were aware of it, and the fifty dollars paid over to me.

Uncle Ben kept his word and put them on to Old Joe for one hundred and fifty dollars, which, at that time, was a very high price for the finest of horses.

The horse I got of him was not worth twenty dollars, while those he got of me were as serviceable horses as ever went to harness. Old Joe put them on to Nathan B. Palmer for about one hundred and seventy-five dollars.

I never saw them afterwards but that I felt like praying for "Uncle Ben" for his disinterested kindness to me as a neighbor, and that he might meet the "bob-tail grey" on the other side of Jordan.

WILLIAM SULLIVAN, ESQ.

Among those of the second decade in the settlement of Indianapolis, and who have been rather prominent before the people for the past thirty-five years, is William Sullivan, Esq., a native of Maryland, who first came among us in 1834, in the character of a schoolmaster, and pursued the business of teaching for several years.

Mr. Sullivan, having married a young lady of this city and made it his permanent home, accepted the office of county surveyor, and subsequently that of city civil engineer in 1836, then first created; it was under his directions our first street improvements were made.

While acting as engineer he constructed a large map for the use of the city, and published a smaller map for the general use of the citizens, a valuable but a very scarce map at the present day.

Mr. S. took an active part in school matters before the introduction of the present system of graded schools, and was instrumental in organizing the Franklin Institute, or High School, then located near the northwest corner of Market and Circle streets, an institution of great utility at that time, and successfully conducted by the Rev. Mr. Chester, now deceased, and afterwards by General Marston, late a member of Congress from the State of New Hampshire, and lastly, I believe, by the Hon. W. D. Griswold, now of Terre Haute, Indiana.

Mr. Sullivan has served as councilman of his ward and as President of the City Council, discharging magisterial duties similar to those of Police Judge now exercised by the Mayor of Indianapolis.

From November, 1841, to November, 1867, twenty-six years, he held the office of justice of the peace for Center township in this city, a longer time than any office has been held by any other person since the settlement of the place, doing a large amount of business, and frequently discharging the duties of City Judge, in the absence or inability of the Mayor.

Meanwhile he has given of his means and devoted his spare time to public improvements, particularly railroads centering at Indianapolis, surveying for several years, as a Director of the Central Railway, from Indianapolis to Richmond during the construction of that road, and subsequently as Trustee of the Peru and Indianapolis Railroad.

Mr. Sullivan is of a quiet and retiring disposition, but has a mind and will of his own, and acts promptly and vigorously as occasions may require. He is a man of genial manners and great kindness of heart, quick to notice an intended injury, and as quick to forgive and forget it when due reparation is made.

He has by close application and attention to business, economy and temperate habits, accumulated a competency sufficient to enable him to live at ease and without business the balance of his life, and leave a handsome property for each of his three children, but I cannot see that he has relaxed his energy or industry of a quarter of a century ago.

Esquire Sullivan is a man of fine conversational powers and at home in any genteel society, and never fails to entertain those he meets with by his great fund of anecdotes and his cheerful spirits.

In politics he was an original Democrat, acted with and gave that party a hearty support until the passage of the "Kansas-Nebraska Acts;" since that time he has voted with the Republicans, but with no very high opinion of the radical wing of that party. He is now chiefly engaged in attending to his own private business.

Mr. Sullivan's oldest daughter is the wife of Mr. May, formerly of Cecil County, Maryland, now sojourning in Helena, Montano Territory, and has been recently appointed Receiver of Public Moneys in that land district.

His second daughter is the wife of that dashing and daring cavalry officer, during the war, Col. Bob Stewart, of Terre Haute. His remaining child, a son quite young, is yet living at home with his parents. Such is Esquire Sullivan, one of our respected citizens of thirty-six years' standing.

ABRAM McCORD

Was among the first carpenters that settled in Indianapolis. He came in the year 1822, and built a shop and residence on the point lot between Virginia avenue and Pennsylvania street, fronting Washington street.

He has been dead several years, leaving four children, all of whom are now dead except Benjamin R., his second son.

His eldest daughter, Adeline, was the wife of Thomas Donnellen, a well known cabinet-maker in his day. His second daughter, Emeline, was never married.

Joseph, the eldest son, has now been dead about twelve years.

Benjamin R. McCord is largely engaged in the lumber, planing, sash, blind and door business in connection with Mr. Wheatley, under the firm of McCord & Wheatley, and they are now doing as large, if not a larger, business in their line than any similar establishment in the city.

Since the above was written that large establishment referred to burned entirely down on the 28th of May, 1870, and was rebuilt and in running order in two weeks. Such is the enterprise of B. R. McCord and his partner, Wm. M. Wheatley.

DR. JOHN H. SANDERS

Was born in Bourbon County, Kentucky, in the year 1791, and there studied his profession and practiced some time in Millersburg; he then removed to New Castle, Henry County, and there remained until his removal to Indianapolis, in the winter of 1829–30.

In the spring of 1830, at the sale of the donation lands, he, in connection with Nicholas McCarty, purchased that portion of the city now lying between Virginia avenue, South street and Fletcher avenue.

He built the house on Virginia avenue, and there resided

Dr. John H. Sanders.

several years, known as the Fletcher homestead; his portion of this property he sold to Mr. Fletcher for fifty dollars per acre, three and one-half acres, which was recently sold by one of Mr. Fletcher's heirs to the Asbury Methodist Congregation, for thirty thousand dollars.

Dr. Sanders then purchased the three lots on the northwest corner of Market and Illinois streets, and built the house which he afterwards sold to the State for a residence for the Governor, for ten thousand dollars.

In 1839 he, with his family, removed to the Ozark Mountains, Missouri, but returned to this place in the early part of 1841.

He then built a residence on South Meridian street, where he resided at the time of his death, and where his family remained for several years afterwards.

In the spring of 1850 he visited a daughter, Mrs. McCrea, then living in New Orleans, and while returning home was attacked with cholera and died on board a steamer on the Mississippi River on the 4th of April.

Dr. Sanders was a kind-hearted and hospitable man, and ardently devoted to his family and friends. He was a member of the Christian Church, and an exemplary man in all the relations of life; as a physician he stood high in this community.

Since his death his widow and second daughter have died. The most of his family yet reside in the city.

The eldest daughter was the wife of ex-Governor David Wallace; another the wife of Robert B. Duncan, one of the oldest citizens of the place, but by no means the oldest man; another the wife of David S. Beaty; the youngest, the wife of Mr. Gatling, resides in Philadelphia.

Dr. Sanders is another of the old and prominent citizens of this city that died before they had witnessed the great prosperity it now enjoys.

LAWRENCE MARTIN VANCE

Was born in Cincinnati, Ohio, in the year 1816. When in his eighteenth year he came to Indianapolis and engaged as a clerk in the dry goods store of Joseph M. Moore & Co., known as the store of the Steam Mill Company, of which Messrs. James M. Ray, James Blake and Nicholas McCarty were the principal owners.

He was married in 1838 to Miss Mary Jane, eldest daughter of Harvey Bates, Esq. He then, with his father-in-law as a partner, engaged in merchandising, and afterwards with other partners, and was a successful merchant.

He was conductor on the Madison and Indianapolis Railroad, and as such brought the first train that ever ran into Indianapolis, in October, 1847.

When the Indianapolis and Cincinnati Railroad was being built he took the contract for and finished several miles of it.

Mr. Vance was one of the seventeen that left the Old School Presbyterian Church and joined the Second Presbyterian Church when it was first founded by Henry Ward Beecher.

He was well known for his generous and obliging disposition, his strict observance of every rule of morality and religion, and his kindness to those that either business or circumstances brought him in contact with.

During the war he was a devoted Union man, using his influence and means, without stint, for its successful prosecution.

One of his sons, after serving in a subordinate capacity for two or three years, was selected as Colonel of one of the city regiments in the hundred days' service, which position he filled to the honor of himself and benefit of the service.

Lawrence M. Vance was one of the enterprising and business men of Indianapolis, and as such enjoyed the confidence of its citizens. He died suddenly in April, 1863, leaving a wife and several children in good circumstances, if not wealthy.

Mrs. Vance owns that splendid business property on the corner of Virginia avenue and Washington street, fronting both on Washington street and the avenue; also the beautiful homestead on East Washington street, and although deprived by death of her partner in life's journey, seems to make the best of it, and enjoy, as best she can, the balance of her pilgrimage on earth.

GOVERNOR DAVID WALLACE

Was a native of Pennsylvania, having been born in Mifflin County on the 24th of April, 1799. When quite young, with his father's family, emigrated to Ohio, and from that State, through the friendship and intercession of General William H. Harrison, received the appointment of cadet, and was educated at West Point.

He afterwards became a citizen of Indiana, and for several years practiced law at Brookville, and represented Franklin County in the State Legislature.

In the year 1834 he was the candidate for, and was elected, Lieutenant Governor on the ticket with Governor Noah Noble.

In 1837 he was the Internal Improvement candidate for Governor against the Hon. John Dumont, the anti-improvement candidate, and was successful.

It was during this canvass that he said that an extra hen and chickens would be sufficient to pay all the extra taxation that would be levied against the farmers for internal improvement purposes. After the scheme proved a failure, he was often twitted by his friends for this expression of false prophecy.

In 1841 he was elected to Congress at the special election ordered by the Governor for members of Congress for the extra session called together by President Harrison.

Governor Wallace's first wife was the daughter of the Hon. John Test, an eminent and early Indiana lawyer, and sister of Judge Charles H. Test, now of Lafayette. By her he has three children yet living. The eldest, William Wallace, is one of our most respected citizens, and a fair lawyer. The second son, General Lew Wallace, now of Crawfordsville, whose history is well known, not only in Indiana but throughout the nation. The third son, Edward, I think, also lives in Crawfordsville.

His second wife is the daughter of Dr. John H. Sanders, late of this city, and one of its prominet physicians. By her he also has three children, a daughter, the wife of Wm. W. Leathers, a lawyer of this city, another daughter yet single, and a son about eighteen years of age.

Governor Wallace was a fine lawyer and one of the most eloquent public speakers of his day, a warm and generous-hearted man, a stranger to anything like duplicity or deceit, and enjoyed the respect and esteem of all who knew him.

He died in September, 1859, in the sixty-first year of his age.

SAMUEL H. PATTERSON.

Mr. Patterson was born in Sumner County, Tennessee, on the 9th of March, 1806. When quite young he came to Indiana a manufacturer of the cases and vender of those old-fashioned clocks, commonly called "wall sweepers," from the fact that they reached from the floor to the ceiling of an ordinary room.

He first located near Paoli, Orange County, thence to the vicinity of Indianapolis in 1829, and made his headquarters at the house of the widow Smock, two miles south of town on the Madison State road; from the latter place his peddler's were traveling in all directions selling his clocks at from thirty to fifty dollars, taking notes for the same at twelve months' time. He finally purchased the clocks of Seth Thomas' manufacture and sold throughout the country for a year or so, or until he was married, which took place on the 19th of February, 1832.

In the spring of the year 1833, he, in connection with Jas. Beard (one of his former peddlers), commenced in this city the wholesale grocery and liquor busineess, the first wholesale establishment of any kind in Indianapolis; this they continued but a short time, as the town and country would not support such an establishment.

In May, 1836, in connection with Benjamin Hensley, of Frankfort, Kentucky, leased the Indiana State Prison, at about three thousand dollars per year; this did not prove very lucrative, as there were only about sixty convicts in it at that time.

In June, 1841, he was superseded as lessee of the prison by Joseph R. Pratt and John McDougall; the intervening time between 1841 and 1846 he spent in farming and trading.

The session of the Legislature of 1845-46 was Democratic by a small majority. Pratt, then the lessee, and Simon Bottrorff, of Jeffersonville, another Democrat, procured the passage of a bill through the Legislature leasing the State Prison at eight thousand dollars per year for a term of ten years, having the bill framed to suit themselves, the lessee to be elected by the present (then) Legislature, not dreaming of, or fearing, opposition in the election.

Mr. Patterson had spent the winter in Indianapolis, seemingly taking but little interest in what was going on, occasionally entertaining his friends with a champaign party or an oyster supper. The election for lessee came off a few evenings before the final adjournment of the Legislature. Pratt and his partner were sanguine of success, as there was not known to be any opposition to them. When the balloting commenced, to the surprise of Pratt the Whigs were voting for Patterson. He yet did not apprehend any danger of the final result, until the roll-call reached the name of David

Herriman, of Noble County (a leading Democrat), who cried out "Samuel H. Patterson." Pratt afterwards said, he "saw in a moment that he had been out-flanked by the adroit wire-worker, for he had never dreamed before the balloting commenced that he was a candidate." As this incident will prove, he never lets his plans be known until they are well matured, and often nearly accomplished.

After his second lease of the prison expired, in 1856, he was the principal stockholder in a line of steamers between Cairo and New Orleans. This was one of the finest as well as largest line of boats ever established on the Mississippi River, a steamer leaving each port daily.

During the fifteen years he was lessee of the State Prison he purchased twelve or fifteen hundred acres of land, lying between Jeffersonville and New Albany, principally for the wood, which he used in burning brick. This land he yet holds, and I understand has been offered one thousand dollars per acre for some of it that lies near the northern terminus of the bridge over the Ohio River.

He is now considered one of the wealthy men of the State. Although in his sixty-fifth year, he is as energetic and industrious and as willing to turn an honest penny as when we first knew him forty years ago, when the price of a "wall sweeper" was fifty dollars. His house has been the hotel of his friends and acquaintance from all parts of the Union since his residence in Jeffersonville, now thirty-four years.

He was a member of the old "National Whig" party from its first organization in 1832 until it was disbanded in 1852; although a Southerner by birth, and the owner of slaves, he was, during the war, a warm Union man, but with no very high opinion of the party in power at the present time.

Mrs. Patterson is the only surviving member (save the writer) of her father's family of nine that came to Indianapolis fifty years ago.

WILLIAM N. JACKSON.

Billy Jackson came to Indianapolis, in the year 1833, quite a young man, and has remained such, in many respects, ever since.

He was the first iron merchant of this city, or the first that dealt in that article exclusively. His store was the second door west from the northwest corner of Washington and Meridian streets. The place at that time would not support an establishment of that kind, hence he continued the business but a short time.

There are few persons throughout the State better known to the public than is Mr. Jackson, nor has any enjoyed the confidence of the citizence of Indianapolis to a greater extent during the thirty-seven years he has called it his home.

He has been identified with the railroads that center in Indianapolis from the start; indeed, he was engaged in the office of the Madison and Indianapolis Railroad sometime before it reached this place, and when the business of the road was transacted at Madison.

He is now, and has been for several years, the General Ticket Agent at the Union Depot, where his genial countenance is very nearly always seen on the arrival or departure of the trains on the various routes that there center.

He is ever ready to assist any unprotected female, whether acquaintance or stranger, on and off the cars, and is assiduous in all the duties that pertain to his position.

Mr. Jackson is a member of the Second Presbyterian Church (generally known by the old settlers as Beecher's); has been one of the elders for several years, and exercises a considerable influence in the government and management of its affairs. He is a very benevolent and charitable man, and I understand from one of his associates and particular friends that the larger part of his salary for several years has been devoted to such purposes. In the meantime he has defrayed the expense in the education of several young ladies whose parents' circumstances precluded the possibility of their doing it. He has also educated some young men, who are now engaged in the ministry.

As intimated in the beginning of this sketch, Mr. Jackson is yet without the pale of matrimony, but is as much of a gallant as was his wont to be thirty years ago, and it is considered a compliment to any lady, young or old, to receive his attention; he seems to be blessed with perpetual youth.

GEORGE PAUL.

There lives within twenty miles of the capital of Indiana, a worthy farmer that counts his 7-30s. and 5-20s., United States Bonds, by thousands, his broad acres by hundreds, his fat bullocks, that graze upon his green pastures, by scores, his barns and graineries well filled with the products of his several farms.

He came to the valley of White River a boy near half a century ago, since which time we have enjoyed his acquaintance and friendship. George is a plain, off-hand, common-sense man, a stranger to the tom-fooleries and fashions of the present day. By industry and economy he was enabled to purchase from the Government eighty acres of land, for which he paid one hundred dollars; on this land he built himself a cabin, and in due time invited the daughter of one of his neighbors, a "well-to-do farmer," to be his partner in life's rugged journey, and share his pleasures as well as toils, which she accepted, and there grew up around them several daughters that were fair to look upon, and at the time of which I am writing were just blooming into womanhood.

George was successful, and when his neighbor, who owned an adjoining farm, wished to sell and emigrate farther West, George was the man that had the means and was willing to buy him out, which he did.

On this farm, in addition to the original cabin, was a one-story frame house of small dimensions.

After this purchase his daughters, who had been from home at school, and had learned something of city life, and the fashions of the day had rapidly gained upon their youthful minds, induced their father to give up their old homestead and cabin where they were born, and around which were entwined in their hearts many pleasing recollections and reminiscences of their childish days.

After he was fairly ensconced in his new domicil, he one day returned from the field, where he had been plowing, with the fresh earth which he had been turning up sticking to his shoes in a considerable quantity. One of the daughters met him at the front door: "Pap," said she, "will you please come in at the back door?" "Why, what is all this?" said George. "This is the parlor," replied the daughter. "Parlor, what is that, daughter?" "A parlor," said she, "is a room where young ladies see their beaux when they come 'sparking,' as you call it."

A few days after this occurrence the worthy farmer visited his old friend and neighbor. After some common-place conversation, said he, "Cyrus what on earth is the world coming to; the other day I had been plowing, and when I went to the house one of the gals met me at the door and asked if I would please walk around to the back door. They had run a table out onto the floor and put a kiver on it, then they laid the Bible and hime-book, and some other books crossways; the dagetypes they spread open on the mantel piece, where were also dishes filled with roses and other flowers. On the walls of the room they had hung up the picters of our Savior on the Cross and the Virgin Mary; the fire-place they had filled with sparry-grass bushes; on one side of the fire-place they had placed a bowl they said was to spit in, and when this was all done they called it a parlor. I don't think much of parlors any how, but if they want a parlor without a bed and chest of drawers in it, why, let them have it. How times have changed since we were young. When the parlor was all fixed the old woman wanted another 'eend put on the house for a kitchen,' to gratify the gals."

The sequel has proved that the improvements suggested by the young ladies were a success, for truly it is a nice, comfortable-looking place, with many vines creeping over the house and its surrounding lattice work, its walk leading from the outer gate to the *parlor* door, with the beds of choice flowers on either side. Such is the homestead of George Paul of Morgan County.

Another farmer, that resides in the same neighborhood, had a son that had just arrived at that interesting period of life called manhood. This young man was named Jesse. He had up to this time seen but little outside the precincts of his father's barn yard. The old gentleman was anxious that his son should see some of the great improvements that were going on in the busy world around him, and in order that he might see the world, he proposed to Jesse to make a trip to "Sinsinnatty," in the stage coach.

This proposition met with a cheerful welcome from the obedient son, who was immediately provided with the necessary means to defray the traveling expenses, and set out for "Sinsinnatty," in the four-horse mail coach.

The first night from home he stopped at the principal hotel in Greensburg, Decatur County. At the supper table the polite and attentive landlord, after helping Jesse to a piece of the fine, juicy beefsteak, asked him if he would be helped to some of the gravy. "Yes," said Jess. "I love sop."

Next morning, when the coaches drove up in front of the hotel to receive their passengers, Jesse inquired for and took the one for Indianapolis. When he arrived at home the indulgent father wished to know how far he went, and why he returned so soon. He said he had gone to Greensburg, Decatur County, and that the tavern-keeper called sop gravy, and he thought that he was far enough from home, for he did not know what they would call it by the time he reached "Sinsinnatty."

So Jesse was well satisfied with his traveling tour to learn the ways of the world, and content to take his sop under the paternal roof.

JACOB COX.

I have known this gentleman (more as a citizen and *friend* than as an artist) since he first set foot in this city, in the year 1833. The three brothers, Charles, Jacob and David, were engaged for several years as tinners, the two former as proprietors, the latter as a journeyman.

Mr. Cox had been married but a short time when, with his estimable lady, he selected Indianapolis as his permanent home, and has here continued to reside since the year above named. He has materially changed his business in this time, and is now esteemed as one of the most accomplished artists of the day. For his career in this profession I would refer the reader to an extract which I clip from the "Art Emporium," published by H. Lieber, of this city. I well remember the Banner, spoken of in that article, which was carried at the head of the Indianapolis Delegation, known as the "Wild Oats of Indianapolis," that attended the convention at the Tippecanoe Battle Ground in the year 1840.

The design was "That same old coon," surrounded by her family of some four or five little coons. After the canvass of that year this banner was presented to the mother of the writer, and is now in the possession of Mrs. Samuel H. Patterson, of Jeffersonville. Although I make no professions as a connoisseur in the fine arts, I will say Mr. Cox's talent in that line cannot be too highly appreciated.

I would not be doing the business I am engaged in, *i. e.*, that of giving sketches of character, were I to omit speaking of Mr. Cox's worthy lady as an antiquarian, and is no less an artist in that line than is her husband with his brush and paints in his.

She has the most complete assortment of specimens of antiquity, and minerals, and very nearly everything that is odd and rare from all parts of the world, either civilized or uncivilized, "from Greenland's icy mountains to India's coral strand," and she takes great pleasure in showing them to her numerous friends when they may choose to call upon her.

The "Art Emporium," speaking of Mr. Cox, says: "His history affords an excellent illustration of the futility of attempting to swerve a person from a strong natural taste or inclination. Born in Philadelphia in 1810, Jacob Cox manifested his taste for art when only thirteen years of years, and wished to study for an artist, but his friends, or family, thought they knew best what was a fit and profitable calling, and he became a tinner. In 1833 he came to Indianapolis and engaged in the business of a tin and coppersmith, and for the next seven years made no advances toward the adoption of the profession of his choice. In 1840 the Harrison campaign called into play his artistic talent, by the demand for transparency and banner painting. While others daubed through political excitement, he worked from love of his work, and painted the banner which was carried at the head of the procession to the Tippecanoe Battle Ground celebration.

"For the next two years he worked assiduously at his new-found and most congenial profession, when, in the autumn of 1842, he went to Cincinnati and opened a studio with John Dunn, a young man with artistic longings. Cox was fortunate in getting into a good run of business in Cincinnati, painting the portraits of Miles Greenwood and several other prominent gentlemen, and remained about five months. Associating with the prominent artists of the city he made great improvement in his art, and when he returned he painted portraits of Hon. Oliver H. Smith, Gover Bigger and Ex-Governor Wallace. Still he did not find painting sufficiently remunerative to justify his retiring from the prosaic business of tinning, and he continued an active partner with his brother, in that business, until about twelve years ago, when he withdrew his personal attention entirely from business, and, about five years later, sold out his interest exclusively. No artist was ever more devoted to his profession than he is, and his works bear evidence of his genius and industry. Among all who appreciate true artistic merit, Mr. Cox has a lasting reputation, and many of his pictures have found purchasers in distant cities."

JOHN L. KETCHAM.

In the short space I design in this work of sketching the characters of the old citizens of Indianapolis, I do not think I could add one word to, nor would I willingly take one from, the eulogy upon the character of Mr. Ketcham, which I find as his obituary notice in the "Evening Mirror," of this city, dated April 21st, 1869.

With Mr. Ketcham I was well acquainted for the entire thirty-six years that he was a resident of this city. I have transacted business with him as a lawyer, as a magistrate, and also as a private citizen, and will add my testimony to his worth in each capacity, and also to his many other noble qualities and christian virtues.

The cause of his sudden and unexpected death that gave such a shock to, and cast such a gloom over the entire city, was by falling through a hatchway in the store of Alford, Talbott & Co., in the Opera House building.

He had stepped into the store but a moment before the sad accident happened, to speak with one of the proprietors, and by a backward step he lost his balance and was precipitated twelve feet into the cellar, and died of the injuries he received, the next morning.

I therefore cheerfully adopt the following, which I clip from the "Mirror:"

"The announcement this morning that the injuries received by Hon. John L. Ketcham, in the fall at the store of Alford, Talbott & Co., yesterday afternoon, had proven fatal, has thrown a saddening gloom over the city. So sudden has been the removal from the activity of life to the stillness of death, that it seems hard to fully realize the painful truth. From the full vigor of a life, unusually earnest and active, he has been taken by one of those terrible decrees of accident that are ever reminding man that his existence is brief, and uncertain in its termination.

"John L. Ketcham was born April 3, 1810, in Shelby County, Kentucky. His father, Colonel John Ketcham, removed to Indiana when he was an infant, but on account of Indian troubles was compelled to return to Kentucky. A few years later he again came to Indiana, and settled in Monroe County, near Bloomington. Colonel Ketcham was a man of strong character, with marked energy and resolute purpose. An early advocate of the Free Soil movement, he continued in that party through all its obloquy and feebleness. His wife was a woman equally marked. She had a quick perception into the right, and was ever ready to sacrifice to it. Her controlling spring seemed to be duty, and she never let pleasure lead her from it.

"From such parentage John L. Ketcham came, and well represented in his life the familiar characteristics of each, more especially being a counterpart of his mother. Colonel Ketcham died two years since. His wife still survives. Mr. Ketcham was educated at the University at Bloomington, under Dr. Wiley, to whom he was much attached. He was graduated in the regular course when quite young. In 1833 he came to Indianapolis and began the study of law under Judge Blackford. Soon after admission to the bar he was elected Justice of the Peace, and held the office one term. This was the only office he was ever a candidate for, his subsequent life being strictly devoted to his profession. In 1836 he married Jane, eldest daughter of Samuel Merrill, Esq. He leaves his wife and a family of eight.

"In his profession he was associated in partnership from time to time with Napoleon B. Taylor, Lucian Barbour, D. W. Coffin and James L. Mitchell, his present partner.

"Such in brief is the history of one who yesterday, in the fullest vigor, was with us. There is, perhaps, no man in the city whose leading traits of character are more marked. For thirty-six years he was a citizen of Indianapolis, for the last twenty of which he has lived in the home he has been so sadly called from. It is a delicate thing to try to portray a character so well known. It lives so in the memory of all that it is a part of the history of the place. But we can but say briefly a little of that that comes quickest to the hearts that are so suddenly called to grieve over a loss so irreparable.

"The hospitality of Mr. Ketcham is well known. It was a part of the duty of life that he never forgot, but made it most pleasant to all who entered his family circle. The nobleness of the man, indeed, was quickest seen in his home. An exceeding tenderness marked his whole intercourse with his family and family friends. Regularity of life was a part of his faith. An untiring worker, he never allowed one duty to overshadow another. His idea of life was to fulfill every duty as it came. The boundaries of duty were never crossed. All his life a Christian, he let his Christianity follow him wherever he went. It is said by those nearest him, that in all his long residence in the city, he never missed a religious meeting of the church to which he belonged, if in the city, or not unwell. A ready speaker at all times, he seemed especially gifted in the prayer meeting, always having something to add which was of value. The main-spring of his life was Christian duty. The influence he silently exerted in the regular observance of his daily devotions is past all expression. Those living near him have often spoken with the deepest feeling of the laborers, when passing his house in the morning, stopping to catch the hymns of praise that were the ushering in of the day to him and his family.

"Strong in his friendship, he never forgot a friend or failed him when needed. During the war his sympathetic patriotism was most marked. Two of his sons were in the army, and every battle was watched and prayed over as if they were there. A man of unostentatious benevolence, he literally did not let his right hand know what his left did. Many instances of his substantial kindness are now known, that before were buried in the hearts of giver and receiver.

"Mr. Ketcham was one of thirteen who left the Old School Church on the division, and founded the Second Presbyterian Church. Mr. Beecher, the first pastor of that church, was accustomed to rely upon him as confidently as he could upon himself. When the Second Church became too full for usefulness, Mr. Ketcham was one of the handful of brave men who founded the Fourth Church. He gave of his time and means without stint to bring that church to its present standing. An elder in the Second Church, he was soon made an elder in the Fourth, in which position he worked faithfully to the last.

"John L. Ketcham died with his armor on. Working nobly for God and man, he was ready at the call. No preparation time was wanted. He stepped from life here to the Life beyond. Vain are our words to say to his family that he has done his work. Vainly can we tender sympathy—vainly speak to the crushed hearts. It is the work of the God he gave his life-service to, and humbly we look to him for comfort for them.

"'Enoch walked with God and was not, for God took him.'"

SAMUEL BECK

Is one of the staid and substantial citizens of Indianapolis, and one that deserves to be, and is, respected by all who know him for his plain, unassuming manner, his strict integrity and upright walk in life.

He is a strict and consistent member of the Methodist Church and a Christian in the true sense of the word, being governed in his intercourse with his neighbors and fellow-men as near as he can by the Golden Rule.

I heard an incident of him the other day that illustrates his true character. A friend of his whose only fault had been that of drinking to excess, through the influence of Mr. Beck was induced to join the church, and for nearly a year had been an attentive member, and had lived up to its rules; but in an evil hour was induced to drink, and fell from grace in that respect. Mr. Beck, hearing of it, instead of informing the controlling powers of the church, sought out his friend and by his persuasive powers induced him to resume his duties to the church as though nothing had happened. Are not such acts more Christian like than to have him exposed and turned out of the church, and, perhaps, seal his fate forl ife? Such, however, is the writer's view.

Mr. Beck has worked at the gunsmith business very near, if not quite, the entire thirty-seven years he has been a citizen of this city, and is yet as industrious and assiduous to his duties as when we first knew him, and at this writing has been longer in the same business than any other person in the city.

Mr. Beck is a native of Pennsylvania, but at an early day came to Connersville, Fayette County, and there resided until his removal this place in the year 1833. Although he has passed the meridian of life he bids fair to live many years, which, if he does, no doubt, as the past have been, will be devoted to doing good, and usefulness to the cause of humanity.

ADAM KNODLE.

Has by pre-emption right become one of the fixed institutions of Indianapolis, and like the worthy gunsmith, whose sketch precedes this, has been longer in his present business than any other person in the city, and next to Mr. Beck has been longer in the same business than any other in Indianapolis, and is the veteran boot and shoe maker and dealer.

He came to Indianapolis from Philadelphia in May, 1835, and has done business on the same square, and very nearly on the same ground he is now, for the whole thirty-five years of his residence here.

In the thirty-five years the writer has been acquainted with him he has never heard a harsh or unkind word spoken of Adam Knodle. He is a plain, unobtursive man, and one that thinks he has quite enough to do to mind his own business and let others, or their attorneys, take care of theirs.

He is not an avaricious man by any means, and has been content quietly to pick up the crumbs that have fallen in his path from time to time and has had the good sense and faculty to take care of them.

I remember seeing him at the southwest window of the Court House in November, 1836, depositing one of the unterrified Democratic tickets for Martin Van Buren, and he still adheres with strict tenacity to the same faith, although he never tries to force his opinions upon others.

Mr. Knodle's son George is now engaged in business with him as a partner, and seems to be in temperament and habits a second edition of the father.

WILLIAM WILKISON,

More generally known as "Billy" Wilkison, was born in New Castle, Delaware, but when a child went to Pennsylvania and there resided until he came to this place in 1836.

He was among the first to rein four horses, attached to a twelve-passenger mail coach, through the streets of Indianapolis, as he did through the summer season when the roads were good. In winter, when the roads were bad, he was equally expert with the same number hitched to the fore wheels of a "mud wagon," on which was placed a queensware crate in which the mail and one passenger were stowed. In this way he plowed through the mud between Richmond and this place at the rate of two miles an hour.

Mr. Wilkison's success is a fair illustration of what perseverance, industry and economy will accomplish. He is now possessed of fine city property, as well as a farm adjoining the city, and is able to live comfortably on his income without physical labor.

During the time he was employed as above stated, he made the acquaintance of the daughter of 'Squire Foley, of Hancock County, and she now rejoices in the name of Mrs. Wilkison. "Go thou and do likewise."

MACKEREL BROWN.

About the year 1832 a merchant employed a young man to clerk in his store. This young man had never been engaged in business of this kind and was inexperienced in the prices and worth of the different articles.

At this time all kinds of merchandize were kept in the same store, from a grubbing hoe to a fine silk shawl, and also all kinds of groceries and produce. In this store was kept a very fine article of No 1 mackerel; they retailed for eighteen and three-fourth cents each, or three for a half dollar.

John Givin sent his son to the store with thirty-one and a

fourth cents, and told him to tell Brown to send him the worth of it in mackerel, supposing that he would send him a large and a small one. His son returned with a half dozen of the finest quality. Mr. Given thought that as Brown was a new hand in the store, he would go over and correct the mistake himself. When he went in, said he: "Brown, you made a great mistake in the number of those mackerel you sent me." "Yes," said Brown, "I thought after your son had left that I should have sent a dozen." From this circumstance he was ever called "Mackerel" Brown while he lived in Indianapolis.

At the time the regiment of mounted volunteers, known, and spoken of on another page, as the "Bloody Three Hundred," was being raised, Brown appeared very war-like, and was very sorry that his engagements were such that precluded the possibility of his joining the expedition. Some doubted his courage and concluded to test it.

Nathaniel Cox and Matthias Nowland went about dark into the woods, near where the Madison and Jeffersonville Depot is now located, and there built several small fires. Robert McPherson was to invite Brown to take a walk in that direction.

When within about fifty yards of the fires McPherson called Brown's attention to them and expressed the opinion that they were the camp-fires of hostile Indians. At the preconcerted time Nat Cox gave a war whoop (which he could equal to an Indian), and fired his pistol or gun. Brown in an instant turned and fled, and did not stop until he reached the residence of Governor Noble, and informed him that the town was surrounded by eight or ten thousand hostile Indians, and that Bob McPherson had been shot down by his side. The Governor at once told him that it must be a mistake, that there were no Indians nearer than the Upper Wabash, and they were known to be friendly. But

Brown was sure and positive, and wanted the Governor to come to town and call out the people. Upon the Governor's refusal to do so, Brown said he did not feel safe to return alone and stayed all night at the Governor's residence.

This and the mackerel story were both more than Brown could stand, and he soon left for other parts less exposed to the depredations of hostile Indians, and where mackerel were sold cheaper by the dozen.

DANIEL M. NOOE,

Like the writer, came to Indianapolis a boy and before his young idea was taught to shoot, and when it was nothing more than an unsightly village of log cabins, and had been an eye-witness to its great and unparalleled prosperity; when I say unparalleled, I mean for a village that has sprung up in the midst of an unbroken and densely timbered forest, and far-removed from any thing like a stream that could be called navigable for commercial purposes.

He partially learned the blacksmith trade with his father, who was among the first to work at that business in this place, After the proprietors of the many lines of stages that centered in this place (James Johnson & Co.) commenced the manufacture of coaches, on the southeast corner of Market and Pennsylvania streets, and where the Post Office and United States Court Buildings now stand, he went to work for them as a coachsmith and continued with them and their successors several years, and was a good workman and efficient in his business.

When the California mania broke out in 1849, he was induced by his particular friend, that distinguished Lafayette lawyer, the late R. A. Lockwood, to join him and go to that distant El Dorado, as many others did, to seek their fortune.

In this he was not successful, and returned to friends and

kindred as he had left them, and among them to seek what he had failed to find in the golden region.

He is yet one of our well known citizens and possesses many good qualities, and never suffers the beggar to go hungry or empty handed from his door, and no man in Indianapolis would do more to relieve distress or want quicker or more cheerfully than Dan Nooe.

CHARLES GARNER.

This good-natured Welchman has been a citizen of this county and city near thirty-four years. He was born and raised in Denbieshire, North Wales, left his native country and landed in New York in the spring of 1836. He immediately came to this county and purchased a farm about four miles southwest of the city, and was for ten years a successful farmer.

He then sold his farm and engaged in active business in town and continued it for ten years more; then again wishing to engage in farming purchased what was then known as the Crowder farm, now known as the Garner farm, on the west bank of White River, and where the Crawfordsville and Lafayette State roads cross that stream.

During his long residence and with his extensive acquaintance in this county, he has moved along in a very harmonious way with his neighbors and others and has the reputation of being governed by the Golden Rule. Although a quiet, good-natured and unobtrusive man, it would not do for any person to try to impose upon his good nature; they might find too late that they were mistaken in the man.

He has raised a family of several children; he has four sons, the eldest, H. S. Garner, is a practical printer, and a member of the Typographical Union of this city, and holds one of the most responsible positions in it, that of Financial Secretary; the second son, Watkin, I think resides in Iowa, a third son is connected with the Clock and Mirror Emporium of Daumont and Company, of this city, the fourth, Charles, is a practicing physician.

From what we have learned of these young men, from those who best know them, Charley may well be, and is, proud of four such sons

"Some men may pause, and say, when some admire,
They are his sons and worthy of their sire."

REV. JAMES B. BRITTON,

The first rector of Christ Church and first Episcopal minister stationed in this city, is now known throughout the land as an eminent and distinguished divine, and one of the purest and best men belonging to that most respectable church organization.

The writer may have some partiality for Mr. B. on account of his having performed for him in that church (the first of the kind in any church of the city), a certain little ceremony that is considered to seal the destiny of at least two persons for weal or woe through life. I must here acknowledge our joint obligation to the reverend gentleman for having performed his part in so beautiful and masterly style.

Mr. B. was born in Philadelphia, Pa., on 26th day of August, 1810. At quite an early age was sent to Columbian College, Washington City, then under the presidency of Dr. Stoughton, a distinguished Baptist minister. He became a member of the Episcopal church in Louisville, Kentucky, then under the ministry of Rev. D. C. Page. Mr. B.'s first charge was in Louisville, after having been prepared for the ministry at Lexington, Kentucky, and ordained by Bishop Smith in 1836.

He came to Indianapolis on the 4th day of July, 1837, as a missionary and worshiped in the Court House, then in the old Presbyterian church. Mrs. McOuat was one of the first members of the communion, which only numbered five in all.

The late Judge James Morrison, Joseph M. Moore and the present esteemed citizen, William H. Morrison, were members of the Presbyterian church, but soon left and joined Mr. B.'s. Here was the nucleus out of which grew the four Episcopal congregations of Indianapolis.

Mr. Britton was at, and assisted in, the consecration of Christ Church, the first Episcopal Church in the place, and made its first rector. In the establishment of this church I am told Dr. George W. Mears and Arthur St. Clair were prominent, and Dr. Livingston Dunlap, Charles W. Cady and William Hannaman were warm friends.

It may be proper here to add that no church in Indianapolis, in that day, was more prosperous and successful or increased in numbers faster than did the Episcopal under Mr. B.'s ministry, many prominent members of other churches leaving and attaching themselves to this. True, when that eloquent and flowery divine, Henry Ward Beecher, organized his church, some of Mr. Britton's members went to him; but accessions came from other quarters, so the church continued to increase, although some of its most prominent members had left.

The first fair under the auspices of the ladies of this church, in the winter of 1838-9, was highly successful, realizing about three hundred dollars profit, a larger amount, in proportion to the number and wealth of the citizens, than is realized from the fairs of the present day.

On account of one of those unfortunate differences of opinion, that sometimes arise in churches as well as other organizations, Mr. B. conceived it to be his duty, to himself as well as to the church, to resign the rectorship, which he did in 1840.

I understand he has been as useful and successful in other fields of ministerial labor as he was here. Long may he live to witness the good he has accomplished.

How changed since he first came here (with his bride), a missionary, thirty-two years ago, he found this place a village, without an Episcopal house of worship, save the Court House. He visited this place a few weeks since, for the purpose of placing a monument to the memory of his infant, now dead over thirty years. What a change there was presented to his view! The place he left but a village, near thirty years since, he found a beautiful city, with four splendid edifices dedicated to the worship of the Most High, in accordance with the peculiar tenets of his own faith.

It is melancholy to think how many of the prominent men and beautiful ladies of that day who contributed so much of their means, and encouraged by their presence the Episcopal church, have passed away and sleep that sleep that knows no waking until the Great Rector shall call them to take their places in his congregation above.

JOSHUA M. W. LANGSDALE.

There are but few persons in Indianapolis but what are acquainted with the familiar name of Josh Langsdale. Mr. Langsdale came to this place from Boone county, Kentucky, in the year 1836, and possessed to a considerable degree the plain, off-hand, blunt manner peculiar to the citizens of his native State.

In former years he was ever ready to accommodate a person with a friendly game of "draw-poker," or stake a "V" on a quarter-race, or, if he had confidence in the success of his favorite Democratic candidate for office, also risk what he called a "sawbuck" (a ten dollar note), on his success.

Mr. Langsdale could not be considered a very immoral man by any means, yet like most every person of that day who were unrestrained by their connection with the church, would sometimes indulge in those sports and pastimes.

After he had been brought to see the error of his ways and

had attached himself to the Methodist church, of which he is now a worthy and respected member, he was as enthusiastic in the good cause in which he had engaged as he had ever been in the success of the Democratic party on election day. It was said of him that on one occasion, at a camp-meeting, near Augusta, in this county (and soon after he had joined the church), that he commenced to sing a hymn. Brother Jimmy Kettleman, in a low tone of voice, said to him, "Brother Langsdale you have the wrong tune to that hymn." Says Josh, pulling out his pocket-book, "Brother Kettleman, I'll go you a 'V' that I am right, and that that's the right tune; and we'll leave it to 'Old Sorrel'" (the Rev. James Havens).

Whether Mr. Langsdale was right or not, I have no means of knowing, but this much I do know, he generally did that which he said he would.

He has now had over twenty years' experience in starting and singing hymns, and if he was not right then, I doubt whether any could beat him at this time.

He has held several offices in the gift of the people, an important one, that of Trustee of Center Township, and discharged its duties with credit to himself and fidelity to the public interests, and there are but few persons in Indianapolis whose check we would rather have, to the bank where they transact business, than that of J. M. W. Langsdale. He now enjoys the confidence and respect of the entire community.

NATHANIEL B. OWENS

Was born in Baltimore, Maryland, October 18, 1806, and with his father's family emigrated to Fairfield County, Ohio, in the spring of 1812. He came to Indianapolis and engaged to help plaster the State House, in the year 1834, and continued to follow the business up to 1862. A large portion of the time he was also engaged in farming near the city.

Mr. Owens has raised a family of eight children, six sons and two daughters, and furnished from his family five soldiers to help fight the battles for the preservation of the Union and the success of the stars and stripes, all of which returned to cheer the hearts of their parents.

Mr. Owens is a worthy and honest man, a member of the Methodist congregation that worship in Asbury Chapel. One of his daughters is the wife of William Wingate, Esq., another of our old and respected citizens, he having been raised in the city.

Mr. Owens has for several years been almost totally deprived of his eye-sight, but is now so far recovered as to be able to attend to his ordinary business, with a fair prospect of entire recovery.

The writer has known him the entire time that he has made this county and city his residence, and cheerfully bears testimony to his many fine traits of character and Christian virtues in this brief but truthful way.

WILLIAM J. BROWN

Was a name as familiar to the people of Indiana as that of any man in the State, he was known and called by his numerous acquaintances as "Bill" Brown.

Mr. Brown was born in Lewis County, Kentucky, in the year 1805. In his fourteenth year, 1819, with his relatives, settled in Richland Township, Rush County, Indiana; he there received a plain English education and studied law.

In the summer of 1835 he was a candidate for and elected to represent Rush County in the State Legislature, and it was while electioneering for this position an incident occured which he often told on himself in after years.

He had gone to the house of an acquaintance, who lived on the bank of Flat Rock, by the name of Jones. He enquired of the wife of the gentleman where her husband was, she told him that he had gone down the creek to the mill. "Well," said Mr. Brown, to the lady, "Mrs. Jones, as Mr. Jones is not at home to-day I will have to electioneer a little with you." Mr. B. said she looked him firmly in the eye for about a minute, and then said "Mr. Brown, I have been a married woman ten years, and you are the first man who ever named such a thing to me." Mr. B. explained that he was a candidate for the legislature and wished her influence with her husband to secure his vote. Said she, "Oh, is that all!" He received Mr. Jones' vote and was elected, and here was the start of the political career which made him so conspicuous in after years.

While a member of the legislature he became very popular, especially so with the Democratic members, and during the session of 1836-7 he was elected Secretary of State, and in January, 1837, with his family removed to Indianapolis and entered upon the discharge of the duties of his office, which he held for four years.

In the political whirlwind that swept over the country in 1840, a legislature was elected which swept him from office, not, however, without leaving him many personal friends of both political parties.

In 1841, some who were opposed to him in national politics, conceived the idea of running him against the nominee of their own party for Representative of the county. Mr. Brown was opposed by some of his own political friends, on the ground that he would only be sacrificing his time and money, as it was deemed almost impossible to overcome the large Whig majority of the previous year, which was about three hundred and sixty, a very large majority, when it is remembered the whole vote of the county was only about fifteen hundred.

Mr. B. contended if his own friends would only give him a clear track and a fair race he could easily overcome the

Whig majority of the previous year. At last, with reluctance, they yielded and he took the field as an independent candidate, untrammeled by party pledges. His first appointment to speak was at Broad Ripple, in Washington township, a precinct that gave about one hundred and ten votes, one hundred of which were Whig. On Mr B.'s arrival he was astonished to find almost the entire voting population of the township present. After the usual salutations with some of his friends, he mounted the rostrum, or stump. He said: "Fellow-citizens of Broad Ripple and Washington township, when the devil took our Savior up into the mountains and told him the cattle upon a thousand hills and all the kingdoms of the world, and the glory of them were his if he would fall down and worship him," said Mr. B., "he made a special reservation of Washington township to himself and his heirs forever. Now, my friends, I have come to dispute and try titles with him." Mr. Brown decreased the Whig majority in Washington township and, to the astonishment of all, was elected to the legislature.

In the year 1843 he was the Democratic candidate against Governor Wallace for Congress, and it was in this canvass he was outwitted by the Governor on one occasion, although he was elected. At the previous session of Congress the Governor had voted for an appropriation of ten thousand dollars to test the efficiency of the magnetic telegraph, then being constructed between Washington and Baltimore. Mr. Brown charged the Governor with voting for a useless expenditure of the public money, wasting it in trying the experiment of transmitting news by electricity. The charge of voting for this appropriation he proved by the Journal of the House.

By some means the Governor got possession of the Journal that Mr. Brown used, and cut that page out. Mr. Brown had made that charge on one occasion and searched the Journal in vain for the proof. Mr. B. politely acknowledged that he was beaten on this occasion, but provided himself with another Journal and was particular to keep it out of the Governor's way.

In March, 1845, he was appointed by President Polk Second Assistant Post Master General, and with his family remained in Washington during that administration.

When General Taylor became President, in the year 1849, Mr. Brown returned to Indiana, and was again elected to Congress from his old district, and was fairly elected Speaker of the House of Representatives by the votes of its members, but before the vote was announced by the chair some of the southern members changed their vote, thereby defeating Mr. Brown, rather than have a member from a free State hold so important a position. They had no cause to be alarmed, for Mr. B. would have been, as he ever had, true to his party, true to his oath, true to the Constitution and the rights of the several States under it. He was ever known to be a State's rights man on the question that was then agitating the public, and throughout the session voted with those who had defeated him.

It was at this session of Congress that the bill known as the Compromise of 1850 was passed, admitting California as a State into the Union, and settling, for the time being, the vexed question of slavery—Mr. Brown voting and acting with the friends of the measure.

He was appointed by President Buchanan's administration Special Mail Agent for Indiana, and filled that position (for which he was peculiarly fitted) up to the time of his death, which occurred in 1859.

Mr. Brown was a fair lawyer, but a much better politician, and possessed a great deal of tact in that way. Whoever saw Bill Brown mount the stump or rostrum to address an audience, can forget his broad grin, which generally convulsed his auditory with laughter before he spoke a word?

He was a very liberal man, and never valued money farther than for the comforts it would furnish his family, to which he was devotedly attached.

His wife resides about three miles south of the city. He left five children, three sons and two daughters. His eldest son, Austin H. Brown, was Collector of Internal Revenue, for the Indianapolis District, during the administration of President Johnson, and has, for several years, represented his ward in the Common Council. His second son, Captain George Brown, of the U. S. Navy, rendered signal service to the Government, during the late war, as Commandant of one of the gun-boats. The third son, William, is engaged in the city as a clerk in a store.

His eldest daughter is a widow, and resides with her mother. The second daughter is the wife of E. L. Palmer (son of N. B. Palmer), a book merchant of the city.

Mr. Brown was a plain, frank man; no duplicity or deceit could be found in his composition, and he will long be remembered as one of Indiana's most successful politicians.

JOSEPH M. MOORE

Was born in the city of New York on the 9th of April, 1813, but with his mother lived in Newark, New Jersey, the most of his life, until he came to Indianapolis in the summer of 1823.

Mr. Moore was the cousin of our esteemed fellow-citizen, James M. Ray, who had sent for him for the purpose of educating and fitting him, as he did, for business.

Mr. Calvin Fletcher had been visiting his friends in the East, and took charge of Mr. Moore (who was only in his eleventh year), and brought him to this place; from the Ohio River they both rode the same horse.

Mr. Moore received the most of his education in the same school with the writer, which was taught by that benevolent and christian man, Ebenezer Sharpe. When he had finished his education he was deputy in the office of county clerk, then filled by his cousin, and it was there, under the instruction of that good man, his habits and character were formed, which afterwards proved to be so useful to society.

He then was the active partner in the store of J. M. Moore & Co.; the other partners were James M. Ray, James Blake and the late Nicholas McCarty. They did business on the west corner of the alley, on the north side of Washington, between Meridian and Pennsylvania streets.

In the year 1840 he was selected to edit the campaign paper, the "Spirit of Seventy-Six," that advocated the election of General Harrison to the Presidency with signal ability.

After the old hero was installed as President, Mr. Moore was appointed postmaster in this city, but after the defection of President Tyler from the Whig party, in 1841. he was the first victim to proscription; he was removed and his predecessor reinstated.

About the year 1844 he was appointed cashier of the branch at Madison of the State Bank of Indiana; when the affairs of that bank were wound up he filled the same position in the branch of the Bank of the State, and continued there until his death in January, 1858.

Mr. Moore was a member of the First Presbyterian Church, and was among the first to leave it and join the Episcopal Church when it was first organized by the Rev. J. B. Britton as its Rector, in 1837.

As a business man he was of more than ordinary ability, and with his strict integrity and attention to business made him a valuable acquisition to any business institution.

He was a fair political writer, and, as such, rendered great service to the Whig cause in editing the paper above mentioned.

After Mr. Moore's death his family returned to this city,

and are still resident here. His oldest son, who bears the father's name, married the grand-daughter of his father's former preceptor, and daughter of Thomas H. Sharpe, Esq.; he was engaged in the wholesale drug business, and was one of the victims to the fire of the Morrison Opera House building that occurred on the night of the 17th of January, 1870.

A second son is engaged as clerk in the wholesale grocery establishment of Alford, Talbot & Co.

His other three children are daughters, one of which is married; the other two reside with their mother on East Michigan street.

CHARLES W. CADY

Was a native of New Hampshire, having been born in the village of Keene; but when his father was elected Secretary of State he, with him, became a resident of Concord, the capital, and there resided until he came to this place, in May, 1837.

He was the first Secretary of the Indiana Mutual Insurance Company, of which James Blake was the President, and they managed its business jointly for about fifteen years.

Mr. Cady was a very liberal and kind-hearted man, and contributed of his means, without stint, for all charitable purposes. Although not a member of any church, he was active in organizing the first Episcopal Church (Christ) in this city, and formed one of its congregation as long as he lived.

In his young days he had been afflicted with white swelling, which caused one of his knees to be stiff, thereby laming him.

He was very fond of hunting, and when he first came to this city the country abounded in game of all kinds.

On one occasion, he and the brother of the writer of this notice went, before daylight, over to Fall Creek bottoms, where it was known several broods of wild turkeys roosted.

Mr. Cady crossed the creek on the bridge on the Crawsordsville State road, and went up on the west side. My brother continued on the east side. When three or four hundred yards above the bridge, my brother commenced calling the turkeys, which he did by using the wing bone of one, imitating them so nearly as to defy detection. While calling in this way, he discovered Mr. Cady approaching on the opposite side of the creek. My brother then slipped behind a tree and called again. Mr. Cady then stepped into the creek, the water coming above his knees, and waded over. My brother, to avoid detection, had left the place of his concealment and gone further into the woods.

On their return, with several fine turkeys which they had killed, my brother told the joke on Mr. Cady, who did not positively deny it, but said it might have been some other person that waded the creek. My brother replied that he could not be mistaken, as he knew Mr. Cady by his limping. This irritated him. He said he had never limped in his life. It was but a few days until this breach in their friendship was healed, and they were ready for another turkey hunt.

On another occasion, he and a particular friend, who was equally irritable, were gunning in company. They both had shot at a flock of wild pigeons at the same moment, but only one bird fell. They both claimed to have killed it, which caused hard feelings between them, and they did not speak to each other for several days, although they boarded at the same house and took their meals at the same table.

He was quick to take any slight, whether intended or not, and as quick to forgive and forget it.

He was a great gallant of the young ladies, as well as a favorite with the sex whether married or single.

Mr. Cady died in November, 1855, leaving a widow and five children—two sons and three daughters—all of whom still reside here.

Doctor Abner Pope.

His wife was Miss Keirsted, of Cincinaati, a niece of the late George H. Dunn, of Lawrenceburg.

DOCTOR ABNER POPE

Was born in Salem, Massachusetts, in the year 1793, a place made famous, during the last century, for the superstition of its inhabitants and the punishment of such as were suspected of witchcraft.

Dr. Pope descended from an English family that came over to this country soon after the arrival of the Mayflower. Dr. Franklin (his mother being a Pope) came over with the same family.

Dr. Pope is a quaker and uses the plain language. "Thee," "thou" and "thine," are upon his flippant tongue. He also dresses in the peculiar style of that religious organization, broad-brimmed white hat and round-breasted coat, generally of the drab color.

He practiced medicine upon the Steam or Thompsonian principle, and had in his shop a long box made water-tight, in which he placed his patients and raised the steam on them to one hundred and twenty-five degrees Fahrenheit, and after limbering in this way for some time, he would douse them head and heels into ice-cold water, and rub them well with a dry towel.

Whether he killed more than he cured, I am not prepared to say; but I occasionally see some of our old citizens that went through this operation walking about the streets, apparently none the worse, if not considerably better for it.

In the Doctor's shop and store, which were together, and located on the north side of Washington street, near where the Trade Palace now stands, was to be found all kinds of merchandise with, perhaps, the exception of bar iron. "*Bitter yerbs,*" all kinds of vegetable medicines, and every other article, from a paper of lettuce seed to a fine shawl, or silver thimble to silk hose. His store was generally the last resort for any article scarce in the market, and when not to be found at Dr. Pope's, the search for it was abandoned.

He was a warm and enthusiastic Whig, and advocated the measures of that party with great zeal and earnestness. In the year 1844, some waggish neighbor played a prank upon him by hoisting a rooster in front of his door.

He left his native town when quite young and lived in Baltimore, Maryland, until the spring of 1836, when he came to Indianapolis, and has resided here ever since. Although now seventy-seven years of age, he is looking hale and hearty, and bids fair to live many years longer.

DAVID V. CULLEY

Was a native of Pennsylvania, but came to Corydon when it was the capital of the State, and, as a journeyman printer, worked on the State work in the office of John Douglass, the father of two of the late proprietors of the "Indianapolis State Journal.'

Mr. Culley then went to Lawrenceburg and edited and published the "Indiana Palladium," a paper in the interest of and advocating the election of General Jackson to the Presidency.

He was an active and enthusiastic politician, and advocated his opinions with a force and fluency that few possessed. He was a man of more than ordinary ability, sound judgment and great stability of character. I remember him well as one of the active and leading men of his party while in the legislature as Senator of Dearborn County.

In the canvass for Governor and Lieutenant Governor, in the year 1831, he was placed on the Jackson ticket as its candidate for the latter, with James G. Read for Governor against Noah Noble and Milton Stapp, the Clay candidates. Although his party were in a majority in the State, the great popularity of Governor Noble carried the election of the Lieutenant Governor, and Mr. Culley was defeated.

In the year 1836, he was appointed, by General Jackson, Register of the Land Office for the Indianapolis district, and, with his family, removed to this place, and resided here until the time of his death, June 4, 1869.

Soon after his removal to this place, he identified himself with the benevolent and charitable institutions of the city, ever taking a deep interest in Sunday Schools, and, afterwards, the general free school system of the State and city. He was, for years, one of the trustees of the latter, and took a lively interest in the cause of education generally.

He was one of the leading members of the Second Presbyterian Church, becoming so while it was under the pastorate of that well known and flowery divine, Henry Ward Beecher.

Mr. Culley was often appointed by will, and selected on the dying bed, as administrator of estates, always complying cheerfully with the request of the dead, and performing the duties to the entire satisfaction of the living.

In writing of so many old and departed but not forgotten friends, brings a sad clearness of the past and crowds my memory with many pleasing recollections, as well as melancholy regrets; and we sometimes feel that we are almost the last of the pioneers of Indiana.

Mr. Culley was of a pleasant disposition, and had a kind word for all. In person he was about five feet eight inches in height, spare made, with mild dark eyes, black hair and dark complexion.

In his attire he was plain and neat, and possessed a great deal of native dignity, with a fine address. We have noticed him, while a member of the Senate, called on to temporarily preside, which he did with a dignity and promptness found in but few presiding officers of the present day; indeed, it was this fact that secured him the nomination for Lieutenant Governor in 1831. But he has gone from among the living.

> So fades, so perishes, grows dim and dies
> All that the world is proud of."

JUSTIN SMITH.

The connection that existed between Mr. Smith and the writer makes it somewhat embarrassing to him to say what he would under other circumstances.

He was a native of the central part of the State of New York, and when quite a young man went south and for a few years engaged in the shipping business in Charleston, South Carolina.

He then returned north and engaged in the wholesale liquor business in Philadelphia, Pennsylvania.

Thence to New York City, and was there married to Miss Maria B. Lloyd, who was the mother of his several children. From New York City he removed to the neighborhood of his birth place, and established a furnace for the manufacture of iron. Thence to Rochester, Monroe County, where he resided until his removal to Indianapolis, in November, 1838.

At the latter place he contributed considerable to the improvement of the city and making it what it is to-day, one of the most beautiful cities of the Union.

When he left this last place to find a home for himself and his family it was a formidable undertaking, as there was no railroads, as now, to facilitate their journey, and when he parted with his friends it was thought to be a last and long farewell, but such has been the progress and improvement in locomotion that they now often meet, in what was then the Western wilds, those whom they never expected to again meet on this side of the grave.

In less than one short year after Mr. Smith's arrival at his new home, she, who had thus far in life's journey been the partner of his bosom, fell a victim to a malignant fever, and left him without the counsel and advice of his best friend, and his children without a mother whom they loved so well.

Mrs. Smith was a lady of fine accomplishments, having been educated at one of the best female institutions in New York, and endowed with such personal attractions that her place was never filled in the heart of him she left behind.

Mr. Smith was not a fashionable christian, but practiced the genuine as he went along in kindness to the poor and acts of charity. He seldom gave to societies, but found the objects of charity on the highway or in the by-ways.

In the year 1844 a distinguished man of the State died. Mr. S. was asked if he was going to the funeral; his answer was, "as this was a rich and distinguished man there would be plenty there to bury him." A few weeks after this a well known pauper died; the funeral procession consisted of the hearse, a country wagon, with the relatives of the deceased, and Mr. Smith in the rear in his buggy.

At the time the Roberts' Chapel congregation worshipped in the Court House, Mr. Smith heard that their preacher (Rev. Mr. Bayliss) was a Democrat, so he attended his meetings quite regular. One evening there was considerable religious excitement in the congregation. The minister invited the mourners to come forward to the altar to be prayed for. Mr. Smith, having a curiosity to know who wanted praying for, rose to his feet, and resting on his cane, was discovered by the minister, who invited him in this way: "Will father Smith come forward?" Mr. Smith very deliberately went forward, took a five-franc piece from his pocket, laid it on the table, and remarked: "If that will pay you for the trouble I've been to you, I shall not visit your church again." So he never again went to hear Mr. Bayliss; he did not like to be called father Smith, nor singled out in that way.

Mr. Smith was a large, portly man, and possessed considerable political information. He said to the writer over thirty years ago, that the seed was then being sown which would produce the bloodiest intestine war the world ever knew of.

Mr. Smith's eldest daughter, Mary Francis, is the wife of V. C. Hanna, eldest son of General Robert Hanna.

The second daughter, Amelia Theresa, the writer claims by right of pre-emption.

The third daughter, Julia Anna (now dead), was the wife of Elwood Fisher, who was one of the readiest political writers of his day. He was, in 1850, the editor of the "Southern Press," in Washington City. This paper was the organ of the extreme southern party that opposed the compromise of that year.

Mr. Fisher went south when the war broke out in 1861, and died at Atlanta, Georgia, in the fall of 1862.

The fourth daughter of Mr. Smith is the wife of Doctor Charles W. Stumm, of Piqua, Ohio.

The eldest son, P. B. L. Smith, died at Marsailles, France, in February, 1868.

The second son, Adolphus Henry, resides at Cincinnati and is a retired banker.

The third and youngest son, Frederick A. Smith, is a resident of this city.

Mr. Smith has several nephews living in the West, two of whom, Generals Morgan L. and Giles A. Smith, were prominent in the war for the preservation of the Union. The latter is now Assistant Postmaster General, and has charge of the appointment office in that department.

Justin Smith died on Friday the 29th of December, 1854, and now sleeps by the side of his daughter (Mrs. Fisher) in that beautiful city of the dead, Spring Grove Cemetery, near Cincinnati.

WILLIAM S. HUBBARD

Is one of the citizens of Indianapolis who has proved by demonstration and success in business that some things can be done as well as others, *i. e.*, that a man with a reasonable share of industry, perseverance and economy can achieve what capital often fails to accomplish—the building up a fortune—and that brain is sometimes indispensable.

Mr. Hubbard is a native of Connecticut, having been born in Middletown in May, 1816. In 1837, at the age of twenty-one, he came to Indianapolis as clerk to the Board of State Fund Commissioners—Dr. Coe, Caleb B. Smith and Samuel Hanna—at a salary of five hundred dollars per year. Doctor Coe advanced him the necessary amount to pay his traveling expenses from the East to this place.

Out of the first year's salary he was enabled to save two hundred and fifty dollars; this moiety of his salary he invested in a lot and cabin which he purchased of Judge Blackford and Henry P. Coburn, and it was here, with that two hundred and fifty dollars, the foundation of a fortune was laid, and proved that it was as necessary to have capital in the cranium as in the pocket.

It is quite unnecessary to my purpose to follow Mr. Hubbard in the different pursuits he has followed and trades he has made; 'tis sufficient to know that with this beginning he now owns some of the most valuable business property in the city. One piece, known as Hubbard's Block, on the southwest corner of Washington and Meridian streets, once known as the Jerry Collins' corner.

He also owns and lives in one of the largest, as well as finest, private residences on North Meridian street, and in that part of the city where the *beau monde* do mostly congregate.

He also, in connection with others, has lately purchased a tract of suburban property which they contemplate laying out in small lots as an addition to the city.

Mr. Hubbard, by his energy and enterprise, has not only built up a fortune for himself, but has added much to the improvement of the city and advancement in price of other persons' property.

About the year 1840 he returned to his native State and was there married, and was fortunate in the selection of a wife that reflected his own disposition and was content to live in a frugal and rational manner, and in their dress and outward appearance showed no disposition to imitate the follies and fashions of the day, and amid the hum and bustle of the more wealthy and showy remained the same they were when they first left the shadow of the parental roof, and by this means they have been enabled to accumulate a competency for the present and any future exigency that may arise, and is indebted to his own industry for what he has heretofore in a manner been indebted to others, and his highest hopes and aspirations have been more than realized.

Although Mr. Hubbard is the architect of his own fortune, he has been aided by the advice and counsel of good and sound-minded men, such as James M. Ray, Edwin J. Peck, and that venerable old citizen, Colonel James Blake, whose friendships are invaluable to any person so fortunate as to possess them. And he has been enabled to retain them by never allowing himself to be guilty of any breach of truth, trust, or good faith, which are the cementing principles of confidence in business men, and which many have made great sacrifices by not observing, and precipitated their own ruin.

Mr. Hubbard is a member of the Second Presbyterian Church, and was active and energetic in building the present fine edifice which has just been dedicated.

He is a man of medium size, quick and active in his movements, and whatsoever his hands findeth to do he does it with all his might. He has a pleasing address and affable manner, and is a much younger-looking man than he really is.

ADAM HAUGH.

We clip from the "Indianapolis Journal" of the 16th of August, 1869, this sketch of the life, and of the funeral sermon of this venerable man. He has three sons engaged in active business in this city. Benjamin F. and Emanuel are large manufacturers of wrought and cast iron railing, bank vaults and improved iron jails. Joseph is cashier of the Citizens' National Bank. A fourth son, John, is a resident of California, having gone to that State in 1850, since which time he had not seen his father's family until a few weeks before the latter's death, and was here at that time.

Mr. Haugh's daughters, I believe, all reside in this city. His sons are universally respected for their strict integrity, temperate and industrious habits and gentlemanly bearing, and are worthy sons of christian parents:

"The Journal of Saturday last contained a notice of the death of Adam Haugh, an old resident of this city, which occurred on the day previous. Mr. Haugh was born February 9, 1789, in Frederick County, Maryland, and was married September 28, 1813, to Mary E. Reck, sister of the Rev. A. Reck, who organized the first Lutheran Church in this city. He emigrated to this city in the fall of 1836, arriving here November 19th. At that time the city had a population of 3,000. For two years he was engaged in blacksmithing, in partnership with James Van Blaricum, and then built a shop on the site of the old Journal building, corner of Circle and Meridian streets. He had a remarkable constitution—was never confined to his bed but one day in his life until his late illness. Raised a family of ten children—five boys and five girls. There have been but two deaths in the family. A son, Adam Haugh, Jr., died in July, 1850, at the age of twenty four years, being the first death in thirty-seven years, and now the subject of this sketch, being the second death in fifty-six years. The balance of the family are all here at present.

"His disease was cancer on the face, from which he suffered most intensely, but with the greatest patience and resignation. His life has been that of an honest, truthful, upright man, and humble, faithful, zealous christian.

"His wife survives him, but can not, at her advanced age, expect to remain very long on this side of the dark valley.

"The funeral services took place at the Second Presbyterian Church, at half-past three o'clock yesterday afternoon, the audience in attendance being a very large one. The opening prayer, which was a touching and appropriate one, was made by Rev. William W. Criley, of the English Lutheran Church. The sermon was delivered by Rev. C. H. Marshall, of the Fourth Presbyterian Church, of which the deceased was a member; the text being from Job 5, 26: 'Thou shalt come to thy grave in a full age, like as a shock of corn cometh in full season.'

"In commencing, he said that death claims all seasons for his own, and claims for his harvest persons of all ages. The infant in its helplessness and budding beauty, youth in the time of its most lofty hopes and anticipations, middle age with its strength and its usefulness, all are liable to be gathered by the reaper, while we tenderly and gently lay away the man of age for his eternal rest. The grave opens to receive all. But here we read what seems to be a promise or a privilege which is granted to comparatively few. The analogy of the text is a beautiful one. Like the ripening wheat, our bodily powers increase for a season, and we steadily gain in strength and power until we reach a time when we gain no longer and gradually pass to the stage of ripeness, and if this season is given to a man it is a great privilege. So it is with our mental powers. By-and-by we come to a time when we can go no further with our imagination or reason. We cease to acquire, and live in the knowledge of the past. So, also, with our spiritual powers. In early infancy we lie in our mother's arms weak and feeble; and again when we are born into a christian life we lie in the arms of Infinite Love, waiting for the growth of the seeds of spiritual truth, which fall into the soul and go on until the full maturity of christian character is reached. To him nothing seemed more beautiful than rich, ripe and full christian old age. It is more beautiful than the autumn leaves, or than any other object in nature.

"We are called to-day to follow to its last resting place the body of one who has passed through the full period allotted to man. Death comes as a shock at any other period of life. It is a great hardship to give up the little child upon whom we have placed our hopes. To the man in middle life, in the very time of his greatest usefulness, and when many are dependent upon his strength, the blow comes still harder. It seems like taking the keystone from the arch, leaving it without the strength to support it. To the young man, just coming upon the stage of usefulness, and when hopes and aspirations are highest, death seems very sad. We find in our graveyards emblems of these events, and when we see the little lamb or the broken bud on our tombstones, we can not feel otherwise than sad and sorrowful. And so, too, with the broken column, emblem of man cut off in the midst of his usefulness and strength. But, for old age, we should have some symbol of beautiful perfection, such as the tree in its strength or the column completed, for of all beautiful things ripe old age is the most so. The work of life has been done, not only in the household, but in society and in the church. Theirs can not be a history broken off in the middle. It is not like a fragmentary form, of which we can read a few stanzas only to regret that there is no more. It is a finished work.

"A long life is beautiful because of the opportunity it

gives of usefulness, and the great influence which may be exerted by it. Here is one who has been for more than fifty years a follower of Christ. His life has not been a striking or brilliant one, but during all this time, as day has followed day and year has followed year, the influence of this christian life has been felt, and the whole sum is wonderful. We may not see the whole result of this influence, but God notes it all, and it will be felt for many years to come. To you, as you noticed his last suffering, with all his peaceful submission, came up afresh all the intercourse of your lives with him, and the recollection of the times when you sat on his knee and listened to his counsel. When we fall in middle age we can have had no chance to exert an influence so perfect and complete.

"It is said by some that death in childhood is beautiful—when the infant is taken from all the trials and difficulties of a long life in this world; but to me it does not seem so. Some may think it beautiful to be stricken down in the harness, in the very midst of activity and usefulness; but to me there is nothing more beautiful than old age, after a life of usefulness and good influence, sitting quietly down and waiting for the Master to open the door and bid them 'come.' It is a blessed thing, at whatever time of life it may come, to find one looking back over well spent days and ready alike for active usefulness, if the time for that has not passed, or for the summons of the Master if the time for the reaper has come.

"The Scriptures liken the perfect christian growth to that of the palm tree. At first it is weak and feeble, but in time it becomes a stately tree, while from year to year the leaves and projections of the early growth, representing sin and deformity, drop off as the love of Christ is strengthened, and in time it stands the perfect trunk, with its perfect crest of beautiful leaves.

"Death at old age, as in this case, reminds us of our gratitude to God. I remember, at an early period of my ministry here, I was called upon to attend a golden wedding, the first one occurring in my congregation. These children of the old couple will all remember that fiftieth anniversary of their parents' marriage. I remember a large picture that was presented to them, containing portraits of all their children and their grandchildren. There was but one space left vacant, and I remember asking who it was for. The answer was, that it was left vacant in memory of one who had died in early life. And this was the only link in the long chain that was missing. How many families of our commnnity have such cause for thankfulness that their home ties have not been broken. Very many there are who have never known a mother's love or a father's guidance. In this case, the father lived to see all his children come to the strength of manhood and womanhood. It was his privilege to welcome home, but a short time before his death, one who had come from a distant shore, and around his bed all were gathered before he breathed his last."

JOHN H. WRIGHT

Was the first merchant of Indianapolis to inaugurate the system of selling goods for cash only, which he did in the fall of 1838, at which time he first made this city his residence; but he soon discovered that the Hoosiers were not willing to give up the credit system, by which they had done business from the first settlement of the place, so he gradually fell into the prevailing custom of the times.

He was born on the eastern shore of Maryland, but when a boy, with his father's family, removed to Philadelphia, from Philadelphia to Richmond, Indiana, where he was principally raised, and was engaged in business previous to his removal to this place.

He was a fine business man, and during his eight years residence in this city did a large business in the sale of dry goods and purchase of produce. He was the first person to purchase and pack pork in this place for a foreign market. He died in the summer of 1846, leaving a wife and two sons, all of whom yet reside in the city. His wife was afterwards married to Dr. Charles Parry and yet resides in her elegant mansion on the northeast corner of Ohio and Meridian streets.

His eldest son, Frank, is engaged largely in the brewing and manufacture of ale, which is well known in this and other markets as " Frank Wright's Cream Ale."

The second son, Dr. Mansur Wright, is one of the practicing physicians of the city. The two sons inherit to a considerable degree the liberality and companionable qualities for which their father was justly celebrated.

DR. CHARLES PARRY

Was a native of the Key Stone State, having been born in Berks County, but was raised and educated in Philadelphia, and was a graduate of the Jefferson Medical College of that city.

I remember having traveled with the Doctor from Philadelphia to Cincinnati, when he, in company with his relative, the late Hon. O. H. Smith, was coming to the West in search of a location, in the spring of 1837.

For eighteen months he lived in the eastern part of Indiana and there practiced medicine. He came to this city in September, 1838, and here he remained up to the time of his death in the summer of 1861.

During his twenty-three years' residence in this city no man was more respected than was Dr. Parry; his genial manners, kind and obliging disposition, and his great liberality, endeared him to all with whom he was acquainted.

As a physician he ranked high, as a surgeon pre-eminently

so, and had a reputation as a skillful and successful operator throughout the State. He had the confidence and respect of the other physicians of the city with scarcely an exception, and was often called by them in consultation.

FRANK MANSUR

Says that he made his first appearance upon the stage of action at Richmond, Indiana, in the year 1828, and that he knows it to be true, for he was there in person; and also, that he is the son of his father, the old gentleman, and that he has ever tried to be a good and dutiful son, as he is.

He first came to Indianapolis in 1840, a boy twelve years of age; just as he alighted from the stage-coach his attention was attracted to a dog fight that was in progress on the corner of Washington and Meridian streets; this he witnessed before he reported to his friends who were expecting him.

He has engaged in various avocations since he has been a resident of this city. No inconsiderable portion of the time has been devoted to fishing and hunting, and when not directly engaged in he was preparing for it; indeed no fishing or hunting party would be considered made up without Frank Mansur. Although he is on the shady side of forty, and a great admirer of the ladies, he still seems unwilling to raise a barrier between himself and his untrammeled liberty in the shape of matrimony, and would rather be "a jolly fellow," than, like Rip Van Winkle, subject to have his hair *yanked* for any delinquency pertaining to conjugal felicity. He has many warm friends in this city who

"Lo'ed him like a vera brither."

Although Mr. Mansur has done considerable in the *fishing* line, I would not have the reader think that he neglects his other business. He is engaged in a first-class livery and sale stable on West Pearl street.

He resides with his venerable father, Jeremiah Mansur, who has been a citizen of this city for several years.

Zachariah and William Mansur, his brothers, are also residents of this city, and prominent among the business men. They are now engaged in banking, Zachariah on his own account, and William a large stockholder in the Citizens' Bank.

AARON GROVER

Was a Yankee in every sense of the word. He was from Bennington, Vermont. In height he was about five feet four inches, broad, stoop shoulders, large aquiline nose, and head entirely bald, except a little hair above the ears; the baldness ran to the back of his head. His eye was as keen and as quick in its motion as that of an eagle. In talking he drawled his words out in true Yankee style. In religion he was a forty-gallon Baptist, and in politics a Democrat of the old school.

He kept a stove store on the southeast corner of Washington and Meridian streets, but liked to talk religion and politics rather better than he did about the sale of his stoves.

On one occasion an old Methodist man, named McCarty, came in to purchase a stove. Mr. Grover was engaged in blacking some second-hand ones and preparing them for sale. The stove dealer, after showing his assortment to Mr. McCarty, sounded him on religion, and found him to be a believer in the doctrine of free agency. "I believe," said the dealer, "that God fore-knew all things from the beginning, and foreknowledge is fore-ordination, and what will free agency amount to when God willed our destiny?" "Don't insult me," said McCarty, "with your h—llish doctrine of Calvin, that would consign infants not a span long to perdition; your heart is as hard as your stoves, and as black as your face; I'll not trade with such a man." He then turned to leave the store in quite a rage. "Friend," said Grover, "don't get excited, let's talk matters over. What might be your name?" "McCarty," was the answer. "Ah, McCarty, McCarty," said the stove dealer; "are you akin to Nicholas McCarty?" "No;" said McCarty, "thank God, I am not, nor to any other Whig." "My friend," said Grover, "give us your hand; we differ on minor questions, but we agree on the main one, and friend you're a *Dimakrat;* we'll merge those minor questions for the sake of the main one, *Dimocracy.*"

In consideration of Mr. McCarty's political faith Mr. Grover sold him the stove for two dollars less than the usual price.

In after years we often saw the two old men sitting in the shade of the stove dealer's store, and we judged by their earnest manner, and the frequent slaps of Mr. Grover's hand upon the side of the house, and hearing him use the name of Henry Clay in no very pleasant manner, that they were not conversing on the subject of free agency or fore-ordination.

Both of those worthy Democrats have passed away, and I hope neither have gone to that place assigned by Parson Brownlow to all of that political faith.

JAMES B. MANN

Was a native of Kentucky, born in Kenton County in the year 1826, and when in his tenth year came to Marion County and resided in Franklin township until he had attained an age suitable to be married.

He then selected the daughter of Mr. Purnel Coverdill, a well known and respectable farmer of that neighborhood, and was married.

Miss Coverdill having become a "Mann" they have not been blessed with any little *Manns* of their own to be the prop and stay of declining years, but he has raised three orphans and proved himself "a father to the fatherless," and that "Mann's a man for a' that."

Mr. Mann has been engaged in the family grocery business on Virginia avenue for several years, and seems to think that a grocer should not be without profits in his own country.

He is a member of the First Baptist Church and a zealous worker in the Sunday School of the Mission Church, at the corner of Noble and South streets. There is no person more respected by his neighbors than James B. Mann.

SAMUEL CANBY

Came to his present residence, one and a half miles southeast of the city, from Boone County, Kentucky, in the year 1837. He is well known as one of our best and most frugal farmers, and the producer of the finest qualities and greatest varieties of fruits. His farm has been well known for its fine productions of choice fruits since the first settlement of the county. On it was the first nursery of the late Aaron Aldridge.

Mr. Canby's familiar countenance may be seen upon our streets every few days; although somewhat advanced in years he yet seems in full vigor of life.

JOHN P. PATTERSON,

One of the leading wholesale business men of South Meridian street, being connected with the house of Alford, Talbot & Co., was a native of Pennsylvania, born and raised in Alleghany County, near Pittsburg.

He came to Indianapolis quite a young man in 1836, and for about three years was a clerk in the store of Russell, Holland & Co., on the northeast corner of Washington and Pennsylvania streets, where Odd Fellows' Hall now stands.

He then went to Noblesville and there engaged in the dry goods business, and remained until 1854, at which time he returned to and has continued in this city ever since.

While at Noblesville he was married to a niece of the late William Conner of that place.

Mr. Patterson was one of the victims to that disastrous fire on the night of the 17th of January, 1870, the Morrison Opera House, but on the next day their firm were again in business, with a good stock of goods, two squares from the scene of their misfortunes of the previous evening, which shows a great industry as well as enterprise.

CHRISTIAN FREDERICK RASENER.

This worthy German came from the City of Minden, Prussia, to this place in the year 1836. He had five children—two sons and three daughters. He brought with him, from the old country, four hundred dollars in coin, with which he purchased land in Hancock County, near Cumberland. This is now owned by his eldest son, bearing the name of the father, who is one of the most prosperous farmers in that German neighborhood. This worthy man I knew well, he having lived with me several years.

The other son, Frederick William, is a resident of this city, doing a mercantile business on East Washington street, near Liberty, and possesses the confidence of his German friends to a great degree, who manifest their confidence in him by bestowing upon him their patronage.

FREDERICK CHRISTIAN HARMENING

Is another German, that came to this place in the month of January, 1846. He was a tailor by trade, and for several years worked for the late Edward McGuire. He has been successful, and is now the owner of some fine city property on South Delaware street, where he resides and keeps a well supplied family grocery. He is a remarkably kind man, and popular with his German friends.

CHARLIE LAUER,

A native of Bavaria, came to the United States in the year 1852. He became a resident of this city a few years subsequent, and has continued to reside here ever since. He is quite popular with all his acquaintances, both German and American. He married, some years since, a Miss Baldwin, the daughter of a respectable Morgan County farmer.

Charlie is now engaged in business opposite Little's Hotel, on East Washington street, and keeps one of the neatest restaurants in the city, where every delicacy calculated to cheer the inner man may be found, and he waits upon his customers in a kind and gentlemanly manner. We commend him to all as a clever man.

JOHN C. HERETH

Was born at Frankfort-upon-the-Main. When a boy he, with his parents, emigrated to the United States and settled in Jefferson County, near Madison, Indiana. When at the proper age, he engaged with William Taylor, a prominent saddler of that place, to learn the business.

In the year 1852, he came to this city and immediately engaged in the manufacture of saddles and harness, and everything that pertains to the wardrobe of a horse. Mr. Hereth is now one of the leading mechanics of this city.

At the State Fair of 1869, he offered a fine side-saddle as a present to the second best lady equestrian, which was won and received by a lady of Shelby County. The superior manufacture of the article and the fine quality of the material of which it was made, were highly creditable to the worthy mechanic, and proved his goodness of heart and his liberality in business. His shop, for the manufacture and sale of his fine harness, is on North Delaware street, opposite the Court House square.

PAUL B. L. SMITH.

Two years ago we wrote the obituary notice of Mr. Smith, he having died at Marseilles, France, on the 2d of February, 1868.

He was born in Brooklyn, New York, but when a mere child he removed, with his father (the late Justin Smith), to Rochester, in his native State, where he lived until he came to Indianapolis, in the fall of 1838.

His father had purchased a large farm, with mills and distillery, near Edinburg, in Johnson County. There he established a dry goods store, and the whole was managed by Adolphus H. Smith, a second son, while P. B. L. Smith was engaged in the mercantile business in this place.

In 1844, P. B. L. Smith determined to gratify a desire, he had long cherished, of visiting the Continent of Europe, and, in the fall of that year, sailed from New York. He spent the winter in Paris, and the summer of 1845 in traveling over the Continent, and returned home in the fall of that year, his business being carried on, in the meantime, by his brother.

Again, in the spring of 1851, he returned to Europe, having taken a partner in his business here that was interested only so far as the profits were concerned. About a year after he left, his partner sold out the establishment and a fine lucrative trade that Mr. Smith had been fourteen years in building up. His place of business will be remembered by most of the old citizens, as situated where Odd Fellows' Hall now stands, on the north-east corner of Washington and Pennsylvania streets.

When he returned from Europe, in the fall of 1852, and found his business closed, he became low-spirited and did not seem to care for business after that, although he had abundant means to engage in any kind he wished.

As there are dark hours in the history of every human being, when despondency and gloom reign supreme, and the future shrouded in melancholy; so it was with him, and he determined to again visit Europe until his mind became tranquil and again prepared for business.

In accordance with this design, he again sailed from New York in April, 1856, taking with him his youngest sister, Justine. Little did either of them dream, as they took a last look at the many church spires of New York, as they receded from their view while the magnificent steamer was leaving the harbor, that he was bidding a long and last farewell to his native land, leaving behind nearly all that was near and dear to him on earth, to find a grave among strangers, and without the sympathetic tear of brother or sister to fall upon his coffin.

The two years his sister remained with him, were spent principally in Paris. After her return to the United States he traversed the Continent from one end to the other, spending the winter seasons in Algiers.

In the last letter one of his sisters received from him, he expressed a desire to once more see his native country; but his health was so impaired as to render it almost impossible.

> "The home of my childhood; methinks I can see
> Those forms that in youth were familiar to me;
> And oft on the tablet of memory I trace
> The image enshrined of each dear loving face."

But he has solved the problem of life, and now sleeps in the Protestant Cemetery at Marseilles, France.

Previous to leaving this country the last time, he placed a large amount of money at interest, the income from which was considerably more than supported him.

There are some men now in business in this city, on the high road to wealth, who did business for Mr. Smith, and acquired much of their business knowledge while with him; among whom are William E. Featherston, who came to him when a boy. Also Charles Bals, who is now a prominent wholesale liquor dealer, on Meridian street.

During the fifteen years residence of Mr. Smith in Europe,

he was proficient in acquiring a knowledge of the French, Italian and German languages, and spoke them with the ease and fluency of a native.

He was a man of fine address and agreeable manners, and was ever a welcome guest at the fireside of his friends and acquaintances.

During his eighteen years' residence in this city, he ranked as a first class business man, punctual with all he had dealings with and expected them to be so with him. His word he valued above money.

From 1838 to 1856 there was no name more familiar to the people of Indianapolis than that of P. B. L. Smith. It is the sincere hope of the writer that he sought and found his portion of that inheritance which fadeth not away.

JOSEPH K. SHARPE.

When I come to write of such men as the one whose name stands at the head of this sketch, and who have by perseverance, industry and economy so successfully carved out their own fortune and standing in society, I am at a loss for language to convey to the reader a proper appreciation of their true worth and merit.

Mr. Sharpe is a man of fine personal appearance, above the ordinary size, and in the prime of life, a smiling and genial countenance, with manners pleasing and captivating, and meets his numerous friends with a welcome recognition and open hands; a pleasant word for all that either circumstances or business brings him in contact with.

He was born in Windham County, Connecticut, raised on a farm, where he acquired the main-springs to success in life, *i. e.*, industry and economy, without which but few succeed.

When quite young he sought a home in the great West, his only fortune a good constitution, temperate habits, sterling integrity and a good education; with this capital he came to

Indianapolis in the year 1845, although he had lived awhile in Illinois and a short time in Ohio.

Mr. S. came to this place for the purpose of settling up the business of a boot and shoe establishment belonging to other parties than those who were managing it. He was not slow in discovering that this was a good point for business; he purchased the establishment, but soon sold it out to Jacob S. Pratt.

Shortly thereafter he commenced the leather and shoe-finding business, which he has successfully carried on without intermission for about twenty-five years, and is now the oldest established house in that line in the city.

In connection with his large commercial business in the city, he purchased a tannery and large tract of land in Monroe County, forty miles south of this place, hauling all his hides and leather from and to the city with his own teams, for at least ten years, and until railroads were made in that direction, adding not a little to our home manufacture and the prosperity of the city.

At this point he also established a country store, which he has carried on for more than fifteen years. This would seem to be enough business to burthen one mind with, but the steady growth of his central business in the city demanded more facilities for supplying the demand and production of leather. To meet this demand he has added another tannery, which is sixty miles north in Grant County. This establishment he has carried on several years. Nor is this all; having been raised on a farm and there labored in his boyhood days, gave him the knowledge and ability to direct, and a taste for agriculture.

He has farmed in this county as well as in several other counties in the State (some of his farms being over one hundred miles apart), raising grain, hogs and cattle in large quantities for this market.

All this business he has managed in addition to his city business, without even apparently losing his equanimity, and its management and success are the natural consequence of great administrative talent and ability.

He owns some fine business property as well as one of the fine residences of the city, the home of his family.

It is a commonly received opinion that men who carve out their own fortunes become penurious, but it is the reverse in this case. He has ever been liberal to the poor, donating largely for the erection of churches and for all charitable or benevolent purposes.

Mr. Sharpe is a member of the Fourth Presbyterian Church, one of its trustees and principal supporters.

Nor has his good fortune and success been confined alone to business, he has been equally so in his domestic relations. He came to this place a single as well as a young man, but soon found one with whom he was willing to join in a lifetime partnership in the person of Miss Graydon, daughter of the late Alexander Graydon, one of our most estimable citizens. In this partnership I understand Mr. Sharpe found his counterpart in many respects.

He has for years been the leader of the choir, assisted by his wife, in the church of which they are both acceptable members.

I have noted this case more particularly than most others I have written of that it may be a stimulant to other young men "to go and do likewise." Verily "honesty and virtue hath its reward."

JACOB B. McCHESNEY.

Among the clever and unpretending gentlemen of Indianapolis is Mr. McChesney, a native of the State of New Jersey, a State that has furnished this city with many of its best citizens. He came to this place in the year 1834.

He was the first Secretary of the State Sinking Fund, and continued as such for near thirty years, and left the office only through the workings of political party machinery. He was a good and efficient official, and had almost the entire charge of the business.

During his thirty-six years as a citizen of this city, by his urbane and gentlemanly deportment, has won the confidence and respect of all who know him. He is the cousin of those two worthy persons, of whom I have already written, James M. Ray and the late Joseph M. Moore.

Mr. McChesney took an active part in the organization of the first Episcopal Church (Christ's), in 1837, and has since that time been a member and vestryman of it.

He has three children, one a daughter, who is the wife of Mr. David E. Snyder, one of the leading insurance men of the city. His two sons are yet single and reside with their father.

HENRY OHR.

This venerable gentleman became a citizen of Indianapolis in April, 1837. He, with his family, emigrated from Frederick County, Maryland, his native State and county.

Mr. Ohr was for several years a well known and popular dry goods merchant of this city, and was universally respected for his upright demeanor and unostentatious piety. He has several children and his companion through life yet living to comfort him in his declining years. Aaron, the eldest son, is now and has been for several years one of the ticket agents at the Union Depot. John H. Ohr has been the principal agent for the Adams Express Company in this city for several years.

Mr. Ohr's eldest daughter is the widow of the late Newton Norwood. The second daughter, Julia, is now deceased; she was the wife of John R. Elder, who is now one of our popular business men.

John Carlisle.

Mr. Ohr's two sons, like their father, enjoy the confidence of all who know them as energetic and industrious business men.

Perhaps the old pioneers of this city did not think that they were destined to supply material to make a chapter in the history of Indianapolis. If their shadow had been cast before them, would their lives have been different? In this case we think not. Mr. Ohr has jogged along through life in the even tenor of his way, and arrived at a good old age, with less to disturb the peace and quiet of his mind than is the fortune of most mortals.

JOHN CARLISLE,

The veteran miller of Indianapolis, was a native of the "Emerald Isle," having been born in the Province of Ulster, county of Down, in the north of Ireland, in the year 1807.

When in his eighteenth year (1825) he came to the United States, landed in the city of New York, and for twelve years was a successful miller at Marlborough, Ulster County, on the Hudson River.

From the latter place he came to this city in the year 1837 and engaged in the manufacture of soap and candles; at the same time he commenced and carried on a distillery and dairy, and was the first to have milk sold from a wagon in this place.

In the year 1840 he built a large merchant mill on the arm of the canal near where it crosses Washington street. It was at this mill he manufactured and packed in barrels the first flour that was manufactured in this part of the country for shipment. In this enterprise he was ridiculed and laughed at by his friends for wagoning flour to the Ohio River to sell at from two to three dollars per barrel. Although not profitable at first, he was building up a reputation for his flour for after years.

In the year 1842 he bought wheat at twenty-five cents per

bushel, corn at ten cents, and sold his flour on the Ohio River at two dollars and seventy-five cents per barrel, corn meal in this city, eight bushels to the dollar, bran at five and shorts at ten cents per bushel, delivered in the city.

In the years 1864 and 1865 his transactions in grain and flour amounted to one million of dollars, his losses being equal to his earnings of several years previous. When the war closed he was the heaviest grain and flour dealer in the West. He had flour on sale in all the Eastern as well as Western cities, and as the article fell he still continued to buy, thereby aiding in keeping up the prices in the West.

When the Government took possession of the railroads to convey the troops home, he found it impossible to have his grain and flour forwarded before such time as it had fallen in the market to make a loss of from five to six dollars per barrel on the flour, and a corresponding loss on grain.

He tells me that in 1866 he paid $3.25 per bushel for wheat and sold flour at $16.00 per barrel, the highest price ever obtained for either article in this market.

A large grain dealer of this city once remarked that the farmers of this and adjoining counties should erect a monument to his memory in consideration of the fact that he was the first to advance and keep up the price of grain, and would suffer loss rather than do anything calculated to depress it.

Mr. Carlisle also tells me that his great error in business was that of holding on too long before selling, and that had he bought and sold *instanter* his profits would have amounted to a large fortune; his great desire was to keep up prices in the hands of the producers, thereby benefiting the whole country. He says he never failed to make money when he bought and sold promptly; but he has the proud satisfaction of knowing that his action has benefited the whole country.

In the years 1864 and 1865 he often bought from 25,000 to 30,000 bushels of wheat, and from 2,000 to 3,000 barrels of flour in one week, paying out in cash therefor nearly one hundred thousand dollars, this amount going directly into the hands of the farming community. It is quite unnecessary to say that his credit was commensurate with his demands for money in carrying on those immense transactions.

Although he lost very heavy, as stated here, I would not have the reader think for a moment that his circumstances were any other than affluent. He and his sons are the owners of two splendid merchant mills in this city, one near the canal, on West Market street, the other on West Maryland street.

Out of his sixty-three years of life forty-two have been spent in the milling business. With this experience it is no wonder his brands of flour stand so high in all the eastern as well as western markets.

Mr. Carlisle is a remarkably active and industrious man, never leaving for to-morrow that which can be done to-day. He is nearly always on the go; more inclined to attend to his own business than that of other people. He don't seem to have any time to spare in idle or frivolous conversation; although decided in his political views, he never tries to force them upon others.

He has occupied his present handsome residence, on the corner of Washington and West streets, about thirty years. He has bought a greater number of bushels of grain, a larger number of barrels of flour, and disbursed more money among the farmers than any man now living in the city. In all his transactions he has been prompt, and he requires others to be so with him. Such is John Carlisle, the veteran miller of Indianapolis.

DOCTOR JOHN M. GASTON,

One of the prominent physicians of Indianapolis, is a native of Pennsylvania, but, when quite young, came with his father to Indiana, and settled in Hancock County. His first residence in this city, for a short time only, was in 1833.

About the year 1838 he returned and commenced the study of medicine with Doctors Sanders and Parry. After finishing his studies and attending the lectures, he entered upon the practice of his profession in this place, and has continued it since that time. Although it is said that a "prophet is without honor in his own country," the Doctor's success has proved that it is different with physicians, as he has ever had an extensive practice. He has gradually worked his way up the ladder until he is now near the top round, and stands high in his profession as well as in his boots.

Hiram Gaston, his brother, made the first buggy ever made in Indianapolis, in 1833. Some years afterwards, Edward and Hiram Gaston commenced the manufacture of carriages of all kinds, and successfully continued until the death of the latter in October, 1866.

Edward is yet working at the business in this city. There were no finer carriages manufactured than at the shop of the Gastons.

CHARLES G. FRENCH.

Charlie tells me he has not the most remote recollection of ever having been born at all, although, from what he has heard, he supposes such an event did occur in Delaware County, Ohio, and says that he there ran wild with bears and "Ingins" until he was large enough to behave himself in white society. I am sorry that the space I have allotted to each sketch precludes my giving his in full, in his own graphic and interesting style.

He received a portion of his education at the college located in Granville, Licking County, in his native State.

After receiving his education he pursued different occupations, such as dispensing the "elixor of life," in the shape of whisky, raising silk worms, thereby destroying all the mulberry trees in his neighborhood to feed them, he finally fought his way into the shop of a watchmaker and jeweller, of Granville, Ohio, where he learned that business.

Charlie came to Indianapolis in the year 1845, and engaged with and worked in the shop of William H. Talbott for many years. He then commenced and has continued business on his own account, and has been quite successful in the accumulation of property, and is rewarded for his industry by the possession of a fine suburban residence at the east end of Washington street, and is doing a fine business at his well filled store on North Meridian street.

He has lately met with a bereavement, in the loss of his amiable wife, that has cast a gloom over his countenance and his usual buoyant and cheerful spirits.

He enjoys the confidence and respect of his numerous friends and acquaintances of this city in a high degree, and the name of Charlie French is synonymous with that of the words liberality and good feeling.

ANDREW WALLACE.

The name that heads this sketch is, perhaps, as familiar to the citizens of this place, as well as to the farming community of Marion and the surrounding counties, as that of any person now doing business in the city.

Although not one of the oldest, he has certainly been one of the most successful produce dealers of his day.

Mr. Wallace was a paper maker by trade, having learned the business with John Sheets, of Madison, Jefferson County. He came to this place in the year 1840, in comparatively poor circumstances. Soon after he bought a small farm in Hamilton County and removed his family thereon; there he remained some time, and, to accommodate his friends, Messrs. Sheets and Yandes, he returned to the city to take charge of and superintend their paper mill, their former superintendent having been burned and otherwise injured to prevent his attending to the duties. Mechanics of that kind being very scarce at that time, Mr. Wallace consented to accommodate them until such time as they should be enabled to employ another.

He remained with them until January, 1847, the high water of that year destroying the aqueduct of the canal wound up for the time being the manufacture of paper and his connection with those gentlemen.

Mr. Robert Underhill, in the meantime, having become acquainted with Mr. Wallace, and learning something of his untiring industry and fine business qualifications, employed him to take charge of his Bridgeport flouring mill, which he did, and managed with profit to his employer until the fall of 1847. It will be remembered by our old citizens that our merchants up to this time had not paid cash for produce, with the exception of pork to be driven to the Ohio River, and by John Carlisle for wheat, which was but a very small portion of the surplus of the country.

Mr. Wallace inaugurated the present system of paying cash for stock and all kinds of produce in this place, and everything he laid his hand to prospered.

He then took charge of Mr. Underhill's City Mills, Mr. Underhill, having the utmost confidence in his integrity, arranged for him to draw money out of bank on his own checks in the transaction of business pertaining to the mill. From the time he took charge of Mr. Underhill's business it prospered, so that in a few years he was enabled to retire with a fortune.

In the year 1848 he was employed by Mr. Jeremiah Foot as a clerk in his store. Mr. Foot wished to make as much as possible out of Mr. Wallace's services, and, like the person that killed the goose that laid the golden egg, very unwittingly got himself rid of his valuable services. One very dull day of trade Mr. Foot requested Mr. Wallace to go into the cellar and saw a half cord of wood, as there was not much doing in the store. This Mr. W. refused to do; he stood upon his dignity, and told Mr. Foot he would rather pay for the sawing out of his own pocket.

Mr. Foot insisted on his doing it himself, as he could not afford to take it out of his own pocket. Mr. W. acceded to Mr. F.'s request, and told him that he would saw the wood, and wished Mr. Foot to make out his account while he was so doing, and that after the wood was sawed he would consider himself free from any obligation to continue in Mr. F.'s employ.

The sawing of that half cord of wood was, perhaps, the dearest Mr. F. ever paid for, as it was to Mr. Wallace time better employed than he had done before.

In the fall of 1848 Mr. W. commenced the purchase of grain and shipping to the house of Pollys & Butler, of Madison, Indiana, and did more business in that line than all the other establishments of the kind in the place, often shipping five or six car lords per day.

He then commenced the business of a family grocer in the Walpole House, a frame building, situated about the middle of the space between where the Odd Fellows' Hall now stands and the alley on the north side of Washington, between Pennsylvania and Delaware streets.

On the vacant ground east of his store, and adjoining the alley, was his wagon yard and salt sheds. On every board in the fence and every barrel of salt was branded the name of "Andy Wallace," much to the annoyance of his competitor, the late P. B. L. Smith, who then did a large business on the corner where Odd Fellows' Hall now stands, and was somewhat jealous of "Andy's," at least, great show of business.

Andy would never suffer a farm wagon to pass his door,

going west, until he had used every stratagem and exhausted all his eloquence to induce its occupants to call in at his establishment first. Often by the time the wagon would be fairly stopped he would have the old lady's baby in his store sitting on the counter, with a stick of candy in each hand and one protruding from its mouth, before the mother had got out of the wagon. Andy, with a large stock of candy with which he sugar-coated the children, and a pretty wiry tongue and an accommodating disposition, became a great favorite with the farmers of the country which built him up an extensive trade.

His competitors in business thought that it would not take long to wind Andy Wallace up. This, reaching Andy's ears, caused him to redouble his diligence and industry, being determined to succeed or risk his all upon the trial; like Richelieu, he thought that "there is no such word as fail."

At this place Mr. Wallace built up a fine business and an extensive acquaintance throughout this and the adjoining counties.

In the year 1855 he engaged in the wholesale grocery business, which he still continues, and has a large share of the wholesale business for both city and country. He is a fair illustration of the truth of the *saw*, "that some things can be done as well as others."

He owns some very valuable business as well as private property in the city, and one of the finest and earliest cultivated farms in the county.

One of the great secrets of his success was that when he made up his mind to do anything he did it with all his might, and when he thought that he had a good investment in property he held on to it.

He was for eight years President of the State Institutions for the amelioration of the condition of the Deaf and Dumb, Insane and Blind, and they, like everything else he put his hands to, prospered under his supervision. But he, like most other successful men, has not been free from the abuse and vituperation of those less successful, and he has hurled back the calumny upon their own heads with a redoubled force.

ELIJAH S. ALVORD

Is a native of the "Old Bay State," having been born and raised in Greenfield, Franklin County. He came to the West in 1834, and for nearly two years resided in Richmond, Indiana, thence to this city in the spring of 1836.

Mr. Alvord brought with him to this place some fifteen or twenty horses, and established himself in the livery business in the stables attached to the aWshington Hall (now Glenns' Block, then kept by E. Browning). He tells us that he here performed, personally, the labor that would require the united efforts of four or five hired men to accomplish, and in order to keep out competition in this line rented the only other establishment of the kind in the place and locked it up. It was then and there the foundation of a fortune was laid, and the reputation of a first-class business man was commenced.

Mr. Alvord was among the first to start the business of a money broker in this place, and was quite successful as long as he continued it.

He then became a partner of Messrs. J. & P. Vorhees in the Ohio Stage Company that owned the various lines of stages that centered to this place and diverged therefrom, East, West, North and South. He was for years principal superintendent of the whole business. He then established some other lines throughout Illinois, Iowa and other Western States, and finally a line across the plains to the Pacific coast. He is now President of the Western Stage Company; President, and a large stockholder in the Citizens' line of Street Railways of this city. He is, also, one of the founders of the Rink, its President, and a large stockholder. This popular place of amusement was the first of the kind in the State. As I said before, he is a fine business man, energetic and industrious, and his indomitable perseverance has been rewarded with a large share of this world's goods.

He possesses great firmness and decision of character, and a stand once taken it is difficult to remove him from it. Although a citizen of this city for the past thirty-four years, he has never sought or asked for office at the hands of the people or any other appointing power.

During the existence of that party he was a warm and enthusiastic Whig, but when it was disbanded, with many others of his political associates, fell in with and supports the Democratic party.

He was, by the State Convention that assembled in this city on the 8th of January, 1870, unanimously chosen Chairman of the State Central Committee of the Democracy of Indiana, which position he has filled thus far to the entire satisfaction of his associates and with credit and honor to himself.

Mr. Alvord owns and lives in one of the palatial mansions of the city, on North Pennsylvania street. He owns a fine business house on South Meridian street, known as Alvord's Block, and other valuable property in the city, both improved and unimproved.

Mr. Alvord is a man of good address, courteous and genial in his intercourse with others. Although he has passed the noon-day of life, he looks quite young, and bids fair for many years of enjoyment in the society of his family and friends, and usefulness to the public.

JOHN BURK

Was a native of the State of New Jersey. He came to Ohio in the year 1832, remaining in that State about a year. He came to Huntington, in Indiana, in the year 1833, and engaged to complete four sections of the Wabash and Erie Canal. About the time of the completion of this contract, he was elected to represent, in the Legislature, the counties of Huntington, Wells, Jay, Blackford and Adams. He made an efficient and working member, just such a man as that new and sparsely settled country needed at that time.

In the fall of 1836 he contracted for building the "feeder dam" at Broad Ripple, seven miles north of this city. He then undertook other important contracts on the Central Canal, and while they were in progress, and before completion, the general and gigantic system of internal improvements by the State was abandoned for the want of the necessary funds to finish them.

While a contractor Mr. Burk frequently worked from eighty to one hundred men at a time, a large proportion of whom were Irish, and they would frequently have riots and quarrels among themselves growing out of their own religious or political opinions in their native land. During these periodical ebullitions of wrath, and often violence, Mr. Burk exercised great influence over them, and often prevented bloodshed and death among them.

Hands working on public works were influenced in the selection of the contractor they would work for by the number of "jiggers" he would give them per day. By jiggers was meant a small cup of whisky, say about a gill; they had cups made on purpose for this use.

About the second question asked by the applicant for work was, "how many jiggers do you give?" Mr. Burk tells me that the number he gave was seven, although some contractors gave eight or nine.

After the public works were abandoned he built a large flouring and saw mill at Broad Ripple, and with his family there resided for several years.

During Mr. B.'s residence at Broad Ripple one of the citizens of the village (Bob Earl) built a flat-bottom canal boat and at the suggestion of Mr. Burk called it David Burr, in honor of the Commissioner of the Wabash and Erie Canal. There are many persons yet living in the city that have had the pleasure of a trip to and from Broad Ripple in Mr. Earl's boat. I remember, very well, that in the summer of 1844, and during the canvass for President between Henry Clay and James K. Polk, Mr. Earl was employed to take a fishing party to the Ripple on his boat. One of our respectable citizens (referred to in another sketch) getting very much excited while talking with a political opponent, unthoughtedly made a back step and went into the canal where it was ten or twelve feet water. This cooled the gentleman's political ardor for the balance of the day, although he was kept quite warm by the laughs and jeers of his friends.

I have digressed to give this little incident. Mr. Burk was active in getting up and forwarding the interest of the Indianapolis and Peru Railroad, negotiated in New York for its first loan, was its first President, and continued as such until the road was finished and became prosperous.

He was the first coal dealer in this city, was the first to open and develop the coal mines of Clay County, from which a large quantity that is now used for manufacturing purposes in this city is derived.

At Mr. B.'s old residence at Broad Ripple may now be seen a large willow tree, two feet in diameter, which, he tells me, sprung from a twig, cut for and used all day as a riding switch in 1843, then he stuck it in a marsh or wet piece of ground, where it took root and has grown since that time to its present proportions.

Mr. Burk was, in the palmy days of that party, an ardent Whig of the old school, and supported the Hero of Tippecanoe for the Presidency in 1836 and that ever-memorable year of 1840. He gives an interesting account of a visit that him-

James H. McKernan.

self and family made to the old Hero in 1840, at his residence at North Bend.

I would have been happy to have finished this short tribute to Mr. B.'s many virtues and noble traits of character without referring to anything of an unpleasant or painful nature, "but such is life" that we often sip from the same cup the bitter as well as the sweet.

On the 28th of October, 1868, at the age of seventy-two years, Mr. Burk, while attending to the receiving of cars loaded with coal, was, in some way, caught between two cars and had his left leg crushed in such a way as rendered amputation necessary; but at this writing he has so far recovered as to be able, with the use of a crutch, to attend to his ordinary business.

JAMES H. McKERNAN,

One of the most enterprising and business men of Indianapolis, was born at New Castle (not upon Tyne, where the worthy apothecary practiced the healing art), but upon the banks of the Delaware.

When he first came to Indiana, in 1842, he was engaged for a short time in the foundry business at Lafayette.

He made this city his home in the year 1845, and was soon recognized as one of the true business men of the place, and since which time he has engaged in various enterprises. In 1853 he engaged in the real estate business, more as a *bona fide* purchaser and seller than as an agent.

Since he first began dealing in real estate he has built about five hundred tenements of different kinds; indeed, near one-half of the houses in the Fifth Ward were built, or caused to be, by him, or with his means.

True, some of those houses were not as large as the Academy of Music, or as elaborate in design; yet they furnished what was demanded by the growth of the city, comfortable and cheap homes for the laborers and mechanics, and within their reach as purchasers or tenants.

During the war he sold many of those houses on credit and at easy payments. After money became scarce, and the laborers were thrown out of employment, those payments could not be made. Mr. McKernan had it in his power to foreclose the mortgages and buy the property for much less than was due him on them, instead of which he took the property back, canceled the notes, and gave the purchasers other property corresponding in value to the amount they had paid. Such acts of generosity are so refreshing, we must be permitted to refer to them when they occur.

The most of those houses west of the canal are yet owned by him, many of which are occupied by poor and non-paying tenants.

He pays taxes on one hundred and forty-seven thousand one hundred and seventy-five dollars' worth of property in the city. I was shown his tax list making seventy pages.

He is, at this time, engaged near St. Louis in manufacturing iron, the ore of which is brought from Iron Mountain, Missouri; the coal used is procured at Big Muddy Mines, in Jackson County, Illinois. When this enterprise was first undertaken various were the predictions of its failure; but since it has proved a success two or three millions have been invested in it by other parties.

Although Mr. McKernan is past the meridian of life, there seems to be no abatement in his energy and industry since I first knew him, over a quarter of a century ago.

When we first made his acquaintance he was a member of the old National Whig party, but, like many others, when that party was disbanded, after the defeat of General Scott in 1852, fell in with and supported the Democratic party, but he still adheres with tenacity to many of the sound and wholesome doctrines of that good old national party.

In benevolence and kindness to the poor he, as well as his amiable wife, allow none to surpass them. They never stop to inquire what caused distress and misery, or to what church or country the applicant for relief belongs, but what can we do to alleviate your suffering or better your condition, is all the inquiry they make.

In their social relations they are equally hospitable, ever glad to meet and entertain at their house their numerous friends and acquaintances.

Mr. McKernan has several children yet living. His eldest son, David, is married, and a resident of the city. Their only daughter, Belle, who was the idol of their affections, has recently deceased and left a vacancy in their hearts that never can be filled this side of the grave.

Since the above was written, we have been shown a most valuable invention of Mr. McKernan's, and of which I deem it proper to mention in this sketch.

The sudden and untimely death of John L. Ketcham, in April 1869, by falling through a hatchway, and which cast such a gloom over this entire community, made such an impression and weighed so heavy upon the mind of Mr. McKernan, that for several nights after the sad occurrence he could scarcely sleep.

He then put his inventive genius to work to see if he could not contrive something that would in the future prevent the recurrence of so dire a calamity.

In the wish to accomplish this great object he was not influenced by mercenary or pecuniary considerations, but solely a desire to benefit his fellow man, although the most valuable improvements and inventions of the age have been brought about by such motives, utility being a secondary consideration.

Mr. McKernan has succeeded beyond his most sanguine expectations, and has an invention that will close the hatch and stairways, windows and doors of a five-story building in two minutes, which, in case of fire, would stop the flames arising from the most combustible material within its walls, thereby saving the loss of property, which is secondary only to life.

The utility of this invention has been tested and demonstrated to the entire satisfaction of all who witnessed it at the Masonic Hall on the 18th of May, 1870.

JOHN B. SULLIVAN,

General Superintendent of the "State Fair" and fair grounds, is a plain, off-hand kind of man, with a stern independence and a lofty resolve about him, with a quick perceptibility of the right, and peculiarly fitted for and adapted to the place he fills with such signal ability. He is proprietor of a first-class livery stable, and is considered by horsemen generally as one of the best judges of that noble animal in the city, if not the State, and understands the *modus operandi* of their training to perfection.

He has been connected with the State fairs since 1854, and the admirable arrangement of the grounds, and distribution and assignment of each particular branch of industry and agriculture to its proper place, and arrangement of stock for exhibition, is attributable to his sound judgment in that particular branch of business.

Mr. S. is blessed with the peculiar faculty of knowing men at first sight, and reads them as they come along with an aptness and certainty as he could the bad or good points of a horse.

In the strict sense of the word, and as I generally use the term, he is not an "old settler." He came to Indianapolis in 1848, when it was but a small town and he quite young. His connection with the fairs has made him well known throughout the State as well as in the city.

John B. Sullivan.

His kind and jovial manners and disposition has won him a host of friends; and when a person once makes the acquaintance of John B. Sullivan he will hardly ever forget him.

John B. Sullivan was born in Annapolis, Maryland, and inherits many traits of character peculiar to Southern people. He is liberal in his opinions as well as with his means, and possesses the faculty of making friends for himself of those that circumstances or business brings him in contact with.

Although the writer has not known him very long, yet quite long enough to learn the truth of this brief tribute to the many good qualities of his head and heart.

He was the personal friend of the late Caleb J. McNulty, of Ohio, and helped to perform the last sad rites to his mortal remains. They both belonged to Company B, Second Ohio Regiment of Volunteers, commanded by Col. George W. Morgan, during the Mexican war.

This Regiment left Cincinnati about the 12th of July, 1846, on board the steamer Jamestown. When opposite Plumb Point, on the Mississippi, Mr. McNulty died, and was buried by his comrades at Helena, Arkansas. Mr. Sullivan there procured the services of a minister and had the burial service read at the grave.

I have digressed from my subject to speak of the eloquent and talented McNulty, who was at one time a member of Congress from one of the Ohio districts, and afterwards chief clerk of the House of Representatives. Who that remembers the Presidential campaign in Ohio in 1844 can forget him?

In that lonely grave yard at Helena, Arkansas, on the banks of "the Father of Waters," sleeps all that was earthly of the eloquent speaker, the fast friend and devoted patriot, Caleb J. McNulty.

The deep respect, mingled with tenderness and admiration Mr. Sullivan entertained for him, caused a natural despondency of feeling in his bosom when he thought of the gulf that separated him from his friend. Though after the first burst of sorrow was over he turned to his companions to look in vain for one to whom he was so devotedly attached, but for a long time the blank was unfilled, as our feelings are often tardy in accommodating themselves to the inevitable decrees of Providence.

WILLIAM JOHN WALLACE.

When I come to write of Mr Wallace, I am at a loss what language to employ to convey to the reader a proper appreciation of his true character, and his many good qualities and great kindness of heart.

He was born in the county of Donagal, Ireland, in March, 1814, although by his language and dialect you would not for a moment suppose he had ever seen the "Green Isle."

With his parents he came to the United States when but a mere boy, and settled at Madison, in Jefferson County, Indiana, and learned the paper-making business with Mr. John Sheets (now deceased), brother of our esteemed citizen William Sheets.

He continued a citizen of Madison and Jefferson County until his removal to this city in 1850; he was, for awhile, the deputy sheriff of that county.

Since his residence in Indianapolis he has been Mayor of the city, and sheriff of Marion County, both of those duties he discharged with credit to himself and to the entire satisfaction of his numerous friends of both political parties. I am told, that although a warm partisan, politics was never known to enter into his official duties.

In writing this short tribute to Mr. Wallace's rare qualities of kindness and goodness of heart, I can discharge but a very small portion of a debt of gratitude I owe him for a recent act of disinterested kindness.

He did not stop to doubt a just and righteous cause, but said "go ahead, I'll stand by you and see you righted;" he did not stop to ask foolish or frivolous questions, but "what can I do to assist you?" He is an off-hand kind of man, and would stake his life on a true principle.

In politics he has ever been an earnest and consistent Whig, always acted upon conservative principles, and advocated with great zeal and all his ability (which is uncommon for a person of his advantages) its cardinal measures.

During the war he was a warm Union man, and contributed liberally of his means, and time without stint, to "make treason odious," and never tired in doing what he thought was for the benefit of the Government and safety of the country of his adoption.

Since the war he imagined and thought he saw corruption growing and thrusting its "hydra head" into his favorite party, and he at once took a decided stand against it; and when he saw he could not reform it, cast his votes for such persons as he thought were capable and honest, and would frown down anything like intrigue or dishonesty either in city, State, or the United States Government. He possesses in a high degree

"The will to do, the soul to dare,"

to oppose anything, in any man or party, that he thinks is not for the interest of the people at large.

In his political opinions he is very liberal, asking nothing for himself he is unwilling to concede to others;' indeed, he asks nothing but what is right, and will submit to nothing wrong.

He is what is called the noblest work of God—an honest man—and a devoted and loving husband, a kind and indulgent father, a steadfast friend, a genial and social gentleman, an upright business man, and the poor and laboring man's friend.

He is possessed of a large share of native talent, and advocates his views with an earnestness and feeling that never fails to convince his auditors that he is honest in their advocacy, and believes and acts upon what he says. Such is William John Wallace.

THOMAS COTTRELL.

Among the prominent and active business men of Indianapolis is the gentleman whose name heads this sketch. He came to this place, in the year 1849, from Cleveland, Ohio, and engaged in the manufacture of tin and sheet iron ware; and when the gas works went into operation he added that of gas fitting.

He is at this time extensively engaged in the wholesale tin plate, copper, sheet brass, sheet iron, Russia iron, sheet zinc, antimony, japanned and pressed tin ware, block tin rivets, iron, copper and brass wire, lead pipe, sheet lead, rubber hose, tinner's tools, brass work, iron pumps, and is also the Western agent for the sale of gas pipe.

For several years Mr. Cottrell has represented his (the Seventh) Ward in the Common Council of the city, and has done a great deal in exposing corruption whenever it was found rearing its hydra head in the municipal government.

He is a wiry, energetic and persevering man, and whatsoever his hands findeth to do he does with might and main.

He has, in connection with his partner, Mr. Knight, just finished a splendid business block on East Washington street, in which is a large public hall, known as that of Cottrell & Knight's. This hall and several of the adjoining rooms have just been leased to the city for a court room and city offices.

Mr. Cottrell possesses business talent of a high order, and ranks as a first-class business man; he has been successful, and is now considered one of the wealthy men of Indianapolis.

Soon after he came to this city he was married to the second daughter of the late Samuel Goldsberry.

JOHN C. NEW

Is a native of Indiana, born in Jennings County July 6th, 1831. He has continued to reside in the State since his birth, with the exception of four years spent at college in Virginia, where he graduated, and received his degree in 1851.

Upon his return to this city he commenced the study of law in the office of Governor David Wallace, and was admitted to the bar in 1852.

In January, 1853, he accepted the position of principal deputy in the County Clerk's office, under William Stewart, and remained as such until the death of Mr. Stewart in November, 1856, when he was appointed to fill the vacancy, and in 1857 was elected for a full term, serving until 1861.

In May, 1862, he was appointed by Governor Morton Quartermaster General of the State, and held the office until the fall of that year when he resigned, having been elected a member of the Senate from this (Marion) County.

In January, 1865, he was appointed cashier of the First National Bank of Indianapolis, which position he still holds.

Mr. New is one among the most enterprising and business men of Indianapolis, and is possessed of some fine property, both business and private, and is considered one of the reliable men of the city; he is yet quite young for one having held so many responsible positions as he has.

He is a gentleman of fine personal appearance and address, genial manners, and possessed of a great deal of general information, quick to discover the difference between a good or bad bargain when offered him.

He scorns anything like duplicity or dissimulation in his business transactions, and is quick to discover it in others, which fact qualifies him in an eminent degree for the responsible position he now holds. The people of Indianapolis might well be proud to have as citizens "a few more of the same sort."

ADAM GOLD

Who has been a citizen of this city about twenty-five years, was born in Philadelphia, but at the age of ten years emigrated with his father's family to Ohio, and there resided until he came to this place, in the year 1845.

He married the niece of the late Jerry Collins of this place and inherited a portion of the property left by the man who dug the grave of the first man buried in the old grave yard, in August, 1821.

Mr. Gold is now engaged in the family grocery business, near the White River Bridge, at the west end of Washington street.

NEWTON KELLOGG

Was the first to start the manufacture of edge tools in this place. He was born in Oswego, New York; for a short time he lived in Dayton, Ohio, and came to this place in 1846 and commenced the manufacture of all kinds of edge tools, which business he yet continues at his old stand at the west end of Washington street. Shortly after making this place his residence he was married to the daughter of Nathaniel Cox, a man well known for his eccentricities, and one of the pioneers of this place.

L. W. MOSES,

The first optician to make Indianapolis his home, although there had been several itinerants of that profession to visit the place, but did not tarry long at a time, as their visits were before the people had been educated up to the use of a first rate article in their line, and such as Mr. Moses furnishes to them now.

Mr. Moses is a native of New England, born and raised in Hartford, Connecticut, a State that is charged with the manufacture of wooden hams and nutmegs. Although this charge may be true, Mr. M. has never yet been charged with making leather spectacles.

He came to this city in the year 1856, and has here resided since that time, and become as popular with his neighbors as his optics have with the public throughout the West.

He has manufactured, directly under his own supervision, all the first class articles in that line he sells, and there is a great demand for them in nearly all the Western States. I have seen them far in the interior of Illinois, that had been ordered from him in this place.

Indeed out there, on people's noses,
Are prominent the specs of Moses.

CHARLES MAYER.

Who is it that has lived in Indianapolis for the last thirty years but knows Charlie Mayer! What stranger that visited the place with the intention of purchasing something for the little ones at home, but have been referred to him!

Among the juvenile portion of this city, for the time above referred to, when they received a present of a dime or a quarter, the first name in their mouth would be Charlie Mayer.

He started with a few dozen ginger cakes, a jar or two of candy, and a keg of beer, and, as his capital would permit, he would add a few toys, until now he has one of the largest establishments of the kind in the West, and I doubt if a more general assortment than he keeps can be found in the Union. In his store is found everything that either fancy or necessity might desire. His store extends from the street to the alley, one hundred and ninety-five feet, three stories high, and is crowded with goods from cellar to attic. He employs seven or eight clerks, and he tells me that it keeps him busy to do the correspondence of the establishment.

Charlie is a native of Wurtemberg, one of the German States, and brought to this country with him that perseverance and industry peculiar to his countrymen. In him we have an illustration of what sterling integrity, business habits and industry will accomplish. He is now one of the wealthy men of Indianapolis.

> "Nothing is difficult beneath the sky,
> Man only fails because he fails to try."

HENRY ACHEY.

It is a very difficult matter to find a starting point to give the reader a true appreciation of the character of Mr. Achey, his many peculiarities, eccentricities and great versatility.

His person was short, rotund in form, with short legs inclined to bow; his whole contour was indicative of wit and humor. He was an American citizen of German descent, having been born and raised in Lancaster County, Pennsylvania.

He was well known throughout the States of Ohio and Indiana as a popular hotel keeper. He had kept tavern in several towns and villages in Ohio. He came to Indianapolis early in 1852, and for several years kept the "Wright House," now transformed into Glenns' Block, where the New York Store is kept.

Mr. Achey always kept a first-class house, and but few ever stopped with him that would not call again, not only on account of his superior accommodations, but he possessed the faculty of making all feel at home under his roof, with his great fund of anecdotes, with which he would amuse his guests.

Henry Achey. 375

He had a smile for all, a frown for none. He seemed to think there was more of sunshine than shade in the lot of man; however, he looked on the bright side, and cast off dull care.

There are many anecdotes of him extant, as well as those he told; his peculiar manner of telling them, and suiting his actions to the words, none ever saw that can forget; his way of drawing up his face and distorting his features, and the fact that he never smiled while relating his stories, was remarkable.

After having kept hotel in several different places in Ohio, he took the Galt House at Cincinnati. It was arranged between him and his predecessor that he should take possession on Saturday evening after supper, at which time the boarders generally paid their week's board in advance. The old proprietor told him that his boarders had been very prompt, with one exception, and that he had not paid any board for six months; that he did not like to turn him off, lest he should lose what he already owed him, and pointed out the person to whom he alluded to Mr. Achey.

After the several boarders had paid their bills, this gentleman stepped up to the office and addressed Mr. Achey in this way.

"I believe you are the gentleman that proposes keeping this house?"

"Yes," was the reply, "that's my intention."

"Your name is Achey, I believe?"

"Achey is my name," was the answer.

"Henry Achey, I think?"

"Yes, Henry Achey."

"You once kept tavern at Dayton?"

"Yes, I kept at Dayton."

"Then at Middleton? Then, I think, at Hamilton?"

"Yes, I kept at both those places."

"Last I believe you kept Sportsman's Hall near this city?"

Early Reminiscences.

"Yes, I kept Sportsman's Hall for awhile."

"Now, you are here. You are a kind of traveling or itinerant hotel keeper."

"Yes, I have moved around considerably," was the answer.

"Now, Mr. Achey," said the boarder, "if I should pay you a week's board in advance, what assurance have I that you will be here a week hence?"

Mr. Achey acknowledged the force of the gentleman's remark by handing him a receipt for the week's board, and inviting him up to the bar.

While Mr. Achey kept the Galt House an old friend, a drover, put up with him; he had several hands that had assisted him with his stock that also stopped at the Galt. During the evening one of those men had bought at auction a cheap fiddle, and was seated by the stove in the office drawing from the bowels of the machine a very doleful, and, to Mr. Achey, disagreeable noise; how to get rid of the annoyance without offending the man he did not know; at last he hit upon this expedient. Said Mr. Achey to his clerk, "Dan, I wish to get rid of that noise, how will we do it?" Without waiting for any suggestion from his clerk, he said, "I have it, we will talk here a few moments in a loud and angry manner as though quarreling, and then I will go out by the stove and get within reach of the fiddle; then you come out and renew the quarrel, and I will snatch the fiddle from his hand and break it over your head; mind, Dan, and keep on your hat."

At the preconcerted time Mr. Achey took a position by the stove, and within easy grab of the fiddle. Dan came out from behind the counter and renewed the quarrel.

"Mr Achey," said Dan, "you are certainly mistaken." "I am not," said Mr. Achey, "and I do not wish you to say so again in my presence." "You tell a falsehood," said Dan. Simultaneous with the word falsehood went the crash of the fiddle over Dan's head.

"Now," said the fellow, "you've broke my fiddle." "Yes," was the reply, "and I have broke his head."

The matter was adjusted the next morning between Mr. Achey and his guest, by Mr. Achey's paying the price of the fiddle, one dollar and twenty-five cents.

On one occasion Mr. Achey had purchased a large number of horses for a distant market, and had lost heavily on them. On his return home his wife inquired of him how he had made out. "Out, out," said he; "all out, horses, money and all." Mrs. Achey was fretting over his loss. "Shut up, shut up," said he; "when you married me you married a man, and if you will only hold on to my coat-tail I'll take you through the world flying."

That the ruling passion is strong in death has been exemplified in his case. A few days before his death an old friend called to see him. During their conversation his friend let him know that he had learned that he had joined the church. "Yes," said Mr. Achey, "Sam I have joined the church, the Methodist Church. My reason for selecting that church was the fact that I have persecuted them more than any other, and this would be the last opportunity I would have of making due reparation."

A few days after this, which was in the winter of 1865–66, he died a firm believer in the Christian religion, a regeneration of his heart, and the forgiveness of his sins.

Mr. Achey possessed many fine traits of character, hospitable and liberal to a fault. He was a man of fair political information, and died, I believe, without an enemy. His death was regretted by many personal friends and his family, who were devotedly attached to him. His wife and two children are still residents of this city.

JOSEPH W. DAVIS.

This jolly, good-natured gentleman, as his very appearance indicates, has been one of the successful business men of Indianapolis for the last eighteen years.

Mr. Davis is a native of Boston, Massachusetts, but came to Cincinnati, Ohio, when a mere child, and there lived until 1852, when, with his family and but little else, he came to this city.

A short time after his arrival here he was preparing to erect a brass foundry in a densely populated part of the city, but was stopped by the Common Council, as they had made the discovery, or been informed, that brass foundries were explosive, and compelled Mr. D. to seek another location.

The present city authorities are not so fearful of a brass foundry, as he is erecting one at this time that fronts on two of our business streets.

Mr. Davis was the first engineer of our steam fire engines, and for many years managed them successfully and to the satisfaction of all who had property exposed to the devouring element.

He has represented different Wards in the Council, made a good and efficient member, ever watching the interest of his constituents, and ready to expose and put down corruption when and wherever found.

He has accumulated property, and now ranks as a first-class business man, and is universally respected for his urbanity of manners and strict honesty and integrity.

JAMES B. RYAN

Is a native of the Emerald Isle, having been born in Thurles, Tipperary County, and with his mother's family came to the United States in 1842 and settled near Washington, Daviess County, where they farmed for about five years.

James B. Ryan. 379

From the latter place he went to Edinburgh, in Johnson County, where he engaged in merchandising for three years; from there he came to Indianapolis, in the year 1850, and engaged as a clerk in the store of the late P. B. L. Smith, then located on the northeast corner of Pennsylvania and Washington streets, and continued with Mr. Smith until that establishment was sold to C. C. Elliott & Bro. He remained with the latter firm until after the death of the senior partner.

He then, in connection with Calvin A. Elliott, continued the business under the Masonic Hall until they built their business house on the northwest corner of Meridian and Maryland streets in 1854, and where Mr. Ryan yet carries on business.

He has been connected with this house in all its changes for twenty years, and to judge from his present health, energy and industry, bids fair to remain for twenty more.

Mr. Ryan is a nephew of the late P. M. Brett, of Daviess County, who was its first Auditor, a man of learning and culture. Although having lived in Indianapolis twenty years, Mr. Ryan yet claims to be a citizen of the "Pocket," as that was his first home in the United States, and many of his relatives yet reside in that portion of the State.

His first wife was the daughter of the late Judge John Smiley, who was the first white man that settled in Johnson County, and its first sheriff; he was, also, the first to represent, in the Legislature, the district composed of the counties of Johnson, Shelby and Bartholomew. The father and daughter both sleep in the family burial ground at Edinburgh.

Mr. Ryan was nominated by the State Democratic Convention three successive times as its candidate for Treasurer of State, *i. e.*, 1866–68–70.

He is a business man in the full sense of the word, but always finds time to keep himself well and correctly posted in political matters, and when before the people makes it a lively and speech-making canvass, and like his lamented brother, the late Richard J. Ryan, possesses the happy faculty of holding his audience spell-bound while he is speaking.

He is a man of sterling integrity, whose word is considered as good as his bond, and he possesses many other fine traits of character, which makes it necessary to be personally acquainted with him to be properly appreciated.

CHARLES BALS,

Who is one of our prosperous business men, came to this place in the year 1839. He is of Teutonic birth, and inherits the peculiar traits of his countrymen.

Charlie was not only poor when he first came to this city, but he owed in the old country a debt of one hundred and thirty dollars, which he was in honor bound and must pay before he could lay by anything in this country.

He was first employed by one of our respectable citizens as a man of all work at five dollars per month, and then for a short time by West & Meeker delivering flour from their mills to their customers in this city.

In the fall of 1847 he was engaged in the wholesale liquor establishment of the late P. B. L. Smith, and there remained nine years, and acquired a thorough knowledge of the rectifying and wholesale liquor business, which knowledge has proved to be of incalculable value to him since.

Soon after leaving Mr. Smith's establishment he engaged in business on his own account, since which time he has been successful, and is now a partner in the house of Hahn & Bals, one of the large and popular wholesale houses of the city.

Charlie arrived at the conclusion that many others had, *i. e.*, that he lost a large amount of money by not having a greater amount of whisky on hand at the time the tax of two dollars per gallon was ordered to be levied on that afterwards manufactured.

The senior partner of this establishment, Mr. Charles F. Hahn, is also from the old country, but a citizen of this city since 1849, and has been engaged in active business since that time. Mr. Hahn is now engaged in building, on South Meridian street, a fine business house, to be occupied by them as a store. This building will rank with any other house of that kind in the city.

AQUILLA JONES.

Prominent among the active business men of Indianapolis is the gentleman whose name stands above. Mr. Jones is a native of North Carolina, came to Indiana in the year 1831, and resided in Columbus, Bartholomew County, until he was elected Treasurer of State in 1857 and removed to this city.

Since Mr. J. has been a citizen of this place he has engaged in many public as well as private enterprises.

He was for sometime a leading wholesale grocer on South Meridian street, but has now retired from that business.

As a State officer he was efficient, never jeopardizing the public money in private speculation, like most officials (however honest in their private transactions) are inclined to do.

He is at this time the Treasurer of the Rolling Mill Company, and also the Gatling Gun Company, positions that he is peculiarly fitted for, as he is well known to possess (as his success in life will prove) financial abilities of the first order.

He married the daughter of John W. Cox, who was for many years a leading politician of Morgan County. We remember seeing him in the Senate from that county during the Presidency of General Jackson, and the old hero had not a warmer or more steadfast friend in that body.

Mr. Jones' only daughter is the wife of H. C. Holloway (a brother to the present Postmaster of this city), and is the Chief Clerk in the Money Order Department of the Post Office.

His oldest son, bearing the name of the father, is in active business, and inherits, to some extent, the business qualifications of his father.

DR. W. CLINTON THOMPSON

Is a native of the Key Stone State, having been born in the town of Zeallia Nople, Butler County. His parents died when he was quite young, and he was thrown entirely upon his own resources to procure an education; but with an energy and earnestness that generally is rewarded with success, he received an education that qualified him for the study of the profession to which he is now an honor.

He is a graduate of the Ohio Medical College. He came to Indiana about the year 1836, and has been a citizen of the State since that time, except six years that he practiced his profession in St. Charles, Missouri.

He has resided in this city during the last twenty-three years, actively engaged in the duties of his profession.

He was appointed Brigade Surgeon, at the commencement of the war, by President Lincoln, at the instance of Governor Morton, and was attached to the armies of McClelland and Pope in their campaign through Virginia.

He resigned this position, by reason of failing health, soon after the battle of Antietam.

Since his residence in Indianapolis Doctor Thompson has held several offices of honor and responsibility, if not of emolument.

He was chosen Councilman of the Third Ward, and, after serving several years as such, he resigned, and without solicitation on his part, was nominated by the Republican party for, and triumphantly elected to represent the county in the State Senate. This office he filled with credit to himself and to the entire satisfaction of his constitutents of all parties.

Since his long residence in this city Doctor Thompson has

ever sustained an unblemished character for honesty and integrity, and a high reputation as a skillful and successful physician.

He is a decided character, whose instincts and impulses are all with the right. He has enjoyed the confidence and friendship of all the Governors of the State from Joseph A. Wright to His Excellency Governor Baker, and has been their family physician.

He has, from his earliest years, had no parents to demand his regard, further than his respect for their memory and regrets for their loss, and no one but strangers to supply their place; with his genial manners he gained many friends, and he has a way of mixing his good feelings with his many jokes, which interests his auditors.

He is still actively engaged in the practice of medicine. and has by economy, industry and honesty acquired a considerable fortune for himself and family, and the sincere wish of the writer is that he may live long to enjoy the fruits of his labor, the society of his family and friends, and be, as he ever has been, of usefulness to the public.

HON. DAVID MACY,

Now one of the prominent men of Indianapolis, is a native of North Carolina, but when a boy came with his parents to Wayne County, Indiana, thence to Newcastle, Henry County, where he successfully practiced law for several years, and represented that county three years in the State Legislature.

From Newcastle he removed to Lawrenceburgh and became the law partner of Judge Major; this (Dearborn) County he also represented one year in the State Legislature.

Mr. Macy was induced to leave Lawrenceburgh in consequence of the too great water privileges of that city, he, not being amphibious, preferred a dry land residence.

He became a resident of this city in 1852; in 1854 he was

chosen President of the Indianapolis and Peru Railroad, and under his supervision that road has become one of the popular as well as paying roads of the State, and is considered a first-class road.

While a member of the Legislature he made the acquaintance of and married the eldest daughter of Robert Patterson, who was one of the pioneers of this city, and for many years one of its most respected citizens.

Mr. Macy built and owns the hotel that bears his name; he is, also, the owner of other valuable city property, and owns and lives in one of the fine residences in the north part of the city.

DR. DANDRIDGE H. OLIVER

Was born in Henry County, Kentucky, and with his father and family he became a resident of Perry Township, in this county, in 1835.

In 1848 his father, John H. Oliver, removed to Montgomery County, and there died in 1859.

Dr. Oliver is a graduate of the Louisville Medical College, and is now one of the practicing physicians of this city.

His first wife was the daughter and only child of Judge Elikem Harding, one of the pioneers who came to this place in the spring of 1820, and was an associate judge in the first court held in this city.

Dr. Oliver is a man of fine personal appearance, courteous and gentlemanly in his intercourse with his friends and those he has business with, and never fails to make a favorable impression upon the minds of those he becomes acquainted with.

WILLIAM H. ENGLISH.

I have digressed from my original design of writing reminiscences and sketches only of the first and old inhabitants of Indianapolis, and have selected a few of the most prominent and enterprising business men of the present day whose career is worthy of emulation.

Prominent among this class is William H. English, President of and principal stockholder in the First National Bank of this city.

He came to this city and organized this bank sometime previous to the removal of his family to this place and making it their permanent home, which was not until 1864.

Being a native of the State and favorably known to our citizens, he immediately took rank as a first-class business man, and identified himself with several enterprises which have proved beneficial to the city and redound to his credit as a man and public spirited citizen.

His career in the southern part of the State, where he was born and raised, was eminently successful. His father was one of the pioneers of that section and a member of the Indiana Legislature for nearly twenty years, and we remember him as one of the leading men of his party in that body.

The son entered political life at an early age. He was principal clerk of the House of Representatives in 1843, and an active participant in the Presidential canvass of 1844 that resulted in the election of Mr. Polk over Henry Clay.

He was an officer in the Treasury Department at Washington during the whole of Mr. Polk's administration, and a clerk in the United States Senate during that ever-memorable session of 1850, when the compromise was effected.

Mr. English was principal Secretary of the Convention that framed the present Constitution of Indiana, a member of the House of Representatives (Scott) in 1851, and was elected its Speaker at that session.

He was a member of Congress during the whole of Mr. Pierce's and Mr. Buchanan's administrations, from the Second Congressional District of Indiana, and Regent of the Smithsonian Institute at Washington the entire eight years.

During his long service in Congress he took a prominent and active part in several important national questions. He was the author of a bill which passed Congress, known as the "English Bill," long a subject of bitter controversy between the political parties of the day.

This bill was a compromise, removing an angry issue between the Senate and House of Representatives, placing it in the power of the people of Kansas, by a vote, to either prevent or secure the admission of Kansas under the Lecompton Constitution as they might determine.

His thoughts and logic were clear, and he depicted facts with a fresh reflection of youth, and with a ready pen he fitted his thoughts to circumstances.

On the breaking out of the war Mr. English retired from Congress, and, comparatively, from an active political life, and without ever having sustained a defeat before the people.

The First National Bank of this city was a pioneer of the system in Indiana, and it has been very successful under his management as the chief executive officer of the institution. I see by the city papers its stock is worth fifty per cent. premium, and holders refuse to sell at these figures; this certainly speaks well for the financial ability of its head.

Mr. English is also one of the two sole proprietors of the various lines of Street Railways that run through the city, as he is also of that fashionable place of amusement and recreation, the Rink.

He is a man of fine native as well as acquired ability, a well-read lawyer, but not in practice for many years, and a man of large wealth.

It is but seldom we see a man who started with such prospects of a brilliant career in politics voluntarily relinquish them for that of an active business life. And it is still more remarkable that an only child as he is, reared in the lap of luxury and ease, and never knew what it was to have a reasonable wish ungratified by indulgent parents, that had never experienced the necessity of exertion of either body or mind, should make the energetic business man he has.

Mr. English is now just in the prime of life, a tall, finely framed and symmetrical figure, dignified and gentlemanly in his bearing, a fine address, his whole contour would at once commend to and attract attention in any intelligent assemblage.

During the time he was engaged in the Treasury Department he met with a young lady of Virginia, then visiting the National Capital, and they were married; she yet shares his great prosperity and the reward of his untiring energy and industry.

He purchased that beautiful property of W. S. Hubbard's, on Circle street, and directly in the center of the city, and there resides.

Mr. English's venerable father and mother, the Hon. Elisha G. English and lady, are citizens of the city and reside with their son.

REV. WILLIAM W. HIBBEN.

Mr. Hibben is, perhaps, as well known to the people of Indiana as any minister now living within its borders.

He was a native of Uniontown, Fayette County, Pennsylvania, but at an early age came to Ohio. He was licensed as a Methodist Minister at Hillsborough, Ohio, in 1832.

In March, 1835, he came to Indiana and was admitted into the Indiana Conference, at Lafayette, in October of that year; after which he was the "preacher in charge" of some of the most important stations within the State.

In 1844, when we first made his acquaintance, he was stationed in Indianapolis, and while located here he raised some seven or eight thousand dollars for the purpose of building Wesley Chapel, and succeeded in stirring up a determination in the congregation to build the church, which they finished the next year.

This church is now owned by Richard J. Bright, and is occupied as the office of the "Indianapolis Daily Sentinel," and Mr. Hibben is the able correspondent for the paper over the signature of "Jefferson."

After being a Methodist Minister for nearly thirty years, a portion of the time as presiding elder, for reasons satisfactory to himself, and believing that he could be more beneficial in another, he severed his connection with the Methodist ministry and attached himself to the Protestant Episcopal Church, and is now one of its honored ministers.

Mr. Hibben is a ready writer, as has been attested by the able articles he has furnished for the columns of the "Daily Sentinel" upon the commercial and manufacturing interests of this city.

During the rebellion he furnished four sons to help fight the battles for the preservation of the Union. Although preachers, especially Methodist, were intensely loyal, I doubt if there are many who can show more substantial evidence of devotion to the "old flag" than Brother Hibben.

He is a man of good address, a pleasant and entertaining speaker, genial manners, and seems disposed to look upon the bright and sunny side of sublunary cares.

ISAAC DAVIS

Is one of the leading hatters of Indianapolis. He has been a citizen of this city since 1862. He was direct from New Albany to this place, and has acquired considerable notoriety in his business capacity.

He is a small, spare-made man, about forty years of age, with a quick and penetrating eye, and can measure at a glance the size of a customer's head, as well as the contents of his pocket-book, the moment he sets foot in his store, and has seldom been mistaken in his man, not even when he encountered "Hoosier Bill," as the sequel proved that Bill was mistaken, and succeeded in waking up the wrong passenger, for he got the worst of it all the way through, and will not wish to encounter another Isaac Davis as long as he lives.

There is no person that has read the city papers for the last seven years but must be familiar with the name of "Ike Davis;" he seems to think and act upon the principal that, next to keeping a fine assortment in his store, printer's ink is essential to success, hence his name in nearly all our daily papers. I believe his business motto is, small profits and quick returns.

On one occasion Mr. Davis was seated in his store ruminating on the uncertainty of sublunary affairs (except taxes), when his attention was attracted to a long, lean, lank, cadaverous individual standing about the middle of his store taking a close survey of his surroundings. His coat sleeves were about six inches too short for his arms, or rather his arms were too long for his sleeves; the waist of his coat seemed to be making an effort to gain the top of his shoulders; one arm was run half-way down his pantaloons pocket, as though to secure his pocket-book; he wore a pair of sunburnt brogans, something of the color of a red fox; his hat had evidently seen better days; his whole contour presented a rather singular appearance.

At the approach of the proprietor, he inquired if they sold hats there? Being answered in the affirmative, and asked what kind he wished to look at, "a nice Sunday hat," said he. Mr. Davis invited him to the back part of the store where the wool or cheap hats were kept.

After looking at and selecting one, he asked the price; one dollar, was the answer. "I shan't gin no such price," throwing the hat down with great earnestness and passion, and picking up his old hat held it up to the view of Mr. Davis, and exclaimed "thar is as nice a hat as wur ever worn by any man, and I only gin eighty cents for it!"

The Hoosier Bill referred to in the first of this sketch was a daring burglar that tried his hand on Mr. Davis' person as well as his premises, but he made a signal failure, as far as the accomplishment of his object was concerned.

Although he dealt Mr. D. a severe blow when he met him at the threshold, he was afterwards captured and sent to the State Prison for a term of years.

Since his incarceration there he was equally unsuccessful. In an attempt to escape from that institution he was shot by one of the guard, and although not killed he was severely injured. As a proper appreciation of the guard's good intention Mr. Davis presented him with one of his "nice Sunday hats."

The extreme counterpart of Mr. Davis' fine store will be found in the sketch of the second hat shop in this place, *i. e.*, of Nathan Davis, more generally known in his day as "Honest Nathan."

I understand Mr. Davis has made many friends since his residence in this place that wish him a long life and continued success in his business of selling "Sunday hats."

BENHAM BROTHERS.

This firm is composed of two young men, Azel M. and Henry L. Benham, who came to this city about ten years since, and without money or friends, have, in the face of strong opposition and capital, succeeded by perseverance, patient industry and upright dealing, built up and now maintain a handsome trade in music and the musical instrument line.

They being connoisseurs in the science of music, as well as performers themselves, have enabled them to secure for the Indianapolis public the very best musical talent of the old as well as the new world.

It has been mainly through their influence that those first-class Opera troops have been induced to visit this city, as the public are already aware through the city papers, that the engagement of those companies have generally been effected through their agency.

They are the editors and publishers of the "Western Musical Review," a twenty page monthly quarto journal of music, art and literature, devoted to the diffusion of musical information, and furnishing their patrons with the latest and most popular pieces.

In their immense establishment may be found all kinds of instruments, from banjo of Cuffey to the finest seven-octave piano that graces the parlors of the upper tendum of the city. In their drawers may be found any piece of music from Billy Barlow, or Captain Jinks, to selections from the most fashionable and standard operas of the day.

Messrs. Benham are natives of the western part of New York, were raised on a farm and used to farm labor, but with a perseverance and energy worthy of emulation, they set out early in life to seek their fortunes among strangers and in a strange land, and we find them to-day enjoying the reward of their indomitable industry, and destined to move in a sphere that at once commands the approbation of the public and the confidence of all who know them.

These gentlemen are endowed with an intellectual cleverness that at once wins upon those they are brought in contact with, either in the ordinary business of the day or in their social relations.

SAMUEL W. DREW

Was born in Dover, New Hampshire, and learned the carriage making business in Exeter, in his native State. From the latter place he removed to Hollowell, Maine, and there carried on his business for several years with considerable success; but he was doomed to misfortune in the loss by fire of his entire manufacturing establishment, as well as his dwelling which was adjoining.

After this disaster, not the least dispirited, he went to Roxbury, Massachusetts, and with a renewed energy again engaged in the business.

From Roxbury he came to Indianapolis in 1852; since that time he has been engaged pretty extensively in the manufacture of carriages of all kinds.

Although Mr. Drew has lived out the three-score years and ten, the time generally allotted to man, he is yet vigorous and energetic, and contains considerable of the true Yankee grit, sufficient for a new lease of life running the same length of time.

The old gentleman is very courteous and accommodating in his intercourse with his customers, and never fails to leave a good impression upon the minds of those who have business with him.

He has, at this writing, carried on the business longer than any other person in that line now doing business in this city, and can furnish as fine a carriage as can be found in any similar establishment in the western country, and there will be found no worm-eaten timber, flawy iron, or streaks of running paint on work that he turns out to his customers.

He makes it a point to be honest and just in business, merciful in religion, and liberal to the poor, never turning the needy away empty handed from his door.

Mr. Drew's oldest son is a resident of the city, and is proprietor of a first-class livery stable on Court street, between Pennsylvania and Delaware streets.

N. R. SMITH, OF THE TRADE PALACE.

Having business a few days since that required me to visit that elegant mart of fashionable merchandise, the Trade Palace, I was astonished to see the improvement that has been made in the style of dry goods, as well as in the manner that they are displayed and offered for sale.

Thirty-eight years ago the writer, as a store boy for Henry Porter, sold the first six yards of calico (then a full dress pattern) that ever was sold on the square where now stands this magnificent establishment; and although I was raised to the business of "cutting tape," I was entirely unprepared to see such a change as has taken place in this particular branch of business, and felt as much out of place as a bull would be in a china shop.

In the Trade Palace are now employed about thirty clerks, male and female, besides several "cash boys" and porters; its business is so systematized that they attend to their various duties and branches without apparently having to speak with each other, at least not so loud as to disturb others transacting business near by.

The moment the customer sets foot on the door-step the door is opened for their ingress and closed noiselessly after them. So soon as they make known the article or style of goods they wish to look at, they are conducted to that part of the immense and beautiful room where the article they wish is kept, and the whole business is transacted in such a quiet and pleasant way as to induce the customer to often purchase for the pleasure attendant thereby.

In the Trade Palace can be found all kinds of fancy or staple dry goods, either of European or American manufacture, and there the most fastidious can be suited. They can select the fabric and have it made in any style they may desire, from a shilling calico dress to a $200 velvet cloak, or a pair of jeans pants to a beaver cloth overcoat without leaving the house.

How different from the country stores of forty years ago, when the first thing that would meet the customer's eye after stumbling over bars of iron, kegs of nails, or piles of bacon to get to the counter, would be an empty whisky barrel turned on end, on this would be a bottle of whisky, a pitcher of water, a bowl of maple sugar and a tumbler of ground ginger, for the use of the thirsty customer before proceeding to purchase their five pounds of coffee, their gallon of molasses, their half dozen of mackerel, or their calico dress pattern. The change in the manner of doing business in Indianapolis is a good deal owing to Yankee enterprise, and the acquisition of such business men as the gentleman whose name stands at the head of this imperfect sketch as the proprietor of the Trade Palace.

N. R. Smith was born in Middlebury, Vermont, August 7, 1831, and is now just in the meridian of life, and at that age when we generally look forward to a bright future. He is of a hopeful and cheerful disposition, and infuses the same spirit into the hearts and minds of those around him. His candor and honesty seems manifest so soon as his acquaintance is made. His genial and smiling countenance is captivating and bears the sterling stamp that at once portrays his goodness of heart and honesty of purpose.

Mr. Smith is emphatically a self-made man, having begun the world without any capital save those personal qualities we have here but briefly referred to, and his attention and assiduity to business gives favorable omens of success in whatever he may undertake.

He has been successful in drawing around him such clerks and assistants as are well calculated to forward his interest and at the same time render his establishment popular.

Indianapolis may well be proud of such an acqusition to her population as N. R. Smith, and welcome all such that may choose to cast their lot among us.

DOCTOR ALOIS D. GALL.

Twenty years' acquaintance with Dr. Gall enables the writer to speak understandingly, and we bear testimony cheerfully of his many good qualities and fine traits of character, and his social and convivial disposition.

We were about the first acquaintance he made in Indianapolis when he first made it his residence in the year 1847, and our friendship and that of our families continued unbroken or marred by a single unpleasant incident up to the time he was so suddenly and unexpectedly called to pass from time to eternity, which gave such a shock to his many friends and acquaintances in this city.

Dr. Gall was very popular with all classes, especially was he so with his German fellow-citizens who venerate his memory as that of one of their most worthy countrymen.

He was a man of fine attainments and well read in his profession. He stood deservedly high with his medical brethren in this city, which will be seen by the proceedings of the "Indianapolis Academy of Medicine," held at their rooms on the evening of February 12, 1867, when the following preamble and resolutions were unanimously adoted, viz.:

"WHEREAS, It has pleased an Allwise Providence to summon from our midst, Dr. Alois D. Gall, a member of this Academy: And whereas, the surviving members desire to express their appreciation of his professional attainments and estimable character: Therefore,

Resolved, That the Academy of Medicine receive the announcement of the death of Dr. Gall with profound grief, as it has deprived them of one of their most worthy, efficient and valuable members.

Resolved, That his many virtues and genial social qualities, as well as his professional attainments, render his loss one that will be painfully felt throughout a wide circle of friends.

Resolved, That the Academy tender their condolence and sympathy to the bereaved members of his family in this grievous affliction.

Resolved, That in testimony of our respect for the deceased the Academy will attend the funeral ceremonies in a body.

Resolved, That the Secretary furnish a copy of the foregoing resolutions to the family of the deceased.

J. H. WOODBURN, M. D., PRESIDENT.

F. B. NOFSINGER, M. D., *Secretary*.

Doctor Gall was born in Weil die Stadt, in the German State of Wurtemburg, on the 16th of March, 1814. About the year 1841 he emigrated to the United States and for five years practiced medicine in Pennsylvania. In the year 1847, as above stated, he removed to Indianapolis and permanently located his family here. He was a successful practitioner of medicine until 1853, when he was appointed by President Pierce as United States Consul at Antwerp, Belgium, where he remained in office six years, having removed his family to that place for the purpose of educating his children.

While holding this high and responsible position, tendered him by the Chief Magistrate of his adopted country, he discharged all its duties with honor to himself and to the entire satisfaction of the appointing power and the people he so faithfully represented.

While at Antwerp the American captains in that port, as an appreciation of his fidelity to his adopted country and the interest he took in American citizens sojourning there, presented him with a beautiful and elaborately wrought gold-headed cane; this was more valuable for the idea it conveyed than for its intrinsic worth.

During the late rebellion he was a warm and devoted Union man, and was Surgeon of the Thirteenth Indiana Regiment, and afterwards promoted to Brigade Surgeon and Medical

Director, and resigned after three years hard and laborious service in the field. While at Norfolk, Virginia, he was presented by the officers of the Thirteenth Indiana Regiment with a fine sword as a testimony of their respect for him and his fidelity to his trust.

Dr. Gall died of appoplexy, after being sick only two hours, on the 11th day of February, 1867, leaving a wife and three children, all of whom yet reside in this city. The only daughter is the wife of Frederick P. Rush, one of the business men of the city.

Albert, the eldest son, at the age of eighteen years, went to California and there remained three years, where he acquired fine business qualifications as a merchant, which laid the foundation for future usefulness as well as a fortune. He is now engaged in a large carpet and general house-furnishing establishment.

Edmund, the second son and youngest child, resides with his mother and manages her business. Dr. Gall left his family in possession of some fine city property, and altogether in comfortable and easy circumstances.

His wife yet retains her widowhood, and mourns her loss as irreparable, as Rachel mourning for her children.

"Death enters and there's no defense;
His time there's none can tell."

EARLY "COLORED SOCIETY" OF INDIANAPOLIS.

The first person of color (I mean African) that came to Indianapolis, was a boy about twelve years' of age, brought here by Dr. Samuel G. Mitchell in the spring of 1821. He remained here about six years, and then, with a party of adventurers, went to Galena, Illinois.

The second was Chaney Lively, a yellow woman, that came as a housekeeper for Alexander Ralston, he being a bachelor.

She was a member of the first Presbyterian Church, and was universally respected by the pioneer ladies of the place, and who often took tea with her. She always behaved herself with propriety, and never took advantage of the attention shown her by them to be in any wise saucy. She was married to a well known barber, named John Britton, who yet resides here. Chaney died about ten years since.

A third was a barber, Obed Miftin. He has been dead near thirty years. Then in turn came "Colonel" Hunter, Fancy Tom, David Mallory and John Alexander.

About the year 1828 a number of blacks came from Bourbon County, Kentucky, the former slaves of John G. Brown.

Among them was "old Sam Brown," Willis, his son, Albert Gallatan, Bill McKinney and several more, nearly all of whom had descended from "Old Sam." Willis and Bill are still living in the city.

Then came Chubb, Parson Layback and Judge Peter Smith, barber-general of the Fifth Judicial Circuit. Parson Layback was a noisy, boisterous preacher, and the back part of his head lay upon his shoulders, so that his face appeared to be on the top of it, hence his name.

Then came one of the present barbers, Augustus Turner, who bought an acre of ground on the corner of Tennessee and Georgia streets, where he still resides.

Then William Bird, Lovel Bass, and a large family named Crawford. The most of these last named are still living, and had learned, long before "Bucktown" existed, to behave themselves, and their persons and property were protected by their white neighbors.

True, there were some colored persons that were temporary residents, and did not come up to Dave Buckhardt's standard of "colored propriety," who were sometimes raided by the "chain gang," and their quarters for awhile were made hot, often so much so that they deemed "prudence the better part

Early "Colored Society." 399

of valor," and emigrated to climes more congenial to their nature.

The first African Church was that of the Methodist, on Georgia street, just west of Kentucky avenue. This church was the scene of many laughable incidents as well as bloody noses, the latter generally happened when some low white man would go there to disturb their worship, and he generally got the worst of it.

On one occasion a fellow went there for that purpose, and the first person he encountered was a large, stout saddle-colored "American citizen," named Bill Manly. Bill gave him a sound thrashing.

The fellow next day informed on him to Esquire Scudder. Mr. Scudder fined Bill one cent, on the fellow's own testimony, and remitted the cost.

In selecting their preachers at this church they did not always get graduates of the best "Theological Institutions" of the country—although they looked fat and sleek as though they had had their share of yellow-legged chickens, and their wardrobes had received proper attention from their colored sisters.

On one occasion a white preacher and a friend had been holding a prayer meeting in "Stringtown" at night, and returning home late they heard a terrible noise proceeding from the church spoken of above. The preacher proposed that they should call by and see what was going on, to which the other assented. The colored preacher was about dismissing his congregation when his attention was attracted to our two friends; he left the pulpit and went to where they were seated, near the door, and requested the white preacher to close their meeting for them "with prar." To this our white friend assented. The colored gentleman returned to the pulpit and called the attention of the congregation in this way. "My dear bredrain, our white brudder do signafy dat he is gwine t> close our meetin' with prar, arter we sing dat good ole hime." He then gave out in this way:

> "Hark from de toons a doleful soun
> My eers atten de cry."

This they sang at the top of their voices to the tune of the "Cannibal Islands."

The colored people are at this time erecting, west of the Canal in that part of the city known as Bucktown, two splendid brick churches, one for the Methodist the other for the Baptist congregations.

DR. J. W. BARNITZ.

Every person is adapted by nature to some particular business or profession, so it is with the subject of this sketch to the art of taxidermy. He can take an animal or bird and prepare and take from its body the skin and again give it the natural shape and life-like appearance it formerly possessed.

Dr. Barnitz is the first of that profession to make Indianapolis his home. With his father's family he came to this place in 1856, and has here resided since that time.

He was born in East Berlin, Adams County, Pennsylvania, on the 23d of June, 1833. When he was two years of age his father removed to Carlisle, where the Doctor was prepared for the higher branches of education. He then entered Dickinson College, and afterward studied medicine with Dr. L. B. Kieffer, an eminent physician of Carlisle; then he attended the medical lectures at Philadelphia. It was while attending these lectures his attention was first turned to taxidermy as his profession; being an admirer of nature and her works the study was an easy as well as a pleasant one to him, and he soon acquired the art and practiced it with success.

He has spent much time and money traveling in foreign countries in search of specimens of the animal creation upon which to gratify his peculiar tastes, and was successful in finding a great variety, and can show quite a museum of the rarest birds and quadrupeds of his native as well as foreign countries.

Dr. Barnitz, with his father, Mr. Charles Barnitz, is engaged in the real estate business in this city, but devotes a considerable portion of his time to the practice of taxidermy, more as an amateur than for a consideration, or as a means of making money.

JEHIEL BARNARD.

Prominent among the business men of Indianapolis is the gentleman whose name stands at the head of this sketch.

Mr. Barnard is a native of that beautiful and prosperous inland city, Rochester, New York, and there resided until he had attained his majority.

His father, the late Jehiel Barnard, of Rochester, was one of the early citizens of that city, and was the first person married within its limits. He was a relative of that eminent and distinguished lawyer and statesman of western New York, Hon. Daniel D. Barnard, who for many years represented the Rochester District in the Congress of the United States.

In the year 1847 Jehiel Barnard removed to New York City and engaged in the wholesale hardware business, and there continued until his removal to Indianapolis in the fall of 1855.

In the year 1856, in connection with his father-in-law (Mr Joseph Farnsworth, formerly of Madison, Indiana), engaged in this city in the manufacture of railway cars, and was successful until the breaking out of the rebellion in 1861, when, in consequence of the large amount due them from Southern Railroad Companies, and not collectable, they suspended operations in that line.

Mr. Farnsworth is at this time a resident of Chicago, Illinois, having retired from active business with a large fortune, the reward of his youthful energy and industry.

Mr. Barnard was elected Secretary of the Indianapolis "Chamber of Commerce" at its first organization in 1863, which position he yet holds; and it may be truthfully said that it is mainly to his personal efforts in its behalf that that organization has become one of the permanent institutions of the city.

He is at this time the agent for seven of the popular and reliable Life and Fire Insurance Companies of the eastern States, and does a large share of that business in this city.

The first and early settlers of Indianapolis were very much prejudiced against people hailing from the Eastern States, all of which they called Yankees without regard to the locality they were from. It is mainly to Yankee enterprise, and such Yankees as Mr. Barnard, that Indianapolis is what it is to-day, one of the most prosperous cities in the Mississippi valley; and if the Eastern States has any more such to spare we will welcome them to citizenship.

Mr. B. is a gentleman of untiring energy and industry, just in the prime of life, with a vigorous constitution, and bids fair for many years of public usefulness, with a good address and pleasing manners, and has since he became a citizen of Indianapolis made many warm personal friends.

THOMAS B. GLESSING.

This accomplished artist and gentleman was born in London, England, in the year 1820, and in his younger years worked with his father at the business of harp and violin string making. In 1840 he came to America on a visit to his brother-in-law, the late William E. Burton, who at that time was the editor of the "Gentleman's Magazine," at Philadelphia, and one of the most distinguished and accomplished actors of the day.

Mr. Glessing remained in Philadelphia one year and then returned to his native land, but soon found that the United States was the country for him, and before the expiration of another year he was again in "the land of the free," where he has remained ever since.

He then went upon the theatrical boards and performed two years; that led him to the paint and scenic room, and there he at last found his forte.

He came to Indianapolis in 1859 to assist a brother artist in the decorations of the Metropolitan Theater, and has never left since, for here he found the first home he could truly call his own, "where none dare hinder or make him afraid." Here he has made many warm friends. We are sorry to learn (and with feelings of deep regret) that he may be induced to give them up for brighter prospects elsewhere.

Mr. Glessing is an artist in every sense of the word, as is attested not only by the decorations of the Academy of Music, but by a visit to his residence. He not only understands the culture and production of the beauties of nature, but also their transcription to canvass, which he does in an artistic and life-like style.

To visit his beautiful home you would not have to be told that he was an artist. In his yard and conservatory will be found nearly every variety of plants and flowers, from the modest field flowers of our own Indiana to those of other climes. In his aquarium will be found some of the most beautiful of the finny tribe.

He is a particular friend of that distinguished actor and gentleman, Joseph Jefferson, whose reputation in the character of Rip Van Winkle is world wide.

Mr. Glessing is a man of more than ordinary culture and refinement, and enjoys the society of his friends and acquaintances, and ever makes them feel welcome when around his hearth-stone.

We should regret very much if Indianapolis could not retain him as one of her permanent citizens, as his place could hardly be filled as an artist as well as a gentleman.

JACOB P. BIRKENMAYER,

A native of the Kingdom of Wurtemburg, Germany, crossed the Atlantic in 1816, and arrived in Louisville, Kentucky, in 1820, where he remained until 1850.

Having heard of the fine opening for business, and some of the great advantages possessed by Indianapolis, he was induced to visit this place, and purchased of the late John L. Ketcham the northeast quarter of section thirteen, in township fifteen, range three east, known as Delaware Camp.

This tract of land the writer has referred to in the sketch of his father as the old Delaware sugar camp, where he made sugar in the spring of 1821, at which time he gave it the name it is yet known by.

This quarter section was purchased by William Sanders at the first sale of lands held in the new purchase at Brookville, in the summer of 1821, and by him made to blossom as the rose.

It has since passed through the hands of John Wood, Robert B. Duncan, John L. Ketcham, and from the latter to Mr. Birkenmayer.

When Mr. B. purchased it, in 1850, at eighty dollars per acre, he was playfully rebuked by some of the citizens for coming here and running up the price of land upon them. Subsequent events proved his sagacity and foresight, for in 1856 he sold forty acres of the same tract to Henry Weghorst for $350 per acre, realizing twelve hundred dollars more than he paid for the whole.

This farm was among the first improved in the county, and produced the finest varieties of fruits and vegetables.

Mr. Wood at one time owned land adjoining this sufficient

to make the whole tract four hundred and eighty acres, most of which is now worth at least $1,000 per acre.

Delaware Camp has, from the time "this town was but a village," been the resort of the belles and beaux of the place, and many has been the wedding engagement made in a ride to and from it.

It was in that house the writer first saw his better half, on the occasion of the wedding of Robert L. Browning to Miss Mary, daughter of Mr. Wood. Little did he dream twenty years before, when he was gathering the sugar water among the nettles knee high, that upon that very ground he would first meet her who was to be his partner in life's rugged journey. Such is life.

At the time Mr. B. purchased this farm it was an almost unbroken forest from what is now called and including Stilz woods to the corner of East street and Virginia avenue.

J. GEORGE STILZ,

Who is at this time engaged in the business of a seedsman and dealer in agricultural implements, was born in the city of Philadelphia, Pennsylvania, in the year 1834, and as a Ward of that grand old commonwealth received at her hands a liberal education in the Public Schools.

Graduating in 1851 from the Central High School of that city, young Stilz entered the mercantile life by engaging with one of the largest commercial houses of his native city, and with whom he continued until the close of 1856, when, being dissatisfied with the limited opportunities for advancement in an overcrowded East, he ventured West in January, 1857, and reaching Indianapolis concluded to settle here, and engaged in the capacity of clerk with Tousey & Byram, and remained with them until March, 1858.

Being of a mechanical turn, and also agriculturally inclined, Mr. Stilz, on the first of June of that year, formed a copartnership with P. S. Birkenmayer, dealer in seeds and agricultural implements, it being the pioneer establishment in this line in the city, of which business, by the withdrawal of Mr. B. in March 1861, Mr. Stilz has been and is now sole proprietor.

Much of Mr. S.'s success in this business is no doubt attributable to his being a practical cultivator and agriculturist, as since his advent into the seed and implement trade he has been actively engaged in the culture of all the varied products of the soil, thus gaining by experience the discrimination and knowledge necessary to the accurate selection of his own wares, and the proper conduct of his business. That the same has been conducted with marked ability and success is evidenced by the steady and permanent growth of his business and the widely extended reputation which this house enjoys.

Mr. Stilz is just now in the prime of life, with a healthy and robust constitution, a fine form and a good personal address, and possesses the happy faculty of making friends of all with whom business or circumstances brings him in contact.

WILLIAM H. H. ROBINSON

Was born in Clark County, Indiana, February 6, 1820. His father removed to Louisville, Kentucky, and after living there a few years returned to his old home in Indiana, and there died in 1831.

In 1837 William H. H. Robinson moved to Rockford, in Jackson County, and there resided until 1851, when he removed to Indianapolis.

Mr. Robinson enlisted in the three months' service at the beginning of the war, and went into Camp Morton as color-bearer; on the next Sunday he was elected Captain of the Company, and went into Virginia with Colonel Lew Wallace.

He was soon elected Major of the Regiment. Was with General Patterson at Martinsburg, then at Winchester; was at Bunker Hill the day of the first Bull Run fight.

After the three months' service terminated he returned home and recruited a Regiment and took them to St. Louis, thence to Paduca, Kentucky, and done honorable service in the field.

In 1864 he was nominated by the Republican party, and elected sheriff of Marion County. This last office he filled with credit to himself and satisfaction to the people.

Since his retirement from office he has engaged in the manufacture of pianos, as one of the partners of the "Indianapolis Piano Manufacturing Company." This establishment turns out three pianos of the best quality per month, and they are shipped to and sold in many of the Western cities, and are considered inferior to none, and far superior to many instruments of the kind of Eastern manufacture. They employ none but the best of workmen, and use only a superior article of material.

The Messrs. Benhams', who are the agents for the sale of these pianos in this place, would sell or recommend none but the best, and their agency is guarantee sufficient to the public for the quality of these instruments, and the public can place the most implicit confidence in what either Mr. Robinson or Messrs. Benhams say in regard to them.

JOSSELYN BROTHERS & CO.,

Are dealers in the Singer Manufacturing Company's Sewing Machines for Indiana, Michigan, Northern Ohio, part of Illinois and Ontario, Canada.

This firm is composed of Alanson K. Josselyn, of Indianapolis, Homer R. Josselyn and John J. Bagley, of Detroit, Michigan.

Alanson K. Josselyn is the managing partner for their immense and splendid establishment in Indianapolis, while his brother is the manager in Detroit.

Alanson K. Josselyn is a native of New York, his brother, of Massachusetts. They possess in a high degree business qualifications that are generally found in persons from those States. They came West for the purpose of taking charge of the Singer Manufacturing Company's business.

John J. Bagley is a prominent business man and capitalist of Detroit, and proprietor of the Tobacco manufacturing establishment of that city, where that well known and popular article of tobacco, called "May Flower," is produced. They established a branch of their sewing machine business in this place in June, 1869, since which time their manager, as well as their articles, have become quite popular, and have grown in public favor.

Their salesroom is splendidly finished and most elaborately furnished, in fact, is the finest in the city, and I doubt much whether it can be surpassed in the West, where all the various kinds of machines of that company may be found, as well as the different silk twist and spool thread manufactured by the company.

In their store will be found the article used by the lone widow or seamstress, as a means of support for herself and family, to the finer and more costly article used by the wealthy for amusement or pastime.

Not the least attractive feature connected with their salesroom are several duplicates of the original sewing machine, first introduced by Adam and used in the Garden of Eden. They are employed to learn their customers how to use the modern article.

In their Indianapolis House they employ five clerks and six shipping clerks, beside the young ladies referred to in the preceding paragraph.

I clip the following from the "Indianapolis Sentinel" of

April 18, 1870. The able correspondent gives a more extended history of the Singer machine:

"This machine is certainly as popular as any other in the United States. The manufactories of this company are located respectively in the city of New York, Newark, New Jersey, South Bend, Indiana, and at Glasgow, Scotland. The New York factory was the original and chief place of manufacture, both for the wood and iron work of their machines, until the erection of their extensive establishment at South Bend, where now nearly all of their cabinet work is done, giving employment to some four or five hundred hands.

"Their Newark establishment is devoted entirely to the manufacture of silk twist, which is the peculiar thread suitable for sewing machines, demanding the capital of a million of dollars, it being the largest establishment of the kind in the world.

"The Singer machine is so called in honor of its original inventor, Mr. Singer, who is now in Paris. He is said to be worth some seven or eight millions of dollars.

"The Singer Manufacturing Company has just purchased thirty acres of ground on Tide Water at Bridgeport, Connecticut, where they are now building a new Eastern factory which will be one hundred feet in length, and which they expect to have completed by fall, so as to be able to meet the demands of their trade, both East and West, and also throughout the different countries of Europe.

"It would, perhaps, to some, seem improbable that this company has over 400,000 of their machines now in use, while during the past year their sales have amounted to 86,781, which far excels any other company, and yet they were not able to meet the demands by over 20,000 machines.

"The wonders of the sewing machine trade of this country may be imagined when the fact is stated that the Singer Manufacturing Company alone gives employment to between seven and eight thousand persons who live through their business and enterprise. This fact certainly demonstrates the utility as well as the excellence of their machines and its appreciation among the people who have had ample opportunities of knowing how they compared with all other machines of like character.

"Their agency was established in this city in 1869, and for the last year has been under the sole direction and government of Josselyn Bros. & Co., of Detroit, whose exclusive territory includes Indiana, nearly one-half of the State of Illinois, Northern Ohio, Michigan, and a portion of Canada. Within these bounds they have sold from this office and that of Detroit, during the past year, some eight thousand of the Singer machines, amounting to a business of nearly eight hundred thousand dollars. The business room of Josselyn Bros. & Co., of this city, No. 74 West Washington street, is one among the neatest and most convenient in the city, and will compare well even with our best finished banking rooms. Indeed, their mode of doing business is somewhat similar to that of banks, for they sell no machines on commission, as their numerous agents are and must be responsible, and purchase before hand every machine they sell.

"The young ladies who superintend the salesrooms of Messrs. Josselyn Bros. & Co., are both polite and attentive to purchasers, and from their intimate familiarity with the Singer machine, will, in an hour or so, initiate any person of an ordinary intelligence into their practical and satisfactory use.

"The fitting up of these machines, after the arrival of the different parts from the manufactory, gives employment to quite a number of men, while the business of the office requires the attention of some three or four clerks.

"The office finds it necessary, in order to meet the demands of the trade at the present time, to keep a large stock on hand. Their basement depository contains now some 2,000 machines.

"The multiplication and sale of sewing machines throughout the United States is one of the progressive wonders of the land, and shows in the footsteps of our civilization what can be accomplished by human genius when it is not only enlightened, but is free and independent of the overreaching dynasty of a stereotyped antiquity.

"The patronage bestowed upon the single article of sewing machines is worthy of an intelligent and free people, as it saves centuries of toil in the use of the needle, and will give to those who make our garments lives of pleasure, instead of a tedious imprisonment in the everlasting flirt of the needle.

"Sewing machines are physical missionaries in the broad field of reform. They lift from the fingers of toil the burden of confinement; they clothe the million in the robes of comfort, and the gentle hum of their song makes much of the music of human progress, as the poetry of its declarations says to the world, 'Be ye well dressed, and then all men will call ye blessed.'"

WILLIAM HENRY TURNER,

Who is one of the leading business men of the city, was born at Whitehall, New York, October 10, 1823.

He removed to Goshen, Indiana, in 1851, and in 1853 became, for the first time, a citizen of Indianapolis, where he engaged in the freight department of the Indianapolis and Madison Railway.

In 1858 he introduced the Russell Reaping and Mowing Machine, and established an extensive business in the sale of this machine and other agricultural implements, and also a large and thriving trade in seeds. He was the first general State agent for the sale of the Grover & Baker Sewing Machine, and built up this branch of business into a large and prosperous trade. In addition he established a grain commission business, which has since become a large and important business, and brought a fortune to his successors. He also introduced the celebrated Morgan stock of horses into this State, for which he is entitled to the gratitude of all lovers and admirers of this beautiful animal.

In 1865 Mr. T. removed hence to Philadelphia, and after an absence of about four years has returned among us with all his old time energy for establishing new branches of industry at the Capital, and has organized and put in operation, on a large scale, the "Indianapolis Mining Coal and Coke Company," of which he is the President.

Out of Mr. Turner's labors among us have sprung four large and prosperous business houses, besides the present enterprise which he is pushing vigorously forward.

But beyond this he is already looking to the establishing of another new branch of business, to be started here as soon as the proper means can be secured. If the East has any more such men send them on, Indianapolis will be thankful for them.

BISHOP UPFOLD.

The Rt. Rev'd Bishop Upfold, D. D., LL. D., was born at Themley Green, County of Surry, England, on the 7th of May, 1796. At six years of age he, with his parents, emigrated to America, arriving at their future home, Albany, New York, in July, 1802. After two years' preparation in Lansingburgh Academy, he was entered a Freshman at Union College, Schenectady, N. Y., in September, 1810, where he graduated at a little over eighteen years of age in July, 1814.

During College vacations he gave himself to the study of medicine, under the direction of Charles D. Townsend, M. D., of Albany, which he pursued after his graduation under Dr. Valentine Mott, of New York, and graduated at the College of Physicians and Surgeons in that city, receiving his degree of M. D. on the 7th of May, 1816, his twentieth birth day.

Bishop Upfold. 413

His attention being soon directed to the work of the ministry he was admitted a candidate for Holy Orders on the 18th of October, 1818, and was ordained a Deacon by the Rt. Rev. John H. Hobart, D. D., Bishop of New York, having meanwhile, on June 3d, 1817, been united in marriage to Sarah S. Graves.

After serving as Minister of Trinity Church, Lansingburgh, and Grace Church, Waterford, he was advanced to the Priesthood by Bishop Hobart in June, 1820, and in December of that year became the first Rector of St. Luke's Church, New York, officiating also as an assistant minister of Trinity Church, New York, from 1821 to 1825.

In March, 1828, he was instituted Rector of St. Thomas' Church, N. Y., which he resigned in 1831, and accepted a call to Trinity Church, Pittsburgh, Pennsylvania, having in August of that year received honorary degree of D. D. from Columbia College, N. Y.

Here he remained until after his election and consecration as the first Bishop of Indiana. In 1849 he removed with his family to this State, and in May, 1850, assumed the Rectorship of St. John's Church, Lafayette, in connection with the duties of the Episcopate. In January, 1854, he resigned his parish to devote himself entirely to the duties of his Episcopal office, and early in 1857 removed his residence to Indianapolis.

In 1856 he received the honorary degree of LL. D. from the University of Pennsylvania.

The subject of this brief sketch still survives, at the advanced age of seventy-four years, but for several years past has been entirely incapacitated for active labor. Full of years and full of honors, his sufferings are soothed by the tender care of her to whom in early youth he pledged his love. He has a cherished sentiment of piety, and there is a religious halo which sheds its light around him. He calmly awaits the call of the Master to the higher ministry, which we trust awaits him in the Church triumphant above.

BISHOP TALBOT.

Rt. Rev. Joseph C. Talbot, D. D., LL. D., was born in Alexandria, Virginia, Sept. 5, 1816, of Quaker parents, and educated at the Alexandria Academy. He removed to the West in 1835, and settled at Louisville, Ky., where for several years he was engaged in mercantile and banking pursuits. There he first became acquainted with the Episcopal Church, and was baptized in Christ's Church, Louisville, by the Rev. William Jackson in 1837, and soon after confirmed by the Bishop of Kentucky, Rt. Rev. Dr. Smith. In the same parish in 1838, was united to Anna M., only child of Captain Samuel Waris, U. S. N.

In 1843 he became a candidate for Holy Orders, and was ordained Deacon by Rt. Rev. B. B. Smith, D. D., of Kentucky, September, 1846, and Priest September, 1848.

With his Deaconate he commenced work for a third parish in Louisville, and soon founded and built St. John's Church, of which he remained the Rector for seven years.

In January, 1853, he accepted a call to Christ's Church, Indianapolis, where he also continued seven years, until his consecration as Missionary Bishop of the Northwest February 15, 1860. During his Rectorship the present beautiful stone church was erected for the parish.

In 1854 he received from the Western University of Pennsylvania the honorary degree of D. D., and in 1867 that of LL. D. from the University of Cambridge, England.

In August, 1865, he was elected by a unanimous vote of the Convention Assistant Bishop of Indiana; and in October of that year returned to the Diocese in that capacity.

He was one of the Council of Anglican Bishops that assembled at Lambeth, England, in 1867.

Bishop Talbot, at the age of fifty-three, is in full vigor of life, and bids fair for many years of usefulness in the good cause in which he is engaged. He is a man of great fertility of thought, with a cheerful and hopeful disposition, and is a very engaging speaker, and beloved by all who know him. He has charge of all the active duties of the Diocese of Indiana. We hope he may live until his hair is bleached as white in the service as that of his venerable predecessor, our good Bishop Upfold.

DR. THOMAS B. ELLIOTT

Has been recognized during the last fifteen years as one of the most enterprising, active and effective workers for the prosperity of the city. He is a native of Brockport, Monroe County, New York, where he was born July 20, 1825.

He received a liberal education, having graduated at Hamilton College, New York, in 1845. He studied medicine with his father, Dr. John B. Elliott, who has been for some years past a venerable and much respected resident of this city, and has reached in good health and vigor the advanced age of eighty-one years.

During the winter of 1846-7, T. B. Elliott attended his first course of medical lectures in the University of New York, then presided over by that eminent surgeon, Dr. Valentine Mott. He continued his studies in New York and Brooklyn during the ensuing spring and summer. In the fall of 1847 and winter of 1848, he traveled in the Eastern States and Canada as agent for a New York publishing house, and during most of the year 1848 traveled through the Southern and Western States, taking full manuscript notes of his travels, occasionally corresponding with Eastern newspapers.

He attended his second term of medical lectures in the winter of 1849-50 at the Jefferson Medical College, Philadelphia, where he graduated in the spring of 1850 with the degree of M. D. He continued his studies in Boston, Massachusetts, during the next year, and in September and November, 1850, he accepted an appointment as Assistant Physician in the Indiana Hospital for the Insane. He remained there four years, and discharged the duties of the position in a manner that secured the approval of all with whom he was associated.

He was married in May, 1853, to Miss Helen Brown, of Goshen, Indiana, and in December, 1855, resigned his trust at the Hospital and commenced the practice of medicine in the city. He was two years physician to the county and three years Secretary to the State Medical Society.

Having entire confidence in the rapid growth of the city, he invested all his means, from time to time, in out-lot property in the then suburbs of the city, which has since largely increased in value.

In June, 1856, he aided in the organization of the Board of Trade, was elected Secretary, and issued a circular showing the advantages of the city for the various industries, which was published with a Railroad Map.

In January, 1857, he presented to the Board of Trade an elaborate paper on "Indianapolis, its Resources or Advantages, Manufactures and Wants," which was printed in pamphlet form, by order of the Board, accompanied with a revised railroad map, and several thousand copies were distributed among distant manufactories and artisans. The influence of these papers has been to establish here a number of our leading manufactures.

In 1858 he relinquished his profession and opened the large brick warehouse, No. 150 South Delaware street, and became a flour and grain merchant.

He was the first merchant in this city to introduce shelling corn by steam power, and preparing and shipping it to the different markets. Previous to this time corn was only used for feed and distillation. During the year 1859 Dr. Elliott shelled, sacked and shipped over one hundred thousand bushels to the markets East and South. At that time there were no through freight lines, and all grain was shipped in sacks or barrels. He conducted another flour and grain warehouse and elevator on the Indianapolis and Cincinnati Railroad track, corner of Alabama street, that was burned in 1866, about which time, owing to serious losses in business, he relinquished warehousing.

In 1863, as Chairman of a committee of citizens, he prepared and published a pamphlet setting forth the advantages of Indianapolis as the site of the new projected National Arsenal. This was sent to each Senator and Representative in Congress, and had its influence in securing the location of that institution in this city.

The Board of Trade, in 1856, had no claims to be considered in any sense a Merchants' Exchange, it was substantially an advertising medium for the city.

In 1864 Dr. Elliott, associated with a number of leading merchants, established the Board of Trade and Merchants' Exchange, and was elected its first President, which office he held until April, 1866, when he was succeeded by James C. Ferguson, Esq.

In 1860 Dr. Elliott was elected one of the Trustees of the Public Schools, and, after years of labor, was appointed President of the Board, which position he continued to hold, by successive appointments, until May, 1869. Our citizens are mainly indebted to his industry, persistence and foresight for the admirable school system which our city enjoys. In 1860 there were not sufficient school buildings, and no adequate funds, and no regular superintendence, and more than fifty per cent. of the pupils of suitable age had no room in the schools.

Under the Presidency of Dr. Elliott Professor Shortridge

was appointed Superintendent, funds were raised by making a levy to the full extent of the law, and new, first-class school houses were built on the corner of Michigan and Blackford, Vermont and Davidson, and Union and McCarty streets, thus adding, with the re-arrangement of the old buildings, room for over two thousand children. The Second Presbyterian Church property, on the corner of Circle and Market streets, was also bought and a High School organized on a grand and liberal scale. Dr. Elliott has at all times cheerfully given whatever aid was in his power to all public enterprises.

CAPTAIN H. M. SOCWELL

Was born in New Jersey "one morning quite early," and when a child came to Indiana. At the age of sixteen he engaged with Captain Tom Wright, on the old steamboat Wisconsin, and was gradually promoted from one place to another until he finally reached the pinnacle of steamboat position.

After fifteen years of "Life upon the ocean wave," he abandoned it, and came to Indianapolis and engaged in the family grocery business on East Washington street, but his steamboat fame had followed him.

A company was formed, with him as one of the stockholders, to build a steamboat to navigate the turbulent waters of White River. This monster of the deep was called "Governor Morton."

When the boat was finished Capt. Socwell was unanimously selected as her commander, which duty he performed with the skill and experience of an old navigator.

On the trial trip to Cold Spring and back the boat was crowded from the hole to the hurricane deck. When but a few minutes out from port the cry of "man overboard" was heard. The Captain ordered the life-boat lowered; the man proved to be a fat Dutchman, who was hard aground laying upon his belly.

The next was a lady, who had stepped into the water up to her armpits. Captain S. cried to the bystanders to save that woman, as she was a young widow worth half a million of dollars.

One of the proprietors of the "Journal," (Mr. Samuel Douglass) who has for sometime been a candidate for matrimony, was standing by and confirmed what the Captain said, and let the golden opportunity slip through his hands. An old widower, whose head had been whitened by the frost of some seventy winters, plunged in, saved the widow, won her heart, if not the half million, and they were shortly after married. "There's a divinity that shapes our ends rough hew them as we will." For particulars call on the Captain.

Captain Socwell has navigated his dry land craft to much advantage, and is yet one of the popular family grocers of the city.

He is just the man to keep such an establishment, good-looking, pleasant manners, accommodating disposition, fond of a joke, and will generally be found with a large and select assortment of goods, and will never be caught placing light weights in the widow's basket. May his business craft never be stranded.

GOVERNOR CONRAD BAKER.

It is but seldom that a public man reaches the highest position in the gift of the people of his State without the tongue of defamation or vituperation being hurled at him by his political opponents, especially when the passions and prejudices of the people are excited to the utmost tension, as was the case during the Gubernatorial canvass of 1868, which was but a month previous to that of the Presidential, when both political parties were straining every nerve, but such was the fact, that not the least charge of private or public misconduct was laid at the door of Governor Baker, although he had been the acting chief executive of the State for sometime. His administration had been characterized as an upright, honest and conscientious one, so much so that his honorable opponent found nothing to attack but the measures of the party of which Governor Baker was the chosen representative.

Conrad Baker is a native of the Key Stone State, born in Franklin County on the 12th of February, 1817; was educated at the Pennsylvania College at Gettysburgh, Pennsylvania; studied law in the office of Stevens & Smyser, the firm consisting of the late Thaddeus Stevens and Judge Daniel M. Smyser. He was admitted to the bar in the spring of 1839, at Gettysburg, and practiced at that place for two years.

He emigrated West and settled at Evansville in 1841, where he has ever since resided until the office of Governor devolved upon him, in January, 1867, by the election of Governor Morton to the Senate of the United States, since which time he has resided at Indianapolis.

He was elected in 1845 to represent Vanderburgh County in the General Assembly and served one term; was elected Judge of the Court of Common Pleas for the district comprising the counties of Warrick and Vanderburgh in 1852, and served about eighteen months, when he resigned. He was nominated for Lieutenant Governor, without his knowledge and without having sought the nomination, by the Republican party in 1856, on the ticket which was headed by Governor Morton as the candidate for Governor. Morton and Baker were defeated, and Willard and Hammond were elected.

He was commissioned in 1861 Colonel of the First Indiana Cavalry, 28th Regiment Indiana Volunteers, and served as such for over three years.

From August, 1861, to April, 1863, he commanded either his own Regiment or a Brigade in the field in Missouri, Arkansas and Mississippi.

In April, 1863, an order from the Secretary of War reached

him by telegraph at Helena, Arkansas, requiring him to proceed forthwith to Indianapolis, Indiana, and report to the Provost Marshal General. He obeyed the order, and on his arrival at Indianapolis he received an order detailing him to act as Assistant Provost Marshal General for the State of Indiana, and as such to organize the Provost Marshal General's Bureau in this State.

He performed the duties of Provost Marshal General, Superintendent of Volunteer Recruiting and Chief Mustering Officer until August, 1864, when his term of military service having expired he was relieved at his own request, and a few weeks afterwards he, together with his regiment, was mustered out of service.

The Republican Convention, which met in 1864, nominated Governor Morton for re-election, and nominated General Nathan Kimball, who was in the field, for the office of Lieutenant Governor. General Kimball declined the nomination, and thereupon the Republican State Central Committee, without his being a candidate or applicant for the position, unanimously tendered him the nomination for Lieutenant Governor. In 1865 Governor Morton convened the General Assembly in special session, and immediately after the delivery of his message started for Europe, in quest of health, leaving Governor Baker in charge of the administration of the Executive Department of the State Government. Governor Morton was absent for five months, during which time Governor Baker performed the duties of Governor. In February, 1867, Governor Morton was elected to the Senate of the United States, and the duties of Governor devolved upon Governor Baker.

He was unanimously re-nominated by the Republican Convention of 1868 for Governor, and was elected over the Hon. Thomas A. Hendricks (one of the most popular men of the State) by the small majority of 961 votes

This canvass was conducted by those two gentlemen with

the best of feeling personally toward each other, nothing having occurred to mar the good feeling, or the social relations existing between them, each party having their ablest exponents of their measures.

There is yet, fresh in the minds of the people, a circumstance that shows that Governor Baker can not be approached with a proposition in "*indecent haste*," which if entertained by him would be derogatory to him as a gentleman, and beneath the dignity of the Chief Executive of the State.

In saying this of one of Indiana's purest public men and popular Governor, the writer can not be charged with being influenced by party considerations, but a desire to "render therefore unto Cæsar the things which are Cæsar's, and unto God the things which are God's."

MAJOR ELISHA G. ENGLISH.

Mr. English is a native of Kentucky, but removed to Scott County, Indiana, about the year 1818. He has made that county his residence ever since, although temporarily residing in Indianapolis at present, and a frequent visitor to this place for the last forty years. In fact, during a great portion of that long period, he has been in attendance during the session of the Legislature either as a member of the House of Representatives or a Senator, having probably served in that capacity a greater number of sessions, and covering a longer period of time than any man now living. We distinctly remember Major English as a member of the Legislature from Scott County nearly forty years ago, about the outgoing of James B. Ray and the incoming of Noah Noble as Governor; when his associates in the House were James Rariden, George H. Dunn, John Vawter, Elish M. Huntington, Geo. H. Profitt, Samuel Bigger, Caleb B. Smith, John H. Thompson, Joseph A. Wright, Amos Lane, and others who made some mark in the world, but have passed away. In fact, of his earlier associates in the Legislature, but few are now living. He is one of the few links in the chain remaining that connects the early history of the State with the present. He was for several years United States Marshal for the State of Indiana, and under his administration of that office the census of the State was taken in 1860. He was several times sheriff of his county and held many other official positions, showing that he always had the confidence of the people who best knew him.

A man of pretty strong prejudices, and an earnest hater where he does hate, he is nevertheless a man of the kindest and most charitable disposition, and particularly devoted to his friends.

During Major English's long public career he was a prominent and leading man with his party, and his public life was characterized by honesty of purpose, fidelity to his principles, pursuing at the same time an open, frank and upright course toward his political opponents. He was a supporter of General Jackson, "the Sage of the Hermitage," and has ever continued a member of the Democratic party.

Although now advanced in years he retains a great deal of the activity and vivacity of his youthful days. Without the benefit of an early education, and a self-made man in all respects, his career, as well as his person, clearly indicate that his is "a sound mind in a sound body."

His only son is our fellow-citizen, Hon. William H. English, long a Representative in Congress from the southern portion of this State, and now President of the First National Bank.

MAYOR MACAULEY.

Daniel Macauley, the present Mayor of Indianapolis, is a native of the Empire City, born in New York on the 8th of September, 1839, of Irish parentage.

When he was seven years of age his parents removed to

Buffalo, where his father died of cholera in August, 1849. He was then apprenticed to learn the book-binding business, and there worked at his trade, with but few years intermission, until 1860, when he came to Indianapolis. He then worked for Messrs. Bingham & Doughty in the Sentinel Book-Binding Establishment until the beginning of the war in 1861. He at once entered as a private in the "Indianapolis Zouaves," and was elected First Lieutenant of the Company, which was assigned to the 11th Indiana Regiment, commanded by Col. Lew Wallace. He was appointed by Col. Wallace Adjutant before the Regiment left for the field. In one year he was made Major. In September, 1862, was made Lieutenant-Colonel; in March, 1863, Colonel, and was twice brevetted Brigadier General for services in battle; was in command of a Brigade about one year; was twice severely wounded, once through the thigh during the battle before Vicksburg, and again on the day of "Sheridan's ride" at Cedar Creek, Virginia, in the hip, this last bullet remaining in his body beyond the reach of extraction.

He was constantly in service for five years, with the exception of thirty days. He was at Donaldson, Shiloh, the siege of Vicksburg; with Banks in Louisiana, Sheridan in the Shenandoah Valley, and in all the battles and campaigns in which the Regiment participated.

Mayor Macauley was married March 26, 1863, and while in the army, to the daughter of Rev. A. S. Ames, and when the war was over he again engaged in the book-binding business.

In April, 1867, he was nominated by the Republican party as their candidate for Mayor of this city and elected in May, and in April, 1869, was re-nominated and re-elected for another term of two years.

The reader will readily perceive that Mayor Macauley has been the architect of his own fortune, and has rose quite early in life to a high and responsible position, and possesses in a high degree the requisite qualifications for the trust reposed in him.

He is a man of pleasing and agreeable manners, and in his intercourse with his subordinate officials seems void of that vanity too often found in persons who reach high positions early in life; this fact renders him quite popular with his colleagues in the city government. Amid the "noise and confusion" that is sometimes observed in the Council as well as in other deliberative bodies, the sound of his hammer never fails to restore order and decorum.

JOSEPH AND MORRIS SOLOMON.

These gentlemen were the first to hang out the three brass, or golden colored balls, in Indianapolis, and the first in the State to do a regular pawnbroking business; although it has been done in this place in a private way since Jacob Landis advanced twenty dollars to a needy painter, on a half bushel of White River bottom corn, supposing the box to contain the *honest* mechanic's tools.

We are aware that there is an unfounded prejudice against this branch of business, but it is generally found among that class of citizens whose necessities never require them to borrow such small amounts as are loaned by the pawnbroker. Still the small dealers sometimes find the pawnbroker's office very convenient, and apply to them for aid. For instance he has a note due in bank for three hundred dollars and has exhausted all his immediate resources, and yet lacks twenty-five dollars, he wishes to keep his credit good for future accommodations, he might, as far as credit is concerned, let it all lay over as to lack the twenty-five dollars. He has a fine watch which he can do without the use of for a few days; he takes it to the broker, raises the money, pays the whole note, saves his credit, saves the cost of protest, which would amount to as much, if not more than he would have to pay for the use of the money.

Again, he might be caught from home without money or friends, and unfortunately gets into trouble, no difference what causes it, it is enough to know he is in trouble and among strangers, and wishes to get out as easy and favorably as possible, to write home would render his family uneasy, while at the same time if he was there he could raise the amount without any difficulty. Suppose he should wait for the answer; his hotel bill would be treble what he would have to pay the pawnbroker for the use of the money, he has a diamond pin, he takes it to the broker and receives on it the amount he wants and goes home. When once at home he quickly raises the money and sends by express for his diamond, without his friends or the public knowing his trouble, consequently saving exposure and mortification.

In the year 1843 the writer arrived in Memphis, Tennessee, on board a steamboat with about sixty horses, and having been detained on the river longer than it was expected, and the transportation more than he had provided for, found himself without a *sou marke*, what to do I knew not; although well aware that I would soon realize all I needed from the sale of horses, but persons knowing my situation would take advantage of it. At that time I did not know what a pawnbroker's shop was. My friend who was assisting me in the sale of the horses had had some experience in that way before. He was the owner of a gold watch worth some two hundred dollars. He seemed amused at my uneasiness, but soon after landing, and without telling me what he intended to do, we stepped into an office, the sign of which was three brass balls, he pulled out his watch and received one hundred dollars, which certainly made me feel one thousand dollars better off, and greatly relieved my mind. The interest we paid was nothing compared to the accommodation we received. No one but the broker knew our situation, consequently no advantage was taken of it.

But there are other and equally beneficial cases when the pawnbroker is useful, a mechanic or laboring man may be sick ; Saturday evening finds him without his weekly stipend for the support of his family. What are they to do ? His house is well provided with the necessary furniture that pertains to house keeping, but his children can not eat the furniture, neither will the corner grocer take it for his coffee, sugar, butter and other necessaries for the use of his family, if he did it would be at a ruinous sacrifice. What is he to do? His children must be fed ; his wife takes some article, the use of which could be dispensed with until the next Saturday night, to the Messrs. Solomon, and gets money enough to purchase what they need for the present. I have no doubt those gentlemen have relieved hundreds of similar cases to this.

I am aware that it would not do to make a business of borrowing large sums from pawnbrokers at their usual rates of interest. No sensible man would pretend to use the accommodations of the pawnbroker as they would that of the banker who loans large amounts for the use of speculation and at comparative small interest, but to the laboring or poorer classes the broker is as useful as the banker is to the wealthier, and perhaps relieve more real want and misery.

In "Harper's New Monthly" for June, I find an article on "Pawnbroking" that gives it great antiquity and originating under the Mosaic Law, and has been considered in all ages and countries useful and handed down to the present generation, and especially to Indianapolis, in the persons of J. & M. Solomon.

From that article I copy to show the delusion that many persons are under in regard to their legitimate business :

" It is not so often as in popularity supposed, perhaps, that the licensed pawnbrokers are brought under the eye of the legal authorities as receivers of stolen goods.

"Not only does their accountability to the police exercise a wholesome influence, but their liability to the lawful owners of goods, fraudulently obtained, has a tendency to render them careful, even if they were otherwise disposed to be unmindful of their duties as citizens, and their acquaintance with certain goods of our criminal population is such that they are not likely to be made the unwitting accomplices of even petty theft.

"Moreover the spoils obtained by the more active thieves of the metropolis are generally of a nature and value to call for the services of a different class of men, some of whom may be herein mentioned."

This article of the New Monthly goes on to show that a very small part of the pawnbroking business of New York is done by the licensed broker, and that that part that is done with thieves and their accomplices is a different kind of persons no better than the thief himself, and their business generally transacted in dark alleys, garrets or out of the way places, not where the three balls hang conspicuous above the door.

This much I have thought proper to say in behalf of those worthy citizens.

Messrs. Solomon tell me they were originally from London, but more directly from Philadelphia to this city, about ten years since. For a while they were in the tobacco business, but for the last five or six years in that of which I have been writing. In their store, No. 25, South Illinois Street, just south of the "Palmer House," may be found almost every article of necessity or utility.

>"From a cambric needle to a crowbar,
> A penny pitcher, or two-penny jar."

Messrs. Solomon belong to that highly respectable class of

citizens known as Hebrews, which Gentiles call Jews. They have been very active and energetic in the interest and contribution to the building of their beautiful temple of worship, the "Synagogue," which is an ornament to our city and a credit to them as a religious denomination.

They have by their kind and obliging disposition, their gentlemanly bearing and manners won the respect, and enjoy the confidence of our business community, and their social qualities make them ever welcome at our firesides.

DANIEL M. RANSDELL,

The present efficient Clerk of the city, is a native of this (Marion) County, born on the 15th of June, 1852, and educated at the Franklin College, Johnson College, Indiana.

In the war for the preservation of the Union he entered the service as a private, on the 28th of July, 1862, and served as such until wounded on the 15th of May, 1864, by which he lost his right arm.

By this misfortune, though a severe one, he was not deterred from making himself useful to the public; he at once set to work to learn to write with his left hand, which he accomplished very readily, and now writes a fine business hand.

He was elected to the office of City Clerk on the first Tuesday of May, 1867, and re-elected to the same office on the first Tuesday in May, 1869. This position he has now filled three years, and to the entire satisfaction of the public.

He is an efficient worker in the Sunday Schools of the city and in the cause of all religious or benevolent institutions generally.

> " May ne'er misfortune's growling bark
> Howl thro' the dwelling O' the Clerk.
> May ne'er his generous, honest heart,
> For that same gen'rous spirit smart "

WILLIAM HANNAMAN

Has been a prominent business man of Indianapolis for over forty years. He came to this place in the year 1826 quite a young man, and for several years worked at his trade, or rather the profession of a printer, in the office of the "Indiana Journal," when that paper was controlled and owned by Douglass & Maguire.

About the year 1832 he engaged with the late Caleb Scudder in the drug business, and continued it for several years. They also erected a carding machine and oil mill on the arm of the Canal at its junction with White River; here was manufactured the first flax seed oil in this part of the country.

Mr. Hannaman was for many years School Commissioner, a Director of the Branch of the State Bank of Indiana located at this place, Trustee of the State University, and during the war Sanitary Agent for Indiana. He has been connected with many of our benevolent and charitable institutions and always gave his aid and influence to any enterprise calculated to redound to the benefit of the city and the public at large. He is yet one of our active business men, and resides in the suburbs of the city. At the present time he is connected with his son in the drug business on the northwest corner of Washington and Delaware streets.

JOHN M. KEMPER,

Who has been a master carpenter of this city for thirty years, is a native of the Blue Grass region of Kentucky, was born and resided in Fayette County until his eighteenth year.

In 1830 he came to this (Marion) County, and for ten years farmed about four miles southeast of the city on Lick Creek.

In 1840 he came to the city, since which time he has been one of the working mechanics of the place.

In 1862 he was appointed city Street Commissioner, served

one term of two years, and made a faithful and energetic officer, always performing his duty to the letter.

Mr. Kemper is a member of the First Baptist Church of this city; his countenance, as well as his name, has been familiar to the writer for forty years, and we have ever regarded him as an upright, honest and conscientious man, which is proven by his every day walk in life. He resides and owns some valuable property on the northwest corner of South and New Jersey streets, where has been his home some twenty-eight years.

CORSON VICKERS

Was a well known citizen of Indianapolis for several years. He was from Campbell County, Kentucky, to this place in 1827, when he was quite a boy.

Soon after he came here he engaged with Thomas M. Smith and learned the tailoring business. After his apprenticeship was finished he worked at his trade a few years. He then engaged in merchandising and was a successful merchant.

After this he was elected sheriff of the county and collector of the State and county revenue. This office he held two terms, or four years. He then became a stockholder and director of the Indianapolis Insurance Company, an institution that did a money brokerage business.

Mr. Vickers was an energetic, industrious man, and accumulated property rapidly. He died in May, 1843, at the age of thirty-four years.

His second wife was the niece of the Hon. Nathan B Palmer. By her he left two children, a son and a daughter, who are yet residents of the city.

The son, William B. Vickers, is the proprietor and editor of the "Saturday Evening Mirror." The daughter is the widow of Lieutenant Colonel Richard O'Neal, late of the 26th

Regiment Indiana Volunteers. Colonel O'Neal served about fifteen months at the beginning of the rebellion. He died at his residence in this city January, 1863.

EDMUND BROWNING.

Mr. Browning is a native of Culpepper County, Virginia, but came to Mason County, Kentucky, when a child, and was there raised.

After keeping a hotel in West Union, Columbus, and Dayton, Ohio, he came to this place in the fall of 1836, and for about thirteen years kept the Washington Hall.

Mr. Browning was ever a popular hotel keeper, and his house was the Whig headquarters of this place, and for members of the Legislature, so long as he kept it.

He retired from hotel-keeping some twenty years since, and has for several years been the Register of the Land Office in this place.

Although he has passed his three-score and ten years, he is yet quite active, and may be seen on our streets daily, as has been his wont for the last thirty-four years.

SCHWABACHER & SELIG.

These two young Bavarians, Jos. Schwabacher and Abram Isaac Jacob Selig, came to this city in the year 1866, and immediately engaged in the wholesale liquor business.

They were directly from Peoria, Illinois, where they were engaged in the same business for a short time.

Since they became residents of Indianapolis they have succeeded in building up a fine trade. Although this city was pretty well supplied with similar business establishments, they have now a trade throughout this as well as other more Western States.

Since he became a resident of this city Mr. Schwabacher has taken a life partner in the person of Miss Matilda Bakrow, one of the belles of Louisville, Kentucky, and daughter of the late John Bakrow, who was a well-known and wealthy dry goods merchant of that city.

Mr. Selig too, like Isaac of old, has found his "Rebekah," whether she was found by his father's servants drawing water at the well I have no means of knowing, but like Rebekah, is perhaps willing to draw water for Isaac's camels. Suffice it to say, he sought and found a prize of inestimable value. May their young loves never be sullied, their lives o'er cast or darkened by sorrow.

DR. JAMES ELLERBY.

Indianapolis has ever been blessed with a superabundance of physicians of both high and low degree, from the graduates of the best Medical Institutions in the world, through all the different systems of practice; from Allopathy, Homeopathy, Hydropathy down to that of the "Indian Yerb Doctor." But we never had a regular graduate of a Veterinary Institution to make this city his residence until Doctor Ellerby made this his home in 1858.

Doctor Ellerby is a native of Yorkshire, England, and a regular graduate of the "Royal Veterinary College," of London, and practiced his profession in Europe until 1849, at which time he came to the United States and commenced the practice of his profession in this city in 1858, and I understand with great success.

Next to the health and life of our fellow creatures is that of the noble animal, the horse, whose health and life should be only secondary to that of the human. I am told that Doctor Ellerby detects the premonitory symptoms of disease in the horse with the certainty and aptness that our best physicians do in the human system.

MISS LAURA REAM.

This accomplished and well-known writer, with the family of her father, (Benjamin Ream) came to this place when she was quite a child. They were direct from Lebanon, Ohio, where, I think she was born.

Soon after their arrival here she was sent to the Episcopal Female School, of this city, where she received such instructions as was common for children of that day, to prepare them for the higher branches of education. She was then sent to the Catholic Female Seminary, at Nazareth, near Bardstown, Kentucky, where she finished her studies.

Soon after her return from the later Institution she was deprived of a father's love and tenderness by his death; her mother soon following. Then she was left alone with a widowed sister and a young brother. In the year 1855 her sister died and she was almost alone in the world as far as female relations were concerned, true she had an aunt, the wife of Mr. Obadiah Harris, who lived in the country.

After the death of her sister she resided with a friend, Mrs. Doctor Livingston Dunlap, where she has ever since made her home.

She had a small income left her by her father, which, by economy would eke out a living. This sufficed for a while, but her proud spirit wished for something more.

It was known to her friends that she possessed abilities of the higher order, but she had never attempted to put them to any use calculated to benefit her in a pecuniary way. Shakspear says:

"Our doubts are traitors,
And make us lose the good we oft might win,
By fearing to attempt."

But at last she did attempt, and has proved successful, as the reading public are already aware. She commenced writing first for our city papers, then occasionally for the Cincinnati papers. Among her writings for the city papers was a novel, "Phebe Doyl," which was read by the ladies with a great deal of interest. Now she is the news correspondent of the "Cincinnati Daily Commercial."

Miss Ream is about the medium height, with a symetrical, well developed form, black hair, a full dark eye, with heavy eye lashes, aquiline nose, brunett complexion, and with a mild, benevolent expression, and intelligent countenance, and would at once attract attention in any assemblage. She is altogether a fine looking lady, and by some would be called pretty.

Her dress is generally of fine material and made in the most fashionable style, but it is worn in such a manner (although properly) to at once lead a person to believe her mind was not upon dress. The fit of the gaiter, the color of the gloves, the elaborate embroidery of the French collar, but upon something of far more importance. In her conversation as well as in her writing, she is plain and frank, and calls things by their right names.

There is none of that affected modesty or prudery either in her conversation or writings too common among females. She would not blush to see the legs of a piano without pantaletts on, or refuse to make her toilet in the presence of potatoes because they have eyes. She has a great deal of common sense, and it is observable in her every act.

Miss Ream, like other mortals, no doubt is subject to her sad as well as pleasant moments, and recurs often to her childish and far gone days, when the voices of father, mother, brother and sister were familiar to her ears, all (save one) are now hushed in death, and the circle that once gathered around the family hearth is broken up, her brother and herself are all that are left, and in her quiet hours no doubt her thoughts are carried back when she and her brothers and sister, with father and mother attended the primitive church, and when with her brother and sister she was in daily attendance at the not to be forgotten school house, where she received her first lessons she has profited by, and turned to her own account and credit.

She has associated widely with the outside world, and knows it in all its phases, no doubt she takes a solemn pleasure in looking over her past life, and thinking of her many departed friends and acquaintances as they pass in review before her mind, but "Earth has no sorrow which Heaven can not cure." No doubt those reflections in all their green and hallowed associations will rush upon her heart and in her melancholy as well as happy moments, and like pleasant dreams for awhile leave a ray of sunshine behind.

What we have said of Miss Ream in this sketch are our opinions, founded upon an acquaintance with her from her earliest childhood.

WILLIAM C. SMOCK.

The present and seventh Clerk of the Marion Circuit Court and County, was born in Perry Township, December 3, 1838, he has descended from the two different families of Smocks, who were among the first settlers of the county.

His grand father on his mother's side, John Smock bought at the Brookville land sale in 1821, the first quarter section of land south of Pleasant Run, on the Madison State Road, about one mile south of the donation line. This he improved and lived on until his death in 1827. This farm is now owned by John Heofgen.

His father, Isaac Smock, was the brother of Simon Smock, who lived about one mile south of John Smock, another brother of his father. Captain Jacob Smock lived just north of Southport.

Those several families of Smocks, and Brewers that had intermarried with them, formed almost the entire population

William C. Smock. 437

on the Madison State Road for twelve or fifteen miles south. So they were called Smocks and half Smocks. Now we not only have Smocks and half Smocks but in the person of our Clerk we have a double Smock.

The family on the father's side of William C. Smock were mostly Presbyterians, and their church at Greenwood was generally filled by Smocks and Brewers. On his mother's side they were Babtists, and their church on Lick Creek, about four miles southeast of town, and where Abram Smock, his grandfather's brother preached, was generally filled with Smocks, Smalls, Pences, Seburns and Woodfills. The two families of Smocks were mostly from the counties of Henry and Shelby, Kentucky, and left that State in consequence of slavery, desiring to raise their families in a free State.

The Smocks and Brewers were honest, upright and successful farmers, and did a great deal toward making the southern portion of this county what it is to-day.

But I have digressed and will return to the subject of this sketch. At the age of fifteen years William C. Smock entered the Recorder's Office as Deputy, under the late Dr. A. G. Wallace, who was then Recorder of the County, in this capacity he remained nearly two years, accumulating a small sum of money with which he designed qualifying himself for higher and more responsible duties.

He then became a student of the Franklin (Johnson County) College, and there remained four Collegiate Terms.

In 1860 he engaged with John C. New as a Deputy in the office of Clerk of the Marion Circuit and Common Pleas Courts.

In 1862, and at the age of twenty-three he received the nomination of the Republican party for the office of Recorder for the County, a coalition having been formed between the Republican and that portion of the Democratic party that favored a vigorous prosecution of the war, and it being desirable in order to secure harmony and unity of action that the County offices should be divided. Mr. Smock very magnanimously declined the nomination, that the object should be effected.

This was a rare case when the nominee of the dominant party surrenders the nomination of a lucrative office for the benefit of the whole party.

In 1865 he was nominated by the same party as its candidate for Clerk of the County, and was elected without opposition, equally as rare a case as the first, being the first instance of the kind in the history of the County, where a candidate for a County office ran without an opponent.

In 1869 the Legislature passed an act known as the "Biennial Election Bill," whereby one year was added to the official term of his office. The term of his office will expire in October, 1870, of course he will retire, not being a candidate.

The citizens of Marion County have been peculiarly fortunate in the selection of their Clerks, from the first the venerable James M. Ray, elected in the year 1822; he was succeeded by his Deputy, Joseph M. Moore, by appointment; then Robert B. Duncan; he by William Stewart; then John C. New; then William Wallace. Men whose capacity and integrity were not questioned, and performed their duties to the satisfaction of their many friends and the public. But we doubt if any gave more satisfaction to the public, or retired from the office with more personal friends than will William C. Smock.

In Mr. Smock's character is exemplified the influence of christian parents in forming the morals and religion of their children, he adheres to the church of his mother, and is a member of the First Baptist Church of this city.

He is also an active member of the "Young Men's Christian Association," an organization that knows no sect or particular religious faith, and is doing much for the cause of true religion by uniting the different branches of the church in the common cause, and putting down Sectarianism.

HON. MICHAEL G. BRIGHT.

We remember Mr. Bright as a regular attendant upon the session of the United States and Supreme Courts of the State, at this place, near forty years ago. He has been a prominent man and lawyer of the State from his earliest manhood.

He was the compeer and associate in the practice of law, of Charles Dewey, Joseph G. Marshall, Oliver H. and Caleb B. Smith, George G. Dunn, Samuel Judah, General Tighlman A. Howard, Governor James Whitcomb, Amos Lane, Philip Sweetzer and many other distinguished lawyers, all of whom have passed away, and Mr. Bright is left as a living evidence of the great legal ability and talent of the Indiana bar thirty years ago.

Mr. B. was never an office seeker, yet he has held some very important ones; he was several times elected to represent his county (Jefferson) in the Legislature, though that county was opposed to him upon national questions. He was a member of the Constitutional Convention which framed the present Constitution of the State, selected for his well-known legal ability, and the people are indebted to him for some of the popular and wholesome provisions of that instrument. He was for many years one of the State Fund Commissioners, and negotiated some heavy and important loans for the State.

Mr. Bright has ever been an active and energetic man, taking a lively interest in railroads and other improvements calculated to benefit the public and the State.

He has lately retired from active life, more in consequence of the feeble state of his health than of his age.

Since his retirement he has made Indianapolis his residence. Mr. Bright is the father of the energetic proprietor

RICHARD J. BRIGHT,

Of the Sentinel Printing Establishment, which he has made one of the most complete in all its appointments of any similar establishment in the Western country. From his newspaper presses are issued two Dailies and one Weekly paper. Connected with it he has also an extensive Book Publishing and Job Office and Bindery, and guarantees work of the best material and modern style.

Richard J. Bright is a fair type in energy and industry of what his father was at his age, and resembles him very much in personal appearance.

Joseph J. Bingham is the leading and political editor of the Sentinel, and is too well known to the reading public as a political writer to require any eulogium from my pen.

The local and city department of the Sentinel is under the control of William A. Winter, of Columbus, Indiana, and John Brough, son of the late John Brough, Ex-Governor of Ohio. Their department also speaks for itself, and the local columns of the Sentinel never fail to give its patrons the latest and most interesting city news in a style pleasing to the reader.

The "Evening News" is the other paper published at Mr. B.'s establishment, and edited by John H. Holliday, quite a young man and a native of Indianapolis. The appearance of the News is looked for with a great deal of interest by its numerous readers and patrons.

How different is this Sentinel establishment from the one it emanated from, the office of the "Indianapolis Gazette." The first number of the Gazette made its appearance on the 28th of January, 1822, and was issued from a log cabin that stood about the center of the square, between the canal and West streets, Washington and Maryland, this cabin was about fifteen by eighteen feet square, and served the proprietors (Smith & Bolton) as a residence as well as a printing office.

Hon. Dillard Rickets.

This was the first printing establishment in the "New Purchase," and has changed proprietors, names and editors, until we now have it as the "Indianapolis Daily Sentinel." The building remodeled and now occupied as the Sentinel building was built and occupied for several years by the Wesley Methodist congregation which was the first Methodist congregation organized in the "New Purchase," and the second of any kind in Indianapolis.

HON. DILLARD RICKETTS

Has been a citizen of Indianapolis since 1867, although he has been well known to our prominent citizens for many years. He is a native of Kentucky, born in Clark county, but lived some time in Henry county previous to coming to Madison, his first residence in Indiana.

He was for several years a successful merchant of Edinburg, and while residing there represented Johnson county in the State Senate.

He was for several years extensively engaged in the purchase and packing of pork, at Jeffersonville, and did a larger business in that way than any other person in the State at that time.

Several years since he was selected as the President of the Jeffersonville and Indianapolis Railroad Company, and at a time its stock was scarcely worth ten cents on the dollar.

Since his Presidency it has gradually advanced in value until it is now at a large premium. Although the Company have purchased the Madison and Indianapolis Railroad and built lateral branches of their own road. One from Columbus to Cambridge City, another from Jeffersonville to New Albany.

Mr. Ricketts and Samuel H. Patterson, of Jeffersonville, as the representatives of the Railroad were active in procuring the building of the Railroad bridge across the Ohio river at the southern terminus of their road, and to them Indiana and the country is mostly indebted for uniting New York with New Orleans by one continuous and unbroken chain of Railroad communication through our State.

Mr. R. has ever been an active and energetic man, contributing largely to the great prosperity of the State.

He possesses a frank and manly bearing and a dignified kindness calculated to win upon those that he is thrown in contact with.

His estimable lady is the second daughter of the Hon. David W. Daily of Clark county, who for many years represented that county in the State Senate. We remember him as one of the firm friends of the administration of General Jackson during his Presidency. Mrs. Ricketts has two brothers well known to our citizens, the first Harry Daily, son-in-law of the late Judge Morrison, is a resident of the city. The second brother, Thomas Daily, is the popular conductor of the passenger train on the Jeffersonville and Indianapolis Railroad.

Mr. Ricketts owns and resides on those beautiful grounds that were the homestead of the late Judge B. F. Morris, in the southern part of the city, on Madison Avenue.

Forty years ago there stood there a heavy and beautiful sugar grove, and it was a place of general resort by the beaux and belles of the village, and by them called " Lover's Green." It is no less beautiful now, although some of the stately sugars have given way to cultivated trees.

ROBERT DOWNEY.

This venerable and pious man is one of the pioneers of Indiana, having came to the State over half a century ago.

Mr. Downey was born in Washington county, Maryland, in 1789, and there resided until 1818, when with his estimable lady, (now in her 76th year) they came to New Albany, Indiana.

After residing three years in that place he removed to Louisville. and there engaged in the Drug business.

In 1825 he returned to New Albany and there remained until 1846. he then removed to St. Louis, Missouri, and engaged in the manufacture of lard oil. In 1851 he came to Indianapolis, and has here resided since that time There are many of the ladies of this city well remember seeing his smiling countenance at the delivery window of the Post Office, of this city.

While a resident of New Albany he was one of the State Board of Directors of the State Bank of Indiana, also for a while a Director of the New Albany Branch of the State Bank.

Out of a family of twelve children this venerable couple have but four left. They were the parents of the late Professor Downey, of the Asbury University. Another son was sent by the Methodist Episcopal Church as Missionary to India and died at Lucknow. They have a son and daughter residing in this city; the son, James E. Downey, is connected with the "Indianapolis Printing and Publishing Company." The daughter is the wife of the Rev. John A. Brouse, and mother of Captain Charles Brouse, who is the Pension Agent for Indiana.

Although Mr. Downey has lived out the time generally allotted to man, he yet seems hail and hearty, and one of the most patriarchial looking gentleman of the city, with a large square frame, high forehead, an arched brow, and hair as white as the driven snow, hanging down upon his shoulders. He is a Methodist of the Wesleyan school, and has no very high opinion of some of the innovations of the present day, upon the primitive customs of the Church. and worships his God in the plain old Methodist style.

CORNELIUS N. BURGES.

The principal portion of the composition work of this book was done by Mr. Burgess, who is one of the veteran typos of this city, having become a citizen of it on the 17th of June, 1846.

He is a native of the "Old North State," born in Camden county on the 27th of November, 1807, and there learned the printing business, and although now in the sixty-third year of his age he is yet a correct compositor.

He has been a professor of the "Art Preservative" for near half a century, and perhaps handled more stick's of type than any man now living in Indianapolis, and if, as said, that "practice makes perfect," he must have nearly attained perfection in his profession.

Mr. Burges has worked in the city of New York, in the Government printing office at Washington City, and resided and worked in Philadelphia some years before he came to the West and made this city his home.

I would be pleased to see the old gentleman able to retire from labor during the remainder of his life; which has been an active and industrious one. I remember Mr. Burges since he first came to Indianapolis, more than twenty-four years ago.

CHARLES G. WARNER

Is another veteran printer that has worked on this book Charles has been well-known to the writer and the citizens of Indianapolis for over thirty years, and we have ever found him a generous, kind hearted man, ever ready to render a brother typo or any other in trouble, such aid as is in his power to bestow. The great fault of Charlie is, he never knew how to value money; always spending it with his friends as though he never expected it to fail him. He is perhaps as well known in the different printing offices of this city as any printer in the place.

Charlie is a quick impulsive man, and sometimes flashes up like powder, but like most all of his temperament he is equally ready to forgive and forget any intended injury when due reparation is made.

He is a native of the State of Delaware, and came to the West in 1837, and to Indianapolis in 1839, since which time, with his family he has here resided.

ELIZABETH NOWLAND.

I can not think of closing this work without paying a tribute of respect to the memory of my departed mother.

From the autumn of 1822 to that of 1856 there was no female whose name was more familiar to the citizens of Indianapolis than that of Mrs. Nowland. Indeed there were but few persons more generally known throughout the State.

We have frequently been asked when traveling through Illinois and other Western States if we were related to Mrs. Nowland, of Indianapolis.

No person who ever knew her could forget her universal good humor. In her kindness to all, both rich and poor, there was no distinction made in their treatment. The poor were never turned away hungry or empty handed from her door, being ever ready to contribute "the widow's mite" for all charitable purposes.

She was left a widow at the age of thirty years, with five small children depending upon her for support. With the determination to keep her children together and have the care of them herself, she labored incessantly. She toiled with willing hands through the day and often late at night, sitting alone by her tallow candle. She found joy in providing for the wants of her children, and she never seemed to think her lot a hard one when her family were comfortable.

What matters it if her remains have long since mingled with earth? There is a sympathetic chord still existing between mother and child, and there is an earlier and more indelible remembrance of her teachings by what is written on the heart in the first susceptibility of childhood, and engraven on Memory's tablet by a mother's tongue, in giving us our first lessons.

I often think of her who could always find an excuse for any delinquency on my part, when I could not for myself. She who was the first to love, was ever the last to censure. The home of my childhood! The very word falls sweetly on my ear, and recalls the many scenes of innocent plays, numbered with the past, but with fond recollections. We delight to dwell on the early events of our life, and before the home circle had been invaded by death. The many years which have passed, have not dimmed the bright colors with which memory has painted those happy hours, spent with my mother in our rustic home. The memory of a mother's care and love should be enshrined in our gratitude and engraven upon our hearts. I venerate the very earth that wraps her slumbering ashes.

A few years before the death of my mother I left the home of my childhood, (Indianapolis) then comparatively but a village, to seek my fortune among strangers, in an Eastern city, leaving the endearing associations of kindred and friends. To me it was a great sacrifice, yet duty and circumstances compelled me to make it.

There was not a brook or tree but brought some pleasing recollections of my early life and school boy days, for the memory which recalls most vividly the happiness of youthful days is generally a more faithless record of their sorrow's. One has said that "They who dwell upon the fragrance of the flower are always the first to forget the sharpness of the thorn." Who, indeed, can recall the griefs and anxieties of his early years. The throng of childish fears and disappointments by which the sunshine of his young spirit was overcast and shadowed.

Well do I remember the little family circle that gathered around me in my mother's family room the evening before my departure, to bid me good bye. I little dreamed that to most of them I was bidding a long and last farewell; and little did I think of the changes a few short years would bring.

About two years after her death I visited my old home, where I had left the unpretending village and I found a city of about twenty thousand inhabitants, with railroad communication to all parts of the Union. It was even then the railroad city of the West, nearly all the old land marks once so familiar to me were obliterated and gone. Where stood the humble shop of the mechanic there stood a large "Palatial Hotel;" where stood the unpretending country Store House there was that magnificent specimen of architectural grandeur—"Odd Fellows' Hall." If I had taken a Rip Van Winkle sleep I could not have expected so great a change as was there presented.

In my wanderings through the city my eye rested upon a place more changed to me than any I had yet seen. It was my mother's "Old Brick House," I entered the family room where but a few years before my friends had met to bid me good bye. It was there I had passed many years with kindred and friends. Oh! what a change was there; already were its walls tottering and crumbling to the earth. Time had laid its heavy hand upon it. It had stood the blasts of thirty winters, and now like its former inmates it must give way for others. This house was the second brick building on Washington street, and the third in the city.

What a multitude of thrilling memories of early years and happy dreams, mingling with the forms of the loved and the dead, and the tones and voices heard no more. A soft but not unpleasant melancholy is sure to steal over us when we enter a house in which we have enjoyed ourselves in a numerous circle of friends and acquaintances. I was forcibly reminded of the language and could almost realize the feelings of the poet when he wrote:

> "I feel like one who walks alone,
> Some banquet hall deserted;
> The lights are fled, the garlands dead,
> And all but me departed."

There was naught but strange voices saluted my ear. No kind mother came forth to embrace me with love beaming in her eye; no loved sister to meet me with a joyous smile; no brother to take me by the hand and bid me thrice welcome under its once hospitable roof.

All were gone! I felt that I was almost the last of my race, and that there were but few whose kindred blood coursed through my veins.

Just beyond the western limits of this city, of which I have been writing for some months, there is another city whose population has grown almost in proportion with this. It is the "City of the dead," whose many marble spires each indicating the last resting place of some loved friend or departed relative.

It was there at twilight and alone, I sought my kindred. In that portion of the city set apart for our family, and corresponding in number with that of my lost friends, I found those little hillocks which so forcibly remind us of the truth: "Dust thou art and unto dust shalt thou return."

Although separated now, I live in the hope of meeting my friends in that other and better land. "Shall we know each other there?" Perhaps if the memory dies we will not, but if thought, lives and love is any reality, then shall "we know as we are known."

CONCLUSION.

In the publication of these sketches I have necessarily, for want of space, to leave out the names of many persons of whom I have written. Should I meet with the success I anticipate in publishing this volume, I shall finish up another in which I shall speak of other prominent business men, as well as the descendants of the old and first settlers of Indianapolis.

In what I here present to the reading public I have endeavored to be truthful and just to all. There may be some to find fault, to such I would say, that what I have written are my own opinions, founded in nearly every instance upon personal knowledge and observation.

I have neither turned to the right nor to the left to make those sketches of character conform to the views of any person.

I have written chiefly of men and things around me. If I have erred there is no one to blame but myself. If on the other hand I am correct, I shall have the proud satisfaction of knowing that I have done no one wrong.

While writing these sketches I have felt some misgivings as to my competency for the task I had undertaken, and have been almost ready to drop my pen and abandon the work. I have never aspired to rank even with the satelites of literary luminaries, but

> "What is writ is writ,"
> Would it were worthier.

INDEX.

	Page.		Page.
Allegory	236	Cool, Dr. Jonathan	102
Alvord, Elijah S	359	Coe, Dr. Isaac	104
Achey, Henry	374	Collins, Jerry	109
Brussell, Conrad	46	Culbertson, Robert	156
Blake, James	60	Campbell, Charles C	189
Basye, Lismond	74	Coburn, Henry P	203
Bradley, Henry	79	Coburn, Hon. John	204
Bay, Billy	87	Cain, Captain John	208
Bolton, Nathaniel	93	Council, Thomas W	262
Bates, Harvey	138	Cox, Jacob	301
Brown, Hiram	160	Cady, Charles W	323
Brady, Henry	171	Cully, David V	326
Burkhart, David	177	Canby, Samuel	342
Beeler, Joseph	180	Carlisle, John	351
Beeler, Fielding	182	Cottrell, Thomas	370
Brown, John G	222	Conclusion	449
Brown, Bazil	236	Dunlap, Dr. Livingston	44
Ballad, A Pathetic	238	Duvall, Joseph P	72
Boatright, Cary H	268	Duke, Samuel	126
Beck, Samuel	308	Douglass, John	185
Brown, Mackerel	309	Davis, Nathan	187
Britton, Rev. James B	313	Davis, Joseph W	378
Brown, William J	317	Davis, Isaac	388
Burk, John	360	Drew, Samuel W	391
Bals, Charles	380	Downey, Robert	442
Benham Brothers	390	Emerson, Benjamin	286
Barnitz, J. W., sen	400	English, William H	384
Barnard, Jehiel	401	Early Colored Society	397
Birkenmayer, J. P	404	Elliott, Dr. Thomas B	415
Baker, Gov. Conrad	419	English, Elisha G	422
Burglary, First	273	Ellerby, Dr. James	433
Browning, Edmund	432	First Winter in Indianapolis	15
Bright, Michael G	439	Fish, Game and Skunks	40
Bright, Richard J	440	Fletcher, Calvin, sen	121
Burges, Cornelius N	444	Foote, Obed	136
Capital, Selection	9	Foudray, John W	175
Carter, Major Thomas	63	Fletcher, T. R	225
Cox, Nathaniel	99	Frasee, James	241

Index.

	Page.		Page.
Fletcher, Stoughton A. sen	249	Kellogg, Newton	372
Fire, First in Indianapolis	273	Kemper, John M	430
French, Charles G	354	Landis, Jacob	144
Good, Richard	88	Lingenfelter, Archibald	186
Givan, John	118	Lockerbie, George	231
Gates, Uriah	127	Lofton, Joseph	233
Gregg, Harvey	143	Lofton, Dr. Sample	233
Griffith, Humphrey	172	Lofton, Dr. Almon	234
Goldsberry, Samuel	205	Langsdale, J. M. W	315
Garner, Charles	312	Lauer, Charles	344
Grover, Aaron	340	McCormick, John	23
Gaston, Dr. John M	353	Morris, Morris	105
Gold, Adam	372	Mitchell, Dr. Samuel G	108
Gall, Dr. Alois D	395	Maguire, Douglass	141
Glessing, Thomas B	402	McCarty, Nicholas, sen	158
Harding Brothers	24	Mallory, David	162
Harrison, Christopher	44	McGeorge, Samuel	173
Hanway, Amos, sen	96	Merrill, Samuel	183
Henderson, Samuel	101	Morrison, James	212
Helvey, Old Bob	115	Morrison, William H	216
Harrison, Alfred	156	Morrison, Major Alexander F.	218
Hanna, Gen. Robert	193	McOuat, Thomas	229
Hogshire, Riley B	195	Mears, Dr. George W	270
Hogshire, William R	197	McCord, Abram	290
Hill, John F	234	Moore, Joseph M	321
Hoosier's Nest	243	Mansur, Frank	339
Holland, John W	248	Mann, James B	341
Holland, Theodore F	248	McChesney, Jacob B	349
Hubbard, William S	331	McKernan, James H	363
Haugh, Adam	333	Moses, L. W	372
Harmening, Fred. Christ	343	Mayer, Charles	373
Hereth, John C	344	Macy, Hon. David	383
Hibben, Rev. William W	387	Macauley, Mayor, Daniel	423
Hannaman, William	430	Nowland, Matthias T	37
Indian attempts to cut a door down	17	Nowland, Matthias R	52
		Norwood, George	152
Incidents, 1821-22	127	Noel, Sam'l V. B	191
Incidents, 1823-24-25	164	Noble, Gov. Noah	201
Johnson, Jerry	31	Nelson, Henry H	285
Johnson, James, Esq	98	Nooe, Daniel M	311
Johnson, Thomas	146	New, John C	371
Jackson, William N	297	Nowland, Elizabeth	445
Jones, Aquilla	381	O'Neal, Hugh	111
Josselyn Brothers & Co	407	Owens, Nathaniel B	316
Kettleman, Jimmy	85	Ohr, Henry	350
Kinder, Isaac	95	Oliver, Dr. Dandridge H	384
Ketcham, John L	303	Preparation for removal	11
Knodle, Adam	308	Pogue, George	20

Index.

Name	Page
Paxton, James	84
Patterson, Robert	120
Pence, Joseph	153
Phipps, Isaac N.	154
Pitts, Stephen	228
Pottawattamie Prophet	240
Peck, Edwin J.	252
Pratt, Hon. Daniel D.	255
Pinney, William H. H.	266
Palmer, Hon. Nathan B.	275
Patterson, Samuel H.	294
Paul, George	298
Pope, Dr. Abner	325
Parry, Dr. Charles	338
Patterson, John P.	342
Russell, Alexander W.	28
Reynolds, Caleb	68
Rooker, Samuel S.	82
Ray, James M.	89
Ralston, Alexander	94
Reagan, Wilks, Esq.	133
Redding, John W.	134
Reid, Archibald C.	153
Ray, Gov. James B.	199
Ray, Rev. Edwin	223
Rasener, Christ. Fred.	343
Ryan, James B.	378
Robinson, William H. H.	406
Ransdell, Daniel M.	429
Ream, Miss Laura	434
Ricketts, Hon. Dillard	441
Spring of 1821	26
Shafter, Daniel	34
Shunk, John	49
Scudder, Caleb	81
Stephens, Daniel	88
Smith, George	91
Smith, Andrew	124
Sulgrove, James	157
Sulgrove, Berry R.	158
Smock, John	199
Stevens, Joshua	207
Smith, James M.	211
Sharpe, Ebenezer	219
Sharpe, Thomas H.	221
Sheets, William	269
Sweetser, Philip	279
Sullivan, William, Esq.	287
Sanders, Dr. John H.	290
Smith, Justin	328
Smith, Paul B. L.	345
Sharpe, Joseph K.	347
Sullivan, John B.	366
Smith, N. R.	392
Stilz, J. George	405
Socwell, Captain H. M.	418
Solomon, J. & M.	425
Schwabacher & Selig	432
Smock, William C.	436
Townsend, Billy	70
Taffe, George, sen.	161
Tom, Fancy	169
Taylor, Robert	173
Taylor, N. B.	173
Tutewiler, Henry	265
Tutewiler Brothers	266
Talbott, John M.	282
Talbott, Wm. H	283
Thompson, Dr. W. Clinton	382
Turner, William H.	411
Talbot, Bishop	414
Upfold, Bishop	412
Van Blaricum, John	114
Van Houten, Cornelius W.	190
Vance, Lawrence M.	292
Vickers, Corson	431
Wilson, Isaac	25
Whitzell family	54
Whitzell, Cyrus	51
Wilkins, John	78
Wilson, Andrew	80
Wick, William W.	137
Walpole, Luke, and family	147
Williams, David	160
Wingate, Joseph	206
Wallace, Gov. David	293
Wilkinson, William	309
Wright, John H.	337
Wallace, Andrew	355
Wallace, William John	368
Warner, Charles G.	444
Yandes, Daniel	76
Yandes, Simon	77
Yohn, James C.	284

www.ingramcontent.com/pod-product-compliance
Lightning Source LLC
Chambersburg PA
CBHW022134300426
44115CB00006B/179